Symbolism of the Ark

Symbolism of the Ark

Universal Symbolism of the Receptacle of Divine Immanence

by

Timothy Scott

THE MATHESON TRUST
Promoting the Study of Comparative Religions

FONS VITAE

First published in 2009 by
Fons Vitae
49 Mockingbird Valley Drive
Louisville, KY 40207
http://www.fonsvitae.com
Email: fonsvitaeky@aol.com

Copyright Fons Vitae 2009
Library of Congress Control Number: 2009933712
ISBN 9781891785368

Printed in Canada.

The Hebrew font in this work is available from
www.linguistsoftware.com/stu.htm, +1-425-775-1130.

Contents

Contents, continued

Preface

In diverse traditions we find an ensemble of symbols, motifs and narratives centring on the idea of a "container" or "receptacle" for the divine Presence. This idea is found in the symbolism of what we might loosely call "the Ark." In the Semitic traditions this symbolism is most conspicuous in the biblical accounts of the Ark of Noah and the Ark of the Covenant. The aim of this book is to uncover the more or less universal significance of Ark symbolism through an exploration of its biblical expressions. The starting point for this inquiry is a set of immutable metaphysical and cosmological principles constituting the *philosophia perennis*, which informs the world's integral mythological and religious traditions. I understand the Ark as the receptacle of Divine Immanence or, what amounts to the same thing, as the dwelling place of God. Immanence may be symbolised by a series of numerical hypostases, the most fundamental of which is the progression from the monad to the quaternary. In turn, the unfolding of the quaternary reveals the fullness of the decad, with the number ten adequately expressing the return of the monad to metaphysical zero. With the account of the Ark of Noah and, to a lesser extent, the Ark of the Covenant in the foreground, we survey the symbolic "progression" from zero to four. Thus the mythology of the Ark of Noah is considered as the movement from zero (the waters of the flood), through the principial monad (the Ark as "seed"), via the duad as both retraction ("two by two") and emanation (the "twin peaked mountains"), to the ternary, both as a hierarchy of constituent elements (the "three decks" of the Ark) and as a creative "power" (the "three sons" of Noah), to the quaternary, which may be said to express Immanence in terms of cosmic stability (the Temple, the *Ka'bah*). The Noah myth is an expedient point of departure for a consideration of the Ark as a universal symbol with two fundamental expressions: the Ark as the divine "vehicle" (boat, ship, chariot) and the Ark as the "house of God." These, however, are only the most obvious expressions of the symbolism under investigation and allusion is made to a variety of other related symbolic motifs (cup, trumpet, conch, heart, amongst others). In the final analysis we are engaged in an inquiry into universal metaphysical and cosmological principles.

The Ark is the receptacle of Divine Immanence. However, such a statement is too simple or even too obvious to bring into focus the vast body of symbolisms and the complex hermeneutics that explicate it. My aim is two-fold: to present an examination of the metaphysics related to the symbolism of the Ark, and to alert the reader to the broad scope of this symbolism. It might help to clarify the nature of this enterprise by first saying what it is not. It is not a work of historical investigation, history of religion, history of ideas, nor speculative or systematic theology, in any limited sense of these words. Neither is this a work concerned with contemplative spirituality, although it is this rich tradition that yields some of the most valuable writings concerning the Ark of Noah and the Ark of the Covenant: one thinks of Hugh of St. Victor's *De arca Noe morali et de arca Noe mystica* and Richard of St. Victor's *Benjamin Major (The Mystical Ark)*, and the influence this last had on *The Cloud of Unknowing*.

This book might best be described as a work of comparative symbolic exegesis. I have attempted to present a study of the traditional symbolisms and metaphysics associated with the idea of the Ark envisaged as a universal principle. Admittedly this is not original in any modern sense of the word. It is not my intention to formulate some new idea, but simply to fathom the depths of the Ark symbol and its related symbolisms. Still, while this is not original it is nevertheless relatively unique among modern scholarly studies, which are more often than not concerned primarily with historical proofs of the Ark of Noah or the Ark of the Covenant.

This work is far from exhaustive; it seeks simply to suggest certain understandings and symbolic relationships that by their very nature are multivalent. When discussing principles I have tried to be direct and concise. Where I engage with examples, be they mythological, symbolical, or literary, I generally let the web of allusions, correspondences and analogies speak for itself. If we appear to wander from what might be thought of as Ark mythology, be this the Ark of the Flood or the Ark of the Covenant, this is due to my central premise: that the Ark symbolises the receptacle of Divine Immanence. Immanence includes every manifested and created thing from the Cosmos itself to the most insignificant speck of dust. God exists in all things and all things exist in God. Thus one might speak of any "thing" as the receptacle of Divine Immanence.

To fully understand the Ark as the receptacle of Immanence one must consider the relationship of Immanence and Transcendence. Thus one moves to a study of Reality in Its fullness, the content of which is infinite. The scope of such a study is limited only by one's intellectual horizon. Yet one is obliged to find a starting place. The notion of the symbolism of the Ark provides that starting place for this book. It is finally, as in fact all symbolism should be, a stepping-stone to an appreciation of the Divine.

Noah's Ark is the symbol of our species,
A boat wandering the ocean.

A plant grows deep in the centre of that water.
It has no form and no location.

Jalāl al-Din Rūmī, *Kulliyat-e Shams*, 546, 561
(tr. C. Barks)

Acknowledgements

The present book is developed from a doctoral thesis that was submitted to La Trobe University in 2003. A debt of gratitude is due to the staff of the Philosophy and Religious Studies program at Bendigo. Acknowledgement is due, above all others, to my supervisor, Dr Harry Oldmeadow, whose guidance, advice and support nurtured my idiosyncratic interests.

For support, friendship, suggestions, and for walking this doctoral path with me I wish to thank my friend Dr Andrew Itter. I am grateful to Graeme Castleman for his aid in the preparation of this text and for his many helpful suggestions and discussions. A debt of gratitude is owed to M. Ali Lakhani, publisher and editor of the journal *Sacred Web*, who gave me my first opportunity to be published.

Lastly I wish to thank my wife, Amanda, who believed in this work and in me when I did not. Without her encouragement and support this work would not have been completed.

A Note on Referencing and the Use of Foreign Terms

As biblical tradition is my starting point I have placed biblical references within the body of the text; all other references are in footnotes. There is a focus on Hebrew as the language of the biblical Ark traditions. However, this is not a work of linguistic analysis; hence, both the use of Hebrew and the general transliteration of languages is kept simple. Spelling, use of accents and italicisation of foreign terms has been standardised throughout.

Abbreviations

Burckhardt, *ISD*	*An Introduction to Sufi Doctrine*
Burckhardt, *MI*	*Mirror of the Intellect*
Charlesworth (ed.), *OTP1*	*The Old Testament Pseudepigrapha Vol.1*
Charlesworth (ed.), *OTP2*	*The Old Testament Pseudepigrapha Vol.2*
Chevalier & Gheerbrant, *DS*	*Dictionary of Symbols*
Cohen, *ET*	*Everyman's Talmud*
Coomaraswamy, *SP1*	*Selected Papers Vol.1: Traditional Art and Symbolism*
Coomaraswamy, *SP2*	*Selected Papers Vol.2: Metaphysics*
Dalley (ed.), *MM*	*Myths from Mesopotamia*
Daniélou, *MGI*	*The Myths and Gods of India*
Meister Eckhart, *Comm. Gen.*	*Commentary on the Book of Genesis*
Meister Eckhart, *Par. Gen.*	*Book of the Parables of Genesis*
Meister Eckhart, *Comm. Jn.*	*Commentary on John*
Meister Eckhart, *Comm. Wis.*	*Commentary on the Book of Wisdom*
Rabbi Gikatilla, *SO*	*Sha'are Orah (Gates of Light)*
Guénon, *SC*	*Symbolism of the Cross*
Guénon, *MB*	*Man and his Becoming According To The Vedānta*
Guénon, *LW*	*The Lord of the World*
Guénon, *GT*	*The Great Triad*
Guénon, *ED*	*The Esoterism of Dante*
Guénon, *RQ*	*The Reign of Quantity & The Signs of the Times*
Guénon, *FS*	*Fundamental Symbols*
Guénon, *MSB*	*The Multiple States of the Being*
Ibn al-'Arabī, *Fusūs*	*Fusūs al-hikam (Bezels of Wisdom)*
Ibn al-'Arabī, *Lubb*	*Lubbu-l-Lubb (Kernel of the Kernel)*
Ibn al-'Arabī, *Futūhāt*	*al- Futūhāt al-Makkiya (The Meccan Revelations)*
Al-Jīlī, *al-insān*	*al-insān al-kamīl (Universal Man)*

Mathers, *KU*   *The Kabbalah Unveiled*

NJB   *New Jerusalem Bible*

Nasr, *NS*   *Knowledge and the Sacred*
Nasr, *ICD*   *An Introduction to Islamic Cosmological Doctrines*

Metford, DCLL   *Dictionary of Christian Lore and Legend*

Oldmeadow, *Traditionalism*   *Traditionalism: Religion in the light of the Perennial Philosophy*

Perry, *TTW*   *A Treasury of Traditional Wisdom*

Rappoport, *AI1*   *Ancient Israel Vol.1*
Rappoport, *AI2*   *Ancient Israel Vol.2*
Rappoport, *AI3*   *Ancient Israel Vol.3*

Schaya, *UMK*   *The Universal Meaning of the Kabbalah*

Scholem, *MTJM*   *Major Trends in Jewish Mysticism*

Schuon, *LAW*   *Light on the Ancient Worlds*
Schuon, *LT*   *Logic and Transcendence*
Schuon, *UI*   *Understanding Islam*
Schuon, *EPW*   *Esoterism as Principle and as Way*
Schuon, *FDH*   *From the Divine to the Human,*
Schuon, *SPHF*   *Spiritual Perspectives and Human Facts*
Schuon, *IFA*   *In The Face Of The Absolute*
Schuon, *G:DW*   *Gnosis: Divine Wisdom*
Schuon, *TUR*   *The Transcendent Unity of Religions*
Schuon, *TB*   *Treasures of Buddhism*
Schuon, *SW*   *Stations of Wisdom*
Schuon, *LS*   *Language of the Self*
Schuon, *SME*   *Survey of Metaphysics and Esoterism*

Snodgrass, *SS*   *The Symbolism of the Stupa*
Snodgrass, *ATE1*   *Architecture, Time and Eternity Vol.1*
Snodgrass, *ATE2*   *Architecture, Time and Eternity Vol.2*

Tishby, *WZ1*   *The Wisdom of the Zohar Vol.1*
Tishby, *WZ2*   *The Wisdom of the Zohar Vol.2*
Tishby, *WZ3*   *The Wisdom of the Zohar Vol.3*

Table of Hebrew Letters

Numerical Value	Letter	Name	Symbolism	Transcription
1	א	alef	Ox	per vocalisation
2	ב	beth	House	v or b, bh
3	ג	gi'mel	Camel	g
4	ד	da'leth	Door	d, dh
5	ה	he	Window	h
6	ו	vav	Peg, Nail	v (u or o as a vowel)
7	ז	zayin	Weapon; Sword	z
8	ח	heth	Enclosure; Fence	ch
9	ט	teth	Serpent	t
10	י	yod	Hand	i, y
20, Final = 200	כ, ך	kaf	Palm of hand	kh, k
30	ל	la'medh	Ox-goad	l
40, Final = 600	מ, ם	mem	Water	m
50, Final = 700	נ, ן	nun	Fish	n
60	ס	sa'mekh	Prop; Support	s
70	ע	ayin	Eye	per vocalisation
80, Final = 800	פ, ף	fe or pe	Mouth	f, p
90, Final = 900	צ, ץ	tsa'dhe	Fishing-hook	ts, tz
100	ק	kof	Back of the head	k
200	ר	resh	Head	r
300	ש	sin or shin	Tooth	s, sh
400	ת	thaw or taw	Sign of the Cross	th, t

Altare holocasti sc̄m hebreos

Introduction

The Traditional Perspective

Tradition, in the rightful sense of the word, is the chain that joins
civilisation to Revelation.

Lord Northbourne[1]

Trust in the Lord with all thine heart; and lean not unto thine own
understanding.

Proverbs 3:5

This book presents an exegesis of the traditional symbolism of the Ark.
The term "traditional" here indicates a perspective most authoritatively
elucidated in the writings of René Guénon, Ananda Coomaraswamy
and Frithjof Schuon.[2] I have attempted to engage Tradition as my mode
of study; to regard the orthodox teachings of the world from a position of humility and respect, learning *from* them as well as *about* them.[3]
Kenneth Oldmeadow observes two complementary senses of the term
"tradition": '*Tradition*: the primordial wisdom, or Truth, immutable and
unformed; *tradition*: a formal embodiment of Truth under a particular
mythological or religious guise which is transmitted through time; or the
vehicle for the transmission of this formal embodiment; of the process
of transmission itself.'[4] To say Tradition is to say Revelation. As Whitall
Perry says, 'Tradition is the continuity of Revelation: an uninterrupted
transmission, through innumerable generations, of the spiritual and cosmological principles, sciences, and laws resulting from a revealed religion'.[5] Tradition is an unbroken "chain" (*shelsheleth* in Hebrew, *silsilah*
in Arabic, *parampara* in Sanskrit).[6]

Tradition is as relevant today as it was in the past; it is not something
to be studied as an oddity of history. On this point, Guénon remarks,
'Tradition, in its integrality, forms a perfect coherent whole, which however does not mean to say a systematic whole; and since all the points
of view which it comprises can as well be considered simultaneously
as in succession, there cannot be any real object in enquiring into the
historical order in which they may have been developed and rendered
explicit'.[7] Nevertheless, as the light is brightest nearest its source it is
somewhat inevitable that the majority of the teachings considered come
from the early periods of human history. Here one must be careful to
avoid the "twin pitfalls" of modern attitudes towards "ancient man" of
either 'pretentious depreciation or that of an overly sentimental romanti-
cism'.[8]

This book is principally concerned with the elucidation of the symbolism of the Ark through the "sacred sciences."[9] As Seyyed Hossein Nasr says, 'The traditional sciences of the cosmos make use of the language of symbolism. They claim to expound a science and not a sentimental or poetic image of the domain which is their concern, but a science which is expounded in the language of symbolism based on the analogy between various levels of existence.'[10]

The symbolism of the Ark is informed by, and itself informs, the *cosmologia perennis* which 'in one sense, is the application and, in another, the complement of the *sophia perennis*'.[11] The *cosmologia perennis* is the science of cosmology. The *sophia perennis*, or universal *gnosis*, is essentially concerned with metaphysics. Both are embraced by the *religio perennis*, which is the language of the relationship between the Divine and the human.[12] A distinction must be drawn between the *religio perennis* and "religion" *per se*. Guénon defines "religion" in respect to its limitation to the 'extensions of the human individuality'.[13] Frithjof Schuon observes that a religion is 'not limited by what it includes but by what it excludes'; still, 'since every religion is intrinsically a totality, this exclusion cannot impair the religion's deepest contents'.[14] A religion, observes Schuon, must satisfy all spiritual possibilities.[15]

The *sophia perennis* lies at the heart of each and every orthodox tradition. "Orthodoxy" provides the starting point in the study of the sacred. By no means should this term be taken as simply indicating the restricted "orthodoxy" of a certain Western religious conception. The "necessary and sufficient condition" of orthodoxy, as Guénon remarks, is the 'concordance of a conception with the fundamental principle of the tradition'.[16] These "principles" are none other than the *sophia perennis*.

At the risk of labouring the point, this work is principally concerned with the symbol of the Ark within the context of the *sophia perennis*. This is to say that my aim is to expound the metaphysical principles that underlie and are expressed through the universal symbol of the Ark.[17] We are here concerned not with information acquired by the discursive mind but with what Guénon calls "genuine knowledge":

> Genuine knowledge, which alone concerns us, has little if anything at all to do with "profane" knowledge; the studies which go to make up the latter cannot be looked upon even as an indirect path of approach to "Sacred Science"; on the contrary, at times they even constitute an obstacle, by reason of the often irremediable mental deformation which is the commonest consequence of a certain kind of education.[18]

Similarly, Schuon:

> The source of our knowledge of God is at one and the same time
> the Intellect and Revelation. In principle the Intellect knows ev-
> erything because all possible knowledge is inscribed in its very
> substance, and it promises absolute certainty because its knowl-
> edge is a "being," or a participation in being, and not merely a
> "seeing."[19]

The Ark refers to a symbol or symbolism expressive of a metaphysical
principle. This is not simply the Ark of Noah or the Ark of the Covenant, to limit ourselves to the Semitic traditions. The reader is asked to
put aside preconceptions associated with this or that symbol of the Ark.
Within the context of an examination of metaphysics, the symbolism
of the Ark of Noah and the symbolism of the Ark of the Covenant are
revealed as two aspects of the one principle. Moreover, these two symbolisms are not exclusive, each containing the other, with the significant
difference being a matter of perspective and emphasis. When talking of
metaphysics and traditional symbolism the question of perspective has
none of the arbitrariness of certain modern relativist theories, but on the
contrary is a matter of precision. Furthermore, the principle of the Ark
can be recognised in various seemingly incongruous forms. These forms
are of secondary interest in the context of this book; in the end we are
concerned principally with the metaphysic of the Ark as expressed in
the language of metaphysics. Having said this, it is necessary to devote a
great part of this work to examining the universal mythologies and traditions related to the Ark, to venture into specific mythologies in order to
decipher certain symbolisms and to explain the metaphysical principles
that inform them.

In recognising the "universality" of these traditions another point
must be made. Guénon refers to the movement from one language or
tradition to another so as to make use of the best fitted form to explain
the principle. While this represents the ideal scenario it nevertheless requires a proficiency in each of the "languages" which I do not claim.
Hence, as discretion is the better part of valour, it may transpire that the
best fitted form is overlooked in preference to the tradition with which I
am most familiar. For this reason the mythological exposition of the Ark
concentrates on the Western traditions—Judaic, Christian and Islamic.
This is, however, only an expedient and we often turn to the Oriental
traditions wherever they throw light on the issues at hand.

The Ark: Principle and Form

'Make me a sanctuary so that I can reside among them.'
Exodus 25:8

The Ark is the receptacle of Divine Immanence. This must be qualified by recognition of the fact that Immanence is, in effect, its own receptacle, in a similar manner to which it might be said that a word is the receptacle of its meaning, while at the say time being identical with it. Divine Immanence, or the Divine Presence, is identical with Being, which is both its own principle and effect. In turn, Being gives rise to the distinction, recognised by Plato among others, between Being and becoming.[20]

Immanence implies Transcendence or Beyond Being.[21] The Divine Reality *per se* may be signalled by the term "The Absolute." A simple overview of the station of Immanence in the context of the Absolute can be expressed thus:

Transcendence = Beyond-Being
Immanence = Being
Being "contains" becoming
becoming = the play of cosmic existence

The existential world is a mode or level of the Divine Immanence. Immanence is itself "contained" or prefigured by the Divine Transcendence. Guénon explains this distinction in terms of Universal (Transcendent) and Individual (Immanent) Existence:[22]

Universal—The Unmanifested
                   — Formless Manifestation
Individual—Formal Manifestation
              —Subtle state
              —Gross state

Guénon is quick to clarify that 'all that is manifested, even at this higher level [Formless Manifestation], is necessarily conditioned, that is to say, relative.'[23] In this sense Formless Manifestation is an aspect of Immanence.

The Unmanifested contains the possibility of Manifestation *in divinis*, this being Formless Manifestation; this gives rise to Formal Manifestation, which, at the level of cosmic existence, gives rise to the Subtle (psychic) and the Gross (corporeal) states. Transcendence, which contains Immanence, is itself embraced by the Divine Totality (the Absolute). Schuon describes this thus: 'The Absolute by definition contains the Infinite—the common content being Perfection or the Good—and

4

the Infinite in its turn gives rise, at the degree of that "lesser Absolute" that is Being, to ontological All-Possibility. Being cannot not include efficient Possibility, because it cannot prevent the *Absolute* from including the Infinite.'[24]

Two difficulties arise with the use of the term "Being." Firstly, there can be confusion between two distinct usages of the term "Being." On the one hand Being corresponds to the Supreme Principle and is identical in this usage with the Absolute, and is therefore, somewhat paradoxically, Beyond-Being or Transcendence. On the other hand Being is sometimes taken as referring especially, if not exclusively, to the level of Manifestation or to Immanence. This is the distinction in the Hindu tradition of *nirguna Brahman* (unqualified *Brahman*) and *saguna Brahman* (qualified *Brahman*). Oldmeadow sees here 'a principle analogous to Meister Eckhart's distinction between god (the ontological, Being dimension of the Absolute; *Īśvara*) and the God-head (the Absolute, Beyond-Being, unqualified; *Brahman*).'[25]

The second difficulty arises insomuch as the term "Being" is used to refer to an exclusive category of the onto-cosmological chain. I have said that Being is synonymous with Immanence and that Immanence is Individual Existence and that this is Formal Manifestation; I have qualified this last identification by noting that Immanence includes Formless Manifestation. However, from a certain point of view, Being, while not itself the Absolute, is nevertheless of the Divine realm, and thus it might be said that in no way can it be identified as part of Manifestation. Here the term "Being" is used to classify the unmanifested ontological principle or cause. Manifestation is consequently the cosmological effect. Being is thus distinct from Manifestation as the category cause is distinct from the category effect. Yet, from another point of view, cause and effect may be identified in the context of the wholeness of a thing itself; in this sense, Being embraces both its unmanifested principle and its manifested realisation.

According to the usage employed herein, Being is both Transcendent and Immanent, both "uncreated" and "created," to use the language of the Christian doctrine of the *Logos* or Intellect. Here it is the case that Being is an interface—a *barzakh* in the language of Islam—between these two "domains." Being is Transcendent inasmuch as it corresponds to, or is prefigured in, the Supreme Principle and it is Immanent inasmuch as it is the principle of onto-cosmological existence.

In talking of the Ark as the receptacle of Divine Immanence we are primarily talking of Being in its role as principle of onto-cosmological existence, although here the distinction between Immanence and Transcendence occasionally becomes blurred. As Schuon remarks,

When we speak of transcendence, we understand in general objective transcendence, that of the Principle, which is above us as it is above the world; and when we speak of immanence, we understand generally speaking subjective immanence, that of the Self, which is within us. It is important to mention that there is also a subjective transcendence, that of the Self within us inasmuch as it transcends ego; and likewise there is also an objective immanence, that of the Principle in so far as it is immanent in the world, and not in so far as it excludes it and annihilates it by its transcendence. ... One finds here an application of the Taoist *Yin-Yang*: transcendence necessarily comprises immanence, and immanence just as necessarily comprises transcendence. For the Transcendent, by virtue of its infinity, projects existence and thereby necessitates immanence; and the Immanent, by virtue of its absoluteness, necessarily remains transcendent in relation to existence.[26]

For the sake of clarifying the basic argument it is acceptable to say that Being is comprised of two modes: efficient and potential. To say efficient is to recognise Being as becoming, as extended through a cycle of cosmic existence. To say potential is to recognise Being *in divinis*, particularly in the intermediate state between the completion of one cycle and the beginning of the next.[27] The symbol of the Ark expresses Being in both its efficient and potential mode. For example, in the Judaic tradition the Ark of the Covenant well expresses the receptacle of Being in terms of the extension of a cycle of cosmic existence: the Ark is the "heart" of the Temple, where the temple is an *imago mundi*; the heart is the container of its extensions, these being the efficient realisations of its virtualities; hence the Ark of the Covenant contains the entirety of cosmic existence *in actu*.[28] The Ark of Noah well expresses the receptacle of Being *in potentia* where the Ark expresses the "seed" for the next cycle of cosmic existence. In his essay on the Hindu Flood, Coomaraswamy observes that during each mythic flood 'the seeds, ideas, or images of the future manifestation persist during the interval or inter-Time of resolution on a higher plane of existence, unaffected by the destruction of manifested forms.'[29] He remarks on the preservation of the seed, from which "future manifestation" may emerge, as being effected through the voyage of an "ark" or "ship": 'in the case of the partial resolution or submergence of manifested form which takes place at the close of a *manvantara*, the connecting link is provided by the voyage of a Manu in an ark or ship.'[30] In the final analysis both modes of Being can be recognised in the symbolism of the Ark of Noah and the Ark of the Covenant.

6

There are two fundamental expressions of the Ark symbol: the Ark as the divine "vehicle" (boat, ship, chariot) and the Ark as the "house of God." The Ark of the Deluge is obvious in the manner in which it is a vehicle. Regarding the Ark of the Deluge as a "house," this connection is made explicit in the *Epic of Gilgamesh* where the ship of Ut-napishtim is constructed from the material of his house;[31] again, Islamic tradition develops a connection between the Deluge and the *Ka'bah*, the Islamic house *par excellence*.[32] The Ark of the Covenant constitutes a house insomuch as the Ark "houses" the Commandments, the Word of God made writ. This is the Word made flesh—or "stone" as it is—which is to say, immanent. The appreciation of the Ark of the Covenant as the house of God is deepened through its role as the heart of the Temple, which is the Judaic house of God *par excellence*. The Ark of the Covenant is also a vehicle in the manner in which it conveys the Divine Presence throughout the exodus in the desert.[33] While these two forms express the two fundamental modes of the Ark symbol there are nevertheless various other forms that also express the idea of the Ark insomuch as they express the idea of the receptacle of Divine Immanence.

The symbols of the vehicle and the house are cosmic models, *imagines mundi*. As Guénon says, 'from the traditional point of view the construction of a ship, just as that of a house or chariot, is the realisation of a "cosmic model."'[34] The *imago mundi* imitates the structure of the universe and embodies a cosmology.[35] It reveals the extension and play of cosmic existence with respect to the ideas of Centre and Origin, which are expressed by the fundamental cosmological aspects: space and time. The *imago mundi* presents an image of a dynamic cosmology. As Adrian Snodgrass remarks with respect to the architectural form, the *imago mundi* 'is an image of the cosmos, not in stasis, but in dynamic procedure from Unity by way of the cosmogenetic diremption of the conjoint principles [Essence and Substance]; it is a likeness of the cosmos in the manner of its production from Principle.'[36] The purpose of the *imago mundi* is the sanctification of the cosmos. Mircea Eliade observes this with respect to the Temple, which 'sanctified not only the entire cosmos but also cosmic life–that is, time.'[37] According to Snodgrass, the 'built-form valorizes space; it confines and determines the limits of a sacred, and therefore meaningful space from out of the unlimited extent of profane and non-significant space.'[38] The *imago mundi* acts as a guide to the spiritual journey, both in the sense of a diagram or map and in the sense of it being a psychopomp.[39]

Hypostatic and Cosmological Numbers

By their wordings they made him logically manifold who is but One.
Rg Veda, 10.114.)

The One brought number into being, and number analysed the one, and the relation of number was produced by the object of numeration.
Ibn al-'Arabī[40]

Make all things according to the pattern which was shewn thee on the mount.
Exodus 25:40 & *Hebrews* 8:5

Immanence may be described by a series of numerical hypostases. Thus, to take but one schema as example: the number one expresses the principial point, both Centre and Origin; the number two expresses duality, subject-object; and the number three expresses the first sense of relationship, knower-knowing-known. The use of number in any symbolic system, properly called, is in no way intended to indicate a quantitative measure of levels or steps in a process of emanation or construction. The first hypostasis is not simply figured by the number one because it is first; rather it is first as an aspect of its integral unity, which is a quality of the number one. This distinction is born out by a deeper appreciation of the nature of symbolism itself.

One of the most explicit examples of a symbolism expressing Reality in terms of numerical hypostases is the ten-fold *sefirot* of Kabbalah.[41] The *sefirot* are commonly expressed as follows:

1	*Keter Elyon*	Supernal Crown
2	*Hokhmah*	Wisdom
3	*Binah*	Understanding or Intelligence
4	*Hesed*	Love or Mercy
5	*Gevurah* or *Din*	Power or Judgment respectively
6	*Tiferet*	Beauty
7	*Nezah*	Eternity or Victory
8	*Hod*	Majesty or Glory
9	*Yesod*	Foundation
10	*Malkhut*	Kingdom

Leo Schaya calls the *sefirot* the metaphysical "numbers" or "numerations" of the divine aspects, which are 'the principal keys to the mysteries of the Torah.'[42] Isaiah Tishby says that the *sefirot* are 'seen as spiritual forces, as attributes of the soul, or as means of activity within the Godhead, that is to say, as revelations of the hidden God, both to Himself and to that which is other than He.'[43] 'The *Sefirot* in their totality' says Schaya, 'constitute the doctrinal basis of Jewish esotericism; they are to the Kabbalah, the mystical "tradition" of Judaism, what the Ten Commandments are to the Torah, as the exoteric law.'[44] This is doubly relevant in the present context where the Commandments are to a degree synonymous with the Divine Immanence. Indeed Tishby reaches the 'crucial and unambiguous conclusion that the Torah is identical with God'.[45] He cites Rabbi Menahem Recanati:

> The commandments form a single entity, and they depend upon the celestial Chariot, each one fulfilling its own particular function. Every commandment depends upon one specific part of the Chariot. This being so, The Holy One, blessed be He, is not one particular area divorced from the Torah, and the Torah is not outside Him, nor is He something outside the Torah. It is for this reason that the kabbalists say that the Holy One, blessed be His name, is the Torah.[46]

Schaya:

> The ten *Sefirot* represent the spiritual archetypes not only of the Decalogue, but also those of all the revelations of the Torah. They are the principial determinations or eternal causes of all things. This decad is divided into nine emanations or intellections by which the supreme *Sefirah*, the "cause of causes," makes itself known to itself and to its universal manifestation.[47]

As "spiritual archetypes" the *sefirot* are analogous, *mutatis mundis*, to the Platonic Realm of Forms or Ideas (Gk. *eidē*) and the Divine Names of Islamic tradition.[48] For Muhyī al-Dīn Ibn al-'Arabī 'the universals, even though they have no tangible individual existence in themselves, yet (sic) are conceived of and known in the mind; this is certain. They are always unmanifest as regards individual existence, while imposing their effects on all such existence; indeed individual existence is nothing other than [an outer manifestation] of them, that is to say, the universals.'[49] In the Introduction to his translation of Ibn al-'Arabī's, *Fusūs al-hikam*, Ralph Austin remarks, 'The term *Allah* is…the Supreme Name, the Name of names, which as the title of divinity establishes the whole quality of the relationship between the two poles, the one being divine and necessary [Absolute] while the other is non-divine and contingent [Relative]. The other names represent the infinite aspects or modes of the relationship in its infinite variety of qualities.'[50] The notion of Forms or Archetypes—and here one is careful to distinguish this term from the lesser "archetypes" of Jungian psychological theory—is given its most definitive European expression by Plato but is also found in the

Eastern traditions. The fifth century Chinese painter, Hsieh Ho, for example: 'The painters of old painted the idea (*i*) and not merely the shape (*hsing*).'[51]

The doctrine of Forms developed a theological interpretation with Philo who places the Forms in the *Logos*, the mind of God.[52] Similarly, Plotinus considers the Forms as thoughts in the Divine Mind or Intellect (*Nous*).[53] For St. Augustine, "The Form," in the final analysis, is God Himself, the ultimate and first Form that constitutes the being of things.[54] As Snodgrass puts it: 'Plato assigned Forms an absolute being; in the thought of Plotinus they became the contents of the World Soul; in St. Augustine they are the thoughts of a personal God. The three doctrines are shifts in emphasis, in turn stressing the metaphysical, the cosmological and the theological aspects of a single concept.'[55] In all cases the Forms are, as it were, the "model" upon which the manifest world is based. 'A form' says Jacob Boehme, 'is made in the resigned will according to the platform or model of eternity, as it was known in the glass of God's eternal wisdom before the times of this world.'[56] The Forms are the unspoken expression of Divine Immanence; and the realm of the Forms, according to Clement of Alexandria, is none other than the Ark of the Covenant.[57]

The Form, as understood by St. Augustine, which is the same with the Intellect as conceived of by Plotinus and Meister Eckhart, is unity. This unity is refracted, so to speak, though the plurality of Forms, like a ray of light shining through a diamond. The symbolism of light is, along with that of sound or speech, the most common symbolism used to express the operation of the Realm of Forms. According to Dante, 'The Divine Light rays out immediately upon the Intelligences, and is reflected by these Intelligences upon other things.'[58] The image of light expresses the illumination of Being from the darkness of Chaos, where Being is identical with the Intellect: 'God in Himself is the Light of all creaturely knowledge.'[59] As Tishby remarks, 'The basic and most commonly used symbol in the *Zohar* is, as its name implies, that of light and splendor.'[60] Light and speech are combined in the symbolism of the *Fiat Lux* of *Genesis*, which, as we will see, is also the symbolism of the river that 'flowed out of Eden to water the garden, and there divided and became four rivers' (Gen.2:10). This is what Guénon calls the "Celestial Ray" or "Divine Ray," which Hindu doctrine denotes by the names of *Buddhi* and *Mahat*.[61]

The *sefirot* number ten. This numbering is neither absolute nor is it arbitrary. In the first place, the quantity of hypostases does not delineate in any absolute way the "structure" of the Absolute; God is not "constructed" of any number of distinct attributes. As Schaya says, 'the fact that God makes himself known under multiple aspects, does not mean that he is in reality any particular number or multitude; "he is One and there is no other."'[62] Moreover, "oneness" is itself a symbolic qualification, and we must recall that Schaya is here considering the monotheism of the Judaic tradition. By contrast, in the Vedantic tradition the Supreme Cause is said to be beyond number, otherwise, as Alain Daniélou remarks, 'Number would be the First Cause. But the number one, although it has peculiar properties, is a number like two, or three, or ten, or a million.'[63] The Vedantists go so far as to say that 'The nature of illusion (*māyā*) is the number one.'[64] Thus they talk of *advaita*, "not-two" or "nonduality," a term, as Coomaraswamy says, 'which, while it denies duality, makes no affirmations about the nature of unity and must not be taken to imply anything like our monisms or pantheism.'[65] This idea of nonduality is also found in Western tradition. Shakespeare: 'Single nature's double name / Neither two nor one was call'd.'[66] As Schuon says, 'one may well wonder what interest God has in our believing that He is One rather than manifold. In fact He has no such interest, but the idea of Unity determines and introduces a saving attitude of coherence and interiorisation which detaches man from the hypnosis, both dispersive and compressive, of the outward and manifold world; it is man, and not God, who has an interest in believing that God is One.'[67] The Absolute is beyond any qualification; it is *neti neti*, "neither this nor that."

In the second place, the quantity of hypostases is precise according to the symbolic adequacy of its number. There are various accounts of Reality that use numerical hypostases and each are in their own way correct and precise. Schuon:

> When one sets out to give an account of metacosmic Reality by means of numerical hypostases, one might without being in the least arbitrary stop at the number three, which constitutes a limit that is all the more plausible in that to some extent it marks a falling back on Unity; it may be said to express unity in the language of plurality and seems to set up a barrier to the further unfolding of the latter. But with no less reason one can proceed further, as indeed various traditional perspectives do.[68]

Certainly the ternary is the most widely used means of expressing, both theologically and mythologically, the Divine Immanence. The *sefirot* number ten; in esoteric Islam there are "Ninety-Nine Divine Names";[69] again, in the esoteric traditions of the Hebrews, where this type of symbolism is common, we find the "seventy-two Names of God" and the "seventy-two lettered Name of God,"[70] or, alternatively, it is said that Reality is built out of the twenty-two letters of the Hebrew alphabet;

in the Taoist tradition Universal Manifestation is expressed by the "ten thousand beings." None of these numerical qualifications denies the others; instead each describes a characteristic of the Divine Reality.[71] In this sense, Tishby says that 'the *sefirot* become specified, limited areas within the Godhead, not, of course, limited in the sense of tangible objects, but as displaying a spiritual pattern of categories, both of content and of character.'[72]

The symbolism of the numbering from one to ten provides an adequate account of the Divine Immanence. Here we have a complete realisation or "unfolding" of the potentiality inherent in the principial number one via the numbers two through nine and the subsequent dissolution of this realised "one-in-many" back into the potentiality from which it has come and from which, in reality, it has never departed. This dissolution is well figured by the "Arabic" numeral, ten, which suggests the return of the one to the metaphysical zero or principial potentiality. Zero is itself not a number. The relationship between zero and one can appear blurred in a similar fashion, and for the same reason, as that between Transcendent Being and Immanent Being. Moreover, we must be careful to avoid the modern rationalistic Western confusion that saw the Sanskrit name for zero, *sunya*, meaning "empty," becoming *chiffre* in the Germanic languages, which carries the meaning of "null" or "nothing."[73] 'Needless to say,' observes Robert Lawlor, '"nothing" is a different concept from "empty."'[74]

There are two further confusions that this type of number symbolism can produce, each, in its own way, derived from the confusion between Transcendent Being and Immanent Being. The first is the confusion that arises with the use of the number one, which is used variously to refer both to Being and the Absolute. In the first case the number one expresses both the unity of Being—the "lesser Absolute"—and its essential principality, demonstrated by its role as Demiurge. In the second case the term "The One" expresses the total Unity of the Absolute. The One, as such, refers to the Unity of the Absolute as, by definition, It includes both Being and Beyond-Being, both Immanence and Transcendence. This distinction between the Absolute and Being might be likened, to varying degrees, to the distinctions that exist, *mutatis mundis*, between Meister Eckhart's Godhead and God, between *Brahman* and *Ātman* in Its guise as *Īśvara*, or, in the Islamic tradition, between *al-Ahadiyah* (Transcendent Unity) and *al-Wāhidiyah* (Unicity). In the context of the current book "The One," where used, indicates the Absolute; "the one" or "the monad" indicates Being as the onto-cosmological principle.

The second confusion that can arise is associated with the use of the number three. Here a distinction must be made between the Trinity—which expresses the three coessential "modes" or "aspects" of the Divine Reality[75]—and the cosmogonic ternary—which arises with the polarization within Being of Essence and Substance. This second use of the number three might best be described by the "mythological" archetype: Being-Father-Mother. A further distinction arises between the ternary Being-Essence-Substance and the ternary Essence-Manifestation-Substance. Again, there is confusion between these "creative" ternaries and the cosmic ternary composed of a hierarchy of constituent elements of the microcosm, such as the ternary, *corpus-anima-spiritus*. There are, of course, numerous other confusions associated with the use of number symbolism; all that can be said here is that one must be aware of two basic, yet seemingly contradictory, guidelines: firstly, symbolism is a precise science and, secondly, symbols are homogenous and hermeneutically dynamic. As Tishby remarks, 'the *sefirot*, which are finite and measurable, are not, however, static objects, like fixed, solid rungs on a ladder of the progressive revelation of the divine attributes. They are on the contrary, dynamic forces, ascending and descending, and extending themselves within the area of the Godhead.'[76]

The dynamism of the *sefirot* means that they can be contemplated from a multitude of points of view. As Schaya observes,

> the *Sefirotic* unity can be contemplated *ad intra* by regarding all its aspects as enclosed in *Keter*, the supreme *Sefirah*, which is identical with *en sof*, pure "infinity." In this case, the *Sefirotic* hierarchy is imagined in the form of concentric circles, the outermost of which is surrounded by *Keter*, and the innermost of which is *Malkhut*, the last of the *Sefirot*...From this point of view the "cause of causes," or "supreme will," concentrates his "thought" (epithet of *Hokhmah*) on his universal "kingdom," *Malkhut*, in order to create the cosmos...On the other hand, the *Sefirotic* "world of emanation" can be contemplated *ad extra*, taking the same symbolism of concentric circles as support, but this time placing *Keter* in the centre and *Malkhut* on the periphery...So, if one looks "inwards" God creates the world by "contraction" or "concentration" of his ontological possibilities, and if one looks "outwards," by their "expansion" or "radiation."[77]

Again, the *sefirot* can be contemplated in terms of the harmonizing synthesis achieved in *Tiferet*, which is here represented as the "medial" *sefirot*, the "heart of God." The classical arrangement of the *sefirot*, as Schaya remarks, is the hierarchical "*Sefirotic* Tree," although here again many variants exist as regards the "channels" connecting each *sefirah* to all the others.[78]

The account of the Ark of Noah—and to a lesser extent the Ark of the Covenant—serves as a framework for our consideration of the receptacle of Divine Immanence. With this in mind it might be said that the mythology of the Ark of Noah is structured by the movement from zero (the waters of the flood),[79] through the principial one (the Ark as "seed"), via the duad as both retraction ("two by two") and emanation (the "twin peaked mountains"), to the ternary, both as a hierarchy of constituent elements (the "three decks" of the Ark) and as a creative source (the "three sons" of Noah), to the quaternary, which may be said to express Immanence in terms of cosmic stability (the altar [*Gen*.8:20], the Temple, the *Ka'bah*). The quaternary expresses the realisation of the ternary as an unfolding of the cosmic conditions of space and time. Space is reflected on earth by the four directions, North, South, East and West. Time manifests as the four seasons, the four parts of the day, the four ages of creatures and worlds. The quaternary expresses fullness and completion, and in this sense it is analogous to the denary by way of the relationship developed and made explicit with the Pythagorean *Tetraktys*.[80] In the unfolding of the quaternary is the fullness of the decad. As expedient to this study I focus on the symbolic "progression" from zero to four, although these naturally give rise to the other numbers of the decad.

REPRESENTATIONS OF THE UNITY OF THE
TEN *SEFIROTH*

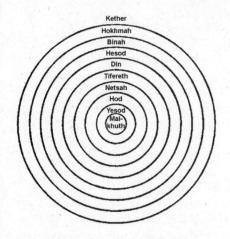

Fig. I. Divine Concentration (or *Sefirothic* Emanation, seen *ad intra*)

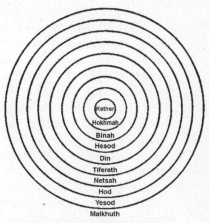

Fig. II. Divine Radiation (or *Sefirothic* Emanation, seen *ad extra*)

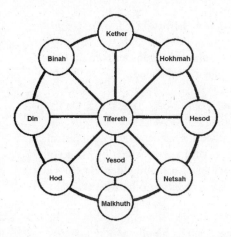

Fig. III. The 'Union' of the *Sefiroth* in the 'Heart' of God (*Tifereth*, inasmuch as it harmonizes and synthesizes all the other *Sefiroth*)

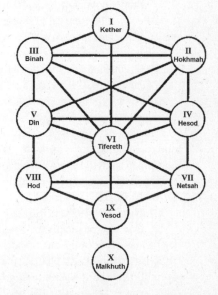

Fig. IV. The 'Tree of the *Sefiroth*' (Representing the hierarchy from the standpoint of prototypical position and relationship)

Fig.1: I-IV — from Schaya, *The Universal Meaning of the Kabbalah*, 1971, p.29.

Notes

1. Lord Northbourne, *Religion in the Modern World*, 1963, p.34.

2. With these can be recognised the writings of Seyyed Hossein Nasr, Marco Pallis, Martin Lings, Adrian Snodgrass, et al. However, most vital in this understanding are the sacred scriptures, texts and commentaries of the various traditions themselves. According to Kenneth Oldmeadow, 'The traditionalists, by definition, are committed to the explication of the *philosophia perennis* which lies at the heart of the diverse religions and behind the manifold forms of the world's different traditions. At the same time, they are dedicated to the preservation and illumination of the traditional forms which give each religious heritage its *raison d'être* and guarantee its formal integrity and, by the same token, ensure its spiritual efficacy' (*Traditionalism*, 2000, p.viii).

3. In the Introduction to his book, Oldmeadow notes the 'political and sentimental accretions' associated with the terms "tradition," "traditionalism" and "traditionalist" (on this point see Guénon, *RQ*, 1995, pp.251-52). Nevertheless, Oldmeadow remarks that 'as these writers would concede the need for some kind of generic label for their thought most would find "traditionalism" the least unsatisfactory' (*Traditionalism*, 2000, p.x).

4. Oldmeadow, *Traditionalism*, 2000, p.61.

5. Perry, 'The Revival of Interest in Tradition' in Fernando (ed.), *The Unanimous Tradition*, 1991, p.4.

6. It is worth noting the onomatopoeia of these names for tradition (*shelsheleth*, *silsilah*, *parampara*), which are themselves "chains" of sounds.

7. Guénon, *MB*, 1981, p.15.

8. M. Perry, 'The Forbidden Door': *Sophia* Vol.7, No.2, 2001, p.155. On the question of "ancient man" see Coomaraswamy, 'Primitive Mentality': *SP1*, 1977.

9. A distinction must be drawn between modern science, which is empirical and quantitative and, as such, limited, and *scientia sacra,* which by virtue of participation in the supra-sensible order transcends these limitations. Herein the term "science" is used in reference to *scientia sacra* unless otherwise stated.

10. Nasr, *KS*, 1981, p.190.

11. Nasr, *KS*, 1981, p.190.

12. Eric Sharpe recalls the attempts of Cicero and Lactantius to derive the basis for the word "religion" respectively from the verbs *relegere* (to re-read) and *religare* (to bind fast). Sharpe concludes that 'there is no way of knowing which is right' (Sharpe, *Understanding Religion*, 1975, p.39). In fact both root meanings express the idea of the relationship between the human and the Divine. Religion is that which "binds" the human to the Divine. It is again the formal transmitter of the Sacred, which is to say, it is a continuous "re-reading" of the Sacred, in respect to both the literal re-reading of the sacred Scriptures and the eternal "re-reading" of the cosmogonic Word (see my 'Preliminary Remarks on Reclaiming the Meaning of "Religion"': *Sacred Web* 7, 2001, pp.59-66).

13. Guénon, *MB*, 1981, p.156. This, then, is to forestall the Western misunderstanding that tends to confuse the relationship between metaphysic and

religion; to appreciate this relationship correctly is to understand that 'between the two viewpoints there is all the difference that exists in Islam between the *haqīqah* (metaphysical and esoteric) and the *shariyah* (sic) (social and exoteric)' (Guénon, *SC*, 1975, p.102, n.4).

14. Schuon, *IFA*, 1989, p.79. Elsewhere: 'A religion is a form, and so also a limit, which contains the Limitless, to speak in paradox; every form is fragmentary because of the necessary formal exclusion of other possibilities; the fact that these forms…each in their own way represent totality does not prevent them from being fragmentary in respect of their particularization and reciprocal exclusion' (Schuon, *UI*, 1976, p.144). 'Each revealed religion' remarks Nasr, 'is *the* religion and *a* religion, *the* religion inasmuch as it contains within itself the Truth and the means of attaining the Truth, *a* religion since it emphasizes a particular aspect of Truth in conformity with the spiritual and psychological needs of the humanity for whom it is destined' (Nasr, *Ideals and Realities of Islam*, 1966, p.15).

15. Hence, according to Schuon, Shintoism is not a total "religion" but requires a superior complement that Buddhism has provided (see *LS*, 1999, p.154).

16. Guénon, *MB*, 1981, p.15.

17. As Guénon remarks, 'it is only in so far as any question, no matter what, is related to principles that it can be said to be treated metaphysically; it is this truth which must never be lost sight of, so long as it is intended to treat genuine metaphysic and not of the pseudo-metaphysic of European philosophers' (Guénon, *MB*, 1981, p.9).

18. Guénon, *MB*, 1981, p.10.

19. Schuon, *LT*, 1975, p.71. Schuon understands the term "Intellect" in the same sense as it is used by Plotinus or Meister Eckhart.

20. *Timaeus* 27D-28A.

21. "Beyond Being" is also Platonic (*Republic* 7.6.509b), although it is more usually associated with Plotinus (for example, *Enneads* 4.3.17; 6.9.11).

22. Guénon, *MB*, 1981, p.34.

23. Guénon, *MB*, 1981, p.33.

24. Schuon, *IFA*, 1989, p.38.

25. Oldmeadow, 'Śankara's Doctrine of *Māyā*': *Asian Philosophy*, Vol.2, No.2, 1992, p.140.

26. Schuon, *EPW*, 1981, p.236.

27. In the Hindu tradition this intermediate state is called a *sandhyā*. According to the doctrine of cycles (*Manvantara*) the end of a particular cycle comes with a *pralaya* or "dissolution," an idea that is well expressed by the symbolism of the deluge.

28. The realisation of cosmic existence unfolds "within" the Heart or the Ark; from the human perspective this relationship is inverted, so that it appears that existence grows "outwards" from the Heart. To avoid any confusion note that the phrase *in actu* refers to the logical order and the phrase *in potentia* to the real order.

29. Coomaraswamy, 'The Flood in Hindu Tradition': *SP2*, 1977 p.398.

30. Coomaraswamy, 'The Flood in Hindu Tradition': *SP2*, 1977, p.400.

31. 'Reed-hut, hearken! Wall, reflect! / Man of Shuruppak, son of Ubar-Tutu, / Tear down (this) house, build a ship!' (*Gilgamesh,* XI, in Dalley (ed.), *MM*, 1991, p.110).

32. According to Shī'ite symbolism the original terrestrial *Ka'bah* was raised to the Fourth Heaven at the time of the Deluge to become the "Temple Frequented by Angels" (*al-bayt al-ma'mūr*) (see Snodgrass, *ATE2*, 1990, p.421, n.34). This corresponds to the ascension of the *Shekhinah* in the Judaic tradition, where it is said that during the time of the Flood the *Shekhinah* ascended to the "fourth region" (see Cohen, *ET*, 1995, p.44). This vertical ascent bears comparison with the ascent of the Ark of Manu up the slope (*pravat*) of heaven.

33. Here the symbolisms of the desert and the waters of the flood are essentially analogous.

34. Guénon, *FS*, 1995, p.228.

35. Snodgrass, *ATE1*, 1990, p.57.

36. Snodgrass, *ATE1*, 1990, p.62.

37. Eliade, *Sacred and Profane*, 1987, p.75.

38. Snodgrass, *ATE1*, 1990, p.57.

39. It may be said that certain structures act to lead the journeying spirit onwards insomuch as their construction draws the intellect deeper through each initiatory level. The construction of the Judaic Temple and the Gothic Cathedrals offer examples of this kind.

40. Ibn al-'Arabī, *Fusūs* cited in Perry, *TTW*, 2000, p.779. Austin's 1980 translation has: 'The number one makes number possible, and number deploys the one' (p.86).

41. The best exposition of the *sefirot* that I have found is Professor Isaiah Tishby's introduction to the *sefirot* in his *The Wisdom of the Zohar.* Leo Schaya's *The Universal Meaning of the Kabbalah*, offers an excellent account of the *sefirot* from the position of the *sophia perennis*, which accords with and complements Professor Tishby's exposition.

42. Schaya, *UMK*, 1971, p.21.

43. Tishby, *WZ1*, 1989, p.271.

44. Schaya, *UMK*, 1971, p.21.

45. Tishby, *WZ1*, 1989, p.284.

46. Rabbi Menahem Recanati, *Sefer Ta'amei ha-Mizvot* (Basle 1581), 3a, cited in Tishby, *WZ1*, 1989, p.284.

47. Schaya, *UMK*, 1971, p.21.

48. On the Islamic doctrine of archetypes see Burckhardt, *ISD*, 1976, Ch.9. Regarding the Forms as Names it is said in the *Tikkune Zohar*: 'Each *Sefirah* has a specific Name, by which the angels are also named, but Thou (the unknowable Essence) has no specific name, for Thou art the One which fills all names and gives them their true meaning' (cited in Perry, *TTW*, 2000, p.666).

49. Ibn al-'Arabī, *Fusūs*, (1980, p.53).

50. Austin, Introduction to Ibn al-'Arabī's, *Fusūs*, (1980, p.30).

51. Cited in Coomaraswamy, *The Transformation of Nature in Art*, 1934, p.15. For worldwide examples of this doctrine see Perry, *TTW*, 2000, pp.670-74.

52. Snodgrass, *ATE1*, 1990, p.26 citing Philo, *Leg. All.* III.9.29.

53. *Enneads* 5.1.4.

54. St. Augustine, *De Libero Arbitrio* II.16-17, cited in Snodgrass, *ATE1*, 1990, p.27.

55. Snodgrass, *ATE1*, 1990, p.27. Snodgrass cites Erwin Panofsky, *Idea: A Concept in Art Theory*, Columbia: University of South Carolina, 1968.

56. Boehme, *Signatura Rerum*, XV, 43.

57. *Stromata* 5.35.5.

58. Dante, *Il Convito*, 3.14.2.

59. Meister Eckhart, cited in Kelly, *Meister Eckhart on Divine Knowledge*, 1977, p.201.

60. Tishby, *WZ1*, 1989, p.290. "Zohar" means "splendor."

61. See Guénon, *SC*, 1975, Ch.24; *MB*, 1981, Ch.7 and also Ch.10 for the symbolism of the "solar ray" (*sushamnā*). It is possible, from a particular state of being, to conceive of two world axii corresponding to the horizontal axis and vertical axis respectively. The vertical axis, the "Divine Ray," includes the horizontal axis by virtue of its greater universality.

62. Schaya, *UMK*, 1971, p.21. As examples of this dictum in the Judaic tradition Schaya cites *Isaiah* Chs. 45 & 46.

63. Daniélou, *MGI*, 1985, p.6.

64. *Maudgala Purāna*, 1, cited in Daniélou, *MGI*, 1985, p.7.

65. Coomaraswamy, 'The Vedanta and Western Tradition': *SP2*, 1977, p.5.

66. Shakespeare, *The Phoenix and the Turtle*, 39-40.

67. Schuon, *IFA*, 1989, p.38.

68. Schuon, *EPW*, 1981, p.70.

69. See Al-Ghazali, *The Ninety-Nine Beautiful Names of God*. Ibn al-'Arabi remarks that there are said to be eighteen thousand universes. This derives from 1. the Intellect, 2. the Soul, 3. the Throne, 4. the Pedestal, then seven Heavens, four Elements and three Births: the total makes eighteen, and in detailed enumeration they total eighteen thousand. 'However,' says Ibn al-'Arabi, 'in reality the truth is that the Universes cannot be numbered' (*Lubb*, 1981, p.14).

70. Alternatively given as "seventy Names" and directly related to the "seventy-two lettered Name of God."

71. The number seventy-two, for example, describes precisely the number of degrees between the principle and its realisation, between the 36 divisions of the Zodiac–representing cosmic existence–envisioned with respect to the perfect number, 10, that is 360, and the 36 divisions envisioned with respect to the spatio-temporal number, 12, that is 432. The difference or number of degrees between 360 and 423 is 72.

72. Tishby, *WZ1*, 1989, p.271. This idea of "areas within the Godhead" raises the theological spectre of the partibility of God. In reality, God the absolute One, has no "parts," but an infinity of possibilities.

73. Lawlor makes this point in his *Sacred Geometry*, 1989, p.19. Lawlor mistakes *"chiffra"* as Latin. *Chiffre* is a Germanic word meaning "a cipher," that is, the arithmetical symbol (0) denoting no amount.

74. Lawlor, *Sacred Geometry*, 1989, p.19.

75. There is a trouble here with the use of terms such as "modes" or "aspects" which we will consider further at the appropriate time.

76. Tishby, *WZ1*, 1989, p.272.

77. Schaya, *UMK*, 1971, p.30.

78. Schaya, *UMK*, 1971, p.30.

79. Zero is generally reserved in spiritual literature for the Absolute Reality as it is in Itself. This symbolism is used here by analogical transposition.

80. $1 + 2 + 3 + 4 = 10$ (see Taylor, *The Theoretic Arithmetic of the Pythagoreans*, 1991).

Symbolism

The Divine Language

God guides towards His Light whoever He wants.
God gives symbols for men. God knows everything.
Sūrah 24: al-Nūr [Light]

And the perceivers shall shine.
Daniel 12:3[1]

It is appropriate that a study of the symbolism of the Ark has as a prolegomenon an exposition of the traditional understanding of symbolism. The symbol, as we are envisaging it here, is the immanent expression of the Divine, which, through participation in both the sensible and the supra-sensible orders of existence, acts as the vehicle by which the human may be lead back to the Divine. According to Snodgrass, a symbol is 'a sensible entity that directs the understanding from the physical towards the supra-physical levels of reality.'[2] The symbol operates through the relationship of the intelligence and the Intellect.[3] The unfolding or unveiling of Reality through a progression of symbolic initiations acts like so many rungs on a ladder leading "upwards" to the Divine. Thus, the symbol is anagogic, from the Greek *anago* ("to lead up to"), as in leading the understanding up to a metaphysical meaning.[4]

The metaphysical is that which resides beyond the physical. It is the archetypal informant and referent of physical existence. Between the metaphysical and the physical realms there is the same difference as between the "intelligible" and the "sensible" worlds of the Platonic doctrine of Forms. Snodgrass describes the Forms as,

> universal, absolute, separate, simple, eternal, immutable, intelligible, independent of the discursive mind and of the sensible phenomena which are their copies. [They] do not change; they are, therefore, outside time: they are eternal. Time is coeval with the cosmos; the coming into existence of the ordered world and the coming into being of time are simultaneous; but the Forms, being eternal, are prior to the manifestation of the world and antecedent to time.[5]

A distinction needs to be made between metaphysics, which has as its point of departure the state of certitude, and the philosophical proposition, which, according to a peculiar modern adaptation of the term philosophy, has as its point of departure the state of doubt. Thus Schuon remarks,

What essentially distinguishes the metaphysical from the philosophical proposition is that the former is symbolical and descriptive, in the sense that it makes use of symbols to describe or translate knowledge possessing a greater degree of certainty than any knowledge of a sensible order, whereas philosophy ... is never anything more than what it expresses. When philosophy uses reason to resolve a doubt, this proves precisely that its starting point is a doubt that it is striving to overcome, whereas we have seen that the starting point of a metaphysical formulation is always something essentially intellectually evident or certain, which is communicated, to those able to receive it by symbolical or dialectical means designed to awaken in them the latent knowledge that they bear unconsciously and, it may even be said, eternally within them.[6]

The symbol partakes of both the Transcendent and the Immanent, both the Divine Unity and the diversity of Its realised or actualised expression.[7] This participation in both levels of existence allows the symbol to fulfil its function as the intermediary—the mode of communication—between the Divine and the human. As Schuon reminds us, 'The language of the sacred Scriptures [the language of symbolism] is divine, but at the same time it is necessarily the language of men; it is made for men and could be divine only in an indirect manner.'[8] Still, it cannot be stressed enough that the symbol is not arbitrary. 'The symbol is not based on man-made conventions,' remarks Nasr, 'It is an aspect of the ontological reality of things and as such is independent of man's perception of it.'[9] Regarding this error of arbitrariness, Schuon writes,

The symbolic language of the great traditions of mankind may indeed seem arduous and baffling to some minds, but it is nevertheless perfectly intelligible in the light of the orthodox commentaries; symbolism–this point must be stressed–is a real and rigorous science, and nothing can be more naïve than to suppose that its apparent naïvety springs from an immature and "prelogical" mentality. This science, which can properly be described as "sacred," quite plainly does not have to adjust itself to the modern experimental approach; the realm of revelation, of symbolism, of pure and direct intellection, stands in fact above both the physical and psychological realms, and consequently it lies beyond the scope of so-called scientific methods.[10]

Similarly, Coomaraswamy:

Symbolism is a language and a precise form of thought; a hieratic and a metaphysical language and not a language determined by somatic or psychological categories. Its foundation is in the analogical correspondence of all orders of reality and states of being or levels of reference; it is because 'This world is in the image of that, and vice versa' (*Aitareya Brāhmana* VIII.2, and *Kathā Upanishad* IV.10) that it can be said *Coeli enarrant gloriam Dei*.[11]

The symbol is infused with the radiance of the divine Light, which is itself a symbol of the Intellect. This shines both through and in the symbol. Mircea Eliade:

> Symbolism adds a new value to an object or to an action without however disturbing their own proper and immediate values. In applying itself to an object or an action, symbolism renders it "open." Symbolic thought makes the immediate reality "shine," but without diminishing it: in its own perspective the Universe is not closed, no object is isolated in its own existentialness; everything holds together in a closed system of correspondences and assimilations.[12]

In the words of Coleridge, a symbol is characterised above all by 'the translucence of the Eternal through and in the Temporal. It always partakes of the Reality which it renders intelligible; and while it enunciates the whole, abides itself as a living part in that Unity of which it is representative.'[13]

The Adequacy of Symbols

> Worship me in the symbols and images which remind thee of me.
> *Srimad Bhagavatam*, 9.5

> For now we see through a glass, darkly; but then face to face: now I know in part; but then shall I know even as I am known.
> *1Corinthians* 13:12

The referent of the symbol is the metaphysical Form, 'not to be known by the senses or the cognitive mind, but only by the immediate and intuitive knowledge, a non-differentiated state of awareness in which the knower, the known and the act of knowing are inseparably fused and non-distinct.'[14] The symbol participates in its referent and likewise facilitates participation with the Form.[15] Snodgrass remarks that this participation 'effects a re-cognition of the referent which, when this is metaphysical rather than physical, is a re-collection or re-membering in the Platonic sense of *anamnesia*.'[16] 'Knowledge' says Plato, 'is simply recollection.'[17] "Re-membering" is a process of knowing leading to absolute knowledge; "a process of becoming";[18] of "awakening," following Buddhist terminology; a process of "identification."[19] To talk of this as a "process" alludes to the distinction between "becoming" and "Being," between "participation" and "identity" *per se*. Thus Paul Tillich says that 'participation is not identity; they [symbols] are not themselves *the* Holy.'[20] On the other hand, the sacramentality of the symbol means that it is in fact ontologically "holy." This is simply to recognise that the Holy is not limited by the extent of all that is made holy by virtue of participation in it.

The symbol participates in both the Divine and human domains. Insomuch as the symbol participates in the human domain it is limited. Nevertheless, as Titus Burckhardt observes, 'the limitation inherent in the symbol cannot lower Him Who is symbolised: on the contrary, it is precisely in virtue of His perfection—or His infinity—that He is reflected at every possible level of existence by "signs" that are always unique.'[21]

The symbol differs from a "sign" *per se* in that the symbol partakes of its referent, whereas, in contrast, for a sign the signifier and the signified are necessarily and by definition distinct. This is due to the fact that they are at the same level of reality, 'the domain of individual experience of particulars'.[22] Tishby:

> There exists a permanent, integral relationship between the symbol and the thing symbolised, for a symbol has its symbolic character impressed upon it from the very beginning of its existence. Consequently, symbolic usage does not divorce the symbolic significance from the actual object utilized. On the contrary, by disclosing the symbolic relationship it has with the hidden divine being, one reveals the real nature of the object, in all its perfection. In mystical symbolism one does not exchange one meaning for another, but one adds to the common, revealed meaning a revelation of its own internal hidden mystery.[23]

In contrast, as Snodgrass remarks, 'the "symbols" of semiology, psycho-analysis, symbolist art, structural anthropology and current postmodernist theories of architecture are "signs," since their referents are knowable by the senses or conceivable by the mind'.[24] Here also we must distinguish clearly between the anagogic nature of "mystic symbolism" and allegory.[25] According to Gershom Scholem,

> If allegory can be defined as the representation of an expressible something by another expressible something, the mystical

symbol is an expressible representation of something which lies beyond the sphere of expression and communication, something which comes from a sphere whose face is, as it were, turned inward and away from us. A hidden and inexpressible reality finds its expression in the symbol. If the symbol is thus also a sign or representation it is nevertheless more than that.[26]

The warrant of a symbol's adequacy is 'its efficiency in producing in a qualified and receptive person an *adaequatio rei et intellectus*, that is to say a condition of true, intellectual knowledge'.[27] Snodgrass:

In one sense all things that exist—images, words, language, physical and mental phenomena—are symbols of the supra-empirical levels of reality. Every existent thing is the "reflection" of an archetypal Form. … In a more specific and restricted sense, however, there is also a deliberate and calculated symbolism, one that crystallizes the doctrinal teachings of a tradition in the form of a prescribed figurative or spatial representation. From this arises the convention of confining the term "symbol" to objects or images which pertain directly to doctrinal formulations, and in which the symbolic content is clearly and explicitly manifest. …These latter symbols, possessed of greater transparency than the usual run of sensible entities, are characterized by "adequacy" ["ad-equate," a "making equal to"], by an efficacy in producing in a qualified and receptive person an *adaequatio rei et intellectus*, which is to say a condition of true, intellectual knowledge. They are capable of provoking a recollection of a supra-mundane paradigm and, by that fact, are imbued with the sacred.[28]

The adequate or sacred symbol is deemed to have been "given"; it is revealed to the tradition from a non-human source.[29] As Coomaraswamy remarks, 'The traditional symbols … are not "conventional" but "given" with the ideas to which they correspond; one makes, accordingly, a distinction between *le symbolisme qui sait* and *le symbolisme qui cherche* [the symbolism which knows and the symbolism which searches], the former being the universal language of tradition, and the latter that of the individual and self-expressive poets who are sometimes called "Symbolists."'[30] Note that "adequation is not equality,"[31] which is to recall that "participation is not identity." The adequate symbol is 'true, analogical, accurate, canonical, hieratic, anagogic and arche-typal.'[32] The hierarchy of adequacy, so to speak, does not necessarily imply that any one symbol is more "perfect" than another, for each will be perfect in respect to its own function.[33] As Tillich remarks, 'Every symbol has a special function which is just *it* and cannot be replaced by more or less adequate symbols.'[34] According to Lama Govinda, 'it is the nature of a symbol to be as manifold as the life from which it grew, and yet to retain its character, its organic unity within the diversity of its aspects.'[35] This highlights the fact that, unlike signs, symbols are not arbitrary.

This does not then mean that the form of a symbol will precede the "need" for it. According to Guénon, symbolism seems to be 'quite specially adapted to the needs of human nature, which is not exclusively intellectual but which needs a sensory basis from which to rise to higher levels.'[36] In the final analysis the symbol is still only a "support." This raises the question of the necessity of the symbol as a means back to the Divine. On this point Guénon says, 'as such and in an absolute way, no outward form is necessary; all are equally contingent and accidental in relation to that which they express or represent.'[37]

The Symbolic Web

We come to this learning by analogies.

Plotinus[38]

The spider spins its web out of its own substance.

Brahma Sutra 2.1.25

The symbol is multivalent, containing and expressing multiple meanings simultaneously. These meanings are derived from the ultimate "diversity in Unity" of the metaphysical referent of the symbol. They are intrinsic and integral, and not contrived by human convention. As Guénon observes, 'every real symbol bears its multiple meanings within itself, and is so from its very origin; for it is not constituted as such in virtue of human convention but in virtue of the law of correspondence which links all the worlds together.'[39] He continues to defend this multiplicity of meaning against those who deny its integrity: 'If some see these meanings while others do not, or see them only partially, they are none the less really there: it is the "intellectual horizon" of each person that makes all the difference. Symbolism is an exact science and not a daydream in which individual fantasies can have a free run.'[40]

The multivalent nature of the symbol precludes a reductionist methodology.[41] As Eliade remarks, 'If we retain only one of its significations, in declaring it the only "fundamental" or "first" or "original" signification, we risk not grasping the true message of the symbol.'[42] Snodgrass stresses this point: 'An exegesis that does justice to the fullness of the symbol in both its horizontal and vertical dimensions will leave its meaning "open" and not confine it within the limiting configuration of a closed hypothesis.' Again, Eliade remarks, 'We compare or contrast two expressions of a symbol not in order to reduce them to a single, pre-existing expression, but in order to discover the process whereby a structure is likely to assume enriched meanings.'[43]

This enrichment of meanings, which is "inward looking" and unifying, should not be confused with an empirical or quantitative awareness of a multiple of corresponding symbols, which, by itself, is "outward looking" and indefinite. The meaning of any symbol is integral with that symbol; the corresponding symbols act as "reinforcements." Each analogous symbol is just that, which is to say that they are analogous but not identical for this would mean that they were in fact not separate but the same symbol. At the same time the "network of homologous symbols," as Snodgrass calls it, does itself reveal the essential principle of Unity in diversity.[44] The enrichment of a symbol through its correspondences is achieved by both reinforcement and by the revealing of the particular symbol in the unified network of homologies. Each of these lead back to an understanding of the Principle, of which they are respectively reflections on their particular levels.

The symbol is multivalent both horizontally and vertically. The horizontal valence of a symbol expresses its homologies on the plane of Existence on which that symbol exists.[45] Snodgrass:

> The symbol ... has a plurality of meanings on the horizontal level. Every symbol forms part of a schema of interlocking referents; it forms part of a *pattern* of concordant interrelationships. It does not stand in isolation but interconnects with other symbols, which fit together to form a mutually reinforcing web of meaning. A deeper understanding of a symbol is gained by studying the grid or net formed by its symbolic homologues. The pattern of meaning that emerges from the juxtaposition of cognate symbols does not exhaust the significance of the symbol, which, as we have seen, is ultimately beyond words, but it reinforces its intimations, indicating a logical cohesion and integrity which in itself is an intimation of the all-persuasiveness of Principle.[46]

The horizontal valence of the symbol is indefinitely extended in accord with the indefinitude of a horizontal plane of Existence.[47]

The vertical homologies guide the intellect "upwards" along the vertical pole of the Divine Ray. It is this aspect of the symbol which can truly be called anagogical. The vertical valence proceeds "into" the metaphysical realm, which is to say that it originates beyond the finite or definable level of onto-cosmological existence. Hence, the vertical valence of the symbol is infinite.[48]

On the horizontal plane the symbol is expressed through various modes. 'The net of symbolic cognates' says Snodgrass, 'is formed not only by visual and spatial symbols, but also by symbolic constructs expressed in other modes: *myth*, which is symbol expressed in a verbal or narrative form; *ritual*, which expresses the symbolic concepts by gestures and words; and *doctrine*, which expresses them conceptually.'[49] These modes are not exclusive. Ritual and doctrine may be found in myth, doctrine may be expressed through ritual, and the eternal Myth— the story of the Divine and the human—is "spoken" through participation in ritual and doctrine. Again, each mode is expressed through various forms. For example, the symbolic dialogue of mythology may be expressed both orally and visually. As Snodgrass observes, 'what the architectural symbol is spatially the myth is verbally.'[50]

The Universality of Symbols

…there is a universally intelligible language, not only verbal but also visual, of the fundamental ideas on which the different civilisations have been founded.

Ananda Coomaraswamy[51]

Languages differ, my son, but mankind is one; and speech likewise is one. It is translated from tongue to tongue, and we find it to be the same in Egypt, Persia, and Greece … Speech then is an image of intellect; and intellect is an image of God.

Hermes Trismegistus[52]

The fundamental derivation of the multiple symbols from the singular Principle means that certain expressions appear universally. This universality may be more easily recognised the greater the adequacy of the symbol. For example, the symbolisms of the "centre," the "cross" and the "circle" are found in nearly every tradition throughout the history of humankind. Each of these symbols may be regarded as pre-eminent in terms of adequacy. Snodgrass explains this universality, as evidenced through a comparative juxtaposition of the Traditions:

The network of homologous symbols, myths, rituals and doctrines that can be delineated by a process of comparative juxtaposition is capable of indefinite extension. Since all symbols within a tradition are so many variant reflections of one and the same Principle, they are all interconnected by way of this common reference, so that the analysis of the pattern of homologies generated from a given symbol as datum, if taken far enough, will eventually extend out to include the symbolic forms of *all* traditions.[53]

The apparent universality of symbols is often dismissed by scholars as the product of eclecticism. In answer to this accusation Guénon stresses the fundamental distinction between synthesis and syncretism.

> Syncretism consists in assembling from the outside a number of more or less incongruous elements which, when regarded, can never be truly unified; in short, it is a kind of eclecticism, with all the fragmentariness and incoherence that this always implies. Syncretism, then, is something purely outward and superficial; the elements taken from every quarter and put together in this way can never amount to anything more than borrowings that are incapable of being effectively integrated into a doctrine worthy of the name. ... Synthesis, on the other hand, is carried out essentially from within; by this we mean that it properly consists in envisaging things in the unity of their principle, in seeing how they are derived from and dependent on that principle, and thus uniting them, or rather becoming aware of their real unity, by virtue of a wholly inward bond, inherent in what is most profound in their nature.[54]

This is to realise that, 'there are symbols which are common to the most diverse and widely separated traditional forms, not as a result of "borrowings," which in many cases would be quite impossible, but because in reality they pertain to the Primordial Tradition from which these forms have issued either directly or indirectly.'[55]

The universality of certain symbols is also sometimes challenged on account of apparent contradictions between the usage of the symbol in this or that tradition. However, as Coomaraswamy remarks, 'this use of symbols which are contrary in their literal but unanimous in their spiritual sense very well illustrates the nature of metaphysics itself, which is not like a "philosophy," systematic, but is always consistent.'[56]

The Cosmic Theophany

The whole world is but a glass, full of lights representing the divine wisdom.

St. Bonaventura[57]

This world is verily an outer court of the Eternal, or of Eternity, and specially whatever in Time, or any temporal things or creatures, manifesteth or remindeth us of God or Eternity; for creatures are a guide and a path unto God and Eternity.

Theologia Germanica, L[58]

> It is not a question of knowing God when the veil be lifted but of knowing Him in the veil itself.
>
> Shaikh Ahmad al-Alawi[59]

According to Guénon, modern "naturalistic" interpretations of symbolism are an error that purely and simply reverse the hierarchy of relationships between the different orders of reality. Guénon:

> Natural phenomena in general, and especially astronomical phenomena, are never looked upon by the traditional doctrines otherwise than as a simple means of expression, whereby they symbolise certain truths of a higher order; and if they do in fact symbolise such truths, it is because their laws are fundamentally nothing but the expression of these very truths, in a particular domain, a sort of translation of the corresponding principles, naturally adapted to the special conditions of the corporeal and human state. It can therefore be seen how great is the error of those who imagine they have discovered "naturalism" in these doctrines, or who believe that the doctrines in question are only intended to describe and explain phenomena just as a "profane" science might do, though in a different form; this is really to reverse the true relationship, by taking the symbol itself for what it represents, the sign for the thing or the idea signified.[60]

> Thus, the purpose of symbols and myths has never been—as often wrongly alleged—to represent the movement of the heavenly bodies, the truth being that they often do contain figures inspired by that movement and intended to express, analogically, something very different, because the laws of that movement are a physical translation of the metaphysical principles on which they depend. … This holds good for historical facts no less than for anything else: they likewise conform to the law of correspondence just mentioned, and thereby, in their own mode, translate higher realities, of which they are, so to speak, a human expression.[61]

In the Traditional view, virgin Nature is a treasury of symbols of the supernatural. As Tishby says, 'The whole of nondivine existence is a great storehouse, as it were, full of symbols of the divine.'[62] Scholem remarks that the whole world is to the Kabbalist a *corpus symbolicum*.[63] According to St. Thomas Aquinas, analogy, which allows one to ascend from the knowledge of creatures to that of God, is 'nothing but a symbolic mode of expression based on the correspondence between the natural and the supernatural orders.'[64]

Nature, at the level of the cosmic environment, presents a symbolic economy that is both essential and effective: essential, as the Cosmos is none other than "one vast complex *Mythos*, or symbolic representation";[65] effective, as symbolism provides the agency for the return of the human to the Divine. Cosmic existence is *the* theophany and *a* theophany, where "theophany" has the literal meaning of "to show God." As Nasr remarks, theophany 'does not mean the incarnation of God in things but the reflection of the Divinity in the mirror of created forms.'[66] 'The cosmos' says Nasr, 'is not only the theatre wherein are reflected the Divine Names and Qualities. It is also a crypt through which man must journey to reach the Reality beyond cosmic manifestation.'[67]

To view the cosmos as symbol is not to deny its contingent reality nor the legitimacy of its *physis*. Nasr: 'To behold the cosmos as theophany is not to deny either the laws or the chain of cause and effect which pervade the cosmos but to view the cosmos and the forms it displays with such diversity and regularity as reflections of Divine Qualities and ontological categories rather than a veil which would hide the splendour of the face of the Beloved.'[68] Moreover, to view the events of sacred Scripture as symbols is not to deny them a phenomenal reality. 'Sacred facts' as Schuon remarks, 'cannot fail to corroborate symbolism since symbolism is in the very nature of things: holy persons have risen visibly to the sky; blasphemers have been swallowed up by the earth. Symbolism is a concrete reality founded on real analogies.'[69]

The Laws of Analogy

That which is below is as that which is above, and that which is above is as that which is below.

The Emerald Tablet

God made this world in the image of the world above; thus, all which is found above has its analogy below…and everything constitutes a unity.
Zohar II, 20a,
Midrash *ha-Ne'elam*

The symbol is reflective of its referent, in accord with it being "made in the image of God." This gives rise to what Guénon calls the "law of inverse analogy": 'Whatever is at the lowest level corresponds, by inverse analogy, to what is at the highest level'.[70] Schuon expands upon this when he notes the two-fold nature of analogy:

If between one level of reality and another there is a parallel analogy in respect of positive content, there is on the other hand an inverse analogy in respect of relationship: for example, there

31

is a parallel analogy between earthly and heavenly beauty, but there is an inverse analogy as regards their respective situations, in the sense that earthly beauty is "outward" and divine Beauty "inward"; or again, to illustrate this law by symbols: according to certain Sufic teachings, earthly trees are reflections of heavenly trees, and earthly women are reflections of heavenly women (parallel analogy); but heavenly trees have their roots above and heavenly women are naked (inverse analogy, what is "below" becoming "above," and what is "inward" becoming "outward").[71]

The inversion of the Subject in its symbolic objectification is not the same as that between analogous symbols. As Schuon remarks,

the universal and fundamental inversion as between Subject and objectification is never done away with as a result of the inversions comprised within the objectification itself, for these are never produced under the same relationship and never under any relationship capable of nullifying that first inversion. Inversion *within* an inversion is therefore never inversion *of* the inversion, never, that is to say, a re-establishment of the "normal" relationship.[72]

The inverse nature of symbol gives rise to a measure of ambiguity according to the perspective of the viewer. Thus a symbol can be both beneficent and maleficent according to the ability of the viewer to perceive and engage the anagogical aspect of the symbol. Guénon recognises this ambiguity with respect to the act of manifestation itself. He writes,

On the one hand if this manifestation is simply taken by itself, without relating it to a much greater whole, the entire process from its beginning to its end is clearly a progressive "descent" or "degradation," and this is what may be called its "maleficent" aspect; but, on the other hand, the same manifestation, when put back into the whole of which it is a part, produces results that have a truly "positive" result in universal existence; and its development must be carried right to the end, so as to include a development of the inferior possibilities of the "dark age," in order that the "integration" of those results may become possible and may become the immediate principle of another cycle of manifestation; this is what constitutes its "beneficent" aspect.[73]

In this connection, the symbol is said to be "revealing," where this term carries the dual meaning of both to "remove the veil" and to "re-veil."[74]

Summary

The symbol is the vehicle directing the understanding from the physical towards the supra-physical levels of reality; from the human to the Divine. The symbol participates in its referent, which is the realm of metaphysical Forms. The symbol is multivalent, having a multiplicity of meanings that do not diminish but instead enrich each other. The horizontal valence of the symbol is indefinite; the vertical valence is infinite. The symbol interconnects with its homologues creating a mutually reinforcing web of meaning. The symbol is open and may not be reduced to a single fundamental meaning. At the same time, with respect to its metaphysical archetype the symbol expresses Principial Unity. The symbol operates analogically and anagogically in both horizontal and vertical valences. The symbol operates according to the laws of analogy: "parallel" analogy, in respect of content; and "inverse" analogy, in respect of relationship. Symbolism operates through complementary modes: myth, ritual and doctrine. The symbol is revealed and adequate. It is exact, having none of the arbitrariness of a sign. The symbol is essential and effective. It is nonetheless contingent on its need and in respect to the Absolute. The symbol effects re-memberance. It is the formal language of the Divine and the human.

Notes

1. In the *Zohar* it is written: ' "And the perceivers shall shine" (*Daniel* 12:3). Who are the perceivers? It is the wise man who, of himself, looks upon things that cannot be expressed orally—these are called "the perceivers"' (II, 23a-23b). They are those who have "ears to hear."

2. Snodgrass, *ATE1*, 1990, p.2.

3. 'The Intellect as seeker penetrates beyond discursive thinking. It goes looking about, seeking, casting its net here and there, acquiring and losing. But above this intellect the seeker is Intellect, which does not seek but rests in the unconditioned isness of its own divine Light' (Meister Eckhart, cited in Kelley, *Meister Eckhart on Divine Knowledge*, 1977, p.236).

4. See Snodgrass, *SS*, 1985, p.3.

5. Snodgrass, *ATE1*, 1990, p.11.

6. Schuon, *TUR*, 1975, p.xxix-xxx.

7. Plotinus: 'The Forms are Unity in diversity and diversity in Unity' (*Enneads* 6.5.6).

8. Schuon, *G:DW*, 1990, p.26.

9. Nasr, *Sufi Essays*, 1972, p.88.

10. Schuon, 'No Activity without Truth': Needleman (ed.), *The Sword of Gnosis*, 1974, p.29.

11. Coomaraswamy, 'The Nature of Buddhist Art': *SP1*, 1977, p.174.

12. Eliade, *Symbolism, the Sacred, and the Arts*, 1992, p.6.

13. As quoted by Snodgrass, *ATE1*, 1990, p.44.

14. Snodgrass, *ATE1*, 1990, p.2.

15. Lévy-Bruhl says of symbols, 'very often it is not their purpose to "represent" their prototype to the eye, but to facilitate a participation' (*L'Expérience mystique*, pp.174 & 180, cited in Coomaraswamy, *SP1*, 1977, p296).

16. Snodgrass, *ATE1*, 1990, p.45.

17. *Phaedo*, 72e. On Platonic recollection see Coomaraswamy, 'Recollection, Indian and Platonic': *SP2*, 1977.

18. See Smith, 'Objectivity and the Humane Sciences' in Oxtoby (ed.), *Religious Diversity: Essays by Wilfred Cantwell Smith*, 1976.

19. Interpretation is an active assimilation concurrent with the realisation of the symbol. As Eliade says, 'creative hermeneutics *changes* man; it is more than mere instruction, it is a spiritual technique susceptible of modifying the quality of existence itself' (*The Quest*, 1969, p.62).

20. Tillich, 'Religious Symbols and Our Knowledge of God' (1955) in Rowe & Wainwright (eds.), *Philosophy of Religion: Selected Readings*, 1973, p.483.

21. Burckhardt, *ISD*, 1976, p.46.

22. Snodgrass, *ATE1*, 1990, p.45.

23. Tishby, *WZ1*, 1989, p.285.

24. Snodgrass, *ATE1*, 1990, p.45; also *SS*, 1985, p.3.

25. Allegory is a fundamental mode of exegesis. St. Augustine says of the Old Testament that it has a fourfold division, 'according to history, aetiology, analogy and allegory' (*De Util. Cred*, III in Aquinus, *Summa Theol.*, 1.1.10; cited in Perry, *TTW*, 2000, p.314). Dante speaks of the *Quadriga* or "four senses": literal, moral, anagogical and allegorical (*Il Convito*, II.2-5).

26. Scholem, *MTJM*, 1995, p.27.

27. Snodgrass, *ATE1*, 1990, pp.49.

28. Snodgrass, *SS*, 1985, pp.2-3.

29. Snodgrass, *SS*, 1985, p.3.

30. Coomaraswamy, 'Literary Symbolism': *SP1*, 1977, p.324.

31. See Snodgrass, *ATE1*, 1990, pp.48.

32. Snodgrass, *ATE1*, 1990, pp.49.

33. The Qur'an teaches that God 'is not ashamed to take a gnat as a symbol' (Qur'an 2:26). Now, a gnat is obviously less adequate a symbol of the Divine than the Sun; nevertheless the gnat is an infinitely more satisfactory gnat than the Sun would be, should it try to be a gnat. The gnat is perfect inasmuch as it expresses the Divine Will that it be.

34. Tillich, *Religious Symbols and Our Knowledge of God* (1955), 1973, p.482.

35. Govinda, *Foundations of Tibetan Mysticism*, 1969, p.51.

36. Guénon, *FS*, 1995, p.13.

37. Guénon, *FS*, 1995, p.14.

38. *Enneads* 6.7.36.

39. Guénon, *FS*, 1995, p.29.

40. Guénon, *FS*, 1995, p.29.

41. Snodgrass, *SS*, 1985, p.8.

42. Eliade, *Symbolism, the Sacred, and the Arts*, 1992, p.5.

43. Eliade, 'Methodological Remarks on the Study of Religious Symbolism' in Eliade & Kitagawa (ed.), *The History of Religion*, 1959, pp.86-107.

44. Snodgrass notes this network as symbolised, in the Hindu tradition, by Indra's Net (*SS*, 1985, p.6); compare the net Hephaestus uses to entrap Aphrodite and Ares, the symbol of the spiders web, and the symbolism of weaving; see Intro.2.; Ch.12.4.c & d.; Guénon, *SC*, 1975, Ch.14.

45. On the "geometry" of Being see Guénon, *SC*, 1975, Chs.11 & 12.

46. Snodgrass, *SS*, 1985, p.5.

47. Guénon: 'a degree of Existence can be represented by a horizontal plane of indefinite extent' (*SC*, 1975, p.58; see Ch.11).

48. See Snodgrass, *SS*, 1985, p.8.

49. Snodgrass, *SS*, 1985, p.6. Titus Burckhardt remarks, 'To carry out a rite is not only to enact a symbol but also to participate, even if only virtually, in a certain mode of being, a mode which has an extra-human and universal extension' (*ISD*, 1976, p.99). According to Martin Lings, 'The symbolism of a rite is its very essence, without which it would lose its ritual quality' (*A Sufi Saint of the Twentieth Century*, 1971, p.177).

50. Snodgrass, *SS*, 1985, p.6.

51. Coomaraswamy, *The Bugbear of Literacy*, 1979, p.80.

52. *Hermetica Lib.*12 (i).13a.

53. Snodgrass, *SS*, 1985, p.7.

54. Guénon, *SC*, 1975, p.x. 'The concordances between all traditional forms may be said to represent genuine "synonymies"; that is how we regard them, and just as the explanation of certain things may be easier in one language than in another, so one of these forms may be better fitted than others for expounding certain truths and rendering them easier to understand. Hence in each case it is perfectly legitimate to make use of the form which seems the most suitable for the purpose in hand; there is no objection to passing from one form to another, provided one is really aware of their equivalence, which can only be the case if one views them in the light of their common principle. In this way no syncretism will arise; indeed the latter can only be a product of a "profane" outlook which is incompatible with the very idea of the "sacred science" to which these studies exclusively refer' (p.xi).

55. Guénon, *FS*, 1995, p.27.

56. Coomaraswamy, 'Some Pali Words': *SP2*, 1977, p.324.

57. St. Bonanentura, *In Hexaem.*, 2.27, cited in Perry, *TTW*, 2000, p.309.

58. Cited in Perry, *TTW*, 2000, p.310.

59. *Hikmatu-hu*, 25, cited in Lings, *A Sufi Saint of the Twentieth Century*, 1971, p.211. Lings adds by way of a note: 'Muhyi 'd-Din Ibn 'Arabi quotes the Qur'an *Naught is like unto Him, and He is the Hearer, the Seer*, to show how in

one verse (XLII, ii) it affirms both his Incomparability and the analogy between Him and His creatures.'

60. Guénon, *MB*, 1981, p.154.

61. Guénon, *SC*, 1975, pp.xii-xiii. Coomaraswamy: 'To speak of an event as *essentially* mythical is by no means to deny the possibility, but rather to assert the necessity of an *accidental*—i.e., historical—eventuation; it is in this way that the eternal and temporal nativities are related' ('The Nature of Buddhist Art': *SP1*, 1977, p.149-50, n.2).

62. Tishby, *WZ1*, 1989, p.284.

63. Scholem, *MTJM*, 1995, p.28.

64. Guénon, *FS*, 1995, p.16, n.5.

65. Coleridge, *Essay XI*.

66. Nasr, *KS*, 1981, p.215, n.6.

67. Nasr, *KS*, 1981, p.200. 'Having journeyed through and beyond the cosmos, man, who is then "twice born" and a "dead man walking" in the sense of being spiritually resurrected here and now, is able finally to contemplate the cosmos and its forms as theophany. He is able to see the forms of nature *in divinis* and to experience the Ultimate Reality not as transcendent and beyond but as here and now. It is here that the cosmos unveils its beauty ceasing to be only externalised fact or phenomenon but becoming immediate symbol, the reflection of the noumenon, the reflection which is not separated but essentially none other than the reality reflected' (p.200).

68. Nasr, *KS*, 1981, p.197.

69. Schuon, *SPHF*, 1987, p.47.

70. Guénon, *RQ*, 1995, p.186, see Ch.25; also *FS*, 1995, Chs.52 & 53; *GT*, 1994, Ch.7. This law follows the oft quoted Hermetic aphorism, "As Above So Below," taken from Emerald Tablet of Hermes Trismegistus: 'It is true without lie, certain and most veritable, that what is below is like what is above and that what is above is like what is below, to perpetrate the miracles of one thing.'

71. Schuon, *TB*, 1993, p.84, n.2; *SPHF*, 1987, p.106, n.1; *LS*, 1999, pp.35-6, where he refers to "direct" and "inverse" analogy.

72. Schuon, *LS*, 1999, pp.24-5.

73. Guénon, *RQ*, 1995, p.334.

74. Guénon, *LW*, 1983, p.19, n.5.

Zero: *Symbolism of Water*

Introduction

The symbolism of water is most commonly recognised as that of potentiality: ontological possibility or *materia prima*. 'Water, thou art the source of all things and of all existence!'[1] This is the immediate symbolism of the Waters of *Genesis*. Potentiality is a reflection, at the ontological level, of the Divine All-Possibility. Thus one can talk of the "Divine Sea," which is none other than the Infinitude of the Absolute. According to number symbolism the Absolute is symbolised by either "The One," expressing Its Unity, or by "zero," expressing both Its Infinite possibility and Its transcendent unknowability. With the symbolism of the Ark, we are considering the symbolism of the deluge, that is, of existence returning to the waters whence it had come, thus to be born "anew." Here the symbolism of water is most immediately that of potentiality. Nevertheless, in framing this study by the progression of zero to four I recognise that potentiality is itself an expression, at the appropriate level, of the Divine All-Possibility. If, as noted earlier, zero is generally reserved for the Absolute Reality as it is in Itself, then it is used here to alert the reader to the analogical relationship between it and the symbolism of water. If the Ark expresses the principle of Immanence, then the waters on which it floats are Transcendence. Hence, this chapter is marked by a study of the Divine Unknowability or Divine Nothingness, as the Reality that underpins the symbolism of water.

The "Divine Nothingness"

The essence of perfect Tao is profoundly mysterious; its extent is lost in obscurity.

Chuang-tse[2]

When I go back into the ground, into the depths, into the wellspring of the Godhead, no one will ask me whence I came or whither I went.

Meister Eckhart[3]

To say Absolute is to say Infinite and thus All-Possibility. The All-Possibility is the Divine Plentitude, which, in a manner of speaking and from a certain perspective, is the Divine Substance (*Ousia* or *hyperousia*). There are two primary symbolisms used here: "Darkness" and the "Divine Sea"—'there was darkness over the deep, with a divine wind sweeping over the waters' (Gen.1:2). The symbolism of the Sea refers to the "depth" and possibility of the Infinite; Darkness refers to its unknowability. In talking of the Infinite we are referring to the Absolute and thus firstly to Transcendence; however, All-Possibility gives rise to Being—which Schuon has described as the "lesser Absolute"—and at this level to ontological All-Possibility or ontological Substance (*ousia*), and thus to Immanence. The element Substance, remarks Schuon, is represented 'at each ontological or cosmic level in appropriate mode; and *a fortiori*, pure Substance or Substance as such underlies each of its secondary manifestations.'[4] Water is the primary symbol of Substance.

When talking of All-Possibility one is talking of both Beyond-Being and Transcendent Being. To talk of Beyond-Being is to allude to the aspect of the Absolute that is unknowable'; accordingly this is expressed through the "negative" symbolism of Darkness. To talk of Transcendent Being is to talk of Being as identical with the Divine Essence, and here the symbolism, which is that of the Divine Sea, is "positive" and alludes to the eventual possibility of knowing God. Two points arise here: firstly, these two symbolisms, Darkness and the Divine Sea, are but two aspects of the one Reality; secondly, the Divine Sea, inasmuch as it emerges from the Darkness or inasmuch as it emerges from itself like a "fountain" (the *Fons Vitae*), is expressive of the Divine Essence; yet at the same time and inasmuch as it is the matrix of Possibility it is expressive of the Divine Substance. Peter Sterry poetically describes this as 'a fountain ever equally unexhausted, a Sea unbounded'.[5] Eliade remarks that the symbolism of the Waters expresses 'the universal sum of virtualities; they are the *fons et origio*, "spring and origin," the reservoir of all the possibilities of existence; they precede every form and *support* every creation.'[6]

According to Schuon, Divine Essence and Divine Substance are 'almost synonymous in practice.'[7] To talk of "Divine Essence" or "Divine Substance" is to consider these terms as symbolic cognomens of the Absolute. To talk of Essence or Substance as "in practice" is to consider these in respect to their ontological realities; here one can talk provisionally of "Pure Essence" and "Pure Substance." Schuon remarks that they 'differ in that substance refers to the underlying, immanent, permanent and autonomous nature of a basic reality, whereas essence refers to the reality as such, that is, as "being," and secondarily as the absolutely fundamental nature of a thing.' He continues, 'The notion of essence denotes an excellence which is as it were discontinuous in relation to accidents, whereas the notion of substance implies on the contrary a sort of continuity'.[8] In the Vedantic tradition the concept of Essence is expressed, at the principial level, by *Ātman*, the Divine Self, which, as Guénon observes, is 'the principle of all states of being, manifest and unmanifest.'[9] According to Guénon, 'The Self must not be regarded as distinct from *Ātman*, and, moreover, *Ātman* is identical with *Brahman* Itself [the Absolute].'[10] Similarly, Schuon notes,

> The essence of the world, which is diversity, is *Brahman*. It might be objected that *Brahman* cannot be the essence of a diversity seeing that It is non-duality. To be sure, *Brahman* is not the essence of the world, for, from the standpoint of the Absolute, the world does not exist; but one can say that the world, in so far as it does exist, has *Brahman* for its essence; otherwise it would posses no reality whatsoever. Diversity, for its part, is but the inverse reflection of the Infinity, or of the all-possibility, of *Brahman*.[11]

The identification of Essence and Substance is found in the Greek word *ousia*, which, as Burckhardt observes, connotes the ideas of both "Substance" and "Essence."[12] In the Islamic tradition, the Aramaic letter-word *ayn*, translated variously as "eye," "fountain" and "individual essence," also expresses both "Substance" and "Essence."[13] From still another perspective, pure Essence and pure Substance are properly speaking the complementary aspects of Being, and here it is incorrect to speak of the Absolute or Beyond-Being in any of these terms. This difficulty is one of human language, which is necessarily limited.

In Islam the ideas of Beyond-Being and Non-Being are equally found with the term *al-'udum*. Titus Burckhardt observes that in Sufism this expression includes 'on the one hand the positive sense of non-manifestation, of a principial state beyond existence or even beyond Being, and on the other hand a negative sense of privation, of relative nothingness.'[14] In the Christian tradition Meister Eckhart taught, 'If I say: "God is a being," it is not true; he is a being transcending being and a transcending nothingness.'[15] In Kabbalah, Beyond-Being is explained metaphorically as "Negative Existence." It is said that there are three veils of "Negative Existence" that serve as the negative background to the positive universe.[16] This schema is a symbolic attempt to explain the ineffable, and it carries the recognition of its own limitation. Z'ev ben Shimon Halevi, a contemporary exponent of Kabbalah, expresses the development of manifest Existence thus,

> God generates, out of the Void of Non Existence, beyond which is All and Nothing, the first state of Unmanifest Existence. From this World without End, crystallizes a realm of Limitless light, in the midst of which, there emerges a point of no dimensions, called the First Crown. These three states of Unmanifest Existence become the negative background to the positive uni-

verse that streams through the primal point of the First Crown to evolve into the archetypal world of Emanations.[17]

We find ourselves here at the limit of rational language as the Kabbalah attempts to express 'the mysterious genesis of the finite in the midst of the infinite.'[18]

The All-Possibility includes, by definition, the paradoxical possibilities of both Being and Its contrary Non-Being, which "is not." According to Parmenides 'being is, and it is impossible that not-being is'.[19] The *Chāndogya Upanishad* examines the question of non-existence, *asat*, in detail with the sage Aruni maintaining the absurdity of the "existence" of non-existence.[20] Plato speaks of the "irrationality" of "not-being": 'You understand then that it is really impossible to speak of not-being or to say anything about it or to conceive it by itself, but it is inconceivable, not to be spoken of or mentioned, and irrational.'[21] Non-being is not. This is a logical truth. Nevertheless, as Ibn al-'Arabī says, 'It is part of the perfection of Being that there is imperfection in it.'[22] Schuon: 'The All-Possibility must by definition and on pain of contradiction include its own impossibility.'[23] This is a paradox, but also a logical truth.

In a certain sense, as Schuon says, the illusion of the Relative (the Hindu *Māyā*) represents the possibility for Being of not being: 'It is in order not to be, that Being incarnates in the multitude of souls; it is in order not to be, that the ocean squanders itself in myriad flecks of foam.'[24] This is to regard manifestation as a "tendency" to "nothingness," an idea also alluded to by Meister Eckhart when he speaks of all creatures as "nothing."[25] This carries two meanings, equally true. On the one hand, creatures are "nothing" in that they have no reality in comparison with the ultimate Reality of the Absolute. This idea is found with the symbolism of "zero"; as Angelus Silesius puts it: 'The zero placed first is worth nothing. The nothing, the creature, when placed before God is worth nothing; placed after Him, thence alone is its value derived.'[26] On the other hand, creatures have as their substance principial potentiality, that is, by symbolic transposition, the "Divine Nothingness," analogous at the appropriate level to the Waters of *Genesis*. In the Buddhist tradition the identification of the nothingness of the creature with the Divine Nothingness is explicit; thus the *Mahā-Prajñāpāramitā-Hrdaya* says: 'Form (*rūpa*) is emptiness (*śūnyatā*), and emptiness is not different from form, nor is form different from emptiness: indeed emptiness is form.'[27] Again, Nāgārjuna observes that 'There is nothing that distinguishes *samsāra* from *nirvāna*'.[28] As Schuon says of the Buddhist tradition, 'the Bodhisattva, since he realises the "emptiness" of things, thereby also realises the "emptiness" of the *samsāra* as such and at the same time its *nirvānic* quality. If on the one hand all is "emptiness," on the other hand all is *Nirvāna*, the Buddhist notion of vacuity being at one and the same time negative and positive'.[29]

In a typically remarkable passage Schuon summarises the nature of the Unmanifested and its relation to manifestation and the world. He writes:

> The idea of the unmanifested has two different meanings: there is the absolutely unmanifested, *Parabrahma* or *Brahman nirguna* ("unqualified"), and the relatively unmanifested, *śvara* or *Brahman saguna* ("qualified"); this relatively unmanifested, being as existentiating principle or matrix of the archetypes, may be called the "potentially manifested" in relation to the "effectively manifested," namely the world; for in the divine order itself, Being is the "manifestation" of Beyond-Being, otherwise manifestation properly so called, or Existence, would be neither possible nor conceivable. To say that the absolutely unmanifested is the principle both of the manifested—the world—and of the relatively unmanifested—Being—would be a tautology: as the principle of Being, Beyond-Being is implicitly the principle of Existence. In the sight of the absolutely unmanifested, the distinction between the potentially manifested—which is relatively unmanifested and creative—and the effectively manifested or the created, the distinction, that is between Being and Existence, has no reality; in the sight of Beyond-Being it is neither a complementarity nor an alternative.[30]

Zero: Void-Plenum

In truth, all possibilities resolve principially into non-existence.
                                                            Ibn al-'Arabī[31]

What is he that calleth it nought? Surely it is our outerman and not our inner. Our inner man calleth it All.
                                                            The Cloud of Unknowing

The clay is moulded to make a pot;
And the clay fits round "nothing":
Herein lies the usefulness of the pot.
                                                            Tao Te Ching, Ch. 11

In terms of numerical symbolism the principial Possibility can be expressed, more or less adequately, by the "metaphysical zero."[32] Zero is strictly speaking not a number but the possibility of number. This pos-

41

sibility is realised virtually in the first number, one, which contains all numbers in pure potentiality. The relationship between virtuality and potentiality gives rise to a kind of identity between zero and one. Thus Macrobius says of the "One" that it also is a not a number, but the source of all numbers.[33] According to Plotinus, 'It is precisely because there is nothing within the One that all things are from it.'[34] The identification of zero and one corresponds with that of the active fountain with the passive Sea: 'a fountain ever equally unexhausted, a Sea unbounded.'

Schuon says of the Infinite that 'it is in the first place Potentiality or Possibility as such, and *ipso facto* the Possibility of things, hence Virtuality.'[35] Schuon's use of the term Potentiality is unfortunate if viewed in a strictly Aristotelian sense where the transference from potentiality to actuality is predicated upon the prior reality of an ever actual principle. Thus it would seem more satisfactory to refer to the Infinite as Actuality, in the sense of *the* Actual or the Real.[36] For the sake of precision, and in the context of this work, we distinguish, as Guénon does, between the terms "possibility," "virtuality" and "potentiality." Thus, possibility primarily refers to the Infinite; virtuality refers to principial Being;[37] potentiality refers to the aptitude of virtual existence to manifest *in actu*, and thus properly to the indefinite. Possibility can be referred to at each level by transposition. However, this does not work in reverse, for it cannot be said of the divine order that it is potential. As Guénon says, 'there can be nothing potential in the divine order. It is only from the side of the individual being and in relation to it that potentiality can be spoken of in this context. Pure potentiality is the absolute indifferentiation of *materia prima* in the Aristotelian sense, identical to the indistinction of the primordial chaos.'[38] Potentiality refers to a change in state and thus to a lack: God lacks nothing.

Materia prima: this is the primordial chaos, expressed by the biblical symbolism of the Waters of *Genesis*. From one perspective this is really the first determination and thus deserves to be represented by the number one. Yet from "below," or from the terrestrial perspective, this presents an indeterminate "face" and thus can be, and in fact is, expressed by zero. As with the Divine All-Possibility, of which it is but a graduation, the primordial chaos is both "void" and "plentitude." This is brought out with the double meaning of the Greek word *khaos*, which, as Schuon observes, means both "primordial abyss" and "indeterminate matter." It is, says Schuon, 'neither nothingness pure and simple nor a substance preceding the creative act, but, together with the demiurge, the first content of creation; the active demiurge being the Centre, and its passive complement, the periphery.'[39] As Guénon remarks, 'the plenum and the void, considered as correlatives, are one of the traditional representations of the complementarity of the active and passive principles.'[40]

Coomaraswamy observes that, in the Indian tradition, zero is denoted by a range of words: *śūnya, ākāśa, vyoma, antariksa, nabha, ananta,* and *pūrna*. 'We are immediately struck' he says, 'by the fact that the words *śūnya*, "void," and *pūrna*, "plenum," should have a common reference; the implication being that all numbers are virtually or potentially present in that which is without number; expressing this as an equation, $0 = x - x$, it is apparent that zero is to number as possibility is to actuality.'[41] This equation further bears out the relationship between zero, infinity and the first point—which is both zero and one—inasmuch as the mathematically indefinite series, thought of as both plus and minus according to direction, cancel out where all directions meet in common focus.[42] Coomaraswamy further remarks that 'employment of the term *ananta* ["endless"] with the same reference implies an identification of zero with infinity; the beginning of all series being thus the same as their end.'[43] Coomaraswamy again: 'the Sea, as the source of all existence, is equally the symbol of their last end or entelechy.'[44]

Tsimtsum: *Creatio Ex Nihilo*[45]

Empty yourself, so that you may be filled. Learn not to love so that you may learn how to love. Draw back, so that you may be approached

St. Augustine[46]

Blessed are the poor in spirit

Matthew 5:3

Meister Eckhart spoke of a "waking dream" that appeared to a man in which 'he became pregnant with Nothing like a woman with child, and in that Nothing God was born, He was the fruit of Nothing. God was born in Nothing.'[47] This "birth" is, in one sense, the birth of the Word in the soul, Meister Eckhart's *durchbrechen* ("breaking through") or *reditus*, the return to the ineffable source. This "birth" is intimately connect with "the inner emanation of the Trinity" or *bullitio*, which is mirrored on the macrocosmic level by the *ebullitio* (the creation of the universe). In this context we recognise the doctrine of *creatio ex nihilo*. The difficulties of this doctrine are explained, to some extent, by the Judaic doctrine of the *tsimtsum*, expounded in the Lurianic School of Kabbalism, founded by Isaac Luria (1534-72). The word *tsimtsum* means literally "concentration" or "contraction"; however, if used in Kabbalistic parlance it is best translated as "withdrawal" or "retreat." According to Luria, *tsimtsum* 'does not mean the concentration of God *at* a point, but his retreat *away*

from a point,' a theory he derived from the inversion of Midrash referring to God having concentrated His *Shekhinah* (lit. "indwelling," the
Divine Immanence) in the Holiest of Holies 'as though His whole power
were concentrated and contracted in a single point'.[48]

The doctrine of *tsimtsum* teaches that God withdraws Himself into
Himself thereby allowing an empty "primordial space" into which "that
which is not God" can come into being. This echoes Meister Eckhart's
image of God as Nothing being born in Nothing, as the fruit of Nothing.
Scholem observes how the doctrine of the *tsimtsum* demonstrates a shift
in appreciation from the God who revealed himself in firm contours to
the God who 'descended deeper into the recesses of His own Being,
who concentrated Himself into Himself, and had done so from the very
beginning of creation.'[49] If we may be allowed a gross oversimplification: in the three Semitic religions the idea of "God" is used, at the level
of exoteric theology, to express the ontological Principle or, even more
simply, the active Demiurge.[50] However, with the *tsimtsum* we are considering the term God as indicating Beyond-Being, the Absolute.

The phrase "that which is not God" is as if to say "that which is not
of itself the Absolute," *ipso facto* the Relative. This is not to say that
the Relative is not of the Absolute or, to put this another way, that the
Relative is not contained within the Absolute, but simply that the Relative does not exhaust the Absolute. The Relative, inasmuch as it is "not
God," is the tendency towards non-existence. Thus, the Divine Nothingness becomes "pregnant with Nothing"—the Relative (*Māyā*)—and
in that "Nothing" God—the Relative viewed positively as the Divine
Immanence—is "born." In this manner the *tsimtsum*, along with the Midrash it derives from, expresses the "concentration" of *En Sof* (the Infinite) at the principial point. The *tsimtsum* is equivalent to the 'unveiling
of God in Himself and by Himself'.[51] Schuon quotes Ibn al-'Arabī: 'According to *Risālat al-Ahadiyah*, "He [the Absolute; *Brahman*] sent His
ipseity [the Self; *Ātman*] by Himself from Himself to Himself."'[52]

Schaya discusses the *tsimtsum* in the language of the *Sefirotic* Tree.
Through the effect of *tsimtsum*, he says, 'the divine fullness withdraws to
a certain extent from the "lower mother" [*Malkhut*, the "plastic cause"],
and awakens creative receptivity in her; the latter, when actualised, takes
on the aspect of the void or "place of the world," ready to receive cosmic
manifestation.'[53] The withdrawal of the *tsimtsum* awakens receptivity in
Malkhut; she is here likened to a womb awaiting the seed. Here, Schaya
remarks that 'all created possibilities spring up from the existential seed
which is left behind by divine fullness on its withdrawal—as a luminous
"residue" (*reshimu*) in the midst of immanent emptiness.'[54] The *reshimu*
is a residue of the *En-Sof*, which, as infinite, can never really not pen-

44

etrate the void except in terms of the "illusion" of the distinction between the Relative and the Absolute. 'You should know,' says Meister
Eckhart, 'God cannot endure that anything should be void or unfilled.
And so, even if you think you can't feel Him and are wholly empty of
Him, that is not the case. For if there were anything empty under heaven,
whatever it might be, great or small, the heavens would either draw it
up to themselves or else, bending down, would fill it themselves.'[55] This
imagery suggests an interesting connection and one that is directly related to the symbolism of the Ark. According to Ovid, at the time of the
Flood, as the rain poured down, Iris, who is identified with the rainbow,
drew up water to nourish the clouds.[56] The rains express the dissolution
of manifest existence into "nothingness" or voidness; this void is, then,
the water of the Flood, which is "drawn" back to heaven.

The *reshimu* is the "mysterious" interface between Transcendence
and Immanence, where the term "mysterious" is used according to its
root meaning of "silence," for this is precisely beyond rational language.[57] In Kabbalah this "mystery" is again expressed through the Holy
of Holies. For Meister Eckhart this is the "spark" that lights existence;
it is Eckhart's famous "something in the soul" that is "uncreated and
not capable of creation," but which is nevertheless the principle of creation.[58] In Islam this mysterious interface is expressed by the mediating
principle, *al-barzakh*, the isthmus between the "two seas" mentioned in
the Qur'an.

According to Schaya, it is 'thanks to the divine "contraction" and
to the void it brings about in the *Shekhinah* [that] the expansion of the
world takes place … everything living in the immanence of God is a
small world created in the image of the macrocosm: it is a void to which
life is given by a luminous "residue" of the only reality, by a central
and divine "spark" that projects onto it the reflection of some eternal
archetype.'[59]

The cosmogonic act of *tsimtsum* entails the "retraction" of the Divine Infinitude so as to allow creation of "one that is another," the Relative. According to the symbolism of Kabbalah, the Divine Infinitude
is the Infinite Mercy of God.[60] The *tsimtsum* is the "limiting" action of
Divine Judgment or Severity upon the Infinite Mercy. Following the
symbolism of the *Sefirot*, the "lightning strike" of creation passes from
Binah (the Upper Mother) through *Hesed* (Abraham; Mercy) before pro-
gressing through *Din* (Isaac; Judgment). Mercy and Judgment are balanced in the creative heart of *Tiferet* (Jacob; Beauty). In the Talmud the
Creator explains, 'If I create the world only with the attribute of mercy,
sins will multiply beyond all bounds; if I create it only with the attribute

of justice, how can the world last? Behold, I will create it with both attributes; would that it might endure!'[61]

When seen from "above," that is to say, from the Divine perspective, *En Sof* is concentrated at *Keter*. *Keter*, the "Crown," is the transcendent aspect of the principial point containing Universal Existence in both its supra-formal (Formless Manifestation) and formal modes. Seen from "below," the human perspective, this first point is *Tiferet*, the central "Heart" of the *Sefirot*: the effective and immanent aspect of the principial point. It is through *Tiferet* that all the other *Sefirot* are synthesized to produce onto-cosmological existence—Individual or Formal Manifestation as such.

Corresponding to and simultaneous with the withdrawal of the *tsimtsum* the infinite Essence "acts" upon virtual Substance bringing forth onto-cosmological existence.[62] The cosmological emanation into the "night of Nothingness" is, in fact, the realisation or actualisation of potential Substance within the infinitude of Divine Substance. The act of manifestation is a "limitation," to speak paradoxically, on the Divine Infinitude. As Schuon remarks, 'To say manifestation is to say limitation.'[63] At the deepest reality, that of the Absolute, this "limitation" is merely the illusion of limitation as viewed from the perspective, illusory of itself, of the Relative.

The *tsimtsum* can be said to be the simultaneous act of "Radiation" and "Contraction." These are again centrifugal and centripetal movement; evolution[64] (de-velopment, "unfolding") and involution (en-velopment, "winding up"); *catabasis* or "going down" and *anabasis* or "going up"; departure into the manifest and return to the non-manifest. This is referred to in many traditions by the symbolism of the expiration and inspiration (or exhalation and inhalation) of the Divine Breath. When one breathes in the lungs expand or "withdraw" as does the air contained within, so to speak. This corresponds in a complementary manner with the influx of "outside" air that expands in filling the lungs. At no time is there an "emptiness" of the lungs. The withdrawal of the "old" air and the expansion of the "new" air are complementary. In fact there is no substantial difference between these two, both are air; neither is there ever a quantitative difference, there is always the same amount of air in the closed system comprising both the "inside" and the "outside." This analogy works similarly if we are to talk of the out breath. When one breathes out the lungs contract like the Infinite contacting on the principial point. This corresponds to the "withdrawal" of the lungs from the space they occupy within the cavity of the chest; again, this simultaneously corresponds to the expansion of the out flowing breath. When we speak of the Divine Breath the distinction of "inner" and "outer" is somewhat removed so that we must say that the Infinite Breath with-draws Itself of Itself so that the indefinite Breath can expand within It.

The "indefinite Breath" is the Relative, in comparison to the "in-finite Breath," which we may here liken to the Infinitude of the Abso-lute. 'The Absolute' says Schuon, 'must by definition and on pain of contradiction include the Relative.'[65] Which is to say: 'If the relative did not exist, the Absolute would not be the Absolute.'[66] This is neces-sary, which is simply to say that God cannot not be God.[67] However this distinction between Absolute and Relative is only legitimate from the perspective of the Relative and then only as an "illusion."[68] As this is a "distinction" it is prefigured *in divinis* by the differentiation between the 'Absolute as such and the Absolute relativised in view of a dimension of its Infinitude'.[69]

This idea may seem to suggest the partibility of God. With respect to this Schaya says,

> In reality, God the absolute One, has no "parts," but an infinity of possibilities, of which only the creatural possibilities have the illusory appearance of separate forms; in themselves these forms are integrated, as eternal archetypes, in the all-possibility of the One. As for that "part from which the light has been withdrawn" to make room for the "place" of the cosmos, it is nothing other than the receptivity of God that actualises itself in the midst of his unlimited fullness; this receptivity has a transcendent aspect and an immanent aspect: "above" it is identified with *binah*, the "supreme mother," which is eternally filled with the infinite and luminous emanation of the "father," *hokhmah*; "below," it is *Malkhut*, the "lower mother," or cosmic receptivity of God.[70]

In accord with inverse analogy the symbolism of breathing is reversed with the human being, for the expansion of the lungs here corresponds to inspiration and the contraction to expiration; likewise the systole and diastole of the heart. *Catabasis* and *anabasis* produce, in the language of Taoism, condensations and dissipations. These correspond to Her-metic coagulation and solution (*solve et coagula*).[71] This is the same with the symbolism of "the power to bind" and "the power to loose."[72] For individual beings these powers are births and deaths—what Aris-totle calls *genesis* and *phthora*, generation and corruption. For worlds, they are what Hindu tradition calls the days of *Brahmā*: *Kalpa* (Day of *Brahmā*) and *Pralaya* (Night of *Brahmā*). As Guénon observes, 'at all levels of reality, on the "macrocosmic" as well as "microcosmic" scale, corresponding phases occur in every cycle of existence, for they are the very expression itself of the law that governs the sum total of universal manifestation.'[73]

The order of these respective terms depends, as Guénon observes, upon one's particular standpoint when viewing them. He explains, 'This is because the two complementary phases…not only alternate but are also simultaneous: hence the order in which they present themselves will depend as it were on which state is taken as point of departure.'[74] From the strictly cosmogonic point of view the movement is from the non-manifest to the manifest (condensation). Dissipation or solution follows, as a movement of return towards the non-manifest.[75] In terms of the cyclic nature of manifestation, this solution will be a "resolution," as Coomaraswamy recognises with respect to the Hindu Flood. Guénon: 'If…we were to take as our point of departure some specific state of manifestation, first we would have to envisage a process tending towards "solution" of whatever is contained in that state, followed by a subsequent phase of "coagulation" involving a return to another state of manifestation.'[76]

In regard to the order of these processes, Guénon remarks,

> There is another factor involved here, which is even more important: namely that things are seen in reverse according to whether they are viewed from the standpoint of the principle or from the standpoint of manifestation … It results from this that what is *yin* from one side is *yang* from the other, and the other way around–although it is only in a manner of speaking which is not strictly correct that one can speak of or imply a direct relationship between the principle itself and a duality such as *yin* and *yang*. In fact … it is the "expiration" or movement of principial expansion which determines the "coagulation" of manifestation, and the "inspiration" or movement of principial contraction which determines its "solution."[77]

This last point alludes to the state of balance between the celestial and the terrestrial (*yang* and *yin*) that is the particular condition of cosmological existence. Guénon:

> All attraction gives rise to a centripetal movement, hence a "condensation"; this will be balanced at the opposite pole by a "dissipation" governed by a centrifugal movement that aims at re-establishing—or rather maintaining—the total equilibrium. One consequence of this is that what from the point of view of substance is "condensation" is, on the contrary, "dissipation" from the point of view of essence; whereas, inversely, what

from the point of view of substance is "dissipation," will from the point of view of essence be "condensation." This means that all "transmutation" (to use the term in its Hermetic sense) will consist precisely of "dissolving" what was "coagulated" and simultaneously "coagulating" what was "dissolved." In appearance these two operations are inverse; in reality they are merely two complementary aspects of one single operation.[78]

The Upper and Lower Waters

God said, "Let there be a vault through the middle of the waters to divide the waters in two." And it was so.

Genesis 1:6

In the beginning the Universe consisted of water within water; as it is written, "The spirit of God moved upon the face of the waters."

Chagigah 77a

There is a fundamental distinction between the Divine Nothingness or Divine Substance (*hyperousia*) and primordial chaos or ontological Substance, for with the former we are talking of a principle and with the latter, a state. With this in mind one can nevertheless recognise here the supreme archetype of the symbolism of the Upper and Lower Waters. It is, as Coomaraswamy has observed, as if over against the Lower Waters of Heraclitus' river,[79] the perpetual flux of *Samsāra*, 'there stands the concept of the silent Sea'.[80] From one perspective this Sea, the Upper and Highest Water, is understood according to its absolute nature as representing the Truth. This reading stretches from ancient Hindu Scripture—'For the waters are the truth'—to the mystical writings of Swedenborg.[81] Similarly, according to Islamic tradition these waters are Divine Gnosis. Al-Ghazali: '*He sendeth down water from heaven so that the valleys are in flood with it, each according to its capacity* [Qur'an 8:7], for the commentaries tell us that the water is Gnosis and that the valleys are Hearts.'[82]

Coomaraswamy observes that in speaking of this Sea, the symbol of *Nirvāna*, the Buddhist is thinking primarily of its still depths: 'As in the mighty ocean's midmost depth no wave is born, but all is still'.[83] Similarly, Jalāl al-Din Rūmī writes: 'the final end of every torrent is the Sea ... Opposites and likes pertain to the waves, and not to the Sea'.[84] Coomaraswamy remarks that the 'eternal source is at the same time motionless and flowing, never "stagnant"; so that, as Meister Eckhart says, there is a 'fountain in the godhead, which flows out upon all things in eternity and in time'; as is also implied by the "enigma" of *Rg Veda*

49

v.47.5, where 'though the rivers flow, the Waters do not move.'[85] Heraclitus' river, *Samsāra*, is not other than the still Sea of *Nirvāna*.

The distinction between the Divine Sea and Heraclitus' river, between *Nirvāna* and *Samsāra*, prefigures the distinctions that exist in Substance *a priori* at each ontological or cosmic level. The Qur'an speaks of this distinction as being between "two seas."[86] In Sūrahs 25 and 35 the two seas are referred to as "sweet" and "bitter": 'It was He who sent the two seas rolling, the one sweet and fresh, and the other salty and bitter, and set a rampart between them as an insurmountable barrier.'[87] Burckhardt remarks that, according to interpretations well known in Sufism, 'the two seas symbolise respectively Quiddity and the Quantities, or, according to other interpretations, the non-manifested and the manifested, the formless and the formal, immediate knowledge and theoretical knowledge, etc. In short, the two seas can represent two more or less exalted, but always consecutive, degrees in the hierarchy of Being'.[88] Here the Divine Sea is envisaged as Transcendent Being, which is paradoxically identical with Beyond Being.

The *Zohar* speaks of "the Upper Waters" and "the Lower Waters": "'And God said: Let there be a firmament in the midst of the waters, and let it divide the waters from the waters" (*Genesis* I: 6). Rabbi Judah said: There are seven firmaments above and they all stand in supernal holiness ... and this firmament is in the midst of the waters and it separates the upper waters from the lower waters, and the lower waters call to the upper, and they drink from this firmament.'[89] According to Tishby, the "seven firmaments above" are the seven *sefirot* from *Hesed* to *Malkhut*; the firmament in the midst of the waters is *Malkhut*, which acts as "a kind of partition" collecting the Upper Waters, the influences of the *sefirot*.[90] These collected Waters nourish the "creaturely world," which is *Malkhut* in its aspect as "garden."

The first three *sefirot*—*Keter*, *Hokhmah* and *Binah*—are unaffected by onto-cosmological conditions, of which they are the tri-unitary principle. Onto-cosmological existence manifests via the lower seven *sefirot*. One might make a distinction between the lower seven *sefirot* as being "wet with existence" and the upper three as "dry." As Heraclitus says, 'For souls it is death to become water ... A dry soul is wisest and best.'[91] The ratio of three "dry" *sefirot* and seven "wet" *sefirot* suggests an interesting comparison with the Chinese legend of Kung Kung, the god of water and cause of one of the floods in Chinese tradition, for 'when Kung Kung was king, the waters occupied seven tenths and the dry land three tenths of the earth.'[92]

The Upper Waters are metaphysical All-Possibility. The Lower Waters are cosmological Substance, primordial Chaos, *prakriti*; mythological examples of this are found with the Babylonian *apsū*, the Hebraic *tehōm*, the Hindu *ap*, etc. From the terrestrial perspective the Upper Waters and the Lower Waters symbolise the two aspects of ontological Substance: essential causality and existential accidentality. This distinction is that of primordial Nature and manifested nature: *materia prima* and *materia secunda*.[93] Guénon likens the distinction between *materia prima* and *materia secunda* to that between the foundation of a building and its superstructure.[94] The active and passive nature of these respective terms is indicated by the use of the designations *Natura naturans* (naturing nature) and *Natura naturata* (natured nature). The term *Natura* denotes not just the passive principle but, simultaneously and symmetrically, both of the two principles associated directly with "becoming." As Guénon observes, 'The essential idea of the Latin word *natura*, just as of its Greek equivalent *physis*, is of "becoming." Manifested nature is "what comes into existence"; the principles involved are "what brings into existence."'[95] In the Hindu tradition this distinction is found in the distinction between *Mūla-prakriti* (Root-Nature) and *prakriti*, the raw material of corporeal existence.[96]

Snodgrass describes Substance as 'the primordial *sub-stratum* which "stands below" (Lat. *sub-stare*) and supports all existences, primordial Nature, the plastic, wholly passive and undifferentiated principle that contains, as in a womb, all the potentialities of existence.'[97] Schuon says that to 'speak of the Divine Substance is necessarily to speak of its ontological prolongation since we who speak owe our very being to this prolongation, which is Existence, manifested Relativity, Cosmic *Māyā*.'[98] This "prolongation" into "relativisation" he explains in terms of Radiation and Reverberation: 'Substance is accompanied—at a lesser degree of reality—by two emanations, one of which is dynamic, continuous and radiating, and the other static, discontinuous and formative. If, in addition to the Substance, there were no Radiation and Reverberation to prolong It by relativising It, the world would not be.'[99] The terms Radiation and Reverberation may helpfully be compared to the Holy Spirit and the Son respectively.[100] Schuon further offers the analogy of the wheel: 'expressed in geometric terms, the Substance is the centre, Radiation is the cluster of radii, and Reverberation, or the Image, is the circle; Existence or the "Virgin," is the surface which allows this unfolding to take place.'[101] The Centre corresponds to *Mūla-prakriti*, Radiation to *Śakti*, and Reverberation to Cosmic *Māyā*. Again, the Centre is essential causality and the circumference is existential accidentality. Essential causality is transcendent and unaffected by its accidents. 'Things' as Schuon says, 'are coagulations of universal Substance, but Substance is not affected (this is crucial) by those accidents in the slightest degree. Substance is not things, but things are it, and they are so by virtue of their existence and of their qualities'.[102] The transcendence of essential causality is explicit in the term *prakriti*, which means "that which is transcendent": 'The prefix *pra* means "higher"; *krti* (action) stands for creation. Hence she who in creation is transcendent is the transcendent goddess known under the name of Nature (*Prakriti*).'[103] Substance, or Nature, insomuch as it is essential causality, is identifiable with the *quinta essentia*, alchemically the "hub of the wheel."[104] This image agrees with Schuon's illustration of the centre as Pure Substance. It is in respect to this essential causality that it can be said that Substance is none other than Essence.

The Kings of Edom

To say manifestation is to say limitation.

Frithjof Schuon

Do not despise the Edomite, for he is your brother.

Deuteronomy 23:8

I called my son out of Egypt.

Matthew 2:15

In the case of the Ark of Noah the state of non-distinction is well expressed by the waters of the deluge. In the case of the Ark of the Covenant this state is expressed by the "desert" or wilderness of the Exodus. Just as the Flood lasted forty years, so Israel wandered in the desert for forty years, and so, might it be added, did Christ undergo his testing and "purification" during his forty days in the desert. Both the Flood and the desert express the idea of purification through a return to primordial chaos. Again, from a perspective that might be described as "linear," both the mythology of Noah's Flood and the story of Moses and the Ark of the Covenant allude to primordial chaos by the "states" described prior to the Flood and prior to the Exodus. In the first case this is expressed by the age of the Nephilim, the "wicked" generation of Noah. In the second case this is the exile of the Israelites in Egypt. Both of these share in the Kabbalistic symbolism of the "Death of the Kings of Edom": 'And these are the kings that reigned in the land of Edom' (Gen.36:31).[105]

'According to the Kabbalah,' remarks Schaya, 'Edom symbolises sometimes the imperfect or unbalanced state of creation preceding its present state–the latter being an ordered manifestation of the *Fiat Lux*'.[106] As Scholem notes, 'This conception of primeval worlds also occurs in the "orthodox Gnosticism" of such Fathers of the Church as Clement of Alexandria and Origen, albeit with a difference, in as much as for them these worlds were not simply corrupt but necessary stages in the great cosmic process.'[107] According to Kabbalah the Edomite kings were constructed of pure Judgment and contained no Mercy. *'Edom* (אדם; *"red"*), derives from the word *'ādām*, (אדם; "to *show blood"*), where red, as Tishby observes, is the colour of strict judgment.[108] The "Death of the Kings" refers to the inability of onto-cosmological manifestation to maintain itself before the advent of the image of supernal Man. Tishby: 'The system of emanation had not yet been prepared in the image of the supernal Man, which constitutes a harmonious structure by balancing the opposing forces. In the idea of the image of Man even the forces of destruction of "the other side" are able to survive. ... Once the image of Man had been prepared all the forces that were not able to exist before existed in it.'[109]

Supernal Man: this is *Adam Kadmon* ("principial man"), also called *Adam ilaah* ("transcendent man"). He is the "prototype" upon which the Universe is modelled—'the Universe is a big man and man is a little universe.' This is the Islamic doctrine of *al-Insānul-Kāmil* ("Universal Man").[110] In his introduction to al-Jīlī's treatise, *Al-Insān al-Kāmil*, Burckhardt remarks, 'With regard to its internal unity, the cosmos is ... like a single being; — "We have recounted all things in an evident prototype" (Qur'an 36). If one calls him the "Universal Man," it is not by reason of an anthropomorphic conception of the universe, but because man represents, on earth, its most perfect image.'[111] A distinction arises between Universal Man and Primordial Man or Pre-Adamite Man (*al-insān al-qadīm*). This, *mutatis mundis*, is similar to the distinction, in the Chinese tradition, between Transcendent Man (*chūn jen*) and True Man (*chen jen*), which is the same as that between "actually realised immortality" and "virtual immortality." Guénon:

> "Transcendent man," "divine man," or "spiritual man" are alternative names for someone who has achieved total realisation and attained the "Supreme Identity." Strictly speaking he is no longer a man in an individual sense, because he has risen above humanity and is totally liberated not only from its specific conditions but also from all other limiting conditions associated with manifested existence. He is therefore, literally, "Universal Man," whereas "true man"—who has only reached the stage of identification with "primordial man"—is not. But even so, it can be said that "true man" is already "Universal Man," at least in a virtual sense.[112]

According to Kabbalah, *Hesed* (Mercy) corresponds to Abraham, *Din* (Judgment) to Isaac, and *Tiferet* (Beauty) to Jacob. Jacob is the balance of Mercy and Judgment, the harmonised "image of Man" who, in his realised state, is Israel. Yet Jacob was not the first born to Isaac: 'When her days to be delivered were fulfilled, behold, there were twins in her womb. The first came forth red, all his body like a hairy mantle; so they called his name Esau. Afterward his brother came forth, and his hand had taken hold of Esau's heel; so his name was called Jacob' (Gen.25:24-6). The name Jacob, *Ya'aqōb* (יעקב), means "*heel* catcher," from the primitive root *'āqab* (עקב; "to *swell*"). The image is of Jacob (order) "swelling" or rising out of the chaotic waters of potentiality (Esau), an image that is common in creation myths. Again, when we think of the "redness" of Esau as "blood" then one is lead to think of the swelling of the woman's belly with the foetal child, which has the same relationship with the "blood" of the placenta as Jacob has with Esau. Esau is potentiality, Jacob is actuality or realisation. Then, as *Genesis* 36:1 tells us, Esau is Edom. The Edomite Kings are 'the kings who reigned in the land of Edom, before any king reigned over the Israelites' (Gen.25:31); as Jacob follows Esau, usurps the birthright and becomes the chosen child, so too Israel follows Edom, and so too creation follows the potential for manifestation.

The symbolism of Edom is found with the Exodus from Egypt, for Egypt is commonly identified with Edom in the Kabbalah.[113] Moreover, the Hebrew word for Egypt, *Mitsrayim*, is the dual of the word, *mātsōwr*, implying the sense of "a *limit*." To say manifestation is to say limitation. In being unmanifest potential, Edom is still the first limitation, as discussed with reference to the *tsimtsum*.

The identification of the wicked generation of the Nephilim with the Edomite Kings is more obscure. The Nephilim are said to have been a race of "giants"; symbolically the Nephilim correspond to the Titans of Greek legend, the Mountain Giants of Norse legend and the *Asuras* of Hindu myth.[114] In each tradition these represent the "unbalanced" state preceding the "Olympian" order. It has further been suggested that the "war of the Titans" corresponds, *mutatis mundis*, with the "war of the kings" (Gen.14:1-16),[115] where the "war of the kings" is again identifiable with the Edomite kings. *Genesis* 36:31 says, 'Bela the son of Beor reigned in Edom, the name of his city being Dinhabah.' Tishby explains that 'the Hebrew word *bela* signifies "destruction," and the whole name is like that of Balaam, son of Beor, who is on "the other side."'[116] Dinhabah we should understand as related to *Din* (Judgment). Here one might suggest the identification, at least symbolically, of "Bela the son of Beor" with "the king of Bela" (Gen.14:8). Added to this, readings from the *Sefirah Dtzenioutha*, the *Book of Concealed Mystery*, and *Ha Idra Rabba Qadisha*, the *Greater Holy Assembly*, suggest the identification

between the Kings of Edom and the kings of *Genesis* 14, albeit in an esoteric way. In the *Book of Concealed Mystery* it is said, 'Thirteen kings
wage war with seven.'[117] These "thirteen kings" are "the measures of
mercies," insomuch as these represent the unity of the Tetragrammaton.
Thirteen answers by Gematria to the idea of unity: 'For ACHD, *Achad*,
unity yields the number 13 by numerical value'.[118] The "seven kings"
are the seven Edomite kings named in *Genesis* 36:31-40. There are, in
fact, eight kings named in this passage; moreover, there are nine principal personages when we recognise the importance of Mehetabel, the
wife of Hadar (v.39). However, concerning the first seven kings it said
of each that "[He] died." Chapter 26 of *The Book of Concealed Mystery*
explains that after Adam was constituted these seven were 'mitigated in
a permanent condition through him'; they ceased to be called by their
former appellations and hence are considered to have "died." Concerning Hadar and Mehetabel it is taught that they were not abolished like
the others because they were male and female, 'like as the palm tree,
which groweth not unless there be both male and female.' Hence, they
did not "die" but remained in a fixed condition.[119] 'Thirteen kings wage
war with seven kings' and, as we are told, there were 'nine vanquished
in war' (i.e. the eight kings of Gen.36 and Mehetabel). Consider then:
Genesis 14:9 is explicit in stressing the odds "four kings against five."
This suggests the nine aspects of Edom (the eight kings and Mehetabel).
When the kings of Sodom and Gomorrah flee (v.10) the odds shift to
four kings against three, which reveals the seven Edomite kings who
died. The "thirteen kings" who waged war with the seven correspond to
Abraham who, as *Hesed* (*Mercy*), is the "measure of mercy."

The relationship between Israel (actuality) and Edom (potentiality)
is complementary. *Deuteronomy* 23:8 says, 'Do not despise the Edomite,
for he is your brother.' Manifestation can never exhaust the indefinitude
of potentiality, which is to say that there is a continuity of potentiality.
A Jewish tradition ties this idea to the mythology of Noah. It is said that
at the time of the Flood the giant Og begged admittance to the Ark. He
climbed on to the roof and refused to leave.[120] In this way the potentiality of the "giants," the Nephilim, remained with the Ark through to the
next generation.

In the *Second Slavonic Apocalypse of Enoch* there is yet another
intriguing reference to Edom that relates it directly to the Flood myth.[121]
According to the story of the birth of Melkisedek (Melchizedek), Nir
("light")—the brother of Noe (Noah)—to whom the new baby had been
entrusted was warned by the Lord that He planned "a great destruction
onto the earth" (the Flood), but the Lord reassured Nir that before this
event the archangel Michael[122] would take the child and put him in the

Paradise of Edem (Eden). Chapter 72 finds Michael taking the child: 'I shall take your child today. I will go with him and I will place him in the paradise of Edem, and there he will be forever.'[123] However in verse nine we find the child placed in "the paradise of Edom."[124] Again, Schaya recalls that during the destruction of the second Temple, itself another case of the dissolution of the Judaic "world," all twelve tribes went into exile in the kingdom of Edom.[125]

Another incident that deserves consideration in light of the symbolism of Edom and the "imperfect or unbalanced state" preceding the "ordered manifestation" is the destruction of the original tablets of the Law (Ex.32:19). Here one recognises a similar relationship between Esau-Jacob and Jacob-Israel; allowing for certain differences of symbolism, what Esau is to Jacob, Jacob is to the Community of Israel. Thus, as Jacob ascended and descended the "Ladder"—the *axis mundi*—to become Israel, so too Moses ascended and descended Mount Sinai bringing the Testimony that transformed the Israelites to the "Community of Israel"—a cognomon of the *Shekhinah*—as such. But, in conformity with the symbolism being considered, the prototype tablets had to be destroyed before the Law could be brought forth in a perfect state.

Eden

A river flowed out of Eden to water the garden, and there it divided and became four rivers.

Genesis 2:10

Between Edom and Eden there is a similar relationship as between Esau and Jacob and, by analogy, between the potential of Jacob and the realisation of Israel, or again, between Eden and the Garden. Here it is all a matter of the hierarchy of Being and of perspective, from "above" or "below." According to Kabbalah there is an Upper and a Lower Eden, respectively *Binah* and *Malkhut*, and these are the "upper firmament" and the "lower firmament,"[126] the "Upper Mother" and the "Lower Mother,"[127] the Upper and Lower Waters.[128]

The name *'Eden* (עדן) derives from the primitive root *'adan* (עדן; "to be *soft* or *pleasant*") expressing the sense of "pleasure" or "enjoyment." However some commentators speculates that the word Eden may originally have meant "open wastes."[129] This suggests the word *tohu* ("formless"; *chaos*), as in the opening of *Genesis*: 'Now the earth was a formless void (*tohu* and *bohu*)'. Eden is the sea of potentiality from which creation stems; it is potentiality of fecundity, as the "ground"—Meister Eckhart's *grunt*—is potentially the garden. According to the perspective adopted, onto-cosmological potentiality presents either a positive (Eden, "pleasure," plenitude) or negative (Edom, "open wastes"; chaos) face.

Eden corresponds to *Binah*, which is called the "Great Sea."[130] As we read, 'a river flowed out of Eden' (Gen.2:10); here again is the symbolism of "the fountain" and "the Sea." The river that flows out of Eden is the active Essence—the same with the Spirit (*Ruah*) that moved on the Waters and, again, with the *Fiat Lux* that brings light from darkness. In the same way that zero contains the possibility for number and one contains all numbers virtually, so too the symbolism of the word Eden (עדן) contains the idea of the "river" that flows out of it. The letter *ayn* symbolically expresses the idea of a "fountain" gushing forth; it is also an "eye," that is, the divine Eye through which the creative Light of the *Fiat Lux* flows out. In accord with the "law of inverse analogy" the human eye is a receptacle through which light, as we perceive it, flows in. *Daleth*, the second letter of Eden, is symbolically a "door"; it is the opening that the river of *ayn* flows through. At the same time this idea of the door partakes of *ayn* insomuch as it is an eye or opening. The letter *nūn*, which completes Eden, is symbolically a "fish"; suffice to remark that the fish expresses the potentiality of water in a living form. It might be noted that Edom expresses a similar symbolism with two informative differences. The first letter of Edom is an *aleph*, symbolically expressing an "ox," where the ox is a well known symbol of Cosmic Substance.[131] The final letter is a *mem*, symbolically expressing "water," that is to say, it precedes the "living form" (the fish) and highlights the unformed or chaotic nature of potentiality.

Eden is unmanifest Existence in its state of biunity: Essence undifferentiated from Substance—recalling the ambiguity of the words *ayn* and *ousia*. The "river" is the vertical ray of Essence in act upon the horizontal garden (Substance). It is said that the river divided and became "four rivers," these being the four symbolic directions of a horizontal plane of existence, the same with the "face of the waters" (Gen.1:2). This same symbolism is found in the *Zohar* (II, 13a-13b), with the difference being that in this case it is the Spirit (*Ruah*) dividing into the "four winds."[132] The details we are given concerning these "four rivers" reveal a cosmogonic symbolism. This, of course, is not to deny a geographical reading but simply to recognise the primacy of the cosmogonic reading in this case. In this respect it is enough to recall that the plan precedes the building.

The first river is Pishon, *Pīyshōwn* (פישון; "*dispersive*").[133] This word is closely related to the word *Pīythōwn* (פישתון; "*expansive*"), which derives from the root *pothāh* (פתה; "to *open*," as implying a secret place). Pishon is said to 'wind all through the land of Havilah' (Gen.2:11), where

Havilah, *Chavīylāh* (חוילה) means "circular" from *chīyl* (חיל; "to *whirl*"). To whirl in a circular manner: the image here may be compared to the analogous symbolism of the Masonic plume line (the vertical axis) set swinging in increasing or "expansive" continuous spirals.

The second river is Gihon, *Gīchōwn* (גחון), from *gōach* (גח; "to *gush* forth" or "to *issue*," in the sense of labour). Gihon moves through the land of Cush. The sense here is more obscure. *Kūwsh* (כוש) is generally associated with Cush, the son of Ham (Gen.10:6). This is far from inconsequential, for Ham plays an active role in the cosmogony as expressed in the story of Noah. On this point, the name Ham, *chām* (חם; "*hot*," to be inflamed) expresses a similar sense as the bringing forth of the ontological waters, where fire and water are recognised as analogous symbols of the state of undifferentiated Being. It is worth noting the similarity here between *Kūwsh* (כוש) and *kūwr* (כור), which means "to *dig*" but particularly to dig "a *furnace*." The two words differ by their final letters, which are subsequent letters in the Hebrew alphabet. *Kūwr* has as its final *resh*, symbolically a "*head*." *Kūwsh* has as its final *shin*, symbolically a "*tooth*." One might say that the tooth is in the head as the heat is in the furnace. This symbolism of the furnace echoes the alchemist's athanor (Arabic *at-tannūr*; "oven") and the Kabbalist's Urn, which are not irrelevant here, for they are both homologues of the Ark.

The third river is Hiddekel, *Chiddeqel* (חדקל). The Hebrew here is of uncertain derivation. In Persian this is *Tigra*, which becomes *Tigris* in Greek, as the *Septuagint* calls it. In the old language of Babylonia this river was termed *Idiglaṭ* or *Digla*, meaning "the encircling."[134] The Hiddekel is said to run to the east of Ashur, which is the same name as Assyria. This name carries the sense of "stepping or coming forth"— suggesting the coming forth of manifestation from unmanifest potentiality; this comes from *'āshūr* (אשור; "a *step*"), which itself comes from the primitive root, *'āshar* (אשר; "to be *level*"). In this context there is an etymological similarity between Assyria, *'Ashshūwr* (אשור) and the word *'ashūwyāh* (אשויה), which derives from an unused root meaning "*foundation*." According to the symbolism of the *Sefirot*, *Yesod* is called "Foundation," as it is the foundation upon which *Malkhut* (the Kingdom) is built; in this connection, note that *Yesod* is symbolically described as a "river."[135]

The fourth river is Euphrates, *Pᵉrāth* (פרת; "to *break* forth"; "*rushing*"). We might compare this with the word *pōrāth* (פרת), which is the same with the primitive root *pārāh* (פרת; "to *bear fruit*"; to be, or cause to be). An interesting connection is suggested here, for *pārāh* derives from *par* (פר), which means "a *bullock*," where the bullock, like the ox, is a universal and common symbol of *prima materia*.[136] Moreover,

Strong's Dictionary suggests that this itself comes from the idea of either *"breaking* forth in wild strength" or, perhaps, from the image of *"dividing* the hoof," and this from *pārar* (פרר; "to *break* up"). Again, *pāras* (פרש), which differs to *pārar* by the shift from the final *resh* to a final *shin*, also means "to *break* apart" in the sense of "to *disperse*," which returns us to the symbolism of the first river, Pishon.

The symbolism described by the "four rivers" is suggestive of Schuon's metaphoric description of Substance through the image of the wheel, excepting in this case the radii appear to be described as "spirals," which is, in a sense, more exact.

The description of "encircling" described by both the name Havilah and the Babylonia word *Digla* remind one of the numerous world encircling rivers of mythology, of which the Greek Oceanus is maybe the most familiar. One feels it is fair to say that this passage contains an esoteric expression of the cosmogony, as opposed to Gerhard Von Rad who claims that this passage 'has no significance for the unfolding action' of *Genesis*.[137] All of the details presented are expressed in the symbolism of the *ayn*, a fountain, which synthetically contains the word Eden.

The Hebrew Scriptures give only the names of the four rivers that divided from the original river yet not the name of this source river. However, according to *Ha Idra Zuta Qadihsa*, the Lesser Holy Assembly, this river is called *Yobel*: 'What is *Yobel*? As it is written, Jer. xvii.8: "VOL IVBL, Va-El *Yobel*, And spreadeth out her roots by the river"; therefore that river which ever goeth forth and floweth, and goeth forth and faileth not.'[138] The word *yōbēl* (יבל) means literally "a *blast* from a trumpet," and comes from a primitive root, *yābal* (יבל) meaning "to *flow*," as a river. The connection of *Yobel* with the sound of a trumpet suggests the idea of creation through the emanation of the primordial sound, the "Word," which is again the "Name," analogous by a shift in symbolism with the *Fiat Lux*. In this connection, *Yobel* is also said to be the same as the angel Yahoel, which is the first of the "Seventy Names of Metatron."[139] According to the Babylonian Talmud, Metatron is the angel who is given the same name as his master.[140] This name is *Shaddai* or "Almighty," which has the same numerical value as "Metatron." According to the *Zohar* the name *Shaddai* is related to the word *sadai* or "field," as in Psalm 104: 'Who sends forth springs into the streams ... they give drink to every beast of the field' (11-12). *Zohar* III, 18a: 'This is [the significance of] the verse "and from thence it was parted and became four heads" (*Genesis* 2:10); these four heads are the beasts of *sadai* ... *Sadai*: do not pronounce it *sadai*, but *Shaddai* (the Almighty), for he receives and completes the name from the foundation (*Yesod*) of the world.' As Tishby remarks, "the beasts of the field" (*sadai*) are the fours beasts of the Chariot.[141] Concerning the connection between the primordial sound and the primordial light, both the Midrash and the *Zohar* says that the *Fiat Lux* of *Genesis* 1:3 is the light of Metatron.[142] He is called 'the light of the luminary of the *Shekhinah*'.[143] Metatron has been identified with Melchizedek,[144] who is seen as prefiguring Christ (Heb.5:7); yet even without this identification having being made it is not hard to see the relationship between the creative sound and light in the Christian tradition. Christ is both the Word and the "light of the world" (Jn.8:12). Jalāl al-Din Rūmī offers the following image of the creation which beautifully sums up all we are considering here: 'But when that purest of lights threw forth Sound which produced forms, He, like the diverse shadows of a fortress, became manifold.'[145]

Schaya remarks that *Yobel* is the "divine state": 'the state of supreme illumination and identity, of total union with God.'[146] He further recognises *Yobel* as *Binah*, the Upper Mother.[147] We have said that the Upper and Lower Mothers are *Binah* and *Malkhut*, but from another perspective they are also *Binah* and *Yesod*, which, as Tishby says are both symbolically "rivers."[148] Furthermore, *Yobel* is the Hebrew word for "jubilee," the fiftieth year beginning on the Day of Atonement (*kol shofar*, the "voice of the trumpet"). Accordingly *Binah* is conceived as having 50 gates through which Mercy flows as a river.[149] It is by the way of the 50 gates of *Binah* that all creation is manifested. In this context it should be noted that the Hebrew word *kol* ("all") has the numerical value of 50.[150] Furthermore, according to Kabbalah, the world is created in and through the 22 letters of the Hebrew alphabet. Manifestation, in both its potentiality and actuality, is thus to be found expressed by the number 72 (50 + 22), which reveals, in part, the meaning of the "Seventy-Two Names of Metatron."

Rabbi Gikatilla observes that it was the angel Yahoel who "performed the slaying of the firstborn."[151] Considering the cosmogony as expressed by the Exile, the slaying of the firstborn and the subsequent Exodus is analogous to the "coming forth" of the *Fiat Lux*. It should also be noted that the slaying of the first-born is prefigured in the "rejection" of Ishmael and again the relinquishing of his birthright by Esau. Moreover, in this context, the *Zohar* recognises Jacob as "a river of praise" and more explicitly say that he is the "river going out of Eden."[152]

Fire and Water

He brought out a single flame from the spark of blackness, and blew spark upon spark. It darkened and was then kindled. And He brought out from the recesses of the deep a single drop, and He joined them together, and with them He created the world.

Zohar I, 86b-87a; *Zohar Terumah* 164b

The state of undifferentiated Existence is principally symbolised by either water or fire. This is the indifferentiation of Essence (fire, Heaven, light, fountain) and Substance (water, Earth, dark, sea). In a remarkable passage the *Zohar* describes the creative act as the distinction of a "spark" of fire and a "drop" of water from the "darkness" and their subsequent merging:

"And Melchizedek king of Salem brought forth bread and wine" (Genesis 14: 18). Rabbi Simeon began by quoting; "In Salem is His tabernacle…" (Psalm 76: 3). Come and see. When it arose in the will of the Holy One, blessed be He, to create the world, He brought out a single flame from the spark of blackness, and blew spark upon spark. It darkened and was then kindled. And He brought out from the recesses of the deep a single drop, and He joined them together, and with them He created the world. The flame ascended and was crowned on the left, and the drop ascended and was crowned on the right. They encountered one another and changed places, one on one side and one on the other. The one that descended went up, and the one that ascended went down. They became intertwined, and a perfect spirit emerged from them. The two sides were immediately made one, and it was placed between them, and they were crowned with each other. Then there was peace above and peace below, and the level was established. *He* was crowned with *vav*, and *vav* with *he*, and *he* ascended and was joined with a perfect bond. Then "Melchizedek [was] king of Salem"—actually "king of Salem": the king who ruled over perfection.[153]

Schaya cites a similar passage, *Zohar, Terumah*, 164b: 'When the Holy One was about to create the world he robed himself in the primordial light and created the heavens. At first the light was on the right'—which, as Schaya says, is the active and spiritual side—'and the darkness at the left'—the receptive and substantial side. According to this tradition the Holy One 'merged the one into the other and formed the heavens'. Schaya notes that the word for heavens, *shamaim*, is composed of *esh* and *maim*, fire (spiritual light) and water (subtle substance), which he also relates to the symbolism of right and left.[154]

Genesis 2:6—'there went up a mist from the earth'—suggests an esoteric identification between the symbolisms of fire and water. The *New Jerusalem Bible* translates the word "mist," `*ēd* (אד) as simply "water," however, this word means *"enveloping,"* coming from the same root as `*ūwd* (אוד; "to *rake* together"; a *poker* for *turning* or *gathering* embers), with Strong suggesting the idea of a "fire-brand." One might well suggest that this "mist" alludes to the indifferentiation of fire and water. According to *Pirke de Rabbi Eliezer*, chapter twenty-three, the waters of the Flood were hot, burning the flesh of the giants.[155] According to an Islamic tradition, at the time of the Flood, the oven (the alchemist's *athanor*; the Kabbalist's Urn) of Noah's wife began to boil from which water flowed, following which water flowed from the arteries of the earth.[156] One is reminded of the "boiling" water that rises up at the base of the tree—the "Tree of Life"—in Chrétien de Troyes story of Ywain.[157] Here the axial symbolism of the tree is analogous to that of the river *Yobel*.

Fire and Water symbolise the dual aspects of the primordial state (Essence and Substance). It is by these elements that the world is most often portrayed "returning" to the primordial state. These "primordial" or "pure" elements purify the "corruption" of the world that has moved from its primordial purity (cf. Gen.6:10: 'God saw that the earth was corrupt'). Chevalier & Gheerbrant's, *Dictionary of Symbols* remarks that 'purification by fire complements purification by water on both the microcosmic level in rites of initiation and, on the macrocosmic level, in alternating myths of floods and great fires or droughts.'[158]

To talk of cosmic purification is, in a sense, to talk of cosmic cataclysm, for purification is the destruction of that which is corrupt, which in this case is the world itself. When talking of cosmic cataclysm or the "end of the world" it is well to take heed of the following words of Guénon:

> This end is doubtless not the "end of the world" in the absolute sense in which some people are liable to interpret the expression, but it is at least the end of *a* world ... In any case the laws governing such occurrences apply analogously at different levels; what is true therefore of the "end of the world" in the fullest conceivable sense, and which moreover is taken usually as referring only to the terrestrial world, remains true also, though on a proportionately reduced scale, of the end of some particular world, understood in a much more restricted sense.[159]

The "end of the world," so to speak, is the end of a particular cycle, be it historic or cosmic. This event can act as the precursor to a "new golden age," born from the ashes or the mud of the previous world. This is the concept of periodic renewal of the world or, as the Stoics called it, *metacosmesis*.[160] Nevertheless, as Eliade explains, for the traditional mind each "ending" was absolute in a "relative sense." This is to say that while there may have been an appreciation of cyclic time, and hence the indefinite continuation of time, nevertheless the end of each cycle was considered as absolute within the relative context of its particular cycle.[161] As Schuon says, 'One must always take account of the difference between the "relative Absolute" which is the Creator-Being and the "pure Absolute" which is Non-Being, the Essence, The Self: the difference is exactly that between the "end of the world" and the apocatastasis, or between the *pralaya* [dissolution] and the *mahāpralaya* [Great Dissolution].'[162]

Myths of cosmic cataclysm principally take two forms: destruction by "water" and destruction by "fire." In the Platonic tradition we find the priest of Saïs telling Solon, 'There have been and will be many different calamities to destroy mankind, the greatest of them by fire and water, lesser ones by countless other means.'[163] In some cases the destruction of the world is effected by a combination of both. In the mythology of the Jains the cosmos is 'annihilated in a cataclysm of fire and flood'.[164] In the Hebraic tradition there is a suggestion of this dual cataclysm in the account of Sodom and Gomorrah, which *Smith's Bible Dictionary* translates respectively as "burning" and "submersion."[165] According to Aztec mythology each of the four elements—water, earth, air, and fire—terminates a period of the world: 'the eon of water ended in deluge, that of the earth with an earthquake, that of air with a wind, and the present eon will be destroyed by flame.'[166] 'Fire' says Heraclitus, 'lives the death of air, and air lives the death of fire; water lives the death of earth, earth that of water.'[167] He also says that the first transformation of "Fire" is into "sea."[168]

There are numerous accounts of cataclysm by water. Theodore Gaster (*Myth, Legend, and Custom in the Old Testament*) cites 302 texts from around the world detailing destruction by flood.[169] The oldest known example of this type is the Sumerian myth of the flood of the patriarch Ziusudra (Nippur, c.1750 BC). In some instances the destruction of the world is said to be brought about by mythic beasts. The Tupinamba tribe of Brazil believed that at the end of the world the sky-god, in the form of a jaguar, would come and eat mankind.[170] It is interesting then that the *Dictionary of Symbols* observes the jaguar and the crocodile as symbolising the 'complementary relationships of fire and water, of which they are the avatars (embodiments) or masters.'[171] In nearly all cases the world is brought to an end by means symbolically correspondent to the primordial principle fire and water.

Destruction by fire can take the form of an actual conflagration, for example, in the Norse tradition, the casting of fire over the earth by Surt at the time of Ragnorok,[172] or, the scorching of the earth by Phæthon in Greek mythology.[173] Alternatively, the destruction by fire may take the form of parching heat, as in the Aryan myth of the drought brought about by the coiled serpent, Vritra ("the Enveloper").[174] Vritra had confiscated the waters and was keeping them in the hollow of a mountain. Here the balance between Mercy (Water) and Judgment (Fire) is disturbed meaning that creation cannot be maintained. This idea of imbalance is again present in the Chinese myth of the Flood of Kung Kung where the deluge comes with the earth being tilted off its axis.[175] Eliade recalls further images of world destruction through "scorching heat" in the Judaic tradition, *Isaiah* 34:4, 9-11; the Iranian, *Bahman-Yašt*, II, 41; and in the Latin, Lactantius, *Divinae Institutiones*, VII, 16, 6.[176] He suspects the vision of the destruction of the world by fire to be of Iranian origin, referring, for example, to *Bundahišm*, XXX, 18.[177] In the Stoic tradition destruction by fire can be found in the *Sibylline Oracles*, II, 253. According to the Stoic doctrine, all souls are resolved into the world soul or primal fire (*ekpyrosis*) to then be formed anew (Cicero's *renovatio*). Description of these destructions can be found in Seneca's *De Consolatione ad Marciam*.[178]

Traversing the Waters

As in a ship convey us o'ver the flood.

Rg-Veda, 1.97.8

The world is my sea, the sailor the spirit of God.
The boat my body, the soul he who wins back his Abode.

Angelus Silesius[179]

Water, in so much as it is "flowing," represents flux, whether this be the ebb and flow of potentiality coming "in" and "out" of being, or the ever running river of time. Both are aspects of Hericlitus' river, which is *Samsāra*. The soul, born into the water of Being, is a wayfarer engaged in the journey back home, to the source, the Silent Sea (*Nirvāna*). This brings us to the symbolism of the "traversing of the waters" or the movement from one state of Being to another. Coomaraswamy has observed that the "traversing of the waters" can be related in three different ways.[180] The voyage can be accomplished either by crossing over the waters to the other shore, by going upstream towards the source of the waters, or by going downstream towards the sea. Now, there are four paradigmic forms of the "boat" or "ship" motif: 1. the "ferry of the dead"; 2. the "ship of the hero"; 3. the "barque of the god"; and 4. the "Ark of the deluge." The first three categories of "boats" respectively correspond to the three forms of the "voyage."

The "ferry of the dead" crosses the "River of Death" from the shore of the living to the "Farther Shore" of the dead. In the Greek tradition this is the ferry of Charon; in Egyptian mythology, the ferryboat of Afu Ra;[181] in the *Epic of Gilgamesh* this is the ferry of Ur-shanabi.[182] There are numerous examples available, so much so that the *Dictionary of Symbols* claims, 'All civilizations have their boat of the dead.'[183] Guénon remarks that this crossing of the waters of death reflects the ultimate transition. As he says, 'the shore which is left behind is the world subject to change, that is, the corporeal state in particular ... and the "other shore" is *Nirvāna*, the state which is definitely set free from death.'[184] In this sense death is to be viewed as a birth, where 'new birth necessarily presupposes death to the former state'.[185] This recalls the "death of the kings" through which cosmological balance is "born." This crossing may likewise be accomplished via a "bridge."

The "ship of the hero" sails upstream to the source of the river, the *Fons Vitae*, the "Well of Honey in Viśnu's highest place,"[186] the Perennial Spring of Plotinus,[187] etc. In the context of the hero's journey this "source" is the hidden goal or treasure, the Golden Fleece, the Grail etc. This is the voyage of the "solar hero" entailing the passage through the symbolic Sundoor.[188] The case of going upstream is, as Guénon observes, 'perhaps the most remarkable in certain respects; for the river must then be conceived as identical with the World Axis.'[189] As such this journey is analogous with the ascension of a "ladder" or more precisely the shamanistic climbing of the "greased pole."[190] To this Guénon adds the "rope trick" in which a rope is thrown into the air and remains or seems to remain vertical while a man or a child climbs it until they disappear from view. As with the voyage upstream, the movement must be continuous. The "hero" must remain focused and always facing forwards or risks being washed back downstream to his eternal detriment.[191] They must be "steadfast in the face of multiplicity," as Meister Eckhart says, so that the "light and grace" of the Source may be revealed to them.[192] In comparison to the "greased pole" the two parallel posts of a ladder represent the complimentary movement up and down along the axis.[193] As Coomaraswamy remarks, 'the Axis of the Universe is, as it were, a ladder on which there is a perpetual going up and down.'[194]

Guénon remarks on the case of the "descent with the current" that 'the Ocean must then be considered not as an extent of water to be crossed but, on the contrary, as the very goal to be reached and therefore as representing *Nirvāna*.'[195] Here again is the realisation of the truth of *Samsāra* as *Nirvāna*. The god upon his "barque" is a symbolic manifestation of the cosmic currents, which, from one perspective, express the flux of potentiality or primordial chaos and, from another perspective, the stability and stillness of cosmic order. The "barque of the god" is the resplendent vessel upon which the god makes his or her endless journey upon the cosmic rhythm of *Samsāra*; and this is to say that the "barque of the god" is none other than Immanence itself. Joseph Campbell remarks on this symbolism as applied to the gods in general:

> As the consciousness of the individual rests on a sea of night into which it descends in slumber and out of which it wakes, so, in the imagery of myth, the universe is precipitated out of, and reposes upon, a timelessness back into which it again dissolves. And as the mental and physical health of the individual depends on an orderly flow of vital forces into the field of waking day from the unconscious dark, so again in myth, the continuance of the cosmic order is assured only by a controlled flow of power from the source. The gods are symbolic personifications of the laws governing this flow.[196]

For the ancient Egyptians the sky was "a vast layer of water" upon which the celestial bodies traversed in boats.[197] The idea of the sun traversing the sky in a vehicle of some description is common and recalls the daily journey of Apollo, as Helios, in his fiery chariot, among others. There are several connections that exist between the boat, the chariot, and the throne. In the *Book of the Dead* it is said of Horus that Osiris has 'made him to have his throne in the Boat of Millions of Years'.[198] The idea of a vehicle as a throne is explicit in the *Merkabah* (throne-chariot) mysticism of the Judaic tradition.[199] The "throne of glory" (Ezek.1:26, 10:1; Dan.7:9; Rev.4:2; 1En.14:18, 71:5-11; 2En.22; 3En.1:6; TLevi 5:1) is an epithet of the *Shekhinah*. The chariot is in turn the dynamic expression of the "throne of glory." As Leo Schaya says, 'The "throne," in its fullness, is the first and spiritual crystallization of all creatural possibilities before they are set in motion in the midst of the cosmos. When the "throne" assumes its dynamic aspect and cosmic manifestation begins to move, it is called the divine "chariot" (*merkabah*).'[200] Elsewhere Schaya remarks on the relationship between the tabernacle and the *merkabah*. 'The tabernacle had provided the presence of God [*Shekhinah*] with no permanent habitation, for it was set up after the model of his heavenly "vehicle" (*merkabah*), in which he would lead His people through the wilderness to the fixed "centre of the world," Jerusalem.'[201] The tabernacle and the *merkabah* are *imagines mundi* in dynamic mode. The throne is an *imago mundi* emphasizing the fixed Centre, complete and Eternal, both Transcendent and Immanent.

The "Ark of the deluge" presents a voyage "upon" the waters rather than "traversing," as this is not a journey from one shore to another. Neither is it like the voyage downstream into the Ocean wherein the "barque" remains endlessly afloat on the currents of divine Harmony. Instead, as Coomaraswamy observes, the voyage of the Ark is 'essentially a voyage up and down the slope (*pravat*) of heaven rather than a voyage to and fro, and quite other than the voyage of the *devayāna*, which is continuously upwards and towards a shore whence there is no return.'[202] The voyage of the *devayāna* ("the way of the gods") is analogous with the voyage of the hero. We may recall how many of the solar heroes are in fact either gods (Apollo, Mithra, Horus, Krishna, etc.) or of divine-mortal birth (Hercules, Gilgamesh, Christ, etc.).[203]

In some instances a particular mythological journey may involve the shift from one to another of these boats, as seen in the move of Afu Rā from his "serpent-boat" to his "river-boat."[204] In the *Epic of Gilgamesh* we have both the ferryboat of Ur-shanabi and the Ark of Ut-napishtim.[205] In each of these forms the journey of the boat expresses a transition between states, a "death" and "rebirth."

As mentioned above, the "traversing of the waters" can also be accomplished via a "bridge."[206] Like the boat, the bridge is associated with the notion of "death" and return to the Source: 'Death is a bridge whereby the lover is joined to the Beloved.'[207] The bridge is often said to be 'broad for the righteous but as thin as a blade for the impious'.[208] Campbell recalls an Eskimo shaman crossing an abyss on a bridge as narrow as a knife.[209] In the *Katha Upanishad* the path is a 'sharpened edge of a razor'.[210] This is the "Sword Bridge" crossed by Sir Lancelot;[211] *Chinvat*, the "Bridge of the Separator" in Zoroastrian tradition; the "narrow" and "hard" way of St. Matthew (Matt.7:14).[212] This symbolism is again found in the assimilation of a bridge to a ray of light, on which point Guénon observes the double sense of the English word "beam" which designates both a girder, in the sense of a single beam or single tree trunk as is the case with the most primitive form of bridge, and a luminous ray.[213] This is a bridge between the terrestrial domain and the celestial or solar domain; its narrowness indicates its treacherous nature—the "hard way"—and it is properly speaking the path of the "solar hero." This bridge both *leads to* the Sundoor and, from a deeper perspective, *is* the Sundoor.

The "sharpness" of the Sword Bridge is again found in the analogous symbolism of the "Cutting Reeds" of Navajo tradition. Here the hero's path is barred by "cutting reeds" that 'tried to catch him, waving and clashing together.' Coomaraswamy observes these as being the same, *mutatis mundis*, with the Clashing Rocks, the Symplegades, which are a form of the "Active Door" or the Sundoor.[214] As Coomaraswamy observes, this is the same symbolism as the crossing of the "Red Sea" (Ex.14:21), where this name, *yam soof*, is said to actually mean the "Reed Sea." Samuel Fohr observes two articles by Bernard F. Batto questioning this reading of *yam soof* and offering instead the translation, "Sea of the End (of the World)."[215] Fohr remarks that the reference is to the primordial chaos.[216] These three apparently contradictory readings in fact confirm each other. The Red Sea, like the "wine-dark sea" of the Ancient Greeks, expresses the "dark" or feminine nature of the colour red, associated with the idea of the womb in which life and death are transmuted the one into the other;[217] this, then, is none other than the "womb" of primordial chaos from which order is "born"; and born, moreover, by passage through the Active Door (the Cutting Reeds; the Symplegades). But this is not all, for the Ark itself, which is analogous to the womb, is variously associated, if not explicitly constructed from, reeds (Noah, Moses, Ut-napishtim); and thus passage from the unmanifest to the manifest is effected through this symbolism of "reeds." Moreover, the "reeds" "growing" in the sea of primordial chaos are the very stuff of creation. Shaikh Ahmad al-'Alawī mentions the reeds of which the cosmic mat is woven as symbols of the manifestation of Divine Qualities out of which the whole universe is woven.[218] R. A. Nicholson recognises, with respect to Rūmī, that the reed (the Persian *ney*) is none other than 'an emblem of the transporting influence of Divine inspiration;[219] that is, the Spirit (*al-Rūh*; *Ruah*) that moves upon the Water; the Spirit, which is the *Logos*, both Uncreated and created, a bridge between the manifested and the Unmanifested.

The symbolic "bridge," in the most general sense, connects the two "shores" which, as Guénon remarks, will always, from a certain level of reference, have between them a relationship corresponding to that between heaven and earth.[220] Guénon:

> The bridge, therefore, is the exact equivalent of the axial pillar that links heaven and earth even while holding them apart; and it is because of this meaning that it must be conceived of as essentially vertical like all the other symbols of the "World Axis"—for example, the axel of the "cosmic chariot" when its two wheels represent heaven and earth. This establishes also the fundamental identity of the symbolism of the bridge with that of the ladder...[221]

The symbol of the bridge is further associated with that of the "rainbow."[222] In the Scandinavian Epic poem, *Gylfaginning*, the great king, High, explains to Gangleri, 'Has no one ever told you that the gods built a bridge to heaven from earth called Bilfrost [or *Byfrost*]? You must have seen it, maybe it is what you call the rainbow.'[223] The rainbow is generally considered as symbolising the union of heaven and earth. However, Guénon, discussing the relationship of the bridge and the rainbow, is less happy with this assimilation or identification. On the whole, he feels, 'the rainbow seems to have been above all connected, in a general way, with the cosmic currents by which an exchange of influences between heaven and earth operates much more than with the axis along which direct communication between the different states is effected'.[224] These "cosmic currents" derive from the action of the cosmic forces: expansion and concentration. The descending current or catabasis, the celestial influence, is symbolised by the analogous symbols of rain and light.[225] The ascending current or anabasis, the terrestrial or human influence, is found in the rising smoke of the sacrifice (cf. Gen.8:21; *Gilgamesh* XI, iv) and again in the flow of blessings or prayers that humankind offers "up."[226]

The curved form of the rainbow is more precisely compared with the spiral[227] that winds around an axis; from another perspective, this spiral corresponds to the two parallel post of the ladder. The difference here, as Guénon remarks, is that 'between the "axial" way, which leads the being directly to the principial state, and the more "peripheral" way which implies the passage through a series of hierarchic states one by one [be they the levels of the spiral or the rungs of the ladder] even though in both cases the final goal is necessarily the same.'[228]

Notes

1. *Bhavisyottarapurāna*, 31.14, cited in Eliade, *Patterns in Comparative Religion*, 1983, p.188.

2. Chuang-tse, *Nan-Ua-Ch'en-Ching*, Ch.11, cited in Perry, *TTW*, 2000, p.995.

3. Meister Eckhart, from Pfeiffer (ed.), *Meister Eckhart Vol.1*, 1924, p.360, cited in Perry, *TTW*, 2000, p.1000.

4. Schuon, *IFA*, 1989, p.56.

5. Sterry, *Vivian de Sola Pinto*, in *Peter Sterry, Platonist and Puritan*, 1934, cited in Perry, *TTW*, 2000, p.31.

6. Eliade, *Sacred and Profane*, 1987, p.130; see also *Patterns in Comparative Religion*, 1983, Ch.5.

7. Schuon, *IFA*, 1989, p.53.

8. Schuon, *IFA*, 1989, p.53, n.1.

9. Guénon, *MB*, 1981, p.30.

10. Guénon, *MB*, 1981, p.38. Throughout the English translations of both Guénon and Schuon there is inconsistency concerning the use of key Hindu terms. This may or may not be an accident of translation. For the sake of consistency I have corrected all quotations in line with current Indological nomenclature. Thus: *Brahman* = the Absolute; *Brahmā* = the creator god; and *Ātman* = the Self.

11. Schuon, *SPHF*, 1987, p.108.

12. See Burckhardt, *Alchemy*, 1974, p.36, n.3.

13. See Burckhardt, *ISD*, 1976, p.62, n.1.

14. Burckhardt, *ISD*, 1976, p.126.

15. Meister Eckhart, Sermon 83 (Colledge & McGinn, 1981, p.207).

16. See for example Mathers, *KU*, 1991, p.20.

17. Halevi, *Adam and the Kabbalistic Tree*, 1974, p.15.

18. Schaya, *UMK*, 1971, p.64.

19. Parmenides, *Frag*.VI, per Fairbanks (tr.), *The First Philosophers of Greece*, 1898, p.91.

20. *Chāndogya Upanishad* 6.2.1-2.

21. *Sophist* 238 c.

22. Ibn al-'Arabi, *Al-Futuhat al-makkiyyah* (*Meccan Revelations*), cited in Austin's introduction to his translation of *Fusūs*, 1980, p.40.

23. Schuon, *SPHF*, 1987, p.102. Schuon again: 'Nothing is external to absolute Reality; the world is therefore a kind of internal dimension of *Brahman*. But *Brahman* is without relativity; thus the world is a necessary aspect of the absolute necessity of *Brahman*. Put in another way, relativity is an aspect of the Absolute. Relativity, *Māyā*, is the *Shakti* of the Absolute, *Brahman*. If the relative did not exist, the Absolute would not be the Absolute' (*LS*, 1999, p.28).

24. Schuon, *LS*, 1999, p.27.

25. See Meister Eckhart, Sermon 4 (Walshe, *Vol.1*, 1987).

26. Angelus Silesius, *Cherubinischer Wandersmann*, V.5, cited in Perry, *TTW*, 2000, p.780.

27. Cited in Govinda, *Foundations of Tibetan Mysticism*, 1969, p.84.

28. *Madhyamakakarika*, xxv. 19-20. As Eliade remarks, 'This does not mean that the world (*samsāra*) and deliverance (*nirvāna*) are "the same thing"; it means only that they are undifferentiated' (*A History of Religious Ideas Vol.2*, 1981, p.225; see §189).

29. Schuon, *TB*, 1993, p.139. In the words of the Sixth Chinese Patriarch (Hui-neng): 'When you hear me speak about void, do not fall into the idea that I mean vacuity...The illimitable void of the universe is capable of holding myriads of things of various shapes and forms' (Goddard, *A Buddhist Bible*, cited in Govinda, *Foundations of Tibetan Mysticism*, 1969, p.117-18).

30. Schuon, *EPW*, 1981, p.52.

31. Ibn al-'Arabī, *Fusūs*, cited in Perry, *TTW*, 2000, p.995.

32. See Coomaraswamy's essay, '*Kha* and Other Words Denoting "Zero," in Connection with the Indian Metaphysics of Space': *SP2*, 1977.

33. *Commentary on the Dream of Scipio*, 1.6.7-9, cited by Meister Eckhart, *Par. Gen.* 15 (Colledge & McGinn, 1981, p.99).

34. *Enneads* 5.2.1.

35. Schuon, *SME*, 2000, p.15.

36. One might describe the Absolute as Actuality and the Infinite as Potentiality, while never forgetting that the Absolute and the Infinite are a single Reality.

37. Guénon warns against dismissing the principial state—the realm of Forms or Ideas—as somehow less real by virtue of the being described as "virtual": 'To consider the eternal ideas as nothing but simple "virtualities" in relation to the manifested beings of which they are the principial "archetypes" … is strictly speaking a reversal of the relationship between Principle and manifestation' ('Les Idées éternelles': *Études Traditionnelles*, 1947, pp.222-223, cited in Perry, *TTW*, 2000, p.772).

38. Guénon, *FS*, 1995, p.300, n.37.

39. Schuon, *SME*, 2000, p.52. Meister Eckhart: 'It is noteworthy that "before the foundation of the world" (Jn.17:24) everything in the universe was not mere nothing, but was in possession of virtual existence'—*Comm. Jn.* 45 (Colledge & McGinn, 1981, p.137), see also *Par. Gen.* 55, 58-72.

40. Guénon, *FS*, 1995, p.309.

41. Coomaraswamy, '*Kha*': *SP2*, 1977, p.220.

42. See Coomaraswamy, '*Kha*': *SP2*, 1977, p.222. Coomarawsamy refers to "the mathematically infinite series." To be precise the term "infinite" should be reserved for the Supreme Principle; mathematical series are properly indefinite.

43. Coomaraswamy, '*Kha*': *SP2*, 1977, p.220.

44. Coomaraswamy, 'The Sea': *SP1*, 1977, p.406. Coomaraswamy continues here to say, 'The final goal is not a destruction, but one of liberation from all the limitations of individuality as it functions in time and space.' The sea is a common symbol of the spatio-temporal domain.

45. This section was originally published in slightly different form as part of my essay, 'Withdrawal, Extinction and Creation: Christ's *kenosis* in light of the Judaic doctrine of *tsimtsum* and the Islamic doctrine of *fanā*', *Sophia*, Vol.7 No.2, 2001, pp.45-64.

46. St. Augustine, *Enarration on Psalm* 30:3.

47. Meister Eckhart, Sermon 19 (Walshe, *Vol.1*, 1987, pp.157-8). On this idea of "nothingness" one is advised to consult this entire sermon.

48. *Ex. Rabba* XXV, 10; *Lev. Rabba* XXIII, 24, cited in Scholem, *MTJM*, 1995, p.410, n.43.

49. Scholem, *MTJM*, 1995, p.261.

50. In Islam the ontological Principle insomuch as it is recognised in the exoteric domain is expressed by *an-nafs al-ilāhiyah* (the Divine Person); the active Demiurge or the Creator is *al-bāri*.

SYMBOLISM OF THE ARK

51. Schuon, referring to "the great theophany," *Māyā* (*LAW*, 1965, p.89).

52. Schuon, *LAW*, 1965, p.97, n.2. The insertions are mine. The *Risālat al-Ahadiyah* or 'The Epistle of the Unity' is a treatise probably by Muhyī al-Dīn Ibn al-'Arabī.

53. Schaya, *UMK*, 1971, p.65.

54. Schaya, *UMK*, 1971, p.65.

55. Meister Eckhart, Sermon 4 (Walshe, *Vol.1*, 1987, p.44).

56. Ovid, *Metamorphoses* I (Innes (tr.), 1961, p.39).

57. Coomaraswamy: 'there are those who ask for a sort of universal compulsory education in the mysteries, supposing that a mystery is nothing different in kind from the themes of profane instruction. So far from this, it is of the essence of a mystery, and above all the *mysterium magnum*, that it cannot be communicated, but only realized: all that can be communicated are its external supports or symbolic expressions' ('The Nature of Buddhist Art': *SP1*, 1977, p.156).

58. See Sermons 13, 48, among others.

59. Schaya, *UMK*, 1971, p.65. As the Sufis say: '*Al-kawnu insanun kabirun wa-l-insanu kawnun saghir*' ('The universe is a big man and man is a little universe').

60. In Christianity this is the Infinite Love of God—'God is love ... and his love comes to perfection in us.' (1Jn.4:8, 12). In Islam this is *ar-Rahmah*, the Divine Mercy.

61. *Genesis Rabba*, 12. 15, cited in Cohen, *ET*, 1995, p.17.

62. This "action" is an "actionless action" as with the *wei wu wei* of the Taoist tradition.

63. Schuon, *IFA*, 1989, p.35.

64. The term "evolution" is here used in its strict etymological sense. This has nothing in common with the way the term is employed in modern "progressive" theories.

65. Schuon, *SPHF*, 1987, p.108.

66. Schuon, *SPHF*, 1987, p.108.

67. Necessity in no way places a limit on the Absolute. As Schuon remarks, "Necessity–not constraint–is a complementary quality of Freedom ... Liberty is related to the Infinite, and Necessity to the Absolute" (*IFA*, p.57). The Absolute is Necessary by definition; the Infinite expresses Freedom by virtue of its Totality, which is to say, by virtue of being Absolute.

68. Schuon: 'To know that the relative comes from the Absolute and depends on It is to know that the relative is not the Absolute and disappears in the face of It' (*UI*, 1976, p.65).

69. Schuon, *IFA*, 1989, p.73.

70. Schaya, *UMK*, 1971, p.64. On the systematic approach of Kabbalistic doctrine in relation to the idea of the unity of God see Tishby, *WZ1*, 1989, Pt.1, section 1, Introduction. For Guénon, 'Being is one, or rather it is metaphysical Unity itself; but Unity embraces multiplicity within itself, since it produces it

by the mere extension of its possibilities; it is for this reason that even in Being Itself a multiplicity of aspects may be conceived' (*MB*, 1981, p.164).

71. The expression, *solve et coagula*, mentions solution first insomuch as the Great Work proceeds from manifestation.

72. Guénon, *GT*, 1994, p.47. Guénon observes these "powers" as the properties of the "two keys" common in various traditions. Of these keys one is gold, referring to spiritual authority, and one silver, referring to temporal authority. These are the two authorities united in the figure of Melchizedek in Hebraic tradition. In the Roman tradition these two keys are the attributes of *Janus*. See Guénon, p.47-48; *FS*, 1995, Chs.20, 39, 60, 70; Coomaraswamy, '*Svayamātrnnā:* Janua Coeli': *SP1*, 1977.

73. Guénon, *GT*, 1994, pp.41-42.

74. Guénon, *GT*, 1994, pp.43-44.

75. 'Every expansive force is *yang*, every contractive force is *yin*' (Guénon, *GT*, 1994, p.43). Hence, in cosmogony, *yin* comes before *yang*. Again, Heaven (*yang*) envelops and embraces all things and thus presents a "ventral" or inward face to the Cosmos, while Earth (*yin*), that supports all things, presents a "dorsal" or outward face (pp.27-28). Only *yin* influences are susceptible to sense perception; *yang* influences elude the senses being graspable by the Intellect alone. From the point of view of manifestation the movement is from what can be grasped most immediately to what is most hidden or, from the outward to the inward. Hence, *yin* proceeds *yang*. This is exactly the opposite of the metaphysical perspective (see p.32).

76. Guénon, *GT*, 1994, p.44.

77. Guénon, *GT*, 1994, pp.44-45.

78. Guénon, *GT*, 1994, p.45. The retraction of the Divine Infinitude is, from the divine perspective, effectively synonymous with the emanation of Cosmological Existence. The *Fiat Lux* coagulates and emanates the Divine Light while simultaneously dissolving and retracting the infinite "Night of Nothingness."

79. 'Upon those that step into the same rivers different and different waters flow' (216); 'Heraclitus somewhere says that all things are in process and nothing stays still, and likening existing things to the stream of a river he says that you would not step twice into the same river' (218)—(Kirk & Raven, *The Presocratic Philosophers*, 1962, pp.196 & 197). Cf. Plato, *Cratylus*, 402A.

80. Coomaraswamy, 'The Sea': *SP1*, 1977, p.406. Coomaraswamy: 'The Sea is the symbol of *nirvāna*, and just as Meister Eckhart can speak of the "Drowning," so the Buddhist speaks of "Immersion" (*ogadha*) as the final goal' (ibid p.406).

81. *Sata. Brāh.*, VII. 4, 1, 6; Swedenborg, *Arc. Cel.*, n.10, 227, *Apoc. Rev.*, n.50, cited in Gaskell, *Dictionary of All Scriptures & Myths*, 1960, p.805. Again, *Brhad-āranyaka Upanishad* 5.5.1: 'In the beginning this was water. Water produced the true, and the true is *Brahman*'.

82. Al-Ghazali, *Mishkāt al-Anwār*, p.128, cited in Lings, *A Sufi Saint of the Twentieth Century*, 1971, p.177.

83. Coomaraswamy, 'The Sea': *SP1*, 1977, p.406.

84. *Mathnawī* iv.3164 and vi.1622 (tr.) Nicholson, cited in Coomaraswamy, 'The Sea': *SP1*, 1977, p.409.

85. Coomaraswamy, 'The Sea': *SP1*, 1977, p.410, n.9.

86. Sūrahs 18: *al-kahf*, 25: *al-Farqān*, 27: *al-naml*, 35: *al-Fātir* and 55: *al-Rahmān*.

87. Sūrah 25: *al-Farqān*. Compare the bitter and sweet waters at Marah (Ex.15:22-25). Here one might note that the Hebrew name Marah derives from the primitive root, *maw-raw*, which is also the root of the name Mary and which has an etymological correlation with the Sanskrit word *Māyā*.

88. Burckhardt, *MI*, 1987, p.193. The terms "Quiddity" and "Qualities" are explained according to their Moslem sense in more detail in Burckhardt (tr.), `Abd al-Karīm al-Jīlī, *al-insān* (Universal Man), 1983. The term "Quiddity" comes from the technical scholastic term "*quidditas*" meaning "what-it-is."

89. *Zohar* I, 32b. This image echoes that of Iris drawing up the waters in Ovid's *Metamorphoses*, and here one recalls that Iris, as the rainbow, is comprised of the "seven colours."

90. Tishby, *WZ2*, 1991, p.581, n.149 & p.582 passim.

91. Heraclitus, fragments 232 & 233 (Kirk & Raven, *The Presocratic Philosophers*, 1962, p.205).

92. Campbell, *Oriental Mythology*, 1973, p.381.

93. See Burckhardt, *Alchemy*, 1974, Ch.7.

94. Guénon, *RQ*, 1995, p.29.

95. Guénon, *GT*, 1994, p.133, n.14.

96. According to the *Devī Bhāgavata Purāna*: 'At the time of the birth of the world the knowing faculty, in the form of Root-Nature (*mūla-prakriti*), unites with Energy (*Śakti*), the ruling deity of life and intellect, which ever instigates and controls all living things' (9.50.6-8, cited in Daniélou, *MGI*, 1985, p.264).

97. Snodgrass, *ATE1*, 1990, p.61.

98. Schuon, *IFA*, 1989, p.53.

99. Schuon, *IFA*, 1989, p.53-4.

100. Schuon, *IFA*, 1989, p.55.

101. Schuon, *IFA*, 1989, p.55.

102. Schuon, *LAW*, 1965, p.77.

103. *Brahma-vaivarta Purāna* 2.1.5. [43] cited in Daniélou, *MGI*, 1985, p.31.

104. Burckhardt, *Alchemy*, 1974, p.96.

105. On the Edomite Kings see *Zohar* III, 128a, 135a, b, 142a, b, 292a, a. See Tishby, *WZ1*, 1991, p.332-3; Schaya, *UMK*, 1971, pp.107-10; Mathers, *KU*, 1991, § § 41, 56, pp.43, 84-5.

106. Schaya, *UMK*, 1971, p.156, n.1.

107. Scholem, *MTJM*, 1995, p.354, n.30.

108. Tishby, *WZ1*, 1991, p.332, n.252.

109. Tishby, *WZ1*, 1991, p.333, n.258, 259.

110. See al-Jīlī, *al-insān*, 1983; also Burckhardt, *ISD*, 1976, Ch.12.

111. Burckhardt, intro. to al-Jīlī, *al-insān*, 1983, p.iv. Elsewhere Burckhardt cites St. Gregory Palamas as saying, 'Man, this greater world in little compass, is an epitome of all that exists in a unity and is the crown of the Divine works' (*ISD*, 1976, p.76, n.3).

112. Guénon, *GT*, 1994, p.124. On the "Supreme Identity" see Guénon, *MB*, 1981, Ch.24.

113. *Zohar* III, 135a-135b associates the "kings who died" to the "king of Egypt who died" (Ex.2:23). Edom is metaphorically identified as both Egypt and Rome (see Schaya, *UMK*, 1971, p.156, n.1). From a socio-symbolic level the civilization of Egypt preceded the civilization of Israel and the civilization of Rome preceded that of Christianity, yet each was necessary for the following civilization to emerge.

114. Bentley (*Hindu Astronomy* Pt.1, 1970, pp.18-27) refers to the famous "Churning of the Ocean" (*Mahabharata* 1.15) as otherwise being called the "War between the Gods and the Giants."

115. See for example Skinner, *The Source of Measures*, 1982, p.207.

116. Tishby, *WZ1*, 1991, p.332, n.256.

117. Mathers (tr.), *KU*, 1991, p.102.

118. Mathers, *KU*, 1991, p.47.

119. See Mathers (tr.), *KU*, 1991, pp.176-7; also Tishby, *WZ1*, 1991, p.332-33.

120. *Pike de Rabbi Eliezer*, Ch.23, cited in Rappoport, *AI1*, 1995, p.212.

121. See Andersen (tr.), *2 (Slavonic Apocalypse of) Enoch*, Appendix: 2 Enoch in *Merilo Pravednoe*: Charlesworth (ed.), *OTP1*, 1983, pp.204-12.

122. The [J] text has Michael while the [A] has Gabriel. On the relationship of Michael and Gabriel see Cohen, *ET*, 1995, pp.50-51.

123. *2 Enoch* 72.5.

124. *2 Enoch* 72.9. It is strange that this apparent anomaly receives no recognition by Andersen.

125. See Schaya, *UMK*, 1971, p.156.

126. *Zohar* I, 85b-86a.

127. *Zohar* I, 247b; III,7b-8a.

128. It is said: 'The two letters of the upper firmament called *Mi* are contained within it [the lower firmament, *Malkhut*], and it is called *Yam* (sea)' (*Zohar* I, 85b-86a). Tishby adds by way of a note: 'The Hebrew letters of the word *Mi*, i.e., m, y, a designation of *Binah*, are reversed in the name for *Malkhut*, forming the word yam (sea)' (*WZ1*, 1991, p.351, n.453).

129. *NJB*, 1994, p.19.

130. Mathers, *KU*, 1991, p.25.

131. See "ox," "bull" and "cow" in Chevalier & Gheerbrant, *DS*, 1996, (pp.730; 131 & 237).

132. According to *hadīth* in the Moslem tradition (Muslim, *īmān*, 264; Bukhārī, *bad'al-khalq*, 6), there are four rivers flowing forth from the *sidra* tree (Qur'an 53:14). The *sidra* or "Lotus of the Limit" is the *barzakh* between manifested and unmanifested existence. Ibn Sina says that these four rivers or

"seas" are the 'ideal realities (*haqīqat*) of substantiality, corporeality, Matter, and Form' (see Corbin (tr.), *Avicenna and the Visionary Recital*, 1960, p.175).

133. On the symbolism of dispersion or "scattering" see Guénon, 'Gathering what is Scattered', *FS*, 1995, Ch.48.

134. Unger, *Unger's Bible Dictionary*, 1965: *Ti'gris*, p.1096. Although the name *Chiddeqel* is of uncertain derivation, if one takes the "*Chi-*" as a typical vowel prostheis, then the consonant series D-Q-L is, in phonological terms, intimately related to T-G-R (*Digla*).

135. Tishby, *WZ1*, 1989, p.433, n.24.

136. As for example in the mythology of Mithras.

137. Von Rad, *Genesis*, 1963, p.77.

138. Mathers (tr.), *KU*, 1991, p.288.

139. On the angel *Yohoel* see Scholem, *MTJM*, 1995, pp.68-9. Note the interchange between there being 70 and 72 names of Metatron, see Charlesworth, *OTP1*, 1983, p.318, n.48D.*a*. On the 72 lettered name of God see Tishby, *WZ1*, 1989, p.318, n.114; also Schaya, *UMK*, 1971, Ch.VIII.

140. See B.T. *Hagigah*, 15a; B.T. *Sanhedrin*, 38 a; B.T. *Avodah Zarah*, 3b.

141. Tishby, *WZ1*, 1989, p.436, n.60.

142. *Midrash ha-Ne'elam*; *Zohar Hadash, Bereshit*, 8d.

143. *Zohar* II, 65b-66b.

144. Z'ev ben Simon Halevi, *Kabbalah The Divine Plan*, 1996, p.14; *The Way of Kabbalah*, 1976, p.16.

145. *Mathnawī* I, 835 (Gupta (tr.), *Vol.1*, 1997, p.74).

146. Schaya, *UMK*, 1971, p.135.

147. Schaya, *UMK*, 1971, p.44.

148. See Tishby, *WZ1*, 1989, p.433, n.24.

149. Rabbi Gikatilla, *SO*, 1994, p.245.

150. See Guénon, *SC*, pp.19-20, in particular n.8.

151. Gen.12:29-34; Rabbi Gikatilla, *SO*, 1994, p.35.

152. *Zohar* I, 247b.

153. *Zohar* I, 86b-87a.

154. Schaya, *UMK*, 1971, p.74.

155. Cited in Rappoport, *AI1*, 1995, p.210.

156. Abulfeda per Rappoport, *AI1*, 1995, p.215.

157. See de Troyes, *Arthurian Romances*, 1991, p.300.

158. Chevalier & Gheerbrant, *DS*, 1996, p.380.

159. Guénon, *Crisis of the Modern World*, 1975, p.xi.

160. See Eliade, *The Myth of the Eternal Return*, 1974, passim.

161. As Eliade remarks, it is this "relative absolute" that allows the primitive man freedom from the "terror of History," see Eliade, *The Myth of the Eternal Return*, 1974, Ch.4, particularly pp.154-59.

162. Schuon, *LAW*, 1965, p.97, n.15. This edition of *LAW* has *prālaya* and *mahāprālaya*.

163. *Timaeus* 22.

164. Campbell, *The Hero with a Thousand Faces*, 1975, p.228.

165. Smith, *Smith's Bible Dictionary*, 1948, *Gomor'rah*, p.221; *Sod'Om*, p.641. According to *Strong's*, Sodom, *C^{e}dōm*, means "to *scorch*"; the word Gomorrah, `*Amōrāh* means "to *heap*." This word is closely linked to the word `*āmaq* meaning "to *be deep*." It seems that being "submersed" under the "deep" leads to the idea of Gomorrah being destroyed by water? Note that the "Sin of Sodom" is not moralistic as such, but the sin of "imbalance." For the traditions concerning the "Sin of Sodom" see Rappoport, *AI1*, 1995, pp.262-74.

166. Campbell, *The Hero with a Thousand Faces*, 1975, p.225.

167. Heraclitus, *Fragment 25*.

168. Heraclitus, *Fragment 21*.

169. Gaster, *Myth, Legend, and Custom in the Old Testament*, 1969, pp.384-87; see also Westermann, *Genesis 1-11*, 1984, pp.82-131. Bailey (*Noah The Person and the Story in History and Tradition*, 1989) provides good summaries and comparisons of many of the flood myths (Chs.1&2). He highlights similarities and divergences in these accounts. Unfortunately Bailey appears unaware of the symbolic concordance of many of the "divergences" he recognises.

170. Chevalier & Gheerbrant, *DS*, 1996, p.551.

171. Chevalier & Gheerbrant, *DS*, 1996, p.245.

172. Sturluson, *Edda*, 'Voluspa', 1987, p.53-5.

173. See Bulfinch, *Bulfinch's Mythology*, 1979, Ch.V.

174. Campbell, *Oriental Mythology*, 1973, p.182; see also, Eliade, *The Myth of the Eternal Return*, 1974, p.19. Joseph Campbell understands this myth as the Indo-Aryan counterpart to the mythology of the Deluge in the Mesopotamian system.

175. Jordan, *Myths of the World*, 1993, pp.166-167.

176. Eliade, *The Myth of the Eternal Return*, 1974, p.66.

177. Eliade, *The Myth of the Eternal Return*, 1974, p.124.

178. See Campbell, *The Hero with a Thousand Faces*, 1975, p.225.

179. *Cherubinischer Wandersmann*, II.69, cited in Perry, *TTW*, 2000, p.386.

180. Coomaraswamy, 'Some Pali Words': *SP2*, 1977, p.324-27; see also, Guénon, *FS*, 1995, Ch.58.

181. See Budge, *The Book of the Dead*, 1995, 'The Abode of the Blessed', passim.

182. Dalley (ed.), Tablet I, Gilgamesh from *MM*, 1991, p.102.

183. Chevalier & Gheerbrant, *DS*, 1996, p.106.

184. Guénon, *FS*, 1995, p.234.

185. Guénon, *FS*, 1995, p.110.

186. *Rg Veda* 1.154.5.

187. *Enneads* 3.8.10.

188. See Coomaraswamy, 'The Sun door and related Motifs': *SP1*, 1977, pp.415-521.

189. Guénon, *FS*, 1995, p.233.

190. Guénon, *FS*, 1995, p.261, n.5.

191. Hence the allusions in myths of every provenance to the danger of going back on one's tracks or of looking behind.

192. Meister Eckhart, from Pfeiffer (ed.), *Vol.1*, 1924, p.147, cited in Perry, *TTW*, 2000, p.383.

193. Guénon, *FS*, 1995, p.229.

194. Coomaraswamy, 'The Inverted Tree': *SP1*, 1977, p.40.

195. Guénon, *FS*, 1995, p.235.

196. Campbell, *The Hero with a Thousand Faces*, 1975, p.225.

197. Budge, *The Book of the Dead*, 1995, p.133. Most notable are the boats of Ra, the two boats of the Sun (Mantchet and Semktet).

198. Ch.CLXXV ii.20-21. It is considering one such mention of this "Boat of Millions of Years" that the eminent Egyptologist M. Naville recognises the Herakleopolitian legend of the Flood.

199. See Scholem, *MTJM*, 1995, pp.42-3.

200. Schaya, *UMK*, 1971, p.84.

201. Schaya, 'The Meaning of the Temple', 1974, p.360.

202. Coomaraswamy, 'The Flood in Hindu Tradition': *SP2*, 1977, p.400.

203. In the case of Gilgamesh 'two-thirds of him was divine and one-third mortal' (Dalley (ed.), Tablet I, Gilgamesh from *MM*, 1991, p.51) which bears comparison with the depth to which the ark of Ut-napishtim sat in the water (see p.111).

204. See Budge, *The Book of the Dead*, 1995, p.146.

205. See Dalley (ed.), Tablet I, Gilgamesh from *MM*, 1991, p.102. Of course Gilgamesh does not actually travel on the ark of Ut-napishtim.

206. See Guénon, *FS*, 1995, Ch.65.

207. `Abd al-`Azīz b. Sulaymān cited in Perry, *TTW*, 2000, p.226.

208. Chevalier & Gheerbrant, *DS*, 1996, p.122.

209. Campbell, *Primitive Mythology*, 1982, p.333.

210. *Katha Upanishad* 3.14.

211. De Troyes, *Arthurian Romances*, 1991, pp.244-46.

212. On this symbolism see Eliade, 'The Bridge and the "Difficult Passage"' in *Shamanism*, 1989, p.482, p.456; see p.455 on "sword ladders."

213. Guénon, *FS*, 1995, p.260, n.2.

214. Coomaraswamy, 'Symplegades', *SP1*, 1977, p.525.

215. The articles are: Batto, 'The Reed Sea: *Requiescat in Pace*': *Journal of biblical Literature, Vol.1*02, 1983, pp.27-35, and 'Red Sea or Reed Sea': *biblical Archeology Review*, Vol.X, No.4, 1984, PP.57-63.

216. Fohr, *Adam and Eve The Spiritual Symbolism of Genesis and Exodus*, 1986, p.98, n.5.

217. Chevalier & Gheerbrant, *DS*, 1996, p.793.

218. Shaikh Ahmad Al-'Alawī in Lings, *A Sufi Saint of the Twentieth Century*, 1971, p.135; see p.148.

219. Nicholson, *Commentary on the Mathnawī*, Bk.ii, 323, cited in Bauman, 'Initiatic Grace in the Masterwork of Jala ud-din Rumi', *Sacred Web* 6, 2000, p.76, as discussing the "reed of the Spirit," a winged horse (*faras*) like *Buraq*.

220. Guénon, *FS*, 1995, p.261, n.4.

221. Guénon, *FS*, 1995, p.261.

222. See Chevalier & Gheerbrant, *DS*, 1996, p.783; Guénon, *FS*, 1995, Ch.66.

223. *Gylfaginning* from Sturluson, *Edda*, 1998, p.15.

224. Guénon, *FS*, 1995, pp.263-64.

225. See Guénon, *FS*, 1995, Ch.62.

226. Rabbi Joseph Gikatilla teaches of the importance for the "children of Israel" or humankind maintaining the recitation of blessings to ensure the flow of the "living waters" from above (see *SO*, 1994, pp.17-19).

227. A circular or semicircular form such as the ouroboros or the rainbow can be considered as the plane reflection of a spiral.

228. Guénon, *FS*, 1995, p.266.

The Monad: *Centre and Origin*

Introduction

The Ark contains and, at the same time, *is* the principle of Immanence, just as a seed contains and is the tree. The Ark of the Deluge is obvious in the manner whereby it contains the principle for the next age. It is the first point of this new age, and the last point of the prior age. "Between" these two ages the Ark identifies with the unmanifested potentiality of the Waters, upon which it rests. This unmanifested Presence remains the heart of the Ark throughout an age of cosmic existence. This is the *Shekhinah*, which dwells within the Ark of the Covenant. The Ark of the Covenant is the centre of the Temple, which, in turn, is the "centre of the world." This chapter begins with a brief consideration of the relationship between the Absolute (The One) and Being (the monad). Immanence or Being is then considered in greater detail, inasmuch as it is the Centre and Origin of onto-cosmological existence.

The One and the Monad

Hear, O Israel: the Lord our God is one Lord.
Shema: *Deuteronomy* 6:4 [5]

God is one, and beyond the one and above the Monad itself.
Clement of Alexandria[1]

The nature of illusion is the number one.
Maudgala Purāna 1

The notion of "oneness" evokes the ideas of both "unity" and "principalis." To talk of unity, without qualification, is to talk of Totality. On the one hand this recognises the exclusivity of Absolute Unity, which *ipso facto* denies that which is not the Absolute; on the other hand this expresses the inclusivity of the Infinite Plentitude. To talk of principalis is to talk of origin and determination, which, *ipso facto*, is to talk of Being. Thus, one might say that to talk of unity is to emphasize the Absolute, while to talk of principalis is to emphasize Being. This of course remains a matter of emphasis: the Absolute is *a priori* principial—it is this that Being manifests—while Being is "relatively absolute"[2] and thus a contingent unity.

From one perspective the use of the cognomen "one" to describe Reality implies the error of limiting the Absolute to its first determination. It is in this sense that the *Maudgala Purāna* calls the number one the "nature of illusion." From another perspective, which is effectively that of monotheism, the recognition of God as "One" implies the identification of Being with the Absolute, the identification of the essence of the ontological—or even theological—principle with the Divine Essence. In a general sense it can be said that these two perspectives, found varyingly in all traditions, express the apophatic and cataphatic paths respectively.

From a purely theological point of view one may talk freely and indiscriminately of God as "one," where this cognomen applies to all levels according to a kind of sincere simplicity. Here it is enough to say that it is believing in the One that saves.[3] 'Reality' says Schuon, 'affirms itself by degrees, but without ceasing to be "one," the inferior degrees of this affirmation being absorbed, by metaphysical integration or synthesis, into the superior degrees.'[4] A superior degree of Reality contains all inferior degrees within it. Therefore from the Divine perspective all is unity. From the human or terrestrial perspective there is a substantial discontinuity between the degrees of Reality, for it is obvious that the lesser cannot contain the greater. Still, when the believer sincerely calls the Creator "one" they articulate the truth of essential identity: the recognition, albeit in most cases unconscious, of the essential continuity of the Divine.

From a metaphysical point of view, both strict and precise, one must distinguish between the application of "oneness" to both the Absolute and to Being. When referring to the Absolute one may talk of "The One."[5] At the same time one may talk of Being as the first determinant or qualification, and here Being is "one" or "the monad." This distinction is that of *nirguna Brahman* and *saguna Brahman*; of *al-Ahadiyah* and *al-Wāhidiyah*; of Godhead and God. Again, I note that reference to "The One" herein indicates the Absolute, while the term, "the monad" refers to Being as the first determination. In proceeding thus we must nevertheless always keep in mind, as Guénon reminds us, that 'although "ontology" does indeed pertain to metaphysic, it is very far from constituting metaphysic in its entirety, for Being is not the Unmanifest in itself, but only the principle of manifestation; consequently, that which is beyond Being is, metaphysically, much more important than Being itself. In other words [and to use the Vedantic terms] it is *Brahman* and not *Īśvara* which must be recognized as the Supreme Principle.'[6]

The Ark is the "receptacle of Divine Immanence." In the ultimate analysis Immanence is "contained" by Transcendence; from a more limited, yet at the same time more precise point of view, this receptacle is Transcendent Being; finally from a general point of view this is Being envisaged as cosmological existence, that is, the world. In the current consideration of the Ark we are primarily, but far from exclusively, concerned with Being, the monad, the first determination, the onto-cosmological principle.

The Naked Essence

Now, both of them were naked, the man and the wife, but they felt no shame before each other.

Genesis 2:25

And while he was drunk, he lay uncovered in his tent. Ham, father of Canaan, saw his father naked and told his two brothers outside.

Genesis 9:21, 22

The Divine All-Possibility gives rise to Transcendent Being, these being identical in essence but not in extent, for Being does not exhaust the Infinite. One thinks here of a drop of water and the ocean. Transcendent Being in turn gives rise to Immanent Being, which manifests as onto-cosmological existence. There is here essential continuity and substantial discontinuity, for each "subsequent"—logically subsequent rather than necessarily temporally subsequent—level towards onto-cosmological existence implies a "limitation" of Divine Substance. Essential continuity means that Immanence fundamentally comprises Transcendence. This is to say that the Relative fundamentally comprises something of the Absolute, and this necessarily so for Relativity to be. As Schuon remarks, 'if the relative did not comprise something of the absolute, relativities could not be distinguished qualitatively from one another.'[7] Again, Ibn al-'Arabī says, 'Were it not that the Reality permeates all beings as form [in His qualitative form], and were it not for the intelligible realities, no [essential] determination would be made in individual beings. Thus, the dependence of the Cosmos on Reality for existence is an essential factor.'[8] At the same time the distinguishing qualifications or limitations that allow relativities to be cannot be themselves absolute: 'The Infinite is that which is absolutely without limits, but the finite cannot be that which is "absolutely limited," for there is no absolute limitation. The world is not an inverted God: God is without a second.'[9]

The manifested has at its heart the Unmanifested. This is to talk, with Meister Eckhart, of the 'something in the soul that is uncreated and not capable of creation'.[10] This same idea is expressed using strikingly similar language in the Buddhist tradition: 'There is, O monks, an Unborn, Unoriginated, Uncreated, Unformed. If there were not this Unborn, this Unoriginated, this Uncreated, this Unformed, escape from the world of the born, the originated, the created, the formed, would not be possible.'[11] This "Uncreated" is the Unmanifested, *al-ghayb al-mutlaq* (Absolute Unknowableness),[12] the Godhead, *Brahman*, the Absolute.

The "Uncreated" is both the "escape" from the created world and the source of it. 'It is precisely because there is nothing within the One' says Plotinus, 'that all things are from it.'[13]

Meister Eckhart uses many metaphors to describe this "something in the soul," the most common being the "spark" (*vünkeīn*) and the "little town, or castle" (*bürgelīn*).[14] At the same time this "something" is none of these things. Meister Eckhart: 'sometimes I have said that it is a spark. But now I say that it is neither this nor that, and yet it is a something that is higher above this and that than heaven is above the earth. … It is free of all names, it is bear of all forms, wholly empty and free, as God himself is empty and free. It is so utterly one and simple, as God is one and simple, that man cannot in any way look into it.'[15] This, for Meister Eckhart, is the Intellect, which along with Aristotle, he describes as "naked":

> Aristotle himself says that the intellect must be an empty or naked tablet.[16] The greater the nakedness, the greater the union. Therefore, prime matter, since among the passive and receptive powers it alone is utterly naked and pure, is worthy to receive the utterly first act, which is existence or form.[17]

This "something," the Intellect, is utterly naked, free and simple. Naked: not veiled or clothed by the conditions of manifest existence;[18] free: unbound by any limitations by virtue of opening onto the Infinite; simple: *esse simpliciter* or *esse absolutum* by virtue of its unity. The essence of Being is one, there is no "other" with which to distinguish it from.[19] Thus, when Meister Eckhart refers to God as *unum* ("one"), or Absolute Unity, he qualifies this saying: 'We must understand that the term "one" is the same as "indistinct," for all distinct things are two or more, but all indistinct things are one.'[20] With respect to the Absolute, this "indistinction" alludes to the obscurity of the Divine Darkness. With respect to Being, this indistinction is the primordial chaos or primordial "nakedness."

In the primordial state Adam and Eve were "naked"[21] in the garden of Eden. This is to say that "prior"—logically rather than temporally—to the "Fall" the ontological principles, Essence and Substance, exist in a state of biunity, not "veiled" by the distinction of Essence *qua* Essence and Substance *qua* Substance. To talk of the "Fall" is to talk of the diremption of the ontological principles and thus the first "downward" movement towards cosmological manifestation. "Downward": firstly expressing the notions of rank and level, and secondly, according with the symbolism of solidification and heaviness, whereby that which is more manifest is more solid and heavy and thus settles lower by virtue of gravity.[22] The diremption of Essence and Substance gives rise to all complementaries and thus the knowledge of distinction, principally the distinction between man and God, or ego-self and Other, and from another perspective, the distinction between Good and Evil. With distinction comes the loss of primordial "nakedness": 'Yahweh God made tunics of skins for the man and his wife and clothed them' (Gen.3:21). These "skins" are at once the psycho-physical "bodies" of the human condition and the spatio-temporal conditions of cosmic existence. These are again the "veils" of *Māyā* in Hindu tradition and the shimmering *paragod* (the "curtain" of onto-cosmological manifestation) of the Kabbalah. With this loss of innocence comes the loss of primordial unity symbolised by the garden of Eden: 'So Yahweh God expelled him from the garden of Eden, to till the soil from which he had been taken' (Gen.3:23).

With Meister Eckhart's "something in the soul" it can be said that man's primordial "nakedness" remains at the heart of his "clothed" being.[23] This is to talk of the uncreated Intellect from which Creation is born and unto which it returns. As the tradition cited above from the *Udāna* says, if this was "not"—that is, "not at the heart of the world"—then there could be no escape from this world. The symbolism of the naked Intellect at the heart of the world is expressed again in the account of Noah's "drunkenness." Noah, it is said, becoming drunk on wine, lay uncovered in his tent (Gen.9:22). Wine is the blood or essence of the grape; by extension to the cosmological plane, wine is a symbol of ontological Essence; from another perspective wine is *gnosis*. One might say that these two readings are identical for, as Nasr remarks, 'The essence of things is God's knowledge of them'.[24] The state of "drunkenness," viewed positively and from a principally symbolic position, is a state of indistinction, a return to the primordial unity. In a passage of particular relevance to our topic St. Cyprian of Carthage says, 'the chalice of the Lord inebriates us as Noah drinking wine in *Genesis* was also inebriated … the inebriation of the chalice … is not such as the inebriation coming from worldly wine … actually, the chalice of the Lord so inebriates that it actually makes sober, that it raises minds to spiritual wisdom, that from this taste of the world each one comes to the knowledge of God'.[25] Again, St. Augustine: 'The light of truth passes not by, but remaining fixed, inebriates the hearts of the beholders.'[26]

Noah's "tent": according to the symbolism of the Hebraic tradition, the tent is the meeting place of God and man. Rabbi Gikatilla remarks that 'through the medium of this *Ohel Moed* (tent) one is spoken to [by YHVH]'.[27] Here the tent displays the same symbolism as Meister Eckhart's *bürgelīn* of which it is in effect a transitory model, in the same manner that the tabernacle of the desert was the transitory model of the fixed Temple. In Shi`ite symbolism the Tent of Adam is the celestial model of the terrestrial "receptacle" that is the *Ka'bah*.[28] Snodgrass: 'The Tent symbolises the Supreme Intellect, the Nous, identified with the Muhammadean Light (*al-nūr al-Muhammadī*).'[29] Concerning the symbolism of "light," and the connection between the symbols of "light" and "city," as with Meister Eckhart's *vünkeīn* and *bürgelīn*, it can be noted that the Hebrew word `*ohel* (אהל) derives from the primitive root `*ahal* (אהל; "to be *clear*"; "to *shine*"). Again, in the *Zohar* the "Opening of the Tent" is equated with the *Shekhinah*, which is symbolised by "light." This, according to the *Zohar*, is also the first *Sefirah* one encounters upon entering the divine realm in which all other *Sefirah* are "reflected."[30] According to Rabbi Gikatilla the 'Aramaic root for *Ohel* is *misSHKaNa*, which is the essence of [and shares the root of] *Shekhinah*'.[31] The word "*mishkān*" denotes the tabernacle. Within this "tent," which is analogous to the "veil" of cosmic existence, Noah enters a state of naked unity with the Divine Essence; within the Divine Immanence (*Shekhinah*), which is the principle of diversity, rests the naked unity of the Divine Transcendence.

It is further written that, 'Ham, father of Canaan, saw his father naked and told his two brothers outside. Shem and Japheth took a cloak and they put it over their shoulders, and walking backwards, covered their father's nakedness; they kept their faces turned away, and they did not look at their father naked' (Gen.9:22, 23). This requires some understanding of the symbolism of Noah's sons, to which we turn later. It is enough here to say that Ham's transgression may be likened to the "sin" of the knowledge of good and evil. Likewise the cloak that covered Noah's nakedness corresponds to the "tunics of skin" given to Adam and Eve, and the "cursing of Canaan" (Gen.9:25) to the expulsion from the garden.

Rest

If they ask you: What is the sign of your Father in you?, say to them: It is movement and rest.

The Coptic Gospel of Thomas, log.50

In all things I seek rest.

Eccesiasticus 24:11

Being, or the monad, is the principle and first point of ontological existence, while remaining unaffected by cosmological conditions; it is the principle of space and time without being of space or time. From a primarily cosmological perspective one can say that the monad is the first point from which cosmological existence expands or emanates.

Considered vertically, existence expands "downwards." This symbolism emphasizes the idea of rank and order, where that which is first is "highest" or situated at the "head." Considered horizontally, existence expands "outwards," where the first is "central" or anthropomorphically at the "navel." From another perspective, primarily metaphysical, the monad is the principle, continuous at all levels of existence, situated at the "heart." These two perspectives coincide in the general symbolism of the Centre, which is both the first point of emanation and the continuous living heart.[32]

'The centre' says Snodgrass, 'symbolises the progenitive Source whence the manifested world deploys. It is the spaceless and timeless Origin of space and time, the One that produces plurality. The centre is the similitude of unitary Being, wherein the virtualities of spatial extension and temporal duration are contained in a state of inseparable fusion, and whence they are actualized by a projection into separativity'.[33] Guénon says that the Centre remains beyond the spatial condition, of which it is the principle.[34] This is to talk of the "naked" or "unconditioned" Centre from which the first point emerges as a conditioned and conceptual "reflected Centre." To be precise, it is this conditioned or created Centre that is the "first" point inasmuch as the unconditioned Centre remains beyond any such qualification. At the same time the unconditioned Centre and the conditioned Centre are the one Centre. This echoes the Christian doctrine of the *Logos*, both uncreated and created. Snodgrass again:

> Because the geometric point-centre is formless, dimensionless and without duration it is an adequate symbol of primordial Unity, the Principle of manifestation. The radiation of the worlds from the centre is a realisation, a bringing in to existence, of virtualities lying dormant within Unity: it is a procession from Unity to multiplicity, from the imperishable One to perishable plurality. It is a disintegration and division of the One into the many: activating itself, the One spreads out and scatters its light into the opacity, and there "rests in a wavering refraction which appears other than itself."[35]

To say that the Divine Light "rests" in a "wavering refraction" is to say that it "rests by changing." This is once more to say that *Samsāra* is *Nirvāna*. To talk of "rest" is to talk of the "stillness" of the Divine Sea. Rest is the state of Harmony or Bliss that is coeval with principial Being, as we find in the Hindu term *Saccidānanda*: *Sat* (Being), *Cit* (Consciousness), *Ānanda* (Bliss). The state of rest permeates manifestation by virtue of being at its very heart, while nevertheless remaining shrouded in

86

the illusion of activity (*Māyā*). Rest is respite from the activity, in reality illusory, of spatio-temporal conditions, which is to say that the symbolism of rest coincides with the symbolism of nakedness.

Considering a horizontal plane of ontological existence one says that the Centre spreads out along the four principal directions of the cross, as with the symbolism of the "four rivers" and "four winds." These have their analogy on earth in the four spatial directions, North, South, East and West, and again in the four elements, earth, wind, fire and water. Cosmological existence is spatial existence and thus entails a shift from planar symbolism to three dimensions: the shift from the circle to the sphere. In this context one says that the Centre spreads out in the six principal directions,[36] being the four directions of the plane together with the nadir and zenith. However, as Snodgrass warns us,

> a description of the genesis of the universe in terms of an emanation from a point outwards in the six directions is, if taken literally, an error, since space is a condition of existence peculiar to our own level in the hierarchy of the states of manifestation. Spatial concepts are not applicable at other levels: the model is to be taken as a spatial representation of processes that are spatial by analogy only.[37]

> The centre of the cross, where its six arms come together, symbolises the Principle that generates the universe; it is the point of origin of all things. Itself dimensionless and timeless, it is the Principle of extension and duration. Lying beyond all spatial and temporal limitations it nevertheless engenders the entirety of spatio-temporal manifestation.[38]

The centre of the six-armed cross is both the origin or "first" point, and the point of reintegration of the six directions, that is, the "seventh" point. It is the first and the last, the beginning and the end, the Alpha and the Omega. Thus Jacob Boehme says that the 'seventh day (of creation) is the origin and the beginning of the first.'[39] This reveals a fundamental aspect of the cosmological meaning of the "seventh day," the day of "rest"—'On the seventh day God had completed the work He had been doing. He rested on the seventh day after all the work He had been doing. God blessed the seventh day and made it holy' (Gen. 2:2, 3). In Judaic tradition this "time of rest" is the Sabbath or *shabbath* (שבח; *"intermission"*), which word derives from the Hebrew word *shabath* (שבח) meaning "to *repose*" in the sense of "a *cessation*" of activity. This is also the sense of the word *nirvāna*, which means "extinction of breath or of disturbance," and of the Islamic term, *fanā* ("extinction").

The symbolism of the Sabbath day is further extended to that of the Sabbath Year (Lev.25:1) and this to the idea of the Jubilee, which is based on the period of seven sabbatical years or seven times seven years, that is forty-nine years. The Jubilee itself is the fiftieth year (Lev.25:8-12), where the number fifty, as noted, expresses the totality and completion of created existence.

This connection between the number seven and the idea of rest is again fleshed out in the account of the Ark of Noah, which came to "rest" on the mountains of Ararat in the "seventh" month of the Flood (Gen.8:4). Furthermore, and even more significantly, the very name Noah or *Nōach* (נח) means *"rest,"* this from the primitive root, *nūwach* (נוח; "to *rest*"). Here one must recognise that Noah and "his" Ark are essentially identical. *Nūwach* should then be compared to the word *nāveh* (נוה), which as an adjective means "*at home*" and as a noun, "a *home*," specifically, "a home of God," that is "a temple." The homologues of "vehicle" and "house" here coincide in the unity of the Centre. It is interesting to compare *nūwach* with the name *Nōwd* (נוד), which is "Nod, the land of Cain" (Gen.4:16). These words differ by their finals, respectively, a *heth*, which has the numerical value of eight and symbolically expresses a "fence," and *da'leth*, which has a numerical value of four and symbolically expresses a "door." The relationship between "fence" and "door" is essentially complementary. The name *Nōwd* derives from *nūwd* (נוד; "to *nod*," the head, i.e. "to *waver*"); this recalls the "wavering refraction" of the Divine Light, as it "rests in change." Figuratively *nūwd* means "to *wander*," and this is the same meaning as the Hindu and Buddhist term *samsāra*.[40] To say that the Centre (transcendent and at rest) is identifiable with immanent flux, is, again, to say that *Nirvāna* is *Samsāra*; from another perspective, this is to recognise that complementarities ("fence" and "door") are resolved in the unity of the *coincidentia oppositorum*.

The Centre is both the first and the seventh and these are one. In fact this symbolism involves a simultaneous reading of two distinct perspectives in light of their eventual union in the single Reality. In the first case, to call the Centre the first is to consider it from the perspective of the Principle. Thus starting from the Centre as one, then the six directions will be counted, so to speak, as two through seven. In this sense the number seven expresses the Centre *ad extra*. In the second case, to call the Centre the seventh implies that one starts from the perspective of Manifestation, whereby the six directions are considered as one through to six with the Centre, the point of reintegration or return, thus being the seventh. Here the number seven expresses the Centre *ad intra*. In the final analysis both perspectives resolve in Unity. However, one may say

88

that in the first case the emphasis is on the radiation of the Principle and in the second case the emphasis is on the contraction of Manifestation. In the first case rest is "hidden" beneath the veil of existence, comprised of the six directions of symbolic space, and symbolised by the number seven. In the second case rest is the "hidden treasure" at the Centre of existence, again, from this second perspective, symbolised by the number seven.

One can take each of these symbolic schemas a step further if one so wishes and in fact various traditional perspectives do. Thus in the first case, which takes the number seven as indicating the radiation of the Principle, one can talk of the contraction of Manifestation back to the Centre-Principle as an eighth "step," so to speak. In this case the eighth is the first viewed "anew," to use the language of Christianity.[41] The second case takes the number seven as indicating the Centre as the point of return, where one can say that this Centre has two levels, created and Uncreated. Here the number seven, influenced as it is by the number six, the number of creation, places an emphasis on the created and creative Centre; the Uncreated Centre can then be symbolised by the number eight. In the first case eight is the Perfection of the manifested world; in the second case eight is the Uncreated Harmony that allows this Perfection. Yet again this is summed up by saying that *Nirvāna* is *Samsāra*.

The above schema might be challenged on the grounds that the distinction inherent in the Centre between created and Uncreated equally exists in the first case, that is, where we started our symbolic numerations with the Centre being one. The Centre, it might then be argued, should therefore be numbered both one and two, as in the second case it is numbered seven and eight. This is only partially correct. The distinction of the Centre into created and Uncreated does indeed exist here. However, as this perspective proceeds from the Principle we must begin with the Uncreated, for which the number one is not symbolically adequate. Instead we must begin, so to speak, with the metaphysical zero. Therefore the Centre is, in this case, zero and one. One might then question the symbolic adequacy of the number eight to express the Uncreated, given that I have denied the adequacy of the number one. To this it can be answered that the major difference in each of the above cases is the initial perspective and that inasmuch as the second case starts from the point of view of Manifestation this necessitates the use of "number," rather than zero, to express the Uncreated, which is to say that it must use the language that is appropriate to it.[42]

The number eight is universally seen as symbolic of cosmic balance.[43] Here it is important, as S. L. MacGregor Mathers remarks, not to confuse this idea with that of equilibrium: 'The balance consists of two scales (opposing forces), the equilibrium is the central point of the beam.'[44] The distinction between balance and equilibrium can be likened to that between the created Centre, and by extension Creation itself, and the Uncreated Centre. There are eight petals on the lotus, upon which *Brahmā* rests on the Waters of All-Possibility; eight paths in the Buddhist Way; eight trigrams in the *I Ching*; eight pillars in the Temple of Heaven; and eight angles that support the Throne of Heaven.[45] In Christian tradition, the "Eighth Day," following the six days of creation and the seventh day of rest, is the 'symbol of resurrection and of transfiguration'.[46] Observe then that the Jubilee, indicating cosmic perfection, is symbolised by the number fifty, that is, one "step" on from forty-nine (7 x 7), just as eight is one "step" on from seven.

Both seven and eight express the notion of "rest." This is born out in the Hebraic Scriptures, which not only talk of the seventh day as the "day of rest" but also say that 'The first and the eighth day will be days of rest' (Lev.23:39). This symbolism is then found in the account of Noah in the eight human occupants of the Ark. This is recognised and stressed in the Christian tradition in the two letters of Peter (1 Pt.3:20-22 and 2Pt.2:5). Noah is undeniably principal among the inhabitants of the Ark, but at the same time, St. Peter also refers to Noah specifically as the "eighth person."[47]

Ibn al-'Arabī recognises the Ark or "basket" of Moses (Ex.2:3) as the 'vessel in which resides the tranqillity [sic] of the Lord.'[48] The idea of rest is also found with the symbolism of the Ark of the Covenant, which is the abode of the Divine Presence or *Shekhinah*. In the Islamic esoteric tradition the *Shekhinah* corresponds to the *al-Sakīnah* ("Great Peace"), which Guénon says carries the same meaning as the *Pax Profunda* ("Great Peace") of the Rosicrucians. He again sees this as analogous to the "Tranquility" with which the Hindu Yogī unites to "possess" the unconditioned Self (*Ātman*).[49] For the Christian this is the 'peace of God, which passeth all understanding' (Ph.4:7).

The Centre is the abode (Eckhart's *bürgelīn*) of rest. Another more commonly used phrase here is "the City of Peace." In the biblical tradition this is Jerusalem and more specifically the "celestial Jerusalem" of the Apocalypse (Rev.21:2). This is again the "Kingdom of Heaven" or the "Kingdom of God" that Christ speaks of as being "within"[50] us. In the Hindu tradition this is *Brahmā-pura*, "the City of *Brahmā*" or "the Divine City."[51] Guénon translates this as the "seat of *Brahmā*,"[52] which recognises the connection between the Divine City and the Divine Throne. This is not only the "centre of rest" but also the "place of power," from which the king as "governor" directs all things. The power of royalty rests in the person of the king and one may say that the kingdom exists solely in virtue of the king. Wherever the king resides is, by his very being, endowed with the quality of the "centre of the kingdom." From this perspective, the throne of the king exists wherever the king is. This demonstrates the relationship of throne and chariot, as in *merkabah* mysticism. The king's chariot is both vehicle and throne. Moreover, the king, by virtue of being the constant Centre, is also *ipso facto* constantly at rest. As such it is not the vehicle of the king that moves, but in fact the kingdom that moves around the king. Nevertheless, from the perspective of the king's subjects, the vehicle of the king appears to move.

Guénon remarks that the "Divine City" is the "centre of being." He continues to say that the centre of being is 'represented by the heart which does in fact correspond to it in the corporeal organism and this centre is the dwelling place of *Purusha*, identified with the divine Principle (*Brahmā*) considered as the "internal co-ordinator" (*antar-yāmī*) who rules the entire collectivity of this being's faculties by "non-acting" activity which is the immediate consequence of his mere presence.'[53] The phrase "non-acting activity" (*wei wu wei*) is borrowed from the Chinese tradition where it appears frequently in Buddhist and Taoist writings. This principle is most commonly known in the West as Aristotle's "unmoved mover."[54] This, according to Aristotle, who cites the authority of Parmenides and Melissos, is the "first principle," "one" and "unmoved."[55] Expressing this in theological language, Boethius says that this first cause is God, whom he describes as 'an immovable good, standing still in himself, untouched and unmoved and moving all things.'[56] In the Hindu tradition it is said, 'O' Arjuna, the Lord dwells in the heart of all beings, causing all beings to revolve, as if mounted on a wheel.'[57] Dante also recognises this principle: 'The nature of the universe which stilleth the centre and moveth all the rest around, hence doth begin as from its starting point. And this heaven (the *Primum Mobile*) hath no other where than the divine mind (the *Empyrean*).'[58] As Coomaraswamy says, 'A first cause, being itself uncaused, is not probable but axiomatic.'[59]

According to the Hindu tradition the Centre, uncaused and first cause, is the *Ātman* (the Self). The Self, as Guénon says, 'is the transcendent and permanent principle of which the manifested being, the human being, for example, is only a transient and contingent modification, a modification which, moreover, can in no way affect the principle'. He explains,

> The "Self," as such is never individualised and cannot become so, for since it must always be considered under the aspect of the eternity and immutability which are the necessary attributes

91

of pure Being, it is obviously not susceptible of any particulari-
sation, which would cause it to be "other than itself." Immutable
in its own nature, it merely develops the indefinite possibilities
which it contains within itself, by a relative passing from potency to act through an indefinite series of degrees. Its essential
permanence is not thereby affected, precisely because this process is only relative, and because this development is, strictly
speaking, not a development at all, except when looked at from
the point of view of manifestation, outside of which there can be
no question of succession, but only of perfect simultaneity, so
that even what is virtual under one aspect, is found nevertheless
to be realised in the "eternal present."[60]

As St. Augustine says, 'Being is a term for immutability. For all things
that are changed cease to be what they were, and begin to be what they
were not. True being, pure being has no one save Him who does not
change. He has it to whom is said, "Thou shalt change them, and they
shall be changed. But Thou art always the self-same"'.[61] 'For I am the
Lord, I change not' (Ml.3:6).

The Seed

Every multitude somehow participates in the One.

Proclus[62]

Just as the whole nature of the large banyan tree is contained in its
tiny seed, so also the whole universe, moving and unmoving, is
contained in the word-seed "*Rāma*."

Rāma-pūrva-tāpinī Upanishad 2.2-3

The seed is the word of God.

Luke 8:11

Being—the "lesser Absolute"—has a direct analogy with the Absolute.
In this sense, All-Possibility has its direct correlation with ontological
All-Possibility or Potentiality. By inverse analogy, the realisation of
Potentiality represents the paradoxical limitation of the Infinite by the
indefinite, where 'to say manifestation is to say limitation'. Ontological
All-Possibility is both a reflection of Divine All-Possibility and itself *a*
possibility plucked from the Infinite to be planted in the Infinite. In this
second sense it is acceptable to say that ontological All-Possibility is,
in essence, identical with All-Possibility. In fact, it is by virtue of this
identity that Potentiality on the one hand brings forth manifestation and,
on the other hand, provides the opportunity or "potential" for deliverance from manifestation. Being is here the interface (*barzakh*) between

the Infinite Unmanifested and the indefinite manifested, facilitating both creation and return to the Uncreated. From another perspective and to use another symbolism, Being is the *reshimu*, "the existential seed," which is a luminous "residue" of *En-Sof* or the Infinite. Coomaraswamy, it will be recalled, describes the Ark as the receptacle of 'the seeds, ideas, or images of the future manifestation'. The Ark, which is Being, is the Divine Seed, a symbolism common in all traditions. Thus Guénon observes that in the Hindu tradition, 'The Divine Principle which resides at the centre of the being is represented … as a grain or seed (*dhātu*), as a germ (*bijā*), because in a way it is in this being only virtually so long as "Union"[63] has not actually been realised.'[64] This qualification relates to the idea of the full realisation of the seed, which is its "return" to the Unmanifested.

The entire existence of the being resides in the "seed germ," which is to say with the *Rāma-pūrva-tāpinī Upanishad*, that the "Universe"[65] is contained in its "seed." Similarly, Sri Ramana Maharshi says: 'The entire Universe is condensed in the body, and the entire body in the Heart. Thus the heart is the nucleus of the whole Universe.'[66] Again, according to the famous *hadīth qudsī*: 'My earth and My heaven contain Me not, but the heart of My faithful servant containeth Me.'[67] The Centre contains the circumference; the heart contains the existence of the human; the tabernacle contains the Temple, and by extension and analogy, the Temple contains the Cosmos. Being is the Cosmic Seed, simultaneously the first point, the Centre and the receptacle of onto-cosmological existence.

In the Vedantic tradition the principial point is called the *bindu* (Tib. *thig-le*).[68] As Lama Anagarika Govinda observes, the word *bindu* has many meanings: point, dot, zero, drop, germ, seed, semen, etc.[69] Alain Daniélou refers to the *bindu* as the "Point Limit," which he describes as the 'determinant of space from which manifestation begins'; 'the centre of the universe'.[70] Daniélou further says that the *bindu* or "Point-Limit" is identical with the Self (*Ātman*).[71] The phrase, "Point Limit" alerts us to the idea that the principial point defines the limits of manifestation; it is, to use Pascal's terminology, the "infinitely small" and the "infinitely big." This idea is expressed beautifully by the third Patriarch of the Dhyana school of Chinese Buddhism, Seng-ts'an, who says, 'The very small is as the very large when boundaries are forgotten; / The very large is as the very small when its outlines are not seen.'[72] Pseudo-Dionysius quotes Batholomew in saying that 'the Word of God is vast and minuscule'[73]. This idea is described in the Gospel saying: 'He that is the least among you all, he is the greatest' (Mt.18:14, 20:16; Mk.9:48, 10:31; Lk.9:48, 18:14).

The Point-Limit is adequately symbolised by the "spatial point." From one perspective this can allude to the Unmanifested. As Schuon remarks, 'One can represent Absolute Reality, or the Essence, or Beyond-Being, by the point; it would doubtless be less inadequate to represent it by the void, but the void is not properly speaking a figure, and if we give the Essence a name, we can with the same justification, and the same risk, represent it by a sign; the simplest and thus the most essential sign is the point.'[74] As Shaikh al-'Alawī says, 'Everything is enveloped in the Unity of Knowledge, symbolised by the Point.'[75] From a more limited and, in a sense, a more precise perspective the point symbolises the principle of Being. Guénon observes that 'Space itself presupposes the point.'[76] Moreover, he remarks that 'the geometric point is quantitatively nil and does not occupy any space, though it is the principle by which space in its entirety is produced, since space is but the development of its intrinsic virtualities.'[77] Meister Eckhart: 'a point has no quantity of magnitude and does not lengthen the line of which it is the principle.'[78] In a similar sense, Guénon observes that 'though arithmetical unity is the smallest of numbers if one regards it as situated in the midst of their multiplicity, yet in principle it is the greatest, since it virtually contains them all and produces the whole series simply by the indefinite repetition of itself.'[79] For Proclus, 'Every multitude somehow participates in the One.' This is again found in the famous Sufic formula: 'Unity in multiplicity and multiplicity in Unity'.[80]

The seed as "container of the Universe" is found with the Christian symbolism of the "mustard seed": 'The kingdom of Heaven is like a mustard seed which a man took and sowed in his field. It is the smallest of all the seeds, but when it has grown it is the biggest of shrubs and becomes a tree, so that the birds of the air can come and shelter in its branches' (Mt.13:31-32; Mk.4:30-32; Lk.13:18-19).[81] In Chinese mythology, *Sumeru*, the Cosmic Mountain, and thus *imago mundi*, is also found contained within a mustard seed.[82] The *Chāndogya Upanishad* describes the *Ātman* in terms familiar to the Christian mustard seed: 'This *Ātman*, which dwells in the heart, is smaller than a grain of rice, smaller than a grain of barely, smaller than a grain of mustard, smaller than a grain of millet, smaller than the germ which is in the grain of millet; this *Ātman*, which dwells in the heart, is also greater than the earth [the sphere of gross manifestation], greater than the atmosphere [the sphere of subtle manifestation], greater than the sky [the sphere of formless manifestation], greater than all the worlds together [that is, beyond all manifestation, being the unconditioned].'[83]

Being unaffected by the conditions of change, of which it is the principle, the Divine Seed is indestructible. In the words of Origen: 'Be-

94

cause God himself has sowed and planted and given life to this seed, even though it may be overgrown and hidden, it will never be destroyed or extinguished completely, it will glow and shine, gleam and burn and it will never cease to turn toward God.'[84] Origen's description again identifies a connection to the symbolism of light and heat.

Guénon sees the symbolism of the "seed" as analogous to that of the "*yod* in the heart."[85] The *yod*, as Guénon observes, is the letter from which all the letters of the Hebrew alphabet are formed. 'The *yod* in the heart is therefore the Principle residing at the centre, be it from the macrocosmic point of view, at the "Centre of the World" which is the "Holy Palace" of the Kabbalah, or from the microcosmic point of view in every being, virtually at least, at his centre, which is always symbolised by the heart in the different traditional doctrines, and which is man's innermost point, the point of contact with the Divine.'[86] A similar use of the symbolism of letters exists in the Islamic tradition. According to two *hadīth qudsī*: 'All that is in the revealed Books is in the Qur'an, and all that is in the Qur'an is in the *Fātihah*,[87] and all that is in the *Fātihah* is in *Bismi 'Llāhi 'r-Rahmāni 'r-Rahīm*', and, 'All that is in *Bismi 'Llāhi 'r-Rahmāni 'r-Rahīm* is in the letter *Bā*, which is itself contained in the point that is beneath it.'[88] There is a similar tradition in Kabbalah where it is said that all that is in the Torah is in the word *Berashith* (the first word of *Genesis*, generally translated into English as "In the Beginning"), and all that is in *Berashith* is in the letter *beth*, and the spoken *beth* (the second letter of the Hebrew alphabet) is in the unspoken *aleph* (the first letter of the Hebrew alphabet). It is interesting to compare these traditions, for in the first case the Essence is symbolised by a point and in the second by the ineffable void.[89] Again, in the classic Russian spiritual tale, *Rasskatz strannika* (*The Pilgrim's Tale*), the Pilgrim says, 'The Gospel and the Jesus Prayer [*Lord Jesus Christ, Son of God, have mercy on me*] are one and the same thing ... For the divine name of Jesus contains in itself all Gospel truths.'[90] Boehme: 'In the sweet name, Jesus Christ, the whole process is contained.'[91] Thus Schuon says, 'It is in the Divine Name that there takes place the mysterious meeting of the created and the Uncreate, the contingent and the Absolute, the finite and the Infinite.'[92]

The symbolism of the Divine Name or Word as the "seed" is echoed universally.[93] Jesus teaches that 'The seed is the word of God.'[94] This is the *logos spermatikos* of the Greek Fathers. In the Hindu tradition the Word-Seed is the sacred *Om*, the 'primordial sound of timeless reality',[95] which "imperishable syllable" is the "whole world" and also "the Self (*Ātman*) indeed."[96] *Om* is the essence of the *Veda*.[97] The *Dictionary of Symbols* describes the *Veda* as the 'seed and potential evolution of future cycles.'[98] According to Hindu tradition, during the cataclysm that separates this *Mahā-Yuga* from the previous one, the *Veda* was enclosed in a state of envelopment in the conch (*shankha*), a homologue of the Ark and one of the chief attributes of *Viśnu*.[99] This notion of the Word-Seed is explicit in the symbolism of the Ark of Noah and the Ark of the Covenant. In the latter this is none other than the Testimony, the tablets of stone upon which God inscribed the Decalogue (Ex.31:18; 32:15; 34:29), the Word of God made writ, or "made flesh" if you will.[100] The Ark of Noah contains the Word of God by way of Noah's son, *Shem* (שם), whose name means "*name*" and more precisely, the "Name of God."

To talk of the seed is to talk of impetus towards growth, which is to say, towards manifestation. Thus the perfection of the ontological seed includes *in divinis* the impetus towards the imperfection of the manifest world. This is prefigured in the paradox of the Relative as a dimension of the Infinitude of the Absolute. To use an analogous symbolism, the Garden of Eden must contain the serpent. As Marco Pallis remarks, 'The perfection of a paradise without the presence of the serpent would be the perfection, not of paradise, but of God Himself. It would be, in Sufic terms, "the paradise of the Essence."'[101] Likewise, the Ark as seed, and here the emphasis is primarily on the Ark of the Deluge, must contain the impetus for manifestation to reemerge from the Waters of nondistinction, which is to say, that it must contain the "serpent," so to speak. Thus, an Islamic tradition tells of how Satan, or Iblis, survived the Flood aboard Noah's Ark. Desiring to board Noah's Ark and survive the Flood, Satan caught hold of the tail of the ass just as the beast was to enter the ark.[102] Noah, growing impatient called out: 'Come on, thou accursed one, come on quickly, even if Satan were with thee.' Satan at once entered the ark with the ass.[103] In a similar story Falsehood came to ask admission to the Ark. However, Noah accepted only pairs. Falsehood paired with Injustice to gain entry to the ark.[104] Again, *Pirke de Rabbi Eliezer* tells of how the giant, Og, the last of the race of Rephaim (Nephilim), climbed on to the roof of the ark and refused to leave, thus being preserved into the next age.[105]

The image of a serpent surviving the Flood is found in Egyptian tradition. The god Tem revealed that he was about to destroy everything that he had made by a flood. Everything was to be destroyed, excepting himself and Osiris, and a very small serpent that no god shall see.[106] The serpent is "very small" in the manner of being "infinitely small." The fact that no god is able to see this serpent expresses the fact that the "gods," like the angels of Judaic tradition and the celestial hierarchies of Pseudo-Dionysius, are themselves of the domain of Manifestation, which the serpent transcends by way of being an aspect of the Principle. The idea of the serpent as the "principle of regeneration" suggests a connection to the symbolism of the Phoenix. Bulfinch recounts the story of how a worm emerges from the dead Phoenix before transforming into a new bird.[107] The worm and the serpent are analogous symbols. Physiologically they suggest the sperm and the phallus, which is to say, the seed and its "extension" or the point and the line.

The symbolism of the seed is found in the native American Huichol account of the Deluge.[108] The flood-hero is warned of the coming deluge by a mysterious woman called Tako'tsi Nakawe, who tells him to make a box from the wood of a fig tree, "as long and as wide as himself," and to take into it five grains of each colour of corn, some fire and five squash stems to burn. These "five grains" represent the four elements, earth, air, fire, water, and the principial ether, which are the "seeds" of manifestation. Symbolically the "five grains of each colour" can be seen in a similar manner as the "seven directions" or, for that matter, the "seven colours of the rainbow." Just as the number seven is symbolic of the centre and synthesis of the spatio-temporal "sphere," so too the number five is symbolic of the centre and synthesis of a horizontal plane of Existence, measured by the four "directions" of the cross. Here one also recalls that the number five is the number of man, and of Christ, measuring the Cross with His body. In this we see again evidence of the fact that the flood-hero is himself the seed of the next Age.

Dogon mythology contains what is maybe one of the most explicit symbolisms of cosmogenesis expressed by numerical hypostases; here again the symbolism of the seed is fundamental.[109] According to the Dogon myth, in the beginning there was Amma, the supreme God. He had four clavicles each containing the archetypes of the principal gods, animals and plants. The southern clavicle contained the *Digitaria exilis* seed, the "little thing," the smallest of the cultivated seeds ("the mustard seed") and symbolically the centre from which the world deploys. In the beginning the *Digitaria* seed contained seven germs, the "seeds of all things"; at the core of the *Digitaria* seed was an oblong plate divided into four sectors, one for each element; in these sectors lay twenty-two signs corresponding to the classification of all things.[110] These twenty-two might be compared with the twenty-two letters of the Hebrew alphabet, which are the "seeds" from which the Torah and thus creation arise. 'The cosmogenesis' remarks Snodgrass, 'was an expansion from the principial Seed-Star and point-source, which vibrated and emanated the seven germ-stars as seven segments of increasing length, following a spiral or helical path so as to fill the World Egg.'[111] 'Man images the primordial Seed-Star'.[112] With the advent of imperfection in creation Amma sent Nommo with an Ark fashioned, in the likeness of a celestial basket, to re-establish order. Into this basket were placed the eight seeds that were to be given to man for his use. As Snodgrass says, the 'basket-Ark was the model of for the Dogon cosmos.'[113]

The Stone and the Pillar

O my son, consider this tiny mustard seed, which God would bring forth were it to be in a rock, whether in heaven or earth.

Ibn al-'Arabī, quoting Qur'an 31:16[114]

This stone I have set up as a pillar is to be a house of God.

Genesis 28:22

Among the meanings of the Hindu term *bindu* is that of "a drop." This same symbolism is found in the *Zohar*, along with the symbols of "a spark" (Meister Eckhart's *vünkeīn*) and "a stone" to express the notion of the first point.[115] The symbol of the "stone" is a well known homologue of the Centre. This symbolism is also associated with the symbolism of the Flood, with probably the best known example being in the Greek account of Deucalion. After the waters had receded Deucalion and his wife, Pyrrah, descended the mountain upon which they had landed to the Temple of Delphi to ask for guidance. Here the oracle instructed them, 'Depart from the Temple with head veiled and garments unbound, and cast behind you the bones of your mother.' These "bones" they concluded to be the stones of Mother Earth. According to the myth, the stones that Deucalion threw became men while those of Pyrrah became women, the "stones" here acting as the seeds for the next generation. This bears comparison with the myth of Cadmus and the serpent's teeth which, planted in the ground, gave rise to a "crop of men" that then build the city of Thebes.[116] Recall, then, that the serpent is a common symbol of *materia prima*. The *Dictionary of Symbols* remarks that Semitic tradition contains accounts of humans being born from stone and that in some Christian legends Christ himself was so born. According to St. Peter, Christ is the "living stone";[117] Christ is the "cornerstone" which knits together every structure into a holy temple, 'a dwelling-place of God in the Spirit' (Ep.2:20-22).[118] The *Dictionary of Symbols* also observes that in Chinese tradition, Yū the Great, the Chinese flood-hero *par excellence*, was born from a stone.[119]

St. Peter, *Petros* (Πετρος)—whose connection to the Ark symbolism we have already noted—is "the Rock" (*petra*; πετρα; "a *rock*") upon which Christ builds his Church (Mt.16:18). The Aramaic here is *kepha*, which, as the Greek name *Kephas* (Κηφας) means "the *Rock*." This derives from the Hebrew *keph* (כף; "a hollow *rock*"), which in turn derives from the word *kaphaph* (כפף; "to *curve*"), which suggests, among other things, the symbolism of the rainbow. This word has numerous phonetic derivations that are all suggestive of the interplay of symbolisms implicit here. The word *kaph* (כף; "the hollow *hand*," by implication a *bowl*), suggests the connection between the stone that fell from Lucifer's forehead and the Grail (as according to Wolfram von Eschenbach). The word *kāphar* (כפר), is a primitive root meaning "to *cover*," and this specifically with "bitumen": compare, then, the accounts of the use of bitumen (pitch) in the making of the Ark (for example, Gen.6:14); moreover, the "cornerstone" is also the "copestone," where the word "cope" expresses the idea of "to cover";[120] this is also "capstone" where "cap," according to Guénon, is obviously the Latin *caput*, "head."[121] The word *kāphār* (כפר), meaning a "village," recalls the Centre as "abode" or "city"; and, the word *kephel* (כפל), meaning "to *duplicate*," recalls the primitive root `uwd* ("to *duplicate*") and the idea that God created man "in the image." Concerning the Ark, the word *kāphar* ("to *cover*") is the root of the word *kappōreth* (כפרח), meaning "a *lid*," but only used as the cover of the Ark of the Covenant and usually translated as "mercyseat."

St. Peter—"the Rock"—is fathered by Jonah, which name is readily associated in the biblical traditions with the symbolism of the "fish."[122] This same connection exists in the Chinese tradition where Yū the Great—who was born from stone—is the son of Kun, whose name means "the Great Fish."[123]

A connection between the symbolism of the stone or stones and the Flood again arises in the Chinese story of the Flood of Kung Kung, sometimes called "Nū Gua and the Hole in the Sky."[124] Kung Kung, it is said, revolted against Nū Gua, whose role it is to engender humankind. Kung Kung was defeated but escaped to the West where he used his body to set off an avalanche on the "Imperfect Mountain," which then dragged down the pillars supporting the heavens in the north-west quarter.[125] As the sky collapsed, a great hole appeared, the earth was tilted off its axis, the sun was obliterated and rain started to cascade through. Nū Gua repaired the sky by building a palace whose roof supports it. She then filled the gap with five different coloured stones that, as Michael Jordan remarks, equate with the "Five Elements" (Wood, Fire, Earth, Metal and Water).[126] The "five coloured stones" compare with the "five coloured grains" in the myth of Tako'tsi Nakawe. In both cases these are the five elements or seeds. On this point it should be noted that Kun, father of Yū the Great, failed in his attempts to stop the flooding by making the mistake of damning up the inundating waters, thereby throwing into disorder the arrangement of the "Five Elements."[127] Jordan notes that another source explains how Nū Gua blocked the hole with the corpse of a dragon while she searched for a boulder to seal the hole permanently. Just as the dragon's body began to sag under the weight of water Nū Gua found a stone of suitable colour and shape and sealed the sky for ever more. Here, as in the story of the serpent Vritra, the dragon and the Waters (Substance in its dual aspects, *materia prima* and *materia secunda*) are united with the "stone" (Essence) to balance or harmonise Creation. Judaic tradition offers a similar account. When David set out to build the Temple, no sooner had the workers begun to dig the foundation than the waters of the deep surged upwards threatening to flood the whole world, as in the days of Noah. However, David was able to stop the waters by setting a stone engraved with the Ineffable Name, the Tetragrammaton, in the orifice through which the waters were surging.[128]

The stone, as Guénon observes throughout his works, is the principal representation of the *Omphalos*, the Centre of the World.[129] Both Guénon and Coomaraswamy recognise connections between the *Omphalos*, which word signifies "umbilical" but also, in a general sense, describes everything that is central, and the Sanskrit *nabhi*, which connotes the "hub of a wheel"; thus by the roots "*nab*" and *nav*" we find the English words "nave" and "navel."[130] Without needing to stress the link here to the umbilical fluid and the waters of the womb, it is worth remarking upon the connection to the English word "naval" and the obvious association with water. Furthermore, it is notable, as Guénon remarks, that 'on certain Greek *omphaloi*, the stone was encircled by a serpent'.[131] An extension of this symbolism is the encircling of the world by a serpent (for example, Midgardorm in the Norse tradition) or by a river (Ocean in the Greek tradition). The world, as Mother Earth—both "mother" and the "Earth" are homologues of the Ark—is a common symbol of the substantial principle; at the same time the substantial Earth is the realised extension of the essential stone.

Essence is, so to speak, "veiled" in Substance, which echoes the cloak that Noah's sons used to hide his nakedness and also the injunction delivered to Deucalion and Pyrrah to depart from the Temple "with head veiled." Again, Essence is "hidden" in Substance, and this evokes the symbolism of the dragon (Substance) that guards the "hidden treasure" (Essence). This "treasure" often comprises "precious stones" or simply a "precious stone." This is of course the famous Philosopher's Stone of the alchemists, and here the symbolism of the stone and of gold is somewhat interchangeable, so that the hidden treasure may be a "chest of gold" or even, most pertinently, the "pot of gold at the end of the rainbow." The treasure can also be a "pearl," and the symbolism here is particularly relevant given that this is "hidden," as it were, beneath the depths of the Sea. For Eliade the pearl has the 'triple symbolism of water, moon, and woman';[132] each of these symbolisms are connected to that of the Ark, with the moon and woman being direct homologues of the Ark.

This connection with the moon is evident in the Hindu tradition where pearls are called "daughters of soma."[133] The *Dictionary of Symbols* refers to the "Aphrodite-pearl" as analogous to the "*bindu* in the conch."[134] Guénon also recalls the *urnā*: 'the frontal pearl which in Hindu iconography often takes the place of the third eye of Shiva'.[135] In Islamic tradition the word for "pearl" may denote "the Qur'an," "knowledge" or "child."[136] For al-Jīlī the pearl (*al-jawhar*) symbolises the Unique Essence.[137] Shabistari saw pearls as 'the heart's knowledge: when the Gnostic has found the pearl, his life's task has been accomplished.'[138] In the Gnostic gospel, the *Acts of Thomas*, the Eastern prince goes in search of the pearl in the same manner as Perceval seeks the Grail. In the Gnostic *Hymn of the Pearl*, the prince searches for a pearl in the possession of a giant serpent. Eliade also recalls the Coptic Kephalaia, 'a Manichaean text that relates how the soul is like a raindrop that falls into the sea and enters the body of an oyster in order to develop into a pearl.'[139] In alchemy, the Philosopher's Stone is known as *margarita pertiosa*, the "precious pearl."[140]

Analogous and often interchangeable with the pearl is the symbol of the "egg," which suggests the symbolism of the "World Egg." This corresponds directly to the Ark, and can even be said to be the symbol *par excellence* of this general principle. The prime symbolism here is that of the Hindu *Hiranya-garbha*, the "Golden Embryo"—embodying the symbolism of the embryonic "seed" and the golden "treasure." This is *aksara purusa*, the Indestructible-Person, from which all destructible forms are made, the principle of vibration or movement which divides itself into the causal mass of potentialities (the causal Waters), after springing forth from *Brahmā* (the universal Intellect).[141] According to Guénon: '*Hiranyagarbha* … is *Brahmā* (determination of *Brahman* as effect *kārya*) enveloping Himself in the "World Egg" (*Brahmānda*), out of which there will develop, according to its mode of realisation, the whole formal manifestation which is contained therein virtually as a conception of this *Hiranyagarbha*, the primordial germ of the cosmic Light.'[142] This is as clear a description of the nature of the Ark as might be found, combining both the sense of the seed of Noah's Ark and the Light (*Shekhinah*) of the Ark of the Covenant. Guénon further adds that *Varāj* (cosmic Intelligence or the created Intellect) proceeds from *Hiranyagarbha* (the seed envisaged as the Uncreated Intellect), and in turn *Manu*—who corresponds to both Adam and Noah—proceeds from *Virāj*.[143] Moreover, as Guénon says, 'This cosmogonic symbol of the "World Egg" is in no wise peculiar to India; it is for example to be found in Mazdeism, in the Egyptian tradition (the Egg of *Kneph*), in that of the Druids and in the Orphic tradition.'[144] The connection between the Egg and the Waters bring to mind the symbolism of the sea urchin, which, as Louis Charbonneau-Lassay remarks, was regarded by the Ancients as a symbol of the "Egg of the World," the *ovum anguinum* or "snake's egg"—recognising the connection between the Waters and the Serpent—of the Druids.[145]

Angelo Rappoport recalls an Islamic tradition that connects many of the elements of the symbolism of the stone that are being considered here. Thus it is said that when it came time for Moses to die he began to lament for those whom he would leave behind. The Lord rebuked him:

> "In whom did thy mother put her trust when she cast thee into the waters of the Nile?"
> "In thee, O Lord," replied Moses.
> "And who protected thee, when thou didst appear before Pharaoh, and who gave thee the wonderful rod with which thou didst divide the sea?"
> "Thou, O God," replied Moses.

Here alone we have the Ark of Moses' infancy linked with the waters of the Red Sea and the "rod," the Divine Ray or polarized power of the principle. The tradition continues with God giving Moses a sign of His omnipotence.

> "Go out once more to the sea and extend thy rod over it, and thou wilt have a sign of My omnipotence."
> Thus spoke the Lord, and Moses at once obeyed. He raised his rod, the sea divided, and he beheld in its midst a black rock. He approached the rock, and once more the Lord said unto him: "Smite it with thy rod." Moses did so and the rock divided, revealing to the astonished gaze of the Prophet a sort of cavity wherein lay a little worm, holding a little green leaf in its mouth, and the worm opened its mouth, lifted up its voice and said: "Praised be the Lord who doth not forget me in my loneliness; praised be the Lord who hath nourished me."
> When the worm was silent, the Lord again spoke to Moses and said: "Thou seest, Moses, that I do not forget even the lonely worm under the rock, in the midst of the sea; how can I forget or abandon thy children who acknowledge Me and My Law?"[146]

The "rod of Moses" is the *Axis Mundi*, which connects Essence and Substance and is the spiritual centre of the cosmos. It expresses the cosmic principles, Essence and Substance, polarized and active. This activity is, by way of the Radiation and Contraction of the *tsimtsum*, both centrifugal and centripetal, its "power" being the ability to move from unity to multiplicity and from multiplicity to unity, or from point to extension and *visa versa*. The waters of the "sea" express the existential illusion of the "veil" (*Samsāra* as *Māyā*). By virtue of the power of the rod (cf. the "reed"), the "veil" of the sea is divided (cf. the waters of the Red/Reed Sea), which is to say that the existential illusion of *Māyā* is "drawn back," or opened like a curtain, through the movement from multiplicity to unity. This "movement" proceeds by way of "the hard and narrow" passage through duality, this being symbolised by the dividing of the sea. At the heart of substantial existence is the "black rock": the "rock" symbolic of Essence; the colour "black" symbolic of the Divine Substance, which is here identical to Divine Essence (*Ousia*). Moses strikes this rock which in turn divides to reveal the "little worm." Here there is a sense in which the "sea" is *materia secunda* and the "black rock" *materia prima*, identical from another perspective with the *quinta essentia*, which is then shown to contain the "worm," which as "semen" is *quinta essentia*, or, as "serpent," *materia prima*. In what is a truly extraordinary passage Substance is identified in its dual aspects (*materia prima* and *materia secunda*); shown to have Essence at its heart; identified with Essence; and then shown to be "contained" by Essence, as indeed the heart contains the "kingdom of God."

There is a striking similarity to this story in St. Matthew's account of the crucifixion of Christ: 'And suddenly, the veil of the Sanctuary was torn in two from top to bottom, the earth quaked, the rocks split, the tombs opened and the bodies of many holy people rose from the dead' (Mt. 27:51, 52). Not only can the "veil of the Sanctuary" easily be seen to correspond to the "sea" but also both accounts contain the subsequent "splitting" of the "rock/s." Moreover, the "holy dead" who rise are like the "small worm" who is sustained even in the intermediate stage of "death" or dormancy, by the "food" of God, which is none other than His Essence expressed in terms of His eternal Substance.

Another point that deserves mention here is the "cavity" wherein the worm lay, which corresponds to the "tombs" or "caves" of the dead in St. Matthew's account. In the first instance the cavity in the rock reminds one of the connection between the Hebrew words *keph* ("a hollow rock") and *kaph* (a "*bowl*"), which symbolism is that of a "cup" or, more specifically, The Cup, the Holy Grail. In the second case the "cave" is closely associated with the Centre and particularly the "heart." While the heart is the "centre of life," the smaller ventricle (Skt. *gunā*) of the heart (*hridaya*) is the "vital centre."[147] According to Guénon, 'The "cave of the heart" is a well known traditional expression.'[148] Beginning from the Hindu tradition Guénon remarks,

> The Sanskrit word *guhā* generally designates a cave, but it is used also of the internal cavity of the heart, and consequently of the heart itself. This "cave of the heart" is the vital centre in which resides not only *jīvātmā*[149] but also *Ātman*, which in reality is identical with *Brahman* itself ... The word *guhā* is derived from the root, *guh*, meaning "to cover" or "conceal" or "hide," as does another similar root, *gup*, whence *gupta* which applies to everything of a secret character, everything that is not externally manifested. This is the equivalent of the Greek *kruptos* that gives the word "crypt," which is synonymous with cave. These ideas are related to the centre insofar as it is considered as the most inward and consequently the most hidden point.[150]

The image of the "black rock" in the above story immediately calls to mind the Holy Black Stone (*al-hajar al-aswad*) of Islamic tradition. This "stone"—in fact this has fragmented into three pieces, which symbolically may not be insignificant, for God hides no truth—is situated in the southeast corner of the *Ka'bah*, the centre of the Islamic world. Shi'ite symbolism of the *Ka'bah* offers some interesting parallels. The *Ka'bah* is said to have been built on the site of the Tent erected by God as a dwelling for Adam. The central pillar of this Tent was a stalk of red hyacinth, which according to a *hadīth* of the fifth Imam, is the revealed Supreme Divine Form (*al-ulūhiyyah al-kubrā*), which, as Snodgrass says, is the first Intelligence, the *Nous* or Intellect.[151] This pillar is red to show that it includes two natures, divine and creatural (cf. the *Logos*, both created and Uncreated): in the science of Islam red is a mixture of white, representing the divine Light, and black, representing the darkness of the created.[152] Recall the Red Sea as the Reed Sea, just as the pillar of the Tent is a stalk or "reed." God sent Adam this Tent, which was made of red jacinth; within this was a white jacinth that served Adam as a seat (the Throne). This white jacinth was later to become the Black Stone. The Tent had four pegs coloured yellow, the colour of gold, which signify Universal Nature. These symbolisms are intimately interconnected. Jacinth is a precious stone, usually reddish; the Latin *jacin(h)us* derives from *hyacinthus* or hyacinth. As Snodgrass remarks, 'the Black Stone, as the secret of the *Ka'bah* and innermost point of man's spiritual life, corresponds to the pillar of red hyacinth'.[153] The symbolic transmutation from the vegetative symbolism of the hyacinth to the mineral symbolism of the celestial jacinth and, in turn, the terrestrial Black Stone correspond, *mutatis mundis*, to the shift from the Terrestrial Paradise as a garden, with a vegetable symbolism, to the Celestial Jerusalem as a city, with mineral symbolism. Concerning this, Guénon remarks that this symbolism expresses the fact that 'vegetation represents the development of seeds in the sphere of vital assimilation, while minerals represent results that are fixed definitively—"crystallised" so to speak—at the end of a cyclical development.'[154] Furthermore, the symbolism of the hyacinth derives, in part, from its "bell-shaped" flowers. The bell— which is an inverted cup and a potent homologue of the Ark—is the means by which Gabriel revealed the Qur'an to the Prophet.

According to the symbolism of the *Sefirot*, *Keter* is also called the Primordial Point (*Nequdah Rashunah*), and is known by the cognomen, *Arikh Anipin*, the Vast Countenance or Macroprosopus. A description of the "eyes" of Macroprosopus offers a strikingly similar symbolism to that of the Tent and the Black Stone. It is written in *The Greater Holy Assembly*:

> When his eyes are opened they appear beautiful as those of doves;[155] in colour, white, red, and black, and golden yellow. ...
> From those colours, when they are uncovered, go forth seven eyes of Providence, which issue from the black of the eye. This is that which is said, Zac. iii.9: "Upon one stone seven eyes." What is the "one stone?" The black of the eye.[156]

These "seven eyes" are the seven onto-cosmological *sefirot*. Viewed from the perspective of the Principle these are the immanence of *Binah* down to *Yesod*; here *Malkhut* is the manifest realisation of these seven. Viewed from the perspective of Manifestation these are *Malkhut* up to *Hesed*; here *Binah* is the transcendent principle of these seven. These "seven" are synthetically prefigured in the "one stone," *Keter*. The *NJB* remarks on this "stone" of Zc.3:9 that it 'presumably stands for the Temple';[157] this is correct, although the full symbolism of the Temple here undoubtedly surpasses what the editors of the *NJB* intend by this supposition.

The term "whirled in the current of the sea" suggests the idea of the essential Principle as it remains at the centre of the whirling Waters of *Samsāra*. Moreover, in its cosmogonic context, this description echoes the famous "churning of the ocean" of Hindu tradition.[158]

The connection between the symbolism of white, red-black, and the stone that falls to earth is expressed in the account of Noah by the symbolism associated with the dove and the raven, which Noah sent forth from the Ark (Gen.8:6-12).[159] The symbolism of the white dove, which returns to the Ark, and the black raven, which remains "flying back and forth above the waters" (which is to say, that remains in manifestation) is analogous to that of the white jacinth (Adam's seat in the celestial Tent) and the Black Stone, in the terrestrial *Ka'bah*. There are numerous connections here of which we will consider but a suggestive few.[160] The dove is Aphrodite's bird, which recalls the symbolism of the Aphrodite-pearl (the *bindu*). In Christian tradition, the dove represents the Holy Spirit, Jesus Christ and, in later times, also the Virgin Mary. However this last identification involves a con-fusion of the symbolisms involved, for while the whiteness of the dove makes it an adequate symbol of the Divine Light (Essence), the Virgin is precisely a symbol of the Receptacle (the Ark; Substance; *prima materia*), and thus is precisely "black"— 'I am black but beautiful' (Sg.1:5-6). In this sense one can recognise the raven—which is of course a red-black bird—as expressive of the Virgin. In *La Queste del Saint Graal* we read: 'By the black bird ... must be understood Holy Church which says: I am black but I am beautiful: know that my blackness is of more worth than the whiteness of any other.'[161] At the same time the raven is identified in devotional writings as the devil himself.[162] This ambiguity is, in the final analysis, a result of the centrifugal and centripetal movement of manifestation away from and back to the Source. Moreover this axial movement between heaven and earth is, in various traditions, attributed to the raven, insomuch as it is the messenger of the gods.[163] This is the same axial role of the Holy Spirit, which is the role of creative power. In Norse mythology, Odin's two ravens, *Hugin* ("mind") and *Munnin* ("memory"), which perch upon his throne, stand for his creative power.[164] It is this creative power that sees the raven "dry" the waters of the Flood.[165] In Chinese tradition, Mencius says it was Yū himself, with his "raven's beak mouth" that 'dug the soil and led the water to the sea'.[166]

According to Guénon, the Black Stone of Muslim tradition is a "stone fallen from the sky" (*lapis lapsus ex cœlis*).[167] The symbolism of the *lapis lapsus ex cœlis*, says Guénon, is connected with that of the Grail, which, according to one tradition, was fashioned by angels from an emerald that dropped from Lucifer's forehead at the time of his fall from heaven.[168] This image of Lucifer's stone suggests the planet Venus as it is the Morning Star or Lucifer's Star (Vulg. *Lucifer* = "brightness"). This is the Star of Light, *Tcholban*, as the ancient Turks called it, the "Shining" or "Dazzling One."[169] The Church Fathers identified the fall of the Morning Star, as told of in *Isaiah* 14:12, with that of Lucifer's fall from heaven. This is commonly seen as the same star that St. John speaks of as falling into the waters, the star called Wormwood (αψινθος; "bitterness"), which turned a third of the waters into wormwood or bitterness (Rev.8:10, 11; 9:1). Recall that the Lower Waters of the Qur'an are said to be "bitter." The ancient Mexicans dreaded the Morning Star as the bringer of disease and death. In his *Mysterium Magnum* Jacob Boehme adopts the positive symbolism of Venus, associating it with the Divine Light of God. Of course, Venus is Aphrodite and this recalls the "Aphrodite-pearl." As Wormwood this symbolism evokes the bitterness of manifestation as *Samsāra* or Illusion; as Venus—the "Aphrodite-pearl"—this symbolism reminds us of the Divine Essence at the heart of manifestation. This ambiguity is inherent in this symbolism with the alternative appearances of Venus as the Morning Star and the Evening Star making Venus a basic symbol of death and rebirth.

As Hesiod tells us, Aphrodite (Venus) was born from the waters when the seed of Ouranos (Uranos) was scattered upon them after his castration by Cronos (the "god-slaying"). According to the ancient Romans, Venus had, as one of her attributes, the emerald, and this recalls the emerald that fell from Lucifer's forehead.[170] These are not the only examples of the emerald as the link between Heaven and Earth. For the Alchemists the emerald is the stone of Mercury, where Mercury is both alchemically and mythologically associated with the "intermediary world." Again, in St. John's vision, the Ancient of Days sits on a throne around which there is 'a rainbow that looked like an emerald' (Rev.4:3). In this connection, the emerald was regarded as a "moist" stone—'watery and lunar as opposed to dry, fiery and solar.'[171]

This net of symbolism can be cast yet further, for Aphrodite is married to Hephaestus, who, like Lucifer, was flung from heaven like a "falling star."[172] Hephaestus, in his role as the divine "blacksmith," is the guardian-keeper of the "divine fire" (Essence) at the heart of the "mountain" (*imago mundi*). Hephaestus corresponds to Agni (Fire) in the Hindu tradition, who is similarly the pillar (*skambha*) between Heaven and Earth.[173] In Chinese tradition the role of blacksmith is taken by the flood-hero, Yū the Great, who cast nine cauldrons—where the cauldron is a homologue of the cup and the Ark—with metal brought from the nine regions he established to balance the cosmos and stop the flooding.[174] Again, in Dogon mythology, Nommo, who corresponds in one sense to Noah and in another sense to Adam, is likewise "the Blacksmith."[175] The Blacksmith is the Demiurge, whose creative prowess involves precisely the combination of fire (Essence) and water (Substance).[176]

Another symbolism associated with the Blacksmith is that of "lameness";[177] this is relevant in the present context, for lameness and "one legged-ness," involve the dual symbolisms of the axis and the imperfection engendered by the entering of manifestation.[178] Thus Hephaestus is made lame by his fall from Olympus; Yū the Great became lame in saving the world from the flood;[179] Nommo is "one-legged";[180] and, Agni, in his form as Aja-Ekapāda, the "One-Footed He-Goat" is 'the uniped whose whole body is a single leg forming one "tall Post" (*stambha*) or "solar standard."'[181] As for Noah, it is said that while aboard the Ark he once forgot to feed the lion—the "solar" animal *par excellence*—which bit his leg so that he became lame.[182] The alchemist, Michael Maier, depicts Saturn as a one-legged gardener watering the earth.[183] The "garden" evokes the symbolism of the axial Tree. For the Semitic traditions, the gardener is firstly Adam (Gen.1:28-29) and then Noah, "the first to plant the [axial] vine' (Gen.9:18).

Hephaestus is the "cup-bearer" of Olympus, this being the cup containing the ambrosial nectar, the "draught of immortality," as with the Grail.[184] Agni is equally associated with the Vedic *soma*,[185] the "draught of immortality" in Vedic tradition; Yū the Great cast the nine cauldrons, which are analogous to the Grail, the receptacle of the "draught of immortality"; and, Noah, of course, is the first person to make wine (Gen.9:21-22). According to Guénon, *Soma*, the fructifying sap of the "World Tree," is identical with the sap of the *Haoma* tree of Zoroastrian tradition, also called *haoma*.[186] This is, to be exact, the white *Haoma* tree, just as *soma* and the analogous symbols of milk and semen are all white. The symbolism of the colour white involves its amalgamation of the spectrum of the rainbow. White is also one of the two colours of Christ along with red, which informs the blood of the Grail and is also the colour of fire. Again, as Guénon says, *soma* is identical with the Hindu *amrita*. He continues to observe the etymological identification of *amrita* with the Greek *ambrosia*. Like the dual symbolism of Venus, *amrita* is both the source of life (*a-mrta*) and death (*mrta*), a symbolism that Alain Daniélou observes expressed in all traditions as the oneness of love and death (*a-mor* and *mor-tis*).[187] This connection is evident in Greek mythology in the love affair of Aphrodite and Aries.

The Greek ambrosia, insomuch as it was distinguished from "nectar," is a food rather than a drink, so that it is a question of a "food of immortality" rather than a draught. This symbolism is found in the biblical symbolism of the Tree of Life and its fruit. Whether "food" or "draught," it is, as Guénon remarks, 'always a product of the tree or the plant, a product that contains the concentrated sap which is in a way the very essence of the plant.'[188] In this context he notes that the Sanskrit word *rasa* means both "sap" and "essence." A further connection emerges when we consider the *apsarases* ("essences of the waters"; Skt. *ap* = "water"–*rasa*) of Hindu tradition. In the *Ramayana* these are presented as "beautiful women" born out of the cosmogonic "churning of the ocean," recalling the birth of Aphrodite. Daniélou says that the *apsarases* are the 'unmanifested potentialities, the possible worlds, which exist in the Divine Mind but may never come to exist physically'.[189]

Their name is also explained as "moving on the waters" (*ap-sārinī*),[190] which echoes the Spirit upon the Waters (Gen.1:2).

The symbolism of a "food of immortality" is again found with the biblical *manna*.[191] Here is another connection to the symbolism of light, for, as Schaya remarks, 'The pure and redemptive light symbolised in the Talmud by "manna," is called *Nogah*, "brightness," in the Kabbalah.'[192] Recall, then, that the Spirit upon the Waters is, in Arabic *ar-Rūh*, which is basically identical with the word for light, *Nūr*, which in turn derives from the same root as the Hebrew word *Ur* ("light"). In the *Slavonic Apocalypse of Enoch* (2 Enoch), Nir ("light") is the younger brother of Noe or Noah.[193] According to the *Gedullath Moshe* (*The Ascension of Moses*), *Nogah* is the name of one of the twin star-angels (*Nogah* and *Maadim*), which are associated respectively with the sun and the moon.[194]

Like the seed sown in the field, or the ray of light shone upon the reflective "face of the Waters," the stone dropped into the Waters adequately symbolises the cosmogenesis. Thus the cosmogonic symbolism of *Genesis* shows the striking of the *Fiat Lux* (infinite, vertical and axial) upon the reflective "face of the Waters" (indefinite, horizontal, planar). The point where the Celestial Ray strikes the Water is the centre to an expanding circle of light comprised of an infinite number of radii each, in effect, being an extension and a reflection of the original Ray. The dropping of a "stone" into the Waters expresses this same symbolism with the radii being expressed by the indefinitely expanding ripples.

The symbolism of the stone "dropped" upon the Waters is both axial and polar, describing both the idea of the Centre and the vertical extension that arises with the diremption of Essence and Substance. The Mishnah talks of the rock of Jerusalem reaching deep into the subterranean waters (*tehom*), indicating the extension of this rock, as well as connecting the ideas of the stone and the Waters.[195] The *Zohar* presents an account of how the Holy One created the world by throwing down a "precious stone" from beneath the throne of His glory that sank into the "deep" or "abyss." This stone is called *even shetiyah* ("foundation stone").[196] It is said that it became lodged in the abyss 'from the upper to the lower worlds, and from it the world was founded': 'One edge of the stone became lodged in the deeps, and another in the realms above. And there was another edge, a supernal one, a single point, which is in the middle of the world, and the world expanded from there, to the right and to the left, and upon all sides, and it is thus sustained by this central point.'[197] In the Lower World this is the foundation stone of the Temple, which stands at the central point of the Holy of Holies. In the language of the Kabbalah this "stone" is said to be a symbol of the *Shekhinah*.[198]

The geometric point adequately expresses both the metaphysical zero and the "first" determination, as one finds with the meanings of the word *bindu*. In the former case it is then the line that must represent the "one," as in fact it is with most numerical systems.[199] Here, while there is polarisation, the emphasis is nevertheless on the line as expressing the virtualities of the point, which must be then seen as emphasising Pure Potentiality. This symbolism of extension has both a vertical and horizontal valency. The stone that falls from the sky traces a vertical axis; the ripples it causes on the face of the Waters express horizontal extension. Similarly, the stone is analogous to the mountain, which demonstrates both a vertical and horizontal symbolism simultaneously. The seed is, by extension, the tree, both vertical (the trunk) and horizontal (the branches). The point expresses a certain static nature, while the line can be said to be dynamic. Thus Jean-Paul Roux remarks that stones 'from the days when our remotest ancestors set them up or carved their messages upon them, are eternal and the symbol of static life, while the tree, subject to the cycles of life and death, but which possess the ineffable gift of perpetual regeneration, is the symbol of dynamic life'.[200] Again, the divine Spark ignites the vertical extension of the divine Ray, which also extends horizontally on the mirror of the Waters. The single drop of water that falls from above, which corresponds by a kind of multiplication to the symbolism of rain, expresses a vertical extension through the tracing of its path. This drop is analogous to the fountain that flows out of the Godhead or the river that flows out of Eden, which both express vertical symbolism, while the waters of Chaos and the four rivers express horizontal symbolism.

A further symbolism that presents itself here is that of the verticality of man (*homo erectus*) and the connection between man and the stone. Thus, in the Deucalion myth, it can be seen that the stone, and here one might equally say the semen or the seed (ovum), becomes the human form. The symbolism of the human form is moreover identified with that of the tree and the Ark in various flood myths. Thus in the Flood myth of the native American Huichol the flood-hero is told to make a box from the wood of a fig tree 'as long and as wide as himself'.[201] This suggests the image of the Ark as a "coffin," which is another homologue of the Ark. This image of the fig-tree as the Ark calls to mind the Egyptian myth of Osiris, who was himself not only entombed in a chest, which was designed to contain "exactly the body of Osiris," but also in the trunk of a tamarisk tree.[202] The trunk of this tamarisk then became the "pillar at the Centre of the king's palace." In fact one can say that the Ark symbol is esoterically expressed five times in the story of the murder of Osiris: Osiris himself, the chest, the tamarisk tree, the pillar, and the wooden phallus, from which Isis famously became pregnant with Horus.[203] The number five is the number of man. In Rosicrucian tradition the image of Noah's encoffined body forms the plan of the Ark.[204]

The *Shekhinah*, as described above, expresses Essence. Yet the *Shekhinah*, as it is symbolically feminine and in the sense that it refers to the Divine Immanence in contrast to the Divine Transcendence, expresses Substance. Of course, as noted above, this ambiguity is inherent at this level of Being and distinctions, properly speaking belong to the differences in perspective between the celestial and the terrestrial or between the Divine and the human points of view. Concerning this ambiguity, the central "stone" of *Zohar* symbolism is said to be "moist"[205] with waters sometimes flowing from it,[206] which is to recognise that this "stone" embodies both symbolisms—(stone / water)—entailed in the bi-unity of Essence-Substance (cf. the emerald). This symbolism can again be seen in the description of "earth" in *Genesis* as "formless and void," which is *tohu* (chaos) and *bohu* (emptiness). According to the Mishnah: '*Tohu* is a green line which encompasses the whole world from which darkness issued; as it is said, "He made darkness His hiding-place round about Him" (Ps.18:11). *Bohu* denotes the slime-covered stones sunk in the depths from which water issued; as it is said, "He shall stretch upon it the line of chaos (*Tohu*) and the stones of emptiness (*Bohu*)" (Is.34:11)'.[207] The "line of Chaos" is the same with the "limitation" of the indefinite extension of a horizontal plane of Existence. This plane of Existence, which is *Tohu* or Chaos, is the pure receptivity of undifferentiated ontological Substance, the Waters of *Genesis*. The circumference is here depicted as a "green line," where green is symbolic of the fecundity associated with potentiality.[208] *Bohu* implies Substance as it is identical with Essence. It is "empty" insomuch as it implies Being in terms of its Uncreated principle. The "depth from which water issued" is the unmanifested and infinitely "deep," the "Upper Waters" of Essence issued forth upon the "Lower Waters" of ontological Substance. That *Bohu* is represented by "stones" accords with the symbolism here under consideration. *Bohu* is said to denote "slime-covered stones" insomuch as the heart of Existence is clothed or veiled in the "slime" of the cosmic illusion (*Māyā*), which recalls the "slime-covered" Pytho of Greek mythology. Moreover, the Qur'an proclaims that man is made from "clay and slime."[209]

The Divine Light

God said, "Let there be light." And there was light.

Genesis 1:3

The principial point is often described in terms of luminous symbolism. Guénon remarks that the expansion of light within and upon darkness expresses the "measure" of creation; the production of "order," the manifested universe, from "chaos."[210] Guénon observes that this production of order is assimilated in all traditions to an "illumination" (the *Fiat Lux*). He says that "chaos" is the 'potentiality from which as starting-point manifestation will be "actualised," that is to say, it is in effect the substantial side of the world, which is therefore described as the tenebrous pole of existence, whereas Essence is the luminous pole since it is the influence of Essence that illuminates the "chaos" in order to extract from it the "cosmos"'.[211]

The centre is indistinguishable by virtue of having nothing else with which it may be referenced. In terms of the symbolism of light, the centre is lost, so to speak, in either the Divine Darkness of the depths of the Infinite or in the blinding super-abundance of Divine Light. In the first case this is the darkness described in the *Song of Songs*: 'I am black, but beautiful'; in the second case this is the "blinding" of the discursive mind, as with the light that blinded Saul upon the road to Damascus (Ac.9:4-9). Moreover, the blackness of the "beloved" in the *Song of Songs* derives precisely from being "burnt" (a super-abundance) by the "sun" (Sg.1:6). This is the Supernal Sun,[212] the "Light Inaccesible," of which Nicholas of Cusa says: 'He who is worshiped as Light Inaccessible, is not light that is material, the opposite of which is darkness, but light absolutely simple and infinite in which darkness is infinite light.'[213]

The reintegration of the manifested world into the Centre involves a "ceasing" of the cosmic or spatializing light. Corresponding with the cessation of space is the cessation of time. Here also the symbolism is of the stopping of the sun and the moon, the celestial timekeepers. Thus, according to Judaic tradition, it is said that during the time of the Flood neither the sun nor the moon shed their light on the world.[214] Again, the *Scroll of Habakkuk*, singing of the coming of Yahweh, describes the coming of "great floods" (3:10) with which the sun and moon where to stay in their "dwellings" (Hab.3:11). These accounts suggest both a temporal and spatial dissolution. The cessation of the solar and lunar cycles is a cessation of time. The cessation of the revealing light is a cessation of spatial extension.

The active Essence (Sun) and passive Substance (Moon) are indistinguishable in the state of biunity. Cusa's description of a "dark-

112

ness that is infinite light" recognises the resolution of contraries that signal the return to the principial Unity. In the Gospels this darkening of the sun and moon is said to indicate the coming of the "Son of man" (Mk.13:24; cf. 15:33, Mt.27:45, Lk.23:44). Again this phenomenon is associated with the institution of the Celestial Jerusalem: 'And the city did not need the sun or the moon for light, since it was lit by the radiant glory of God, and the Lamb was a lighted torch for it' (Rev.21:23). This description is common with respect to the Celestial City: 'The sun shines not there, nor the moon and stars; ... This whole world is illumined with His light'[215]; 'That the sun does not illumine, nor the moon, nor fire; going there, they (the wise) do not return. That is My Supreme Abode'[216]; 'Here the Sun and Moon lose their distinction.'[217] The *Skanda Purāna* describes the Paradise of Vaikunth, the celestial abode of Viśnu, by saying: 'In this self-luminous, brilliant sanctuary, no sun is shining, no moon and no stars.'[218] This symbolism speaks of the dissolution of created and creating light in the "infinite" and "self-luminous" light of the Uncreated Principle.

The connection between Light and the Divine City (*vünkeīn* and *bürgelīn*) is explicit in the symbolism of the Chinese Emperor's palace-temple, the *Ming T'ang*. This name means literally, "House of Light" or "Hall of Light."[219] Snodgrass observes that the character *ming* (明) comprises the characters for the sun and the moon, 'thus expressing light in its total manifestation, both direct and reflected.' Guénon likens this to the symbolic association, in the Judaic tradition, between light and the *Shekhinah*; moreover, he remarks on the *Ming T'ang* as an image of the Cosmos 'viewed as the realm or "field" of manifestation of the Light.'[220]

In the Judaic tradition mentioned above (*Pirke de Rabbi Eliezer*, Ch.23) it is added that, even though the sun and moon had ceased to shed their light, still Noah knew when it was day or night because the pearls and precious stones, which he had taken with him into the ark, sparkled at night time, but lost their lustre during the day. These "pearls and precious stones" remind one of those that encrust the Heavenly Jerusalem (Rev.21:18-21). Both "pearls" and "precious stones," as noted, are symbols of Essence, or, what is effectively the same thing, of *gnosis* or the Intellect. Nasr remarks, 'The pearl is the universal symbol of the gnosis which purifies, sanctifies, and delivers'.[221] The *Dictionary of Symbols* observes "precious stones" as being 'the symbol of the transmutation of the opaque into the translucent and, in a spiritual sense, of darkness into light and imperfection into perfection.'[222] This is to say they express the active and ascending nature of the creative Intellect. The *Dictionary of Symbols* remarks on the universal consistency of the pearl as a lunar symbol.[223] Precious stones, in respect to their "fire," display a solar symbolism. Thus this reference to "pearls and precious stones" suggests the creative Intellect in both its passive, or lunar aspect (the pearl), and its active, or solar aspect (the precious stones). This tradition refers to the "pearls and precious stones" as "sparkling" together; thus we see this solar-lunar "light" of the "pearls and precious stones" as a single light that expresses the biunity, and potential polarity, of the Intellect at this level. "At this level": for it should not be forgotten that Noah brought these with him onto the Ark, and that they thus symbolise the Intellect insomuch as it is the created Intellect, as distinct from the Uncreated Intellect. The distinction here may be likened to the distinction in the Islamic tradition between *al-'Aql* (the intellect) and *al-'Aql al-Awwal* (the first Intellect), or, from another perspective, between *al-Rūh al-Kullī* (the Universal and created Spirit) and *al-Rūh al-Ilāhī* (the Divine and Uncreated Spirit).

The Centre by its very nature appears, according to the perspective from which it is viewed, to express either Manifestation or Principle. Thus, when we are told that the pearls and precious stones sparkled during the night this implies that "within" the Centre the Intellect acts to illuminate the pole of Manifestation, which here exists as the potentiality of chaos (night). That they lost their lustre during the day implies that the light of the Intellect is indistinguishable in the Infinite Light of the Supernal Intellect (day).[224] Again, directed towards the potentiality of "night" the light of the creative Intellect—which implies the biunity of ontological Essence (precious stones) and ontological Substance (pearls)—acts as the creative Light or *Fiat Lux*. Directed towards the Principle, the light of the creative Intellect dissolves in the Infinite Light of the Supernal Sun.

The creative Intellect: the *Fiat Lux*, the Divine Ray, *Buddhi*, Universal Spirit. According to Fohr, this symbolism is expressed in the account of Noah by the 'sunlight shining through the top of the ark after the flood'.[225] This idea is supported by the description of the Ark as having a "window" (Gen.6:16), where this word is *tsōhar* (צהר; "a *light*"). Fohr: 'Thus, as creation is said to take place due to the influence of *Purusha* on *Prakriti* [in the Vedantic tradition], in the biblical story [of Noah] it is the result of the influence of sunlight on the contents of the ark.'[226] Fohr further notes the Gothic cathedral with its rose window as an 'architectural representation of the ark with its opening near the top'.[227] According to *The Golden Legend* the window of the Ark was made of crystal.[228] Eliade remarks that crystal is 'a foetus, born from the rocks in the ground'[229]; it is the "embryonic diamond," evoking the "diamond wall" of Jerusalem (Rev.21:17), which, as we will see, is identifiable with the Divine Ray. Moreover, the symbolism of the crystal is linked to that of the divine Palace and the Grail, both homologues of the Ark, and the emerald. According to J. Servier, the crystal 'represents a level intermediate between the visible and the invisible [cf. the *Logos*] ... Heroes in both Eastern and Western romance encounter crystal palaces as they emerge from gloomy forests in their quest for the royal talisman. An identical belief links the quartz of the Australian Aborigine initiates with the Holy Grail of Western chivalry, carved from a mystical emerald.'[230] For Angelus Silesius the image of light striking crystal symbolises the Immaculate Conception: 'Mary is crystal, her son heavenly light which passes through leaving the whole intact'.[231]

Centre and Origin

The origin inspires the centre, and the centre perpetuates the origin.
Lord Northbourne[232]

The Centre is an image of God. For Nicholas of Cusa, God is 'both circumference and centre'.[233] According to the famous formula of Hermes Trismegistus, 'God is an infinite sphere whose centre is everywhere and whose circumference is nowhere.'[234] For Giordano Bruno this became: 'the centre of the universe is everywhere and the circumference nowhere.'[235] This lead to Pascal: 'Nature is an infinite sphere, whose centre is everywhere and whose circumference is nowhere.' The purely divine symbolism of Nicolas of Cusa and Hermes Trismegistus stands true; however, as Guénon rightly observes, from the strictly metaphysical point of view the formula of Pascal 'should and indeed, must, be reversed.' Guénon: 'It is the centre that is rightly speaking nowhere, because it is not to be found anywhere in manifestation, since it is absolutely transcendent in respect thereof, while being the centre of all things ... it is therefore really the circumference that is everywhere, since all places in space, or more generally, all manifested things (space being here only a symbol of universal manifestation), "all contingencies, distinctions and individualities," are only elements in the "stream of forms," points on the circumference of the "cosmic wheel."'[236]

The Centre is both the point of origin and ultimate return. The movement of expansion "outwards" along the radii of the Circle—symbolically the arms of the Cross—may correspondingly be traced "inwards" as a retraction into the Centre. Snodgrass explains:

There are two possible directions of movement along the radii that join the points on the circumference of the circle to their centre, firstly from the centre to the circumference, and secondly, from the circumference to the centre. These complementary phases of movement, centrifugal and centripetal, comparable to those of respiration or the action of the heart, give the image of the successive manifestation and reabsorbtion of existences.[237]

The Centre as projected on Earth is an hierophany, an opening between the three cosmic levels: Heaven, Earth and Hell.[238] The Centre is unique in Heaven; it is only relatively so on Earth, which is to say that there can be a plurality of "centres" on Earth.[239]

The spatial Centre is directly related to the temporal Origin. 'In the spatial world we live in,' remarks Schuon 'every value is related back in one way or another to a sacred Centre, to the place where heaven has touched the earth; ... Similarly for the Origin, the quasi-timeless moment when heaven was near and when terrestrial things were still half-celestial ... the Origin is also, in the case of civilizations having a historical founder, the time when God spoke thereby renewing the primordial alliance for the branch of humanity concerned. To conform to tradition is to keep faith with the Origin, and for that very reason it is also to be situated at the Centre'.[240] Lord Northbourne recognises this relationship in the principles of "tradition and hierarchy." 'Tradition and hierarchy' he says, 'are inseparable. Together they constitute a chain linking civilisation with the Spirit in successional mode and in simultaneous mode respectively; that is to say, in time to a spiritual origin and in space to a spiritual centre. The origin inspires the centre, and the centre perpetuates the origin.'[241]

The Centre and the Origin respectively correspond to the cosmic aspects, space and time. Guénon observes how space and time express the cosmic phases of compression and expansion.[242] He remarks that the principle of compression is represented by time, and the principle of expansion represented by space.[243] However, he stresses that 'both these two principles [compression and expansion] are manifested in time and space, as in everything else.'[244] They exist in a complementary relationship. Guénon also remarks that the sedentary mode of living corresponds to time, as the nomadic mode corresponds to space. This appears counterintuitive but is really another example of the "law of inverse analogy." Thus:

...the works of sedentary peoples are works of time: these peoples are fixed in space within a strictly limited domain, and develop their activities in a temporal continuity which appears to them to be indefinite. On the other hand, nomadic and pastoral peoples build nothing durable, and do not work for a future which escapes them; but they have space in front of them, not

facing them with any limitation, but on the contrary always offering them new possibilities.[245]

Guénon further relates sight to space and hearing to time, observing that
'the elements of visual symbol occur simultaneously, and those of the
sonorous symbol in succession'.[246] In the Hindu tradition space is represented as female and time as male. Moreover, time is associated with the
"primordial vibration" (*nāda*) which is the creative Sound (the Word;
Om). 'The male principle is also represented as Fire, the devourer, while
the female principle is Soma, the devoured offering.'[247] Similarly, Guénon observes that 'time uses up space'.[248]

'According to ancient Indian tradition' says Lama Govinda, 'the
universe reveals itself in two fundamental properties: as *motion*, and as
that in which motion takes place, namely *space*. ... This space is called
ākāśa (Tib.: *nam-mkhah*) and is that through which things step into visible appearance, i.e., through which they posses extension or corporeality.'[249] This "space" corresponds to the three-dimensional space of our
sense perception, however, this does not exhaust it: 'it comprises all
possibilities of movement, not only the physical, but the spiritual one:
it comprises infinite dimensions.'[250] To recognise space as comprising
infinite dimensions is to recognise the Centre, which is the principle of
space, as it touches the Infinite.

Space is the container of the Universe, but the Universe cannot be
said to be in space, as if space itself was something different to the Universe. According to the teachings of certain Sufis, 'there is no space
outside the Cosmos and the Universe cannot be said to be in space.'[251]
There is neither a vacuum nor plenum outside of the Universe. From a
physical point of view, space is the boundary of bodies; from a more
inward point of view, space is an abstract, intelligible idea, 'a form ab-
stracted from matter and existing only in the consciousness'.[252] Space, as
Guénon says, 'is not homogeneous, but is determined and differentiated
by its directions.'[253] It is, as such, "qualified space."

Similarly, time exists only in the sense of being "qualified time."
The only "real time" exists exclusively in the present, which is without
extension, is instantaneous and evanescent, and occupies no space. 'The
interval we measure when we measure time, then,' says Snodgrass, 'can
not be time itself, which has no extension, but is a memory; time inter-
vals are measured in the mind.'[254] The mind engages time through the
threefold activity of memory, attention and anticipation (past, present,
future), in the flux of temporal succession.[255] As such, time is illusory.
The Now which is strictly speaking "timeless" is the principle of time.
For Aristotle, 'time is only made up of the past and the future ... the

Now is not a part of time at all.'[256] 'What the dimensionless point is to spatial extension the timeless is to temporal duration and succession; just as the dimensionless point equates to the Infinite, so the atemporal instant equates to the Eternal.'[257] Eternity is the principle of Time; however, it is not temporal. 'Whereas time is succession, Eternity is a timeless simultaneity.'[258] Thus, Snodgrass remarks that 'Eternity is not to be confused with a continued existence in time. Eternity is not time extended for perpetuity, but rather is the Timeless, that which is wholly unconditioned by temporal limitations.'[259] He continues,

> The indefinite extension of time is properly aeviternity, from the Latin word eavum, denoting the mean between time and eternity. In Eternity there is neither past nor present nor future but only the static Now (*nunc stans*); in the *aevum* there is no succession in essential being but nevertheless 'a liability to accidental modification of temporal duration'. The gods, angels and the souls of men are aeviternal in that their essential being is eternal, but in generating nature they also generate time...[260]

Eternity contains time in "total simultaneity (*tota simul*)."[261] According to Plotinus Eternity 'is centred in the One, arises from the One and is turned to the One'.[262]

Immortality is the experience of Eternity. Thus the Centre is the abode of immortality. This idea is explicit in the account of the Mesopotamian flood-hero, Ut-napishtim, who was granted immortality for his role. In the case of Noah there is a "virtual" immortality, which is to recognise that his role as the "new Adam" and God's promise 'never again to strike down every living thing' (Gen.8:21) effectively means the immortality of the line of his descendants. According to the *Dictionary of Symbols*, the Ark was made from "immortal wood," *Met*.[263] This is "gopher-wood" or "resinous wood" (Gen.6:14). An interesting connection arises here to the tamarisk tree, which, as Udo Becker remarks, 'is universally regarded as a symbol of immortality.' He also observes that in China, where it is seen as thus, its resin was used as a drug to prolong life.[264] This is doubly interesting as it was a tamarisk that encased the body of Osiris in the Egyptian story of his murder by Set. This tamarisk then became the central pillar of the palace of King Melcarthus.[265] In the first case the tamarisk demonstrates a homology with the Ark, and is thus the principial point; in the second case, the tamarisk as pillar expresses the diremption of the point into the axial pillar; this pillar is then the centre to the "royal palace" (*imago mundi*). Moreover, Unger observes that the resin of the *Tamarix mannifera* is known to the Arabs as *mann*,[266] suggesting a link with the scriptural *manna*. Unger discounts this link. However, *manna* shares in the symbolism of immortality with *soma*, the "draught of immortality," which accords with the symbolisms being considered.

The "draught of immortality" returns us to the symbolism of the Grail, which is prefigured in the Hebrew Scriptures by the "oracular" cup of Joseph (Ex.17:5). Likewise, the symbolism of the stone includes this dimension so Guénon remarks that what we are considering are "oracular" stones or "talking stones."[267] This is the same with the baetyl, which, as Guénon says, 'was a "prophetic stone," a "stone which speaks," that is, a stone that yields oracles'.[268] In this context, Shi'ite tradition says that on the Last Day the Black Stone will be given a tongue to bear witness against men.[269] Guénon further compares the emerald that fell from Lucifer's forehead with the Hindu frontal jewel, the *urna*, associated with the third eye of Shiva and representing the "sense of eternity."[270] This oracular nature is by virtue of being situated in the Centre, from where all things can be seen in the instant of the eternal Now, it is not "foreknowledge" but the "sense of Eternity."

Notes

1. Clement of Alexandria, *Paedagogus*, 71, 1.
2. Schuon talks of Being as the "lesser Absolute" (for example see *IFA*, 1989, p.38), which is to recall that Manifestation or the Relative is made "in the image" of the Absolute; hence Being is a "relative Absolute" a phrase that Schuon admits is 'an unavoidably ill-sounding expression, but one that is metaphysically useful' (*IFA*, 1989, p.57).
3. See Schuon, *EPW*, 1981, pp.236-37 on this idea of 'believing in the One both wholly and sincerely'.
4. Schuon, *TUR*, 1993, p.38.
5. Plotinus' "The One" (*to hen*).
6. Guénon, *MB*, 1981, p.37.
7. Schuon, *LS*, 1999, p.17.
8. Ibn al-'Arabī, *Fusūs*, (1980, p.57).
9. Schuon, *SPHF*, 1987, p.168.
10. See Sermons 13 & 48, among others.
11. *Udāna* VIII. i.4.3.
12. See Ibn al-'Arabī, *Lubb* (1981, p.10).
13. *Enneads* 5.2.1.
14. For examples of Meister Eckhart's use of the metaphor of a "spark" see Sermons 22 and 48. The use of the symbolism of "light-fire-heat" to describe the "heart-centre" is common universally. For Meister Eckhart's use of the *bürgelīn* see Sermon 2.
15. Meister Eckhart, Sermon 2 (Colledge & McGinn, 1981, p.180).

16. Aristotle, *De anima* 430a. According to most modern interpretations Aristotle is here putting forward the idea of the mind as a "blank tablet" (*tabula rasa*) as opposed to Plato's doctrine of innate Ideas or Forms. Meister Eckhart here applies this to the Intellect or *nous*, the spiritual or mystical faculty, as distinct from the *dianoia*, the analytical and discursive "mind."

17. Meister Eckhart, *Par. Gen.* 32 (Colledge & McGinn, 1981, p.105); see Aristotle, *On the Soul* 4.4 (429b31).

18. 'The Creation of the World was a Vail cast upon the Face of God, with a figure of the Godhead wrought upon this Vail, and God *seen* through it by a dim transparency' (Peter Sterry, cited in Perry, *TTW*, 2000, p.27).

19. Meister Eckhart: 'When I go back into the ground, into the depths, into the well-spring of the Godhead, no one will ask me whence I came or whither I went' (Pfeiffer, 1924, *Vol.1*, p. 143 cited in Perry, *TTW*, 2000, p.1000). The *Sefirahh Yetsirah* asks, 'Before one, what canst thou count?' (cited here in Guénon, *SC*, 1975, p.20). Again, from the *Brihad-Aranyaka Upanishad*: 'How could the Knower be known?' (4.5.14).

20. Meister Eckhart, *Comm. Wis.* 144.

21. 'Now, both of them were naked, the man and his wife, but they felt no shame before each other' (Gen.2:25). After eating of the fruit of the tree of Knowledge the man and woman "saw that they were naked" and were ashamed (Gen.3:7). This passage has lead to a strong biblical and Qur'anic moral perspective that condemns nudity. However, as Schuon has said, this moral perspective does not represent the whole truth, the positive symbolism of *nuditas sacra* being much more profound. Schuon: 'If in the biblical and Qur'anic symbolism the sexual parts evoke shame and humiliation, it is because they remind man of blind and God-fleeing passion that is unworthy of man because it ravishes his intelligence and his will … [but] the Bible does not reproach Adam and Eve for their nakedness; it records that they looked upon it with shame, but this refers to the fall and not to nudity as such' (*EPW*, 1981, p.84).

22. The law of gravity expresses both a metaphysical and a physical truth which coincide with respect to their symbolism. Metaphysically it expresses a movement towards the Centre, to the point of greatest stability. Terrestrially this results in the gravitational "pull" towards the centre of the earth; celestially this results in the "pull" towards the Sun, the manifest symbol of Divinity. Thus something like Christ's ascension is not, as might be contested, a contradiction of the law of gravity but an example of its celestial or divine mode, whereby Christ's movement "upwards," from a terrestrial point of view, is a movement "inwards" to the Sun.

23. Schuon: 'According to Islam, clothing is a divine revelation, and this accords with the biblical story; but the Qur'an adds: "and the clothing of the fear of God is better" (*Sura of the Heights*, 26), meaning that awareness of the Divine is a better protection than clothing against deifugal concupiscence, an idea that evokes the principle of sacred nudity, of which all religions, moreover, provide at least some examples' (*EPW*, 1981, p.84, n.92).

24. Nasr, *KS*, 1981, p.21, n.61.

25. St. Cyprian from Hamman (ed.), *The Mass: Ancient Liturgies and Patristic Texts*, 1967, cited in Urban, '*Oblatio Rationabilis*: Sacrifice in East and West', *Sophia*, 2002, p.183.

26. St. Augustine, *In Ps.* XCIII, cited in Perry, *TTW*, 2000, p.638. For numerous other examples of the positive symbolism of wine and drunkenness see Perry, pp.637-640.

27. Rabbi Gikatilla, *SO*, 1994, p.30.

28. See Snodgrass, *ATE2*, 1990, pp.419-422.

29. Snodgrass, *ATE2*, 1990, p.421.

30. Matt (tr.), *Zohar*, 1983, p.65-68.

31. Rabbi Gikatilla, *SO*, 1994, p.30.

32. The concept of the "Centre" is fundamental in traditional thought. Amongst the multitude of possible references mention might be made here of the following, all especially pertinent to the subject at hand: Guénon, *MB*, 1981, Ch.3; *FS*, 1995, Chs.74-76; *LW*, 1983, Ch.7; and *SC*, 1975, passim.; Eliade, *Sacred and Profane*, 1987; Eliade, *The Myth of the Eternal Return*, 1974, pp.12-17.

33. Snodgrass, *ATE1*, 1990, p.58.

34. See Guénon, *SC*, 1975, Chs.16 & 29.

35. Snodgrass, *SS*, 1985, p.21-22.

36. Guénon warns that one should not confuse the "directions" and "dimensions" of space: 'there are six directions but only three dimensions, each of which comprises two diametrically opposed directions' (*SC*, 1975, p.14, n.1).

37. Snodgrass, *SS*, 1985, p.20.

38. Snodgrass, *SS*, 1985, p.21.

39. Boehme, *Mysterium Magnum*, 16. 6.

40. As translated in Coomaraswamy & Sister Nivedita, *Hindus and Buddhists*, 1994, p.394. *Samsarati* = "wander," in the sense of trans-migration. On "transmigration" see Coomaraswamy, 'On the One and Only Transmigrant': *SP2*, 1977.

41. 'Look, I am making the whole of creation new' (Rev.21:5).

42. Even here one notes the obvious connection between the zero and the number eight (8)—as it appears in al-Banna al-Marrakushi's form of the "Arabic" numerals—which one might say is like the zero placed against a mirror; and this is just so, for eight expresses the harmony of the Uncreated realised in the mirror of Creation.

43. See Chevalier & Gheerbrant, *DS*, 1996, pp.342-43.

44. Mathers, *KU*, 1991, p.45.

45. Chevalier & Gheerbrant, *DS*, 1996, p.342.

46. Chevalier & Gheerbrant, *DS*, 1996, p.343.

47. 2 Pt.2:5 following *The Parallel Bible* (1886). The *NJB* has 'Noah, the preacher of uprightness, along with seven others'.

48. Ibn al-'Arabī, *Fusūs* (1980, p.253).

49. See Guénon, *MB*, 1981, respectively, p.172, n.2 & p.173, citing Shankarāchārya's *Ātmā-Bodha*.

50. Lk.17:21. The *NJB* translates this as 'the kingdom of God is among you', feeling that the more traditional "within you" does not furnish as direct an answer to the Pharisee's question. This is simply an example (all too common) of the translators not being fully aware of the symbolism inherent in even the simplest words. The Greek word translated here as "within," *entos* (εντος; "*inside*") derives from the primitive root *en* (εν) denoting "a fixed position," and is related to the idea of "rest" as an intermediate between the words *eis* (εις; "*to* or *into*," indicating the "point reached") and *ek* (εκ; the "*origin*" and moreover the "point whence motion or action proceeds").

51. See *Chāndogya Upanishad* 8.1.1; see Guénon, *MB*, 1981, Ch.3; *FS*, 1995, Chs.74, 75, 76.

52. Guénon, *MB*, 1981, p.40.

53. Guénon, *FS*, 1995, p.308.

54. Aristotle, *On the Soul*, 3. 10.

55. Aristotle, *Physics*, 1.2; 184 b 16.

56. *Consolation of Philosophy* 3, poem 9, as cited in Meister Eckhart, Sermon 15 (Colledge & McGinn, 1981, p.191).

57. *Bhagavad-Gita*, 18.61.

58. Dante, *Paradiso*, 27.106.

59. Coomaraswamy, *Time and Eternity*, 1993, p.42.

60. Guénon, *MB*, 1981, p.29.

61. St. Augustine, Sermon vii, 7, cited in Perry, *TTW*, 2000, p.773.

62. *Elements of Theology*, prop.1.

63. Schuon: "'Union' (*yoga*): the Subject (*Atmā*) becomes object (the Veda, the *Dharma*) in order that the object (the objectivized subject, man) may be able to become the (absolute) Subject' (*SPHF*, 1987, p.109). On Union as "Deliverance" see Guénon, *MB*, 1981, Chs.22 & 23.

64. Guénon, *FS*, 1995, p.300.

65. "Uni-verse" from *uni* "one" - *versus* "turn," indicating the idea of existence as a cycle. Again, "verse" implies the notion of the "word," spoken or written and particularly associated with metric rhythm. This suggests the not inconsequential reading of "universe" as "one word."

66. Ramana Maharshi, *Talks With Sri Ramana Maharshi Vol.3*, 1955, p.247, cited in Perry, *TTW*, 2000, p.826.

67. Cited in Ibn al-'Arabi, *Lubb* (1981, pp.16; 42); also Perry, *TTW*, 2000, p.822.

68. On the *bindu* see Daniélou, *MGI*, 1985; in the Tibetan tradition see Govinda, *Foundations of Tibetan Mysticism*, 1969.

69. Govinda, *Foundations of Tibetan Mysticism*, 1969, p.116.

70. Daniélou, *MGI*, 1985, p.203 & p.229.

71. Daniélou, *MGI*, 1985, p.50.

72. Cited in Perry, *TTW*, 2000, p.826.

73. Pseudo-Dionysius, *Mystical Theology* 1000B-C (1987, p.13).

74. Schuon, *EPW*, 1981, p.65.
75. From 'Le Prototype unique', in *Etudes Trad.*, 1938, p.300, cited in Perry, *TTW*, 2000, p.778.
76. Guénon, *SC*, 1975, p.77; see Ch.16.
77. Guénon, *MB*, 1981, pp.41-2.
78. Meister Eckhart, *Par. Gen.*, 20. See also Albert the Great, *On Indivisible Lines* 5-6; Euclid, *Geometry*.
79. Guénon, *MB*, 1981, p.42. Each number is composed of "units" or "ones"; see Aristotle, *Metaphysics* 10.1 (1053a30); Aquinas Ia.11.1.ad1.
80. Cited in Perry, *TTW*, 2000, p.776.
81. See Guénon, *MB*, 1981, p.41, n.1; 'The Mustard Seed', *FS*, 1995, Ch.74.
82. *His-yu Chi*, see Yu, *The Journey West Vol.1*, 1980, p.180, & n.3.
83. *Chāndogya Upanishad* 3.14.3. (The inserted comments are Guénon's, *MB*, 1981, p.41).
84. Origen, *Homilies on Genesis* 13.4.
85. Guénon, *FS*, 1995, Ch.73.
86. Guénon, *FS*, 1995, p.297.
87. The *Fātihah* is the first Sūrah of the Qur'an (literally "the Opening").
88. Cited in Lings, *A Sufi Saint of the Twentieth Century*, Allen & Unwin, London, 1971, p.148. These traditions are quoted by al-Jīlī at the beginning of his commentary on them, *Al-Kahf wa 'r-Raqīm*.
89. On this symbolism of letters see Lings, *A Sufi Saint of the Twentieth Century*, 1971, Ch.7.
90. *The Pilgrim's Tale*, Second Meeting, 1999, p.75.
91. Boehme, *Signatura Rerum*, VII.14.
92. Schuon, *TUR*, 1993, p.145.
93. See Perry, *TTW*, 2000, pp.1031-1037 for numerous examples.
94. Meister Eckhart says that the "beginning"—"In the beginning is the Word"—'is preexistent in it (the Word) as a seed is in principle (*in principium*, both "beginning" and "principle")' (*Comm. Jn.* 4 – Colledge & McGinn, 1981, p.123).
95. Govinda, *Foundations of Tibetan Mysticism*, 1969, p.47.
96. See *Mandukya Upanishad* 1, 8-12.
97. *Chāndogya Upanishad* 1.1.1-3; *Brihad-Ārayaka Upanishad* 5.1.1.
98. Chevalier & Gheerbrant, *DS*, 1996, p.229.
99. Guénon, *FS*, 1995, p.107.
100. 'Inside the ark you will put the Testimony which I am about to give you' (Ex.25:16). The word translated as "Testimony," *'eduwth* (עדוח) is derived from the primitive root *'uwd* (עוד) meaning "to *duplicate*," which leads one to recall that God created man "in the image."
101. Pallis, *A Buddhist Spectrum*, 1980, p.39.
102. The ass is a potent example of the duality of symbolism. Guénon suggests that the ass may be identical with the 'scarlet Beast of the Apocalypse' (see *FS*, 1995, p.101). In the tale of Balaam the part played by the she-ass was clearly beneficent: 'Mgr Devoucoux unhesitatingly makes her the symbol of

learning and esoteric knowledge' (Chevalier & Gheerbrant, *DS*, 1996, p.51). The ass is also a vehicle of transition similar to the Ark. Christ rode a she-ass on Palm Sunday; Joseph set Mary and Jesus on a she-ass; a donkey carried the chest that was used as a cradle for Dionysus; see "ass (donkey)" in Chevalier & Gheerbrant, *DS*, 1996; also Apuleius, *Metamorphoses* 'The Golden Ass.' In the Islamic story of Satan and the ass it appears the beast is expressive of its malefic aspect in carrying aboard the Ark the seed for the destruction of the next age.

103. Per Rappoport, *AI1*, 1995, p.215-16.

104. *Midrash Tehillim*, Ps.7.

105. *Pirke de Rabbi Eliezer*, Ch.23.

106. Budge, *The Book of the Dead*, 1995, p.312, following Naville, E., Ahnas el Medineh (Heracleopolis Magna), Tylor, J. J. & Griffith, L., *The Tomb of Paheri at El Kab*, London, 1894, p.28.

107. *Bulfinch's Mythology*, 1979, p.311.

108. See Jordan, *Myths of the World*, 1993, pp.114-15.

109. References to the Dogon myth follow Snodgrass, *ATE2*, 1990, Ch.35; Snodgrass cites the works of Marcel Giaule and Germaine Dieterlen.

110. Snodgrass, *ATE2*, 1990, pp.450-51.

111. Snodgrass, *ATE2*, 1990, pp.451. Snodgrass adds that these seven seed-stars are also within the human body, so that the myth has both a macrocosmic and microcosmic reference. This helical path gives rise to what Guénon calls the "cosmogonic spheroid." See Guénon, *SC*, 1975, Chs.10-13.

112. Snodgrass, *ATE2*, 1990, pp.452.

113. Snodgrass, *ATE2*, 1990, pp.453.

114. Dawood's 1995 translation of the Holy Qur'an has: 'My son, God will bring all things to light, be they as small as a grain of mustard seed, be they hidden in a rock or in the heaven or the earth.' This translation directly compares the "mustard seed" and the "rock," while Ibn al-`Arabī's (*Fusūs*, 1980, p.237) alludes to the "seed *within* the seed," so to speak, or the "cavity in the heart." Both are equally correct and illuminating.

115. See for examples, *Zohar* I, 86b-87a; I, 231a-231b; II, 222a-222b.

116. See Bulfinch, *Bulfinch's Mythology*, 1979, p.95-6.

117. 1Pt.2:4. Christ is the "cornerstone." In this connection see Guénon, *FS*, 1995, Ch.45, who here reminds us that one must not confuse the "cornerstone" and the "foundation stone" (the "rock"), or Christ and Peter. These are connected of course by way of analogy but not by identification.

118. See Guénon, 'The Cornerstone', *FS*, 1995, Ch.45; see also Ch.47.

119. Chevalier & Gheerbrant, *DS*, 1996, pp.933-34.

120. Guénon, *FS*, 1995, p.191.

121. Guénon, *FS*, 1995, p.192.

122. See Guénon, *FS*, 1995, Chs.20, 21, 24, 25, 39 & 40; also see Chevalier & Gheerbrant, *DS*, 1996, pp.383-84. The symbol of the fish is a homologue of the Ark. Viśnu appeared as a fish (the *Matsya-avatara*) to guide the ark of Manu through the flood (see Daniélou, *MGI*, p.166-7); Christ Himself is the

Ichthus, 'the Fish that guides the Ark of the Church' (Chevalier & Gheerbrant, *DS*, 1996, p.383). Note the suggestive phonological link, in the sense of the Hindu science of *nirukta*, between the words *ketos* (κητος; "a huge *fish*"), *Kephas* (Κηφας; "*the Rock*") and *kibotos* (κιβωτος; "the sacred *ark*").

123. See *Shu Ching*, 5.4.1.

124. The following account follows Jordan, *Myths of the World*, 1993, pp.166-167.

125. Recall the location of the pillars of Hercules as in the northwest.

126. Although the correspondences here are different to those noted above the essential symbolism is the same.

127. *Shu Ching*, 5.4.1.

128. *Jerushalmi Sanhedrin*, X, 29a; *Succah*, 52b-53a, cited in Rappoport, *AI3*, 1995, pp.116-17.

129. See for examples Guénon, *LW*, 1983, Ch.9; *FS*, 1995, Chs.5, 6, 27, 45, & 46.

130. Guénon, *LW*, 1983, Ch.9; Coomaraswamy, 'Kha': *SP2*, 1977, pp.222-24.

131. Guénon, *LW*, 1983, p.53, n.13.

132. Eliade, *Patterns in Comparative Religion*, 1983, p.439. On the wealth of consistent symbolism associated with the pearl see Chevalier & Gheerbrant, *DS*, 1996, p.744; Eliade (ed.), "Pearl" in *The Encyclopedia of Religion Vol.11*, 1995.

133. *Atharva-Veda* cited in Chevalier & Gheerbrant, *DS*, 1996, p.744. Soma, the sacrifice—which is the "seed of life"—is also the moon. On soma see Daniélou, *MGI*, 1985, passim.

134. Chevalier & Gheerbrant, *DS*, 1996, p.744.

135. Guénon, *FS*, 1995, p.18.

136. Chevalier & Gheerbrant, *DS*, 1996, p.745.

137. Al-Jīlī, *al-Insān*, 1983, p.6. Burckhardt adds: '*al-jawhar al-fard*, literally: "The singular jewel," means the essence of the being; it is also the Intellect in so far as this is connected to the individual being and his eternal principle. "*Al-jawhar*" (from the Persian "*gawhar*") means a pearl or precious stone and in philosophical language the essence of the substance; the incorruptible character of the precious stone symbolises the immutability of the essence. One may remember here the Buddhist expression "jewel in the lotus" (*mani padmē*)' (p.6, n.19).

138. Chevalier & Gheerbrant, *DS*, 1996, p.744.

139. Eliade (ed.), "Pearl" in *The Encyclopedia of Religion Vol.11*, 1995, p.225.

140. Eliade (ed.), "Pearl" in *The Encyclopedia of Religion Vol.11*, 1995, p.224.

141. On *Hiranya-garbha* see Daniélou, *MGI*, 1985, pp.237-8.

142. Guénon, *MB*, 1981, p.101.

143. Guénon, *MB*, 1981, p.101, n.4.

144. Guénon, *MB*, 1981, p.101, n.3. On the symbolism of the World Egg see further Guénon, *FS*, 1995, Chs. 34 & 35.

145. Charbonneau-Lassay, *The Bestiary of Christ*, 1992, p.310.

146. Rappoport, *AI2*, 1995, p.393.

147. See Guénon, *MB*, 1981, Ch.3.

148. Guénon, *FS*, 1995, p.145.

149. *Jīvātmā*, "living soul," 'the particularised manifestation of the "Self" in (*jīva*) and consequently in the human individual' (Guénon, *MB*, 1981, p.40).

150. Guénon, *FS*, 1995, p.145.

151. Snodgrass, *ATE2*, 1990, p.420. For a thorough examination of this symbolism see Snodgrass's incisive analysis (pp.415-424). Snodgrass references A. J. Wensinck's essays, "Kibla" and "Ka'ba" in the *Encyclopaedia of Islam* (1927).

152. Snodgrass, *ATE2*, 1990, p.420.

153. Snodgrass, *ATE2*, 1990, p.422.

154. Guénon, *ED*, 1996, p.65, n.88.

155. 'Your eyes are doves behind your veil' (*Song of Songs* 4:1).

156. Mathers (tr.), *KU*, 1991, p.187.

157. *NJB*, 1994, p.1579, n.i.

158. *Mahabharata*, 1.15; *Ramayana*, 1.45.31.

159. In Mesopotamian mythology Ut-napishtim released a dove, a swallow and finally a raven.

160. For general discussions on the symbolisms involved here see Charbonneau-Lassay, *The Bestiary of Christ*, 1992, pp.229-242; also "dove" and "raven" in Chevalier & Gheerbrant, *DS*, 1996, (pp.306-307 & 789-790).

161. Cited in Charbonneau-Lassay, *The Bestiary of Christ*, 1992, p. 240.

162. St. Eucher, *Liber formuarum*, V; Dom Pitra, *in Spicilege de Solesmes*, T. II, p.80, 12, cited in Charbonneau-Lassay, *The Bestiary of Christ*, 1992, p.238.

163. See Chevalier & Gheerbrant, *DS*, 1996, pp.789-790.

164. Chevalier & Gheerbrant, *DS*, 1996, p.790.

165. Here the symbolism of "drying" is opposite to that of Hericlitus' "dry soul," for it expresses the rising of "dry lands" (the Cosmos) out of chaos.

166. *Mencius* 3.1.4.7, cited in Campbell, *Oriental Mythology*, 1973, p.389. Campbell is following Karlgren B., 'Legends and Cults in Ancient China,' *Bulletin of the Museum of Far Eastern Antiquities*, No. 18, 1946, p.303.

167. Guénon, *FS*, 1995, p.198.

168. Guénon, *FS*, 1995, p.18.

169. These general comments are drawn from Chevalier & Gheerbrant, *DS*, 1996, p.926.

170. See Chevalier & Gheerbrant, *DS*, 1996, p.352.

171. Chevalier & Gheerbrant, *DS*, 1996, p.353.

172. Milton, *Paradise Lost* Bk.1, 745.

173. *Rig Veda* 4.5.1; 5.29.4; 1.67.5; 6.8.3. On this symbolism see Snodgrass, *SS*, 1985, pp.163-176.

174. Chevalier & Gheerbrant, *DS*, 1996, p.166.

175. Nommo, in fact, takes on the form of "a Blacksmith and his Wife" (the Divine Androgyne) at the centre of the Ark, which descended to earth along a rainbow (see Snodgrass, *ATE2*, 1990, pp.453-54).

176. For the symbolisms associated with the blacksmith see Eliade, *The Forge and the Crucible*, 1976.

177. *The Dictionary of Symbols* remarks, 'In many …mythologies we find such blacksmith gods as Varuna, Tyr, Odin or Alfodr, gods with knowledge of fire and metal-founding, wizard-gods who were either lame, one-eyed, one-armed, or otherwise disabled' (1996, pp.587-88).

178. See "lameness"and "onelegged" in Chevalier & Gheerbrant, *DS*, 1996, (p.586 & 721).

179. See Campbell, *Oriental Mythology*, 1973, p.390. Campbell is following Karlgren, citing *Shih Chi*.

180. *The Dictionary of Symbols* considers Nommo as "one-legged" inso-much as his upper half is human and his lower half is in the shape of a fish, that is tapering to a single tail or "leg." This "man-fish" symbolism (cf. Christ as the *Ichthus*) is not unrelated here.

181. See Snodgrass, *SS*, 1985, pp.166-67.

182. *Genesis Rabba*, 30, cited in Rappoport, *AII*, 1995, pp.213-14.

183. Maier, *Symbola aueae mensae* (1817) in Klossowski de Rola, *The Golden Game: Alchemical Engravings of the Seventeenth Century*, 1997, p.113.

184. On the "draught of immortality" see Guénon, *FS*, 1995, Ch.55.

185. The Moon is the vessel of *soma*. The Moon's light is the colour of milk which again expresses the idea of the essential drink of life. A Gallo-Roman dedicatory inscription in Autun, France, identifies the 'chalice from which flows grace' with the 'breast from which flows the milk which nourishes the city' (Devoucoux, cited in Chevalier & Gheerbrant, *DS*, 1996, p.178). This further alludes to the relationship between the "cup" and the "city."

186. Guénon, *FS*, 1995, pp.225-26.

187. Daniélou, *MGI*, 1985, p.16.

188. Guénon, *FS*, 1995, p.226.

189. Daniélou, *MGI*, 1985, p.304.

190. Daniélou, *MGI*, 1985, p.305.

191. The *Zohar* considers *manna* as a product of divine emanation; see Matt (tr.), *Zohar The Book of Enlightenment*, 1983, p.246.

192. Schaya, *UMK*, 1971, p.94.

193. Andersen (tr.), *2 (Slavonic Apocalypse of) Enoch*, Appendix: *2 Enoch in Merilo Pravednoe*: Charlesworth (ed.), *OTP1*, 1983.

194. Rappoport, *AII*, 1995, p.32.

195. Eliade, *The Myth of the Eternal Return*, 1974 , p.15.

196. Guénon is right to distinguish between the symbolism of the "black stone" and the "foundation stone" (*FS*, 1995, Ch.50), insofar as the first is celestial and the latter terrestrial. He does, however, continue to recognise that there is one case in which there is a certain connection between the "black stone" and the "cubic stone": 'this is where the cubic stone is not one of the "foundation stones" placed at the four angles of a building, but rather the *shethiyah* stone at the very centre of its base, corresponding to the point of impact of the fallen "black stone," just as, on the same vertical axis but at its opposite

extremity, the "corner stone" or "summit stone" … corresponds to the initial and final "celestial" position of the same "black stone'" (p.212).

197. *Zohar* I, 231a-231b; II, 222a-222b.

198. Tishby, *WZ2*, 1991, p.571, n.76.

199. As a generalisation one can say that in the "West" this will usually be a vertical line, placing the emphasis on Transcendence, while in the "East," this will usually be a horizontal line, emphasising Immanence.

200. Jean-Paul Roux, *Faune et Flore sacrées dans les sociétés altaiques*, Paris, 1966 cited in Chevalier & Gheerbrant, *DS*, 1996, p.934.

201. Jordan, *Myths of the World*, 1993, pp.115. The fig tree shares in the symbolism of the olive-tree and the vine. For an account of the symbolism of the fig tree see "fig-tree" in Chevalier & Gheerbrant, *DS*, 1996, p.376.

202. See Budge, *The Book of the Dead*, 1995; Spence, *Egypt Myths and Legends*, 1994; Jordan, *The Encyclopedia of Gods*, 1994.

203. On the wooden or stone phallus see Eliade, *Patterns in Comparative Religion*, 1958, p.VI., § 76, 77.

204. See the engraving of Lugdani Batavorum (1593) in Spence, *The Encyclopedia of the Occult*, 1988, facing p.340.

205. *Zohar* I, 16a.

206. *Zohar* I, 231a-231b; *Chagigah* 12a; cf. Ex.17:6.

207. *Chagigah* 12a.

208. Green is both the colour of birth, new growth, and the colour of death, putrescence, death being but a change of state from potentiality into actuality. On the symbolism associated with the colour green see Chevalier & Gheerbrant, *DS*, 1996, p.451. Of course green is the colour of the emerald.

209. Qur'an 15:27.

210. Guénon, *RQ*, 1995, p.39.

211. Guénon, *RQ*, 1995, p.38.

212. 'The divine sun shines much more brightly than all the suns in the firmament ever shone' (Johannes Tauler, cited in Perry, *TTW*, 2000, p.834).

213. Nicholas of Cusa, *De Docta Ignorantia*, (tr.) Fr. Germain Heron, 1954, cited in Perry, *TTW*, 2000, p.834.

214. *Pirke de Rabbi Eliezer*, Ch.23; cf. Jos.10:12-13, Hab.3:11-12.

215. *Katha Upanishad*, 5.15; *Mundaka Upanishad* 2.2.10; *Svetasvatara Upanishad* 6.14.

216. *Bhagavad-Gita* 15.6.

217. Saraha, from Perry, *TTW*, 2000, p.833.

218. Cited in Burckhardt, *MI*, 1987, p.108. Burckhardt's essay, 'The Heavenly Jerusalem and the Paradise of Viakuntha', offers a compelling comparison.

219. On the essential symbolism of the *Ming T'ang* see Guénon, *GT*, 1994, Ch.16; for a detailed consideration of its architectural symbolism see Snodgrass, *ATE1*, 1990, Ch.30.

220. Guénon, *GT*, 1994, p.114, n.17. On this last point Guénon refers the reader to *The Reign of Quantity & The Signs of the Times*, 1972, Ch.3.

221. Nasr, *KS*, 1981, p.36.
222. Chevalier & Gheerbrant, *DS*, 1996, p.939.
223. Chevalier & Gheerbrant, *DS*, 1996, p.742.
224. In his *Mathnawī* Rumi writes: 'Say the body is like this lamp ... it's always burning ... up, trying to die. But where is the sun in this comparison? It rises, and the lamp's light mixes with the day. Oneness, which is the reality, cannot be understood with lamp and sun images. The blurring of a plural into a unity is wrong.' This translation follows Barks, *The Essential Rumi*, 1995, p.177, who cites Nicholson's ed.1925-1940 (IV, 419-33).
225. Fohr, *Adam and Eve*, 1986, p.42.
226. Fohr, *Adam and Eve*, 1986, p.42.
227. Fohr, *Adam and Eve*, 1986, p.42, n.8.
228. De Voragine, *The Golden Legend, Vol.1*, 'The History of Noah', 83, 1900.
229. Cited in Chevalier & Gheerbrant, *DS*, 1996, p.267.
230. Servier, J., *L'homme et l'invisible*, Paris, 1964, pp.102-3, cited in Chevalier & Gheerbrant, *DS*, 1996, p.267. One might add the symbolism of crystal ships and, for that matter, the crystal slipper of Cinderella, which reveals her "true" nature.
231. Cited in Chevalier & Gheerbrant, *DS*, 1996, p.267.
232. Lord Northbourne, *Looking Back on Progress*, 1970, p.14.
233. Cited in Chevalier & Gheerbrant, *DS*, 1996, p.173.
234. *Book of Propositions or Rules of Theology, said to be by the Philosopher Termegistus*, prop.2.
235. *Della causa, principio ed uno*, V.
236. Guénon, *SC*, 1975, p.129-30.
237. Snodgrass, *SS*, 1985, p.22.
238. Eliade, *Sacred and Profane*, 1987, p.36; *The Myth of the Eternal Return*, 1974, p.15.
239. See Eliade, *Sacred and Profane*, 1987, pp.37-47.
240. Schuon, *LAW*, 1965, p.7.
241. Lord Northbourne, *Looking Back on Progress*, 1970, p.14.
242. Discussing the biblical myth of Cain (sedentary) and Abel (nomadic) Guénon demonstrates the inter-relationship between time and space; see Guénon, *RQ*, 1995, Ch.21.
243. Guénon, *RQ*, 1995, p.180. Guénon cites the works of Faber d'Olivet on this cosmological interpretation.
244. Guénon, *RQ*, 1995, p.180. This is obvious in so much as the complementary duality of compression and expansion is the principle of cosmic Existence, of which Space and Time are the expressive aspects.
245. Guénon, *RQ*, 1995, p.180.
246. Guénon, *RQ*, 1995, p.181.
247. Vijayananda Tripathi, "Devata tattva," *Sanmarga*, III, 1942, cited in Daniélou, *MGI*, 1985, p.203.
248. Guénon, *RQ*, 1995, p.180.

249. Govinda, *Foundations of Tibetan Mysticism*, 1969, p.137.

250. Govinda, *Foundations of Tibetan Mysticism*, 1969, p.137.

251. *Risālat al-jāmi'ah*, II, 24 (Damascus, 1949), cited in Nasr, *ICD*, 1978, p.64.

252. *Rasā'il*, II, 9-10 (Cairo, 1928), cited in Nasr, *ICD*, 1978, p.64.

253. Guénon, *RQ*, 1995, p.46. See Ch.4.

254. Snodgrass, *ATE1*, 1990, p.63.

255. Snodgrass, *ATE1*, 1990, p.64.

256. Aristotle, *Physics* 218A & 8.8, 263B, cited in Snodgrass, *ATE1*, 1990, p.65.

257. Snodgrass, *ATE1*, 1990, p.65.

258. Snodgrass, *ATE1*, 1990, p.68.

259. Snodgrass, *ATE1*, 1990, p.74.

260. Snodgrass, *ATE1*, 1990, p.74.

261. Snodgrass cites numerous examples of this idea from the Greek, Christian, Islamic and Buddhist traditions, see Snodgrass, *ATE1*, 1990, Ch.8 particularly 'Eternity as the Punctual Now.'

262. *Enneads* 3.7.4.

263. Chevalier & Gheerbrant, *DS*, 1996, p.42.

264. Becker, *The Element Encyclopedia of Symbols*, 1994, p.297.

265. See Budge, *The Book of the Dead*, 1995, p.55. Budge also observes how Philae, as resting place of Osiris, was overshadowed by a tamarisk tree (*Legends of the Gods*, 1994, p.231). Similarly, according to the Hebrew Scriptures, the bones of Saul and his sons were buried beneath a tamarisk tree in Jabesh (I Sam. 33:13).

266. Unger, *Unger's Bible Dictionary*, 1965, p.1139.

267. Guénon, *FS*, 1995, p.198

268. Guénon, *FS*, 1995, p.122.

269. Snodgrass, *ATE2*, 1990, p.421.

270. Guénon, *LW*, 1983, p.26.

The Duad: *Two by Two*

Introduction

Cosmological existence is marked by duality, inasmuch as "order" (*cosmos*; κοσμος) requires at least two points: a point of reference and an "other." This duality is prefigured *in divinis* by the principial ontological complementarity: Essence and Substance. The biblical symbolism of entering the Ark of Noah by "pairs" expresses the retraction of duality to the unitary principle (the monad). These are precisely "pairs" or complementaries: masculine and feminine. Cosmological existence returns to the unitary Ark via the *coincidentia oppositorum* ("coincidence of opposites"). Likewise cosmological existence emerges from the Ark via the *coincidentia oppositorum*. In the symbolism of the deluge this "emanation" is generally symbolised by the Ark coming to rest on a "twin-peaked" mountain, which, in turn, is an *imago mundi*. The symbolism of the *coincidentia oppositorum* is found with the Ark of the Covenant in the form of the two *cherubim* that flank the mercy-seat, upon which rests the *Shekhinah*. This chapter considers the relationship of the ontological principles and the soteriological role of the *coincidentia oppositorum* in its guise as the "Sundoor."

Knowing God through the *Coincidentia Oppositorum*

God is known to God alone.

Nicolas of Cusa[1]

Between the Divine and the Human, between the Absolute and the Relative, between Principle and Manifestation, there is discontinuity and continuity. Discontinuity, for there can be no common measure between God and man. Continuity, for nothing can be other than God.[2] At the meeting of such two states lies an interface, an isthmus between the Upper and the Lower Waters, or what Islamic esotericism calls *al-barzakh*. This isthmus is the same with Nicholas of Cusa's famous *coincidentia oppositorum* ("coincidence of opposites").

In the introduction to his 1997 translation of Cusa's *De visione Dei*, Hugh Bond makes the following distinction between types of coincidence:

> First of all, we may separate *coincidence of opposites* from *coincidence of things that are not opposing*. Examples of the former would include the coincidence of rest and motion, past and future, diversity and identity, inequality and equality, and divisibility and simplicity. However, God and human beings, though

131

distinct, cannot be said to be opposites, for God has no opposite. Second, we may speak of *coincidence in theory*, such as the coincidence of all polygons in the triangle, and *coincidence in fact or being*, such as the coincidence of the divine and the human natures in Christ. Third, we may speak of *coincidence as derived* and *coincidence as given and formative*, from which other coincidence can be construed. An example of the former, the *complicatio-explicatio* couplet, describing the work of the divine in nature, is derived from an example of the latter, the creative activity of the Trinity, of the three persons of the Godhead acting in coincidence. ... Finally, we may distinguish between *coincidence in epistemology*, as a way of viewing problems, and *coincidence in mythology*, as a way of solving them.[3]

Of these last two, Bond remarks that Cusa's famous "learned ignorance" (*De docta ignorantia 1440*) is an example of both. "Learned ignorance" is one of the most famous examples of *coincidentia oppositorum*; it is through this that one "knows" God by "unknowing."

Cusa describes the *coincidentia oppositorum* using the metaphor of "the wall of paradise":

> Therefore, I thank you, my God, because you make clear to me that there is no other way of approaching you except that which to all humans, even to the most learned philosophers, seems wholly inaccessible and impossible. For you have shown me that you cannot be seen elsewhere than where impossibility confronts and obstructs me. O Lord, you, who are the food of the mature, have given me courage to do violence to myself, for impossibility coincides with necessity, and I have discovered that the place where you are found unveiled is girded about with the coincidence of contradictories. This is the wall of paradise, and it is there in paradise that you reside. ... Thus, it is on the other side of the coincidence of contradictories that you will be able to be seen and nowhere on this side.[4]

The image of a wall has biblical precedent, for this is none other than the "diamond wall"[5] of the celestial Jerusalem (Rev.21:17). Again, and from another perspective, this wall is personified, so to speak, by the "guardians of paradise": the 'great winged creatures and the fiery flashing sword' that guard Eden (Gen.3:24). This is to recognise that the celestial Jerusalem is none other than the terrestrial Paradise or Eden, which is principally shown by the identification of the 'river of life, rising from the throne of God' (Rev.22:1) with the 'river that flowed from Eden'

(Gen.2:10).[6] Now, according to Judaic tradition, it is the angel Uriel who stands at the gate of Eden with the "fiery sword." The *Zohar* says that Uriel is the key-holder to the three hundred and sixty-five lights that came from 'the light that emerges from the supernal, innermost secluded and concealed *hashmal*'.[7] These "three hundred and sixty-five lights" are associated with the light of the solar year, as are the twelve fruit or "Suns" of the biblical Tree of Life (Rev.22:2), as Guénon points out.[8] This is not to imply that this symbolism is simply astrological; indeed the solar year is much more than simply astrological but itself expresses the Divine Cycle: the cycle of creation from God and return to God. As it is, the return to Eden through the "wall of the guardians" expresses a complete cosmic cycle.

The *hashmal* is both the fiery creatures of Ezekiel's vision (Ezk.1:4-5) and the unified mystery that they symbolise.[9] This is the mystery of the river that flowed out of Eden (*Yobel*), which divided to make four streams, for likewise the light of *hashmal* 'radiates its beams of light to the four corners'.[10] According to *sefirotic* symbolism, the *hashmal* is represented by *Tiferet*, the "centre" or "heart" of the lower seven cosmological *sefirot*. *Tiferet* is personified by Jacob, who, as we have seen, is the "river of praise" that flowed out of Eden. This correspondence confirms again the identification of the *hashmal* with the river *Yobel*. The "fiery creatures" of Ezekiel's vision moreover prefigure the *Tetramorphs*, which surround the "Throne" in St. John's vision (Rev.4:6-8), recalling that the throne is a homologue of the city.

The *New Jerusalem Bible* translates the Hebrew term *k͏ᵉrūwb*, (כרוב) as "winged creatures." *The Parallel Bible* (1886) translates this by the more traditional term, *cherubim*.[11] Just as *cherubim* guard Eden so they guard the mystery of the Ark of the Covenant. *Exodus* 25:17-22:

> You will also make a mercy-seat of pure gold two and a half cubits long and one and a half cubits wide, and you will model two great winged creatures (*cherubim*) of beaten gold, you will make them at the two ends of the mercy-seat. Model one of the winged creatures at one end and the other winged creature (*cherub*) at the other end; you will model the winged creatures of a piece with the mercy-seat at either end. The winged creatures must have their wings spread upwards, protecting the mercy-seat with their wings and facing each other, their faces being towards the mercy-seat. You will put the mercy-seat on the top of the ark, and inside the ark you will put the Testimony which I am about to give you. There I shall come to meet you; from above the mercy-seat, from between the two winged creatures

which are on the ark of the Testimony, I shall give you all my orders for the Israelites.

Interestingly, the word translated as "wings," *kānāph* (כנף), means "an *extremity*" and is used to refer to the four quarters of the earth and also the pinnacle of a building.[12] The four wings of the two *cherubim* can be seen as analogous to the four "streams" and the "four corners" that are revealed by the light of *hashmal*. The four corners of the earth, which is to say the manifold universe, are brought to meet with God through the two *cherubim*, where these two express the passage of duality and *oppositio* back to the unity of the mercy-seat, for the *cherubim* are 'modelled of a piece with the mercy-seat' (Ex.25:19). Thus Pseudo-Dionysius says that the *cherubim* 'are found immediately around God and in a proximity enjoyed by no other. ... No other is more like the divine or receives more directly the first enlightenment from the deity.'[13] He also says that the name "cherubim" means "fullness of knowledge" or "outpouring of wisdom" and signifies 'the power to know and to see God'.[14] Just so Cusa says that it is only through the "wall of paradise," the *coincidentia oppositorum*, that God can be seen.

Learned ignorance is the knowledge of God that comes with "identification." This knowledge is so utterly without objectification as to imply absence of knowing. This notion is explicit in Hindu tradition: '*Brahman* is known to him to whom It is unknown, while It is unknown to him to whom It is known. It is unknown to those who know and known to those who do not know'.[15] Again: 'Although he does not know, nevertheless he knows; he does not know but there is no loss on the knower's part, since he is indestructible; it is just that there is no second thing other than and distinct from himself that he might know.'[16] For Erigena this is the "ignorance that surpasses all knowledge": 'God does not know what He himself is, because He is not any what; this ignorance surpasses all knowledge'.[17] St. Gregory Palamas is quick to stress that this is not simply a pure negation: 'God is not only beyond knowledge, but also beyond unknowing'.[18]

Cusa talks of the "courage to do violence to myself"—'O Lord, you, who are the food of the mature, have given me courage to do violence to myself, for impossibility coincides with necessity'. This "violence" inflicted upon "my-self" refers to the sacrifice of the individual ego-self: the self of the "I" rather than the true and only Self, the Hindu *Ātman*. As Swami Ramdas says, 'This "I" is an illusion which must be eliminated from our life and thought.'[19] This is only achieved when there is identification. In the words of the *Yoga Darshana*: 'When alone the object of contemplation remains and one's own form is annihilated, this is known as "identification."'[20] Thus Shiva Samhitā says, 'The word "I" does not exist for him who always sees the Self.'[21] As Coomaraswamy remarks, 'To sacrifice our self is to liberate the God within us.'[22] This paradox—this "impossibility"—is the "necessary" condition of the return to God. For this one must have the "courage" to face one's own death. In the words of the famous *hadīth qudsī*: 'Die before you die.' Then it will be death that is conquered, as we are told in St. Paul's first letter to the Corinthians: 'The last enemy that shall be destroyed is death.' (1Co.15:26) 'O, death, I am to thee a death,' proclaims Jacob Boehme.[23] This is a paradox readily found in the Gospels: 'Anyone who tries to preserve his life will lose it; and anyone who loses it will keep it safe' (Lk.17:33; Mt.10:39; Jn.12: 25). In "losing" the life of the ego-self one is born anew so that it is no longer the "I" that knows by distinction but the Self that knows by identification. As St. Paul proclaims, 'I live, yet not I, but Christ in me' (Ga.2:20). Likewise Muhammad is able to say, 'Who hath seen Me, the same hath seen the Truth.'[24] And so St. Augustine, 'Let me know myself, Lord, and I shall know Thee.'[25] In the final analysis to know God is to be God. Meister Eckhart: 'In the case of God, being and knowing are identical.'[26]

This sense of "violence" is also portrayed by Meister Eckhart's image of "breaking through" (*durchbrechen*), which he uses to describe the second stage of the *reditus* or return to God. The *durchbrechen*, remarks Bernard McGinn, is the 'penetration of the soul into the divine ground that is the God beyond God.'[27] As Meister Eckhart says, 'in this breaking-through (*durchbrechen*) I perceive that God and I are one. Then I am what I was, and I neither diminish nor increase, for I am then an immovable cause that moves all things.'[28] This last point recognises that the result of the "breaking though" is the return to the "unmoved mover," which is the "first principle," Meister Eckhart's *unum*, Absolute Unity.

The *coincidentia oppositorum* is the point of resolution of contraries, of dissolution of duality into Unity, the return of Manifestation to the Principle. In the words of Shabistarī: 'Unity will not embrace plurality / For the point of Unity has one root only.'[29] As Sahl al-Tustarī, says, 'One knows God by the union of the contraries which relate to Him.'[30] Again, Ibn al-'Arabī observes, 'Kharrāz … declared that God is not known save by His uniting all opposites in the attribution of them to Him.'[31] In the resolution of contraries one knows God as essential Unity.[32] The distinction of subject and object disappears; knower, known and the act of knowing are indistinct.[33] They are, in the words of Meister Eckhart, "fused but not confused."

To stress an earlier point: knowledge of the Divine comes through identification. 'If you do not make yourself equal to God, you cannot apprehend God; for like is known by like.'[34] So says Hermes Trismegistus. In the *Theologia Germanica* we read: 'God can be known only by God';[35] or, in the words of Nicolas of Cusa, cited above, 'God alone knows Himself.' In the Hindu tradition there are again many such statements: '*Brahman* knows *Brahman*, and is established in Its own Self.'[36] 'Anyone who knows that supreme *Brahman* becomes *Brahman* indeed.'[37] 'Being but *Brahman*, he is absorbed in *Brahman*.'[38] This is a universal maxim which Alighieri Dante describes with typical eloquence: 'O Light Eternal who only in thyself abidest, only thyself dost understand, and self understood, self-understanding, turnest love on and smilest at thyself!'[39] In the end, as Ibn al-'Arabī says, it is not a question of "becoming one" with God or the Godhead, rather becoming conscious of the Divine Unity which is.[40]

The Essential Complementarity

The Being of all beings is but one only Being, but in its generation it separates itself into two principles.

Jacob Boehme[41]

God is both One and All does not mean that the One is two, but that the two are One.

Hermes Trismegistus[42]

'The Tao' it is said, 'produced one; one produced two.'[43] The extension or realisation of the Cosmic Seed (the monad) produces a polarity (the duad); the diremption of the principial ontological singularity produces the complementary ontological principles: Essence and Substance.[44] In his exegesis of the opening chapter of *Genesis*, Meister Eckhart says, '"In the principle God created heaven and earth," that is, two principles of everything that exists, the active and the passive. "Heaven" is the active, the first "unchangeable thing that changes others";[45] "earth" is the passive inasmuch as it is especially material.'[46] Meister Eckhart equates the first "principle" with the Christian *Logos* and the Greek *Idea*.[47] This is Being. 'It is true' says Guénon, 'that Being is beyond all distinction, since the first distinction is that of "essence" and "substance" or of *Purusha* and *Prakriti*; nevertheless *Brahmā*, as *Īśvara* or Universal Being, is described as *savishesha*, that is to say as "implying distinction," since He is the immediate determining principle of distinction'.[48] This diremption gives rise to an axial symbolism (*Axis Mundi*).

The essential ontological complementarity: Essence and Substance. In the Vedantic tradition these terms most readily correspond to *Purusha* and *Prakriti*, however, these principles can be recognised, at the respective levels, as both *Ātman* (the Divine Self) and *Māyā* (the "Great

Theophany") and as *nāma* (name) and *rūpa* (form). Furthermore, this complementarity is identifiable, *mutatis mundis*, with Being and becoming; Platonic *nous* (Intellect) and *psyche* (soul); Aristotelian *eidos* (*forma*) and *hyle* (*materia*) and, again, Aristotelian Act and Potency; Heaven (*T'ien*) and Earth (*Ti*) of the Chinese Great Triad; *yang* and *yin* of Taoism;[49] Sulphur and Quicksilver of Hermetic Alchemy; Christian Spirit and Soul; *Keter* and *Malkhut*, and, again, *Hokhmah* and *Binah* of Kabbalah; etc. Guénon recognises this complementarity in terms of "Quality" and "Quantity,"[50] while Whitall Perry discuss this in terms of "Subject" and "Object."[51]

Symbolically, Essence and Substance are respectively the active and passive principles: male and female; communicative and receptive; positive and negative; right and left; light and dark; above and below. Fohr recognises this symbolism in the colours of the raven and the dove, which Noah released from the Ark. 'Much has been made of the personality and habits of these birds,' says Fohr, 'but as far as their spiritual symbolism is concerned the only thing that matters is their colours— black and white. Here again we have the symbolism of the Spiritual Ray—white—and the undifferentiated or prime matter—black.'[52] Moreover, the "Spiritual Ray" (the *Fiat Lux*) is the Word, and this reveals further associations of symbolisms. The Hebrew term for "dove," *yōwnāh* (יונה) is the same as the name *Yōnāh* or Jonah. The connection between the symbolism of "Jonah in the whale" and "Noah in the Ark" is immediate.[53] J. R. Skinner remarks on this while also noting the name *Yōnāh* as the same as the name "John."[54] Both Skinner and Guénon regard the symbolism of the name "John" as relevant to both John the Baptist and St. John the Evangelist, who must both be thought of as "bringing forth" the Word.[55] According to the practice of *Gematria* the value of this name is seventy-one, a variation on the number seventy-two,[56] recalling the association of this number with the Word via the "Seventy-Two Names" of Metatron.[57]

According to Jewish tradition the dove is a symbol of the *Shekhinah*.[58] In Christian tradition the dove is associated principally with the Holy Spirit following the account of Jesus' baptism: 'and the Holy Spirit descended on him in a physical form, like a dove' (Lk.3:22; Mk.1:10; Jn.1:32). Again, St. Matthew says: 'And when Jesus had been baptised he at once came up from the water, and suddenly the heavens opened and he saw the Spirit of God descending like a dove and coming down on him' (Matt.3:16). This passage is likened by Christian tradition to the Spirit (*Ruah*) that hovered over the Waters in the story of *Genesis*, with the Spirit now anointing Christ as the "new Creation." In fact the word variously translated as "moved" or "rested" in the second verse of

Genesis—'and the Spirit *moved* over the Waters'—is a primitive root, *rāchaph* (רחף), meaning "to *brood*," as a bird brooding over its eggs. This suggests the Hindu tradition of *Brahmā* riding on the swan *Hamsa*, brooding over the "Golden Embryo," *Hiranyagarbha.*

Raven, *'ōrēb* (ערב; "a *raven*" from its *dusky* hue): this word derives from the primitive root *'ārab* (ערב; "a *covering*," as in dusk) hence the covering of "night," which is a cognomen of Substance. Moreover, the raven is a red-black colour recalling our earlier observations on this symbolism. Here another symbolism arises, for, according to the *Epic of Gilgamesh* there were three birds released from the Ark: a dove, a swallow and a raven. Fohr suggests that the brown-orange colour of the common swallow is close enough to red, so that here also is the symbolism of the colours black, red and white. Fohr interprets these colours with respect to the three colours of the Hindu *gunas*: *sattva* (white); *rajas* (red); and *tamas* (black).[59] This is a matter of symbolic valency and stress. As Fohr remarks, 'In the biblical version stress is being put on the idea that creation proceeds from the action of *Purusha* on *Prakriti*. In the version from the *Epic of Gilgamesh* stress is being put on the idea that the world is made up of the three gunas.'[60]

The degree of the complementary qualities must be distinguished according to the perspective from which these principles are viewed. Thus Guénon, discussing the Chinese tradition, observes,

> Within the Universal, and viewed from the side of their common principle, Heaven is "active perfection" (*Ch'ien*) and Earth is 'passive perfection' (*K'un*). Neither of these is Perfection in the absolute sense: a distinction already exists, and a distinction inevitably implies a limitation. Viewed from the side of manifestation, they are merely Essence and Substance, which necessarily posses a lesser degree of universality because they are observed in correlation with each other, Heaven is always an active principle and Earth always a passive principle.[61]

Whitall Perry recognises three principal categories of polarities: (1) *reciprocal or complementary*, hence *neutral*, e.g. right / left; (2) *opposite but symmetrical*, e.g. night / day; (3) *contradictory and dissymmetrical*, e.g. real / unreal.[62] The distinction between Absolute and Relative, inasmuch as it be granted, is of this last kind. In this sense there cannot really be said to be any "meeting" of these two terms. However, insomuch as the Absolute is the principle of Being—without being limited to this designation—and the Relative is Manifestation, then they may be said to be a polarity or complementarity of the second category: opposite but symmetrical. They are, in this sense, "cause" and "effect."

Essence and Substance are "almost synonymous in practice"; still we can talk provisionally of "Pure Essence" and "Pure Substance" in respect to their being metaphysical realities. Both Essence and Substance exist only in terms of their essential complementarity or biunity. As Guénon says, 'complementarism is essentially a correlation between two terms.'[63] Essence and Substance constitute the poles of existence: the ontological poles of the *Axis Mundi*. It is through the union of Essence and Substance that cosmological existence is brought into being. Neither Essence nor Substance can be said to "exist" independently of the other, by virtue of the fact that cosmological existence is by its very nature the actualisation or effect of this union. This "union" can be seen in the entwined lovemaking of *Purusha* and *Prakriti*, and in the sexual intercourse of Moses and the *Shekhinah*.[64] The perfection of this "celestial union" is again witnessed in the marriage of the King and Queen in the Chemical Wedding of Alchemical tradition.[65]

All dualities are complementarities expressing the vicissitudes of a multivalent singularity. Hot and cold, dry and wet, light and dark, good and evil: these are the asymptotic poles between which a creatural being measures its state of temperature, moistness, visibility, and morality respectively.[66] On their particular plane of activity, and from the perspective of the Relative, each complementarity reflects the principial distinction of Absolute and Relative. God is One but creation is born from duality. 'Once and for all God has spoken two things' (Ps.61:12). 'I have spoken once, I shall not speak again; I have spoken twice, I have nothing more to say' (Job 40:5). 'Everything that falls away from the One, the First of all things,' says Meister Eckhart, 'immediately falls into two and into the other numbers by means of duality.'[67]

According to Boehme: 'one separates into two'; but it must not be thought that this implies the extinction of the one with the concurrent creation of the two. In reality this "separation," as such, is an internal recognition of the virtuality inherent in the eternal monad. From a certain perspective the first distinction is that of Absolute and Relative. However, this distinction exists only when viewed from "below" and then only as the illusion of duality. As this is a distinction, remarks Schuon, it is necessarily prefigured *in divinis* by the differentiation between the 'Absolute as such and the Absolute relativised in view of a dimension of its Infinitude'.[68] Moreover, this distinction is "illusory" precisely because this difference 'is real only from the standpoint of Relativity.'[69] In the ultimate reality the Absolute is "One without a second."[70] Thus according to the *Hermetica*, 'the plenitude of all things *is* one and *is in* one, not because the one duplicates itself but because both are one.'[71]

What then is the nature of the distinction between the monad and the duad? In the introduction to his translations of the *Sefirah Dtzenioutha* and *Ha Idra Rabba Qadisha*, Mathers approaches this problem by first considering the integrity of the monad:

> We now come to the consideration of the first *Sephira*, or the Number One, the Monad of Pythagoras. In this number are the nine other hidden. It is indivisible; it is also incapable of multiplication; divide 1 by itself and it still remains 1, multiply 1 by itself and it is still 1 and unchanged. Thus it is the fitting representative of the great unchangeable father of all. Now this number of unity has a twofold nature, and thus forms, as it were, the link between the negative and the positive. In its unchangeable one-ness it is scarcely a number; but in its property of capability of addition it may be called the first number of a numerical series. Now, the zero, 0, is incapable even of addition, just as also is negative existence.

Mathers then explains the origin of the duad, offering the concepts of "reflection" and "definition":

> How, then, if 1 can neither be multiplied nor divided, is another 1 to be obtained to add to it; in other words, how is the number 2 to be found? By reflection of itself. For though 0 be incapable of definition, 1 is definable. And the effect of a definition is to form an *Eidolon*, duplicate, or image, of the thing defined.[72] Thus, then, we obtain a duad composed of 1 and its reflection. Now also we have the commencement of a vibration established, for the number 1 vibrates alternatively from changelessness to definition, and back to changelessness again. Thus, then, is it the father of all numbers, and a fitting type of the Father of all things.[73]

The Divine Androgyne

The One which is called Unity is both male and female.

> Macrobius[74]

"You say, then, Trismegistus, that God is both sexes?"

> Hermes Trismegistus[75]

He divided his body into halves, one was male and the other female. The male in that female procreates the universe.

> *Manu Smrti* 1.32

When considering the creative process it is entirely appropriate that a sexual symbolism come into play. The distinction between the Absolute and the Infinite, inasmuch as it might be granted, expresses the two fundamental aspects of the Real, that of essentiality and that of possibility; this, as Schuon remarks, 'is the highest principial prefiguration of the masculine and feminine poles.'[76] Schuon does not say that these are the principial masculine and feminine poles; rather, this is precisely a "prefiguration." With respect to the Absolute, it is inappropriate, if occasionally symbolically profitable, to assign gender.[77] Thus Guénon remarks that '*Wu Chi* corresponds to the neuter, supreme *Brahman* of Hindu tradition (*Para-Brahman*)'.[78] Again, according to the symbolism of the *Sefirotic* Tree, *Keter*, the "Crown," presupposes *Keter Elyon*, the "Supreme Crown," which like *Wu Chi* and *Para-Brahman* must be considered as neuter. It is only with *T'ai Chi* or, in the Hindu tradition, *Īśvara* (*apara-Brahman*) that we can talk of gender. Nevertheless, the prefiguration of the masculine and feminine poles in the distinction between Absolute and Infinite gives rise, at the ontological level, to Being as the Divine Androgyne, neither masculine nor feminine yet "implying the distinction" (*savishesha*) of the principial ontological complementary, Essence and Substance, *Purusha* and *Prakriti*, masculine and feminine. This distinction is also found in the distinction between the Upper and Lower Waters, with the *Ethiopic Book of Enoch* saying that, 'That which is from the heavens above (the Upper Waters) is masculine water, that which is underneath the earth (the Lower Waters) is feminine.'[79]

Being contains both the masculine and feminine principles in princial non-distinction, *in divinis*. This is Being envisaged as the Divine Androgyne.[80] *Purusha* and *Prakriti* are coeval as *Īśvara*. Śiva appears united in a single body with Śakti, his spouse–he the right and she the left—in the manifestation known as Ardhanārīśvara, the Half-Woman Lord." *Keter* comprises Father (*Hokhmah*; wisdom) and Mother (*Binah*; intelligence). This is again King and Queen. In Buddhist tradition the Bodhisattva Avalokiteśvara (male) manifests as the feminine Kwan Yin. The Great Original of Chinese chronicles, the holy woman T'ai Yuan, combines in her person the masculine *yang* and the feminine *yin*.[81] According to the Greeks, Eros, who Plato says is the first of the gods, is both male and female.[82] *Genesis* tells us that 'God created man in his own image, in the image of God he created him; male and female he created them' (Gen.1:27). The Midrash explains this: 'When the Holy One, Blessed be He, created the first man, He created him androgynous.'[83] The *Zohar* adds, '"He blessed him and called his name Adam." A human being is only called Adam when male and female are as one.'[84]

To talk of the Principle as the Divine Androgyne is to talk of Adam as *Adam Kadmon*; in the language of Islam this is *al-insān al-kamīl* ("Universal Man").[85] This is again the "King" (*Wang*) of Taoist tradition, and *Ādibuddha* in Tibetan Buddhism.[86] With respect to the Judaic tradition, Leo Schaya remarks, 'Transcendent man, *adam ilaah*—also called *adam kadmon* ("principial man")—is God in his essence and his ontological emanation'.[87] Gershom Scholem calls *Adam Kadmon* "primordial man" stressing that the Divine Being Himself cannot be expressed. All that can be expressed are His "symbols," the *Sefirot*.[88] Elsewhere Scholem explains the Lurianic doctrine: '*Adam Kadmon* is nothing but a first configuration of the divine light which flows from the essence of *En-Sof* into the primeval space of the *Tsimtsum*—not indeed from all sides but, like a beam [the Divine Ray], in one direction only. He is therefore the highest form in which the divinity begins to manifest itself after the *Tsimtsum*.'[89]

The homogeneity of the diverse aspects of the unified Reality can be explained in a sense by this androgynous symbolism. As Mathers remarks, each of the *sefirah* of the *Sefirot* 'will be in a certain degree androgynous, for it will be feminine or receptive with regard to the *sefirah* which immediately precedes it in the *sefirotic* scale, and masculine or transmissive with regard to the *sefirah* which immediately follows it. But there is no *sefirah* anterior to *Keter*, nor is there a *sefirah* which succeeds *Malkhut*. By these remarks it will be understood how *Hokhmah* is a feminine noun, though marking a masculine *sefirah*.'[90] In this manner the *sefirot* are homogeneously concomitant or coexistent, expressing unity as multiplicity, in accord with the first of the four Kabbalistic laws that govern the Universe: All is One.[91]

While *Keter* is intrinsically androgynous it is nevertheless extrinsically masculine. It is Macropropus, the "Crown" or "King," where these two terms are synonymous. There is then a relationship between *Keter* ("King") and *Malkhut* ("Queen"), who is also *Matrona*, the "inferior Mother" (the Supernal Mother is *Binah*), the Bride of Micropropus. This relationship is the "Marriage of Heaven and Earth," the Chemical Wedding of Alchemical tradition, and it is from this that the androgynous "Son" is born. In the Greek tradition this is Hermaphrodite, born from the union of Hermes and Aphrodite.[92] Moreover, as Campbell says, 'Hermes, too, is androgyne, as one should know from the sign of his staff.'[93]

Malkhut is synonymous with the *Shekhinah*, which, remarks Schaya, is 'the immanence of *Keter*, the presence of divine reality in the midst of the cosmos.'[94] Thus, according to the point of view adopted, the *Shekhinah* is identifiable with either the female *Malkhut* or the male

Keter.[95] The androgynous nature of both the Principle and Manifestation explains the apparent divergences between traditions with respect to the gender of the Divine Immanence. Thus the *Shekhinah* is commonly regarded as female, yet *Īśvara* ("Lord"), which is the personification of Being in the Hindu tradition, and Christ, who is the "Word made flesh" (i.e. "immanent") are male. Again, the *Shekhinah* is the source of spiritual inspiration, a trait that leads Alan Unterman to consider Her as interchangeable with *ruach ha-kodesh* ("the holy spirit").[96] Yet Guénon asserts that, where one must talk of sexual attributes with respect to the Persons of the Trinity, the Holy Spirit is 'fundamentally masculine and "paternal"'.[97] Of course this involves a difference between the symbolism of the Judaic and Christian traditions, which difference is itself connected with the ambiguity of the Spirit as mediating principle. Furthermore, the *Shekhinah* is associated with *Metatron*, which name has as one of its principal meanings that of "Lord,"[98] the same with *Īśvara*, demonstrating that in talking of the *Shekhinah* and of *Īśvara* we are talking about the same principle seen from alternate perspectives. From the celestial perspective the Divine Immanence resides in the Principle (*Ātman*), which is to say the active or male Essence. From the terrestrial perspective the Divine Immanence is recognised in the play of cosmic potentialities within the passive or female Substance (*Māyā* envisaged as *līlā* or "cosmic play").[99]

Sexual symbolism is also evident in the fundamental cosmological aspects of space and time. According to Hindu cosmology, 'the power of deliberation (*vimarśa*) and the power of expression (*prakāśa*) first manifest themselves respectively in "the determinant of space," the point-limit (*bindu*) from which manifestation begins, and "the determinant of time," the primordial-vibration (*nāda*). Space is represented as female, time as male. Their union in the Hermaphrodite is known as Lust (Kāma).'[100]

One of the most interesting descriptions of the androgyne or hermaphrodite is found in Plato's *Symposium*. Aristophanes' takes up the task of describing the ἀνδρόγυνον ("man-woman"):

> In the first place there were three sexes, not, as with us, two, male and female; the third partook of the nature of both the others ... The hermaphrodite was a distinct sex in form as well as in name ... each human being was a rounded whole, with double back and flanks forming a complete circle; it had four hands and equal number of legs, and two identically similar faces upon a circular neck, with one head common to both faces, which were turned in opposite directions. ... To run quickly they used all

their eight limbs, and turned rapidly over and over in a circle, like tumblers who perform a cartwheel and return to an upright position.[101]

This description of "a rounded whole" recalls Parmenides' description of Being as 'like the mass of a well rounded sphere stretching equally in all directions from the centre.'[102] According to Guénon, 'the form as a rule symbolically assigned to the Androgyne is the spherical one, which is the least differentiated of all, since it extends equally in all directions, being regarded by the Pythagoreans, for example, as the most perfect figure of universal totality.'[103] This is most eloquently demonstrated in the Taoist *yin-yang* symbol.

Aristophanes' hermaphrodite displays certain interesting attributes. The description of "one head" with two faces "turned in opposite directions" immediately recalls the symbolism of *Janus Bifrons*. Perhaps even more astounding is the detail supplied concerning the "eight limbs." The number eight is universally regarded as expressing the idea of balance. Guénon remarks that the octagon is associated with the "intermediary world," 'the world of the eight directions, the eight gates, and the eight winds,'[104] between the circle of heaven and the square of earth. One recalls the eight-legged horse, Sleipnir, of Norse mythology, and its association with the hermaphroditic Loki. Of particular interest in the context of the present study, Sturluson observes that the name Sleipnir is used in the *Skaldskaparmal* to indicate a "ship." Moreover, with respect to the androgyne, the story of Sleipnir's parentage is the story of a mountain-giant's attempt to steal the sun and the moon.[105] The union of the Sun and the Moon, or Gold and Silver, as the case may be, is the subject of the Chemical Marriage of the Hermetic tradition. This union is analogous, at its level, to the union of Heaven and Earth. Thus, in the story of *Genesis*, Being, which is identical to the Unmanifested *Logos*, undergoes a first polarisation (Gen.1:1) engendering Heaven (Essence; *Purusha*; *Hokhmah*) and Earth (Substance; *Mūlaprakriti*; *Binah*). This is the masculine and feminine at the level of Being. Their union gives rise to the manifested *Logos*, which in turn polarises into the Universal Intellect (Sun) and Universal Substance (Moon), and this is exactly described by the creation of the 'two great lights: the greater to govern the day, and the smaller to govern the night'(Gen.1:16). This relationship is alluded to by Aristophanes, who explains that of the three sexes 'originally the male sprang from the sun and the female from the earth, while the sex which was both male and female came from the moon, which partakes of the nature of both sun and earth.'[106] Regarding "light," the moon is passive with respect to the sun and active with respect to the earth. It is, in this sense, the intermediary world.

One must be careful here to realise that the vertical multivalency of a symbol can mean that the same symbol appears simultaneously at different levels with varying levels of significance. Thus, in the polarisation of Heaven and Earth, the Sun may be used to represent Heaven. Here, Heaven is the Essence of the Unmanifested *Logos*, and thus it is a matter of a "Black Sun" or, what has been called a "nocturnal day." Clement of Alexandria believes it was the "universal essence" that Plato referred to, in the seventh book of the *Republic*, as a "nocturnal day."[107] In the context of the onto-cosmological chain, the union of Heaven and Earth gives rise to the manifested *Logos*, which, in its turn, is symbolised by the Supernal Sun; and this in turn polarises into the Universal Intellect and Universal Substance, the Sun and the Moon. Thus the Moon is both a horizontal pole of the Universal Intellect, and the Substantial result—on a lower plane of Existence—of the union of Heaven ("Black Sun") and Earth, as with Aristophanes' hermaphrodite.

The eight limbs of Aristophanes' hermaphrodite allow it to turn 'rapidly over and over in a circle, like tumblers who perform a cartwheel and return to an upright position'. This is a remarkable description considering the context of a union of Sun and Moon, for it is precisely by the number eight that the solar and lunar cycles are balanced or "married." This symbolism is found in the *Vāstu-purusa-mandala*. Snodgrass:

> In one of its many meanings the *Vāstu-purusa-mandala* is a diagram of the movements of the sun and the moon. The squares of the eight *Vāstuparusas*, the deities of the eight directions, ... correspond to the eight planets that rule over the eight positions of the ecliptic (the equinoctial, solstitial and intermediate points) passed through by the sun in the course of the year. ... The squares in the next layer of the mandala are the 16 digits (*kalā*) of the moon, the total number of its phases; and the squares in the outer layer correspond to the thirty two stations of the moon in the lunar month and also the twenty eight lunar mansions plus the four points that mark the equinoctial and solstitial positions of the sun in the year. ... In the mandala the cycles of the sun and the moon form the numerical series 8, 16 (= 2   8) and 32 (= 4   8), arranged in relation to the cross of the directions and its divisions and subdivisions. By this juxtaposition the mandala marries the solar and lunar motions and figures their nuptial integration; the cross of the mandala reconciles the disjunct rhythms of the two primary celestial cycles.[108]

This is to recognise a complete solar-lunar cycle turned "over in a circle" and "returned to an upright [balanced] position."

The Isthmus

He has let loose the two oceans: they meet one another. Yet between them stands a barrier which they cannot overrun.

Sūrah 55, *al-Rahmān* [*The Merciful*]

Moslem tradition describes the *coincidentia oppositorum* as an isthmus (*al-barzakh*) between the "two seas": 'It was He who sent the two seas rolling, the one sweet and fresh, and the other salty and bitter, and set a rampart between them as an insurmountable barrier.'[109] Schuon refers to the *barzakh* as 'a dividing line between two domains [which] line appears, from the standpoint of each side, to belong to the other side.'[110] He adds, 'The archetype of the *barzakh* is the half-divine, half-cosmic frontier separating, and in another sense uniting, Manifestation and the Principle; it is the "Divine Spirit" (*Rūh*) which, seen "from above" is manifestation, and seen "from below" is Principle. Consequently, it is *Māyā* in both its aspects; the same thing appears, in a certain manner, in the Christian expression "true man and true God."'[111] Similarly, Burckhardt remarks that, when seen "from the outside" the *barzakh*, must necessarily have the definite meaning of "partition" or "seperative element" ("an insurmountable barrier") but, looking at it in regard to its ontological situation, if one may so put it, 'it appears as a simple partition only from the point of view of lesser reality, whereas seen "from above," it is the very mediator between the two seas. … The *barzakh* is thus separation only in that it is itself the starting point of a seperative perspective, in the eyes of which it appears to be a limit.'[112]

Nasr, discussing the *Hayy ibn Yaqzān* of Ibn Sina, says of the *barzakh* that it is 'the *intellectus materialis*, or *al-'aql al-hayūlānī*, which with respect to the intelligible forms acts as *materia prima*.'[113] This is to view the Intellect, *al-'Aql*, with respect to its Substantial mode or polarity, but the Intellect is equally Essence, these being "almost synonymous." Thus the *barzakh* is also *al-'aql al-Awwal*, the First Intellect, analogous to *al-Qalam al-a'lā* (the Supreme Pen), and here we might recall that the symbolism of the Pen implies both active instrument and passive ink; moreover, the ink will then be active to the Guarded Tablet (*al-Lawh al-mahfūz*), the symbol of universal receptive Substance, which is here passive. To compare the Intellect to the *barzakh* is to agree with Plotinus who places the Intellect as the mediating principle or hypostasis "between," if this phrase be allowed here, the One and the World Soul.

In the *Recital of Hayy Ibn Yaqzān* Ibn Sina describes the soul's journey across the *barzakh* thus:

> Thou hast heard of the darkness that forever reigns about the pole. Each year the rising sun shines upon it at a fixed time. He who confronts that darkness and does not hesitate to plunge into it for fear of difficulties will come to a vast space, bound and filled with light. The first thing he sees is a living spring whose waters spread like a river over the *barzakh*. Whoever bathes in that spring becomes so light that he can walk on water, can climb the highest peaks without weariness, until finally he comes to one of the two circumscriptions by which this world is intersected.[114]

The "living spring" (*fons et origio*) is the "mediator between the two seas," which flows "vertically." Here again is the river *Yobel*. The *barzakh* or isthmus is the "seperative element," and in a sense might be described as the "horizontal" divide between the Upper and Lower Waters. In one sense the horizontal isthmus and the vertical "living spring" are the two "faces" of the one *barzakh*; here the symbolism of the *barzakh* coincides with the symbolism of the Cross.[115]

Schuon's comment on the "archetype of the *barzakh*" alerts one to the fact that this term refers both to *an* intermediary and to *the* intermediary, the archetypal interface between Transcendence and Immanence. This is similar to what we may note of the Tibetan term *bar-do* or "in between," which usually refers to the state in between death and rebirth but equally refers to the sense of a phase between two successive states of being.[116] In the Hindu tradition this intermediate state is called *sandhyā* (twilight).[117] This word, as Guénon observes, is derived from *sandhi*, the point of contact or of junction between two things. It is used in an ordinary sense to describe twilight (morning and evening); in the theory of cosmic cycles (*manvantara*) it is used to indicate the interval between two *Yugas*.[118] Mention can be made here of the planet Venus, which, as the Morning and Evening Star, appears at each twilight as the intermediary between Day and Night and, more specifically with respect to the celestial bodies, between the Sun and Moon. Moreover, insomuch as the *barzakh* is equated with the *'aql al-hayūlani* or the *materia prima* of the intelligible forms, it is worth noting that the planetary symbolism of al-Jīlī makes Venus correspond with the imagination (*al-khayāl*), with al-Jīlī noting that this is the 'materia prima of the world of forms.'[119]

In the Taoist tradition this intermediary or interface can be recognised in the "line" that marks off the two halves of the *yin-yang* symbol.[120] Throughout his writings Guénon often remarks that this symbol, far from affirming any "dualism," stresses the unity of this single principle, the *T'ai-chi* or Great Ultimate of Chinese tradition.[121] Guénon:

> The two halves [of the *yin-yang* symbol] are marked off from each other by a line that curves, which indicates an interpenetration of the two elements; if on the other hand they were divided by a diameter one would be inclined to deduce a simple juxtaposition. It is worth noting that this curved line consists of two semi-circumferences whose radius is half the radius of the circumference forming the outline of the whole diagram. Accordingly the total length of the line is equivalent to half the total length of the circumference, which means that each of the two halves of the diagram is contained by a line equal in length to the line containing the whole diagram.[122]

The circumference of the whole may be said to symbolise the Infinite. The symbolism of the circumference alludes to this "boundless" nature. The white *yang* is marked off by a black line marking out a circumference; the black *yin* is marked off by a white circumference; these two then cancel each other, so to speak, such that it can be said that there is really no circumference to this infinite "circle." Guénon's observation that each colour is bound by a line of equal length to the circumference alludes to the idea that each of these colours or principles is infinite and thus non-distinct within the unity of the *T'ai-chi*. It is only from the perspective of manifestation that we recognise these principles as distinct and even then the *yin-yang* symbol reminds us of their complementary nature through the small circle of *yang* that resides in *yin* and vice versa.

It might be objected that there is no "line" between the *yin* and the *yang* in this symbol and in truth there is no line as such that is distinct from either *yin* or *yang*. Rather this line is implied where the two principles meet, but it is precisely not articulated because of the "mysterious" nature of this interface. In this connection, Perry says that the Islamic *barzakh* equates with the mystery of the "Cloud of Unknowing."[123] In Kabbalah this mystery is expressed by the Holy of Holies, the domain of the Ark; this is again, *Tiferet*, the "heart" of the *Sefirot*.

The likening of the interface to the "heart" is similarly found in the Islamic tradition. Shaikh Si Mohammad Tādīlī of Jadīda: 'All *barāzikh* (plural of *barzakh*) of man depend on his central *barzakh*, which is the heart (*qalb*), mediator between the domain of the Spirit (*Rūh*) and that of the individual soul (*nafs*). ... What is called the *barzakh* of a given realm of existence is nothing other than the pole (*qutb*) that governs this realm and gives it its growth.'[124] Burckhardt observes that, in Sufism,

148

the term *barzakh* is sometimes used synonymously with the term *qutb*, "pole." Burckhardt points out that it is significant that the root of the word *qalb* (heart), QLB, implies the idea of "turning upside down" or inversion. Thus, according to the Midrash, during the time of the Flood the sun rose in the west and set in the east.[125] One is reminded here of Dante's "perplexing" inversion whilst climbing out from Hell, which occurs precisely at the "centre" of the earth, the point that is likewise the essential pole of Hell and the lowest or "substantial" pole of Mount Purgatory.[126] The word *qalb*, moreover, has the meaning of "mould," given the inversion of "negative" and "positive" in the process of moulding.[127] There is here also a philological metathesis from the root QLB to QBL, which latter is the root of the word, *qabil*, "receptacle." The root QBL means to "receive," "to placing one in front of the other," "to be in face of." As Burckhardt observes *al-qābil* is the receptacle, the passive and receptive substance.[128]

Burckhardt notes two functions of the *barzakh*: 'the first consists in meditation in an "ascending" sense, in other words in the passage from the manifested to the non-manifested, a passage or transformation which always traverses the blind spot of an extinction, or of a death; while the second is that this point is the point of reversal of relationships.'[129] It is this nature of the *barzakh* that gives rise to the laws of analogy.

Burckhardt further remarks that the different aspects of the *barzakh* are represented in the diagram of the Seal of Solomon, and this, as he says, 'leads us to consider the relationship of the *barzakh* with *al-insān al-kamīl*, "Universal Man," who by expressing the constituent analogy of the microcosm and the macrocosm, is truly the *barzakh* par excellence or, what amounts to the same thing, the symbol par excellence.'[130] This identification of the *barzakh* with Universal Man agrees with Schuon's recognition of the *barzakh* envisaged as "true man and true God." Again this is to recognise that this interface between the Transcendent and the Immanent is none other than Christ, where Christ is identical with the Spirit (*Rūh*), as 'These three are one', and where 'No one can come to the father except through me' (Jn.14:6).

The Symplegades

I am the door. No one comes to the Father except through me.
John 10:9; 14:6

Die before ye die.
Muhammad[131]

From the human perspective the *barzakh* appears as an "insurmountable barrier." However, this is just to say that it is "insurmountable" without a kind of active negation or death. 'Die before ye die' says the Prophet. Again, St. Thomas Aquinas remarks, 'No creature can attain a higher grade of nature without ceasing to exist.'[132] In this light the symbolism of the *barzakh* corresponds to that of the Symplegades, the "Clashing Rocks" or, in Ananda Coomaraswamy's terms, the "Active Door."[133] The passage through the Symplegades is, strictly speaking, the prerogative of the Hero.[134] The Symplegades form a passageway to the "Otherworld." Passing through this passageway the Hero relinquishes the mortal element, undergoing a purification, which is a birth and a death, for, as Guénon says, 'new birth necessarily presupposes death to the former state'.[135] Coomaraswamy: '"No one becomes immortal in the flesh," (SB x.4.3.9), and whoever reaches the Otherworld and the attainment of all desires does so "going in the spirit"... "having shaken off his bodies" (JUB iii.30.2-4)—the Platonic *katharsis* (*Phaedo* 76C).'[136]

In Greek mythology the *Argo* came to the Symplegades on the quest for the Golden Fleece.[137] The Fleece with its double symbolism of gold and the solar ram, is the hidden goal or treasure, the *Fons Vitae*, the Grail, etc. Its solar symbolism expresses the light of illumination of the Intellect. The Active Door is here the "Sundoor." The *Argo* is the vessel of the spiritual journey, and in this sense corresponds to the human condition. That the *Argo* is a "winged ship" expresses its potential for "flight" or transcendence.[138] The *Argo* here symbolises the human intellect, which may transcend its created state by identification with the Uncreated Intellect. This is the Christian doctrine of the *Logos*: one with two states, created and Uncreated, the "bridge" between man and God.[139] Meister Eckhart calls the Intellect—created and Uncreated—the "spark in the soul," and again, the *Synteresis*. On this point, Coomaraswamy remarks that the word, *synteresis*, is etymologically equivalent of the Sanskrit word, *samtāraka*, "one who helps to cross over."[140] The Intellect is the Self (*Ātman*) of Hindu tradition, and thus we read: 'Now, the Self (*Ātman*) is the bridge, the separation for keeping these worlds apart. Over that bridge there cross neither day, nor night, nor old age, nor death, nor sorrow, nor well-doing, nor evil doing.'[141]

According to tradition, the seer Phineus advised Jason that to successfully pass through the Symplegades they should release a dove between the rocks, and if they saw it pass safely between them, to sail through in full confidence, but if it was destroyed, to make no attempt to force a passage. The Argonauts released a dove from the prow; and as she flew through only the tip of her tail was snipped off as the rocks clashed together. Following suit the Argonauts waited for the rocks to part and then rowing hard made their way through, although the tip of the vessel's poop was shorn. Ever afterwards, the Symplegades have stood motionless.

In Greek tradition the dove is associated with Aphrodite—recall the dual symbolism of Venus. In Christian tradition the dove is a well-known symbol of the Holy Spirit. In both cases this is the intermediary principle—created and Uncreated. In passing through the Symplegades the dove lost its tail feathers, so too the *Argo* only makes it through with the loss of her tail. This shows that passage through the Symplegades entails the "death" of the created state: 'No one becomes immortal in the flesh.' Coomaraswamy notes several variations on this myth. In Greenland the Eskimo hero Giviok is confronted by "two clashing icebergs," which he passes through only after having the stern-point of his kayak "bruised." In the South American Tupi saga of the Sky-journey of two brothers, respectively human and divine, the way leads between clashing rocks, by which the mortal is crushed.[142] And of course, passing between Scylla and Charybdis, Odysseus lost his six ablest men, which highlights the fact that the passage through the Symplegades is the retraction of the six created directions though the seventh point, the Uncreated Centre.

Coomaraswamy remarks on the fact that these Clashing Rocks are to be recognised as a "mouth."[143] This, as he says, is really the "fiery Jaws of Death" (*Rg Veda* 10.87.3). The image of the interface as a mouth not only expresses the maleficent notion of "devourment" but also alludes to the beneficent reading of this symbol in the context of the creative Word. Similarly expressing this idea of creativity, the passage through the Symplegades is also expressed by the image of the birth canal and vagina. Coomaraswamy notes one North American myth in which the door of the king of heaven is made of his daughter's toothed vagina, uniting the two ideas. Again, he remarks on the Polynesian tale of Maui's brother crushed between the thighs of the Night Goddess.[144] The association between sex and death is common: 'The stroke of death is a lover's pinch, which hurts, and is desir'd.'[145]

In the *Rg Veda* 6.49.3 the "Clashing Rocks" are Day and Night. Coomaraswamy quotes from the *Kansītaki Brāhmana*: 'Night and day are the sea that carries all away, and the two twilights are its fordable crossings'.[146] The two twilights (*sandhyā*) are at once the "insurmountable barrier" or *barzakh* and the "fordable crossing" or the "bridge." In this sense the two twilights are Parmenides' "gates of the paths of Night and Day" that both bar and allow passage.[147]

Coomaraswamy observes the obvious parallel of this passage from the *Rg Veda*, with it description of Night and Day as "seas," to the crossing of the Red Sea. This is again paralleled in the crossing of the Jordan (Jos.3:14-17), which of course was accomplished via the "power" of the

Ark of the Covenant. We should also note here that the word "Hebrew" (עבר) can signify "one that passes over from, or to, a place";[148] as such, it has been suggested that "Abram the Hebrew" (Gen.14:13), may be "Abram who crossed the River" (Jos. 24:2, 3).[149] Sir William Drummond sees in this name an esoteric relationship to the meaning of the *Passover*.[150] Meister Eckhart: 'Blessed are they who make this passover: all things are known to them in truth and they themselves unknown to any creature.'[151]

The Symplegades express the principle of complementarism. In the final analysis, as Guénon observes, complementarism vanishes in the "resolution of opposites": 'Complementarism itself, which is still duality, must at a certain degree, vanish in face of unity, its two terms being balanced and as it were neutralized when uniting to merge indissolubly in the primordial indifferentiation.'[152] After the *Argo* had passed through them the Symplegades stood motionless. Connected with this idea, Perry discusses the "split gates" of the Balinese northern temple, Meduwe Karang, at Kubutambahan.[153] These "gates" are iconographically carved on either side, both facing outwards and inwards; however, the opposing faces between the gates are smooth, expressing the state of nondistinction "within" this unity.

Coomaraswamy concludes his article on the Symplegades thus: 'It remains only to consider the full doctrinal significance of the Symplegades. What the formula states literally is that whoever would transfer from this to the Otherworld, or return, must do so through the undimensioned and timeless "interval" that divides related but contrary forces, between which, if one is to pass it must be "instantly."'[154] As St. Paul says, this "mystery" will occur 'instantly, in the twinkling of an eye' (1Cor.15:52).

The Twin-Peaked Mountains

And in the seventh month, on the seventeenth day of the month, the ark came to rest on the mountains of Ararat.

Genesis 8:4

The mythologist H. A. Guerber sees the *Argo* as 'a symbol of the earth as a living parent, which contains in itself the germs of all living things.'[155] A comparison with the Ark of the Deluge is immediately apparent. Still, with the Ark of the Deluge it is more the case that the Ark enters the "space"[156] between the symbolic Symplegades but does not proceed to the "other side," the higher state. Instead the Ark returns from this mysterious interval concurrently with the withdrawal of the waters of the flood. It is equally true, from the perspective of the Principle, to say that the emergence of the Ark causes the withdrawal of the waters.

Among mythologies of the Flood the resting place of the Ark is often said to be a "twin peaked" mountain. In the Greek tradition this is explicitly stated with Mt. Parnassus.[157] In the Babylonian *Epic of Gilgamesh* we find the Flood-hero, Ut-napishtim, residing with his wife at Mt. Mashu or "the mount of the twin."[158] In Hebrew Scripture, Noah landed 'upon the Mountains of Ararat' (Gen.8:4), which, according to tradition, are identified with the double conical peaks of Mt. Massis in the Causasus Mountains, called by the Persians, Kuhi-Nuh, "the mountain of Noah."

Josephus remarks that the Armenians called Ararat, *Apobatērion* or "The Place of Descent."[159] In his notes to this, William Whiston observes that 'this is the proper rendering of the Armenian name of this very city [he refers here to the city at the base of Mt. Ararat]. It is called in Ptolemy *Naxuana*, and by Moses Chorenensis, the Armenian historian, *Idsheuan*; but at the place itself, *Nachidsheuan*, which signifies *The first place of descent'*.[160] Whiston notes that Moses Chorenensis says elsewhere that another town in this area was 'related by tradition to have been called *Seron*, or "The Place of Dispersion," on account of the dispersion of Xisuthrus's or Noah's sons, from thence first made.' These twin notions of "descent" and "dispersion" correspond respectively to the vertical and horizontal extensions of Being from the ontological Origin, in this case, Ararat—the "one that is two."

Considered in light of its Kabbalistic symbolism the word "Ararat" (אררט) reveals further esoteric meaning:

$$ט \quad ר \quad ר \quad א$$

serpent / head / head / ox

Symbolically this word expresses a shift from "ox" (*aleph*) to "serpent" (*teth*). The ox, in its relationship to the cow and the bull, is an aspect of the symbolism of Cosmic Substance. While it is a gross oversimplification we might nonetheless say that the bull expresses the terrifying strength and vitality inherent in the potentiality of Cosmic Substance or Chaos;[161] the cow expresses the fertility or fecundity inherent in the birth and nurturing of Creation; and the ox expresses the sacrificial nature of Cosmic Substance. The ox is further associated with the symbolism of Water, which is the symbol of Cosmic Substance *par excellence*.[162] In the *Zohar* the ox is explicitly associated with the power of sorcery or magic, the power of the "other side."[163] This symbolism is again expressed by Water.[164] The serpent also relates, as part of its complex symbolism, to the notion of Cosmic Substance. The serpent is also associated, in an active sense, with the concept of the Fall and thus can be said to suggest Cosmic Substance in its productive nature.

We are here primarily concerned with the "isthmus" created between the "Upper Water of the ox" and the "Lower Water of the serpent" by the two "heads," the two letters *resh*. The letter *resh* is symbolically a "head." The two "heads"—faces of the one letter/head—recall the symbolism of *Janus Bifrons*. These two "heads" form the "Active Door," the Symplegades, between the Upper and Lower worlds. It may be suggested that the double letter structure implies the idea of the one letter/symbol seen from two perspectives, as with the *barzakh*. Thus the first *resh* is influenced by the *aleph* and the second *resh* by the *teth*; yet they nevertheless remain the one letter.

Aleph is the first letter of the Hebrew alphabet; *teth* is the ninth letter of the Hebrew alphabet. When one considers the number nine in terms of the creative decad it is the last number in the "unfolding"; in this sense it represents the completion of the series, where the ten is the return of the whole to a state of potentiality. Considered in this way the *aleph* and the *teth* are the "beginning" and the "end" of the decad series, or, in other words, the Alepha and the Omega. As such the *resh* becomes the principle that partakes of both; like Christ, who is also the Alpha and Omega, the *resh*/head is both "true God and true man," both Principle and Manifestation. In this context it is said that 'Christ is the man's head' (1Co.11:3).

It is interesting to consider this meeting of two heads in light of *Genesis* 1:27—'God created man in the image'—and this in the context of the law of inverse analogy. As such the meeting of the Transcendent and the Immanent might well be figured by an image of two human forms, one erect and one inverted, with their respective heads meeting. Coomaraswamy has considered this idea briefly in his work on 'The Inverted Tree.'[165] He remarks: 'What we are concerned with is that the coming into being of the man presupposes a descent, and that of the return to the source of being an ascent; in this sense, the man, *qua* tree, is inverted at birth and erected at death.'[166] Thus, in the *Acts of Peter* 37-39, Peter beseeches his executioners, 'Crucify me thus, with the head downwards, and not otherwise ... For the first man, whose race I bear in mine appearance, fell head downwards'.

Numerically the two letters *resh* add to forty. The Hebrew letter that corresponds to the number forty is *mem*, symbolically "water." The number forty symbolises an intermediate state, as with the isthmus. This is also a state of perfection; both King David and Solomon reigned for forty years (1 K.11:42 & 2S.5:4). This is also a state of transition.

The Flood of Noah lasted forty days (Gen.7:4); Moses remained upon Mt. Siani for forty days; Israel wandered in the desert for forty years (Nb.32:13). Jesus underwent his temptation in the desert for forty days (Matt.4:2); he preached for forty months and the risen Christ appeared to his disciples during the forty days preceding his Ascension (Acts 1:3). Lent lasts forty days. The number forty also plays an important part in the death rituals of many peoples. It is the number of days needed ensure that the corpse is free of living matter, it is thus the length of time of mourning taboos. Similarly the same period of time applies to women after childbirth.[167] The association of the number forty with both death and the intermediary or transitional state is in perfect accord, for death is merely a state of transition.

The word Ararat (אררט) totals fifty according to its numerical symbolism. This, as noted, is the number of the word *kol*, "all," recalling the Jubilee as the totality of time. Ararat, as the Cosmic Mountain, is "all," the totality of Cosmic Existence. Furthermore, the *sefirot Binah* is said to have "fifty gates."[168] It is by the way of the 50 gates of *Binah* that all creation is manifested. Schaya:

> When the Kabbalah says that the total duration of the world is fifty thousand years, this figure should be taken as symbolic of the law which constitutes its eternal foundation. This law resides in the mystery of the seven *Sefirot* of construction, each one of which recapitulates, in its way, the whole. Thus one is faced with a unity of 'seven times seven' or forty-nine *Sefirotic* degrees, which are manifested through as many cyclic phases, its total duration being that of the indefinite existence of the cosmos; these forty-nine degrees issue from *Binah* and return to it. *Binah*, as the "fiftieth" degree, of the supreme and prototypical "Jubilee."[169]

Josephus identifies Ararat as *Apobaterion* or "The Place of Descent." J. Ralston Skinner takes this to be "Mount Jared,"[170] where *Jared* (ירד), the sixth antediluvian patriarch (Gen.5:18-20), comes from a primitive root meaning "to *descend*." Numerically the name Jared also totals fifty. The patriarch, Jared, is the fifth generation in the Adamic chronology; again, there are five generations from Jared to Noah. In this sense the symbolism of Jared combines that of the number five, the number of "man," with that of the mediate station, from which, moreover, begins the descent.

If we correspond the Adamic chronology with the *Sefirotic* Tree, starting with Adam as *Keter* and thus proceeding, then Jared corresponds to *Tiferet*. This is to say that he is the "heart" of the system. It should be little surprise to anyone familiar with the Kabbalah, or indeed esotericism in any true form, to find that I have here related Ararat to *Tiferet* where above I related it to *Binah*. The fact is that all diverse forms lead to the unity of the principle. As such, the more adequate a symbol the more unifying its symbolism. Thus the Centre is the circumference and *visa versa*. This is perfectly true, yet at the same time distinction exists and retains its precise meaning within itself, and this insomuch as diversity is a contingent reality. Thus, in the case of Ararat we have been considering the idea of the first point of ontological manifestation, which itself partakes of the Unmanifested and here we have been talking of *Binah*. Yet this is also the centre point or heart of Cosmic Existence, and this is *Tiferet*.[171]

The symbolism of the name Jared is that of a "hand" (*yod*), a "head" (*resh*) and a "door" (*daleth*). There is something here of the symbolism of the Roman *Janus Bifrons*, who is not only pictured with two faces joined in one head but who is, like St. Peter, the "doorkeeper," the "holder of the keys."[172] Both Guénon and Coomaraswamy have variously discussed the symbolism of Janus.[173] As Guénon observes the two faces are often pictured as male and female, expressing the image of "Janus the androgyne" or "*Janus-Jana*." This, as Guénon remarks, calls attention to the close relationship of this form with certain Hermetic symbols such as the *Rebis*.[174] The two keys, which Janus is depicted as holding, are respectively gold and silver. These are the keys of the solstitial gates, *Janua Coeli* and *Janua Inferni*, corresponding respectively to the Winter and Summer solstices, for Janus is the 'Janitor who opens and closes this cycle.'[175] *Janus* is further the god of initiation, and these keys are those of the "greater mysteries" and of the "lesser mysteries." In his essay, 'Some Aspects of the Symbolism of Janus,' Guénon remarks, with Charbonneau-Lassay, on the identification of *Janus* with Christ. The symbolism of *Janus Bifrons* corresponds, *mutatis mundis*, to the symbolism of Christ crucified upright and Peter crucified upside down.

As Guénon remarks, to treat the subject of *Janus* fully would need a whole volume. There are however several particular points that are pertinent to the study of the Ark. Guénon remarks that Charbonneau-Lassay's discussion of Christ's depiction as *Janus* shows Christ crowned, with the sceptre in one hand and a key in the other hand. This demonstrates the dual authority of the royal power (the sceptre) and the sacerdotal power (the key—symbol of St. Peter and through him the papacy). In the Hebraic tradition this dual authority is united by Melchizedek (Gen.14:18), who is seen in Christian tradition as prefiguring Christ (Heb.7:3). The figure of Melchizedek is intricately tied to the symbolism of the Flood.

In the *Jerusalem Targum* Melchizedek is identified with Shem. *Genesis Rabba*, 44 says that it was Shem 'who was now priest of the most high God and ruled at Salem under the name of Melchizedek'.[176] In another tradition Abraham questions "Shem-Melchizedek" on the virtue that merited the saving of his father and his brothers on the ark.[177] In 2 *Enoch* Melchizedek is said to be the son of Noah's brother (Nir). Moreover, during the Flood it was none other than Melchizedek who was removed to the Garden of Eden, analogous here to the Ark.

Again linking *Janus* to the symbolism of the Ark, Guénon remarks that the barque was a symbol of *Janus*. He says, 'The barque of Janus was one that could move in both directions, forward and backward, which corresponds to the two faces of Janus himself.'[178] With this we could add that Peter was a fisherman. Here again is another example of the homogeneity of symbolism.

Coincidentia Oppositorum in Ark Symbolism

> From all living creatures, from all living things, you must take two of each kind aboard the ark.
>
> *Genesis* 6:19

> He gave him the two tablets of the Testimony, tablets of stone inscribed by the finger of God.
>
> *Exodus* 31:18

The notion of the retraction of duality into the *coincidentia oppositorum* is explicit in the mythology of the Deluge. As Whitall Perry remarks, one of the aspects of the symbolism of the "pairs" in the biblical Flood story 'is that manifestation was not to be consummated at the end of the cyclic period in question, but rather temporarily withdrawn "into the Ark," and hence the polarities were maintained, but in a state of "suspension" for an interval.'[179] This retraction expresses the movement at the end of a cycle from the state of duality and hence relativity and indefinite multiplicity, to a state of virtual unity.[180]

According to chapter six of *Genesis*, God told Noah to gather "two of each kind" of "all living things," these being "male and female" (Gen.6:19). In chapter seven this is specified as, 'Of every clean animal you must take seven pairs, a male and its female; of the unclean animals you must take one pair, a male and its female and of the birds of heaven, seven pairs, a male and its female' (Gen.7:2-3). Modern biblical scholarship tends to regard this as an anomaly caused by the interpolation of a Priestly narrative into a Yahwistic narrative; however, viewed symbolically, which is to say, in the fashion of the peoples for whom the Scriptures were and are a living text, these two supposedly distinct narratives are in fact a single cohesive and complementary description of the retraction into the *coincidentia oppositorum.*[181]

In chapter six the emphasis is on the general idea of duality and the "masculine-feminine" complementarity by which cosmological existence ("all living things") proceeds to the Ark-Centre. This emphasis highlights the first "stage," so to speak, of the retraction, that is, from multiplicity to duality. In chapter seven the emphasis shifts to the Centre itself, to the *coincidentia oppositorum* viewed not simply as the meeting of two complementary principles, but as these complementarities viewed with respect to their biunity. In the first case it is as if the *coincidentia oppositorum* is viewed from "outside" and in the second, from "inside."

Viewed from "inside" the Ark-Centre is, from the appropriate perspective, both "first" and "seventh." This symbolism is alluded to by the command to take one pair of every unclean animal and seven pairs of every clean animal. The number seven expresses "fullness" (שבעה, *shib'ah*). This symbolism is associated here with the idea of "cleanliness" or "purity" (טהור, *tahowr*), where this word derives from the primitive root *taher* (טהר) meaning, "to *be bright.*"

The *coincidentia oppositorum* is evident in the symbolism of the Ark of the Covenant, in the image of the *cherubim* that frame the mercy-seat. This is not all, for in turn the *cherubim* are prefigured by the Testimony, which is the fundamental "content" of the Ark: 'Inside the ark you will put the Testimony which I am about to give you' (Ex.25:16).[182] Moses ascended Mount Sinai where at the summit he received the "two tablets of the Testimony."[183] Here again the meeting of man and God occurs at the summit of the World Mountain via (one might say, between) two "tablets" of stone: 'When he had finished speaking to Moses on Mount Sinai, he gave him the two tablets of the Testimony, tablets of stone inscribed by the finger of God' (Ex.31:18). Recalling the sense in which the symbolism of the stone expresses *prima materia* it is not hard to think of these "two" tablets as being a single *tabula rasa* prior— logically rather than temporally—to being "written" upon by God. This is the Guarded Tablet (*al-Lawh al-Mahfūz*) of Islamic tradition.

Moreover, as the river *Yobel* becomes four rivers and as the Light of *hashmal* radiates its beams of the four corners, so too the Word of God given to Moses is first one, then two and then four. This idea, although presented in an esoteric fashion, is nevertheless explicit. As we read, 'Moses turned and came down the mountain with the two tablets of the Testimony in his hands, tablets inscribed on both sides, inscribed on the front and on the back' (Ex.32:15). That is to say, inscribed on the *four*

158

sides. Furthermore these four gives rise to the number eight, the number of cosmic balance. Thus, in an ancient Egyptian inscription Thoth says,

I am One which transforms into Two   (polarity)
I am Two which transforms into Four   (surface, $2^2 = 4$)
I am Four which transforms into Eight (volume, $2^3 = 8$)
After all of this, I am One.[184]

The word variously translated as "tablet" or "table" is in Hebrew לוח, *lūwach*, a primitive root that *Strong's* feels probably means "to *glisten*," thus "a *tablet*" in the sense of being a polished piece of stone, wood or metal. If it is correct that *lūwach* means "to *glisten*," then this draws attention again to the relationship between the symbolism of the stone and the idea of "brightness." Even more striking is the close connection between this word and the word *lūwz* (לוז) with its relation to Bethel and the symbolism of the stone. The difference lies in the respective finals; in the case of *lūwz* this is a *zayin*, symbolically associated with "a sword"; in the case of *lūwach* this is a *heth*, associated with "a fence or enclosure." These two images are, of course, far from unrelated, and one thinks of the fiery sword (Gen.3:24) which, along with the winged creatures, acts to enclose Eden.[185]

This connection between *lūwach* and the idea of "light" offers one of the most interesting developments to the account of Moses bringing the stone tablets down from Mount Sinai. *Exodus* 34:29: 'When Moses came down from Mount Sinai with the two tablets of the Testimony in his hands, as he was coming down the mountain, Moses did not know that the skin on his face was radiant because he had been talking to him [God].' This has led to portrayals of Moses with rays of light emanating from his head. One of the most famous and intriguing of such portrayals is Michelangelo's statue of Moses for the tomb of Pope Julius III, which shows Moses with two horns. These horns are commonly believed to be the result of a confusion of the Hebrew for "rays of light"[186] with the Latin *cornu*, "horn," in the Vulgate text—'*et ignorabat quod cornuta esset facies sua*' ('Moses wist not that the skin of his face shone'). This may be so, but it is nevertheless interesting to remark on the fact that the symbolism of horns is tied to the idea of the two complementary principles (left and right) between which exists the point of resolution (the *urna* or "sense of eternity").[187] Campbell recalls the image of the yogi in Hindu myth as having a 'curious headdress with a high crown and two immense horns'. He observes that Heinrich Zimmer considered these to resemble the Buddhist sign of the Three Jewels, the *Triratna* (*Buddha, Dharma, Sangha*).[188] In Dogon mythology the celestial ram is pictured bearing a calabash between its horns. 'The ram's horns are testicles, balancing the calabash which it fertilizes by means of the penis growing out of its forehead'.[189] The calabash, a homologue of the Ark, is quite interesting in that it is a female, solar symbol. This is to say that it reconciles these two symbolic principles that would usually be thought of as opposites. The Dogon ram is a "golden ram"[190] echoing the Golden Fleece, which Jason sailed through the Symplegades to retrieve. A further interesting point is the manner in which the word "horns" is sometimes used to denote the crossbeams of the Cross.[191] The Cross reconciles, so to speak, the vertical and horizontal axes. Likewise, Christ, who is symbolised by the Cross, reconciles the Divine and the human.

The Hebraic word *qeren* (קרן) means "horn," the horn of a ram or a goat. It is from such a horn that the Hebrews fashion the trumpet or *shofar* that traditionally signals the Jubilee (*Yobel*; "a *blast* of a trumpet"). This is the same with *Yobel*, the river that flowed out of Eden and *Yobel* or *Yahoel*, the first of the names of Metatron, the Word of God. The descent of the tablets of the Testimony thus corresponds to the descent of the Word; this is the same as the "descent" of the *Fiat Lux*, which is none other than the Light of *hashmal*. Michelangelo's depiction of Moses with two "horns" may be the result of an error of translation. Then again, it may well suggest a deeper understanding of these complexes and intertwined symbolisms.

The descent of the tablets of the Testimony, in the terms in which we have been considering it, expresses a cosmogonic symbolism. In a sense this symbolism is prefigured by that of Jacob, who ascended the "ladder" and returned as Israel. Now it is Moses who ascends the "mountain" to return with the Law that establishes Israel as a people. Furthermore, Jacob or Universal Man has his complementary/prototype in Esau, who expresses the Edomite Kings, the "kings who died." This symbolism is also found in the account of Moses, for, as it is written, when Moses first came down with the tablets of the Testimony he found the Israelites worshipping the golden calf and in his anger, 'He threw down the tablets he was holding, shattering them at the foot of the mountain' (Ex.32:19). Here the prototype is destroyed, just as the kings are "killed." In chapter thirty-four God instructs Moses, 'Cut two tablets of stone like the first ones and come up to me on the mountain, and I will write on the tablets the words that were on the first tablets, which you broke' (Ex 34:1). These tablets are "like" the first ones: made "in the likeness" (Gen.1:27). Moreover, these tablets ascend to God,[192] thereby balancing the tablets that descended, in accord with the universal law: 'That which is below is as that which is above, and that which is above is as that which is below.' Thus the tablets of the Ark are the balance between the Divine and the human.

The two tablets of the Testimony suggest a connection between the Ark of the Covenant and the Ark of Noah, for these echo the two tablets upon which Seth inscribed the story of Adam and Eve so that it might survive the future cataclysms of fire and water. In the *Life of Adam and Eve* it is said that after the death of Adam Eve gathered together Seth with thirty brothers and thirty sisters and instructed them: 'Make now tablets of stone and other tablets of clay and write in them all my life and your father's which you have heard and seen from us. If he [God] should judge our race by water, the tablets of earth will dissolve and the tablets of stone will remain; but if he should judge our race by fire, the tablets of stone will break up and those of clay will be thoroughly baked.'[193] In *2 Enoch* it is specifically said that the "handwritings" of Enoch and his fathers are to be preserved 'so that they might not perish in the future flood which I [God] shall create in your generation.'[194] According to Josephus, the tablets made by Seth and his children were in fact two "pillars,"[195] which alludes again to the relationship between the stone and the pillar. Moreover, these two pillars are identified with the two pillars of Solomon's Temple, *Jachin* and *Boaz*. Here Rabbi Gikatilla says that the essence of these pillars is stated in the verse: 'His legs are like ShaySH (marble, also the word for six) pillars, MeYuSaDIM (set) in sockets of fine gold (*Song of Songs* 5:15).'[196] These two pillars (which correspond to the *sefirot Nezah* and *Hod*) give rise to the "six Names," that is six "powers," which are the six directions of onto-cosmological existence.

Notes

1. Nicolas of Cusa, *De Docta Ignorantia*, 88 (1997, p.127).

2. Schuon: 'The separation between man and God is at one and the same time absolute and relative. Were it not absolute, man as such would be God. Were it not relative there would be no possible contact between the human and the Divine, and man would be an atheist by ontological definition, and thus irremediably so. The separation is absolute because God alone is real and no continuity is possible between nothingness and Reality; but the separation is relative—or rather "non-absolute"—because nothing is outside God. ... In a sense it might be said that this separation is absolute as from man to God and relative from God to man' (*SPHF*, 1987, p.167).

3. Bond, Intro. to *Nicholas of Cusa Selected Spiritual Writings*, 1997, pp.26-27.

4. Cusa, *De visione Dei*, 9.37 (1997, pp.251-52).

5. Considering the symbolism of diamond one notes that the "unity" of light is separated into the spectrum by the "action" of the earthly diamond; by inverse analogy the celestial diamond reunites the diversity of the spectrum into the Unity of the Divine Light.

6. Guénon observes the identification of the Celestial Jerusalem with the Terrestrial Paradise, whereby 'the Celestial Jerusalem represents the very re-constitution of the Terrestrial Paradise, according to an analogy applied in an inverse sense' (*ED*, 1996, p.65, n.88).

7. *Zohar* II, 78a-78b.

8. Guénon, *FS*, 1995, p.226.

9. See *Zohar Hadash*, *Yitro*, 38a & d.

10. *Zohar Hadash*, *Yitro*, 38a & d. This identification is further confirmed by *Zohar* II, 15b, *Midrash ha-Ne'elam* which provides a commentary on *Song of Songs* 6:11 (Tishby, *WZ1*, 1991, p.620, cites Sgs.1:11): 'I went down into the nut garden'. The "nut" is the 'supernal chariot of the four head rivers that went out from the garden, like the nut that has four holy heads inside'. The nut which is the river is also the chariot.

11. The *NJB* notes the word *cherubims* is akin to the Assyrian word *karibu*, creatures with a human head, the body of a lion, the hooves of a bull and the wings of an eagle; their effigies stood guard outside the palaces of Babylon. This description of the *karibu* is obviously reminiscent of Ezekiel's "winged creatures" and the *Tetramorphs*.

12. Combined of course this gives a description of a pyramid. Without going into the complex symbolism of the pyramid, we may add that the Ark of Noah was seen by some to have had a pyramidal form (Chevalier & Gheerbrant, *DS*, 1996, p.1145).

13. Pseudo-Dionysius, *The Celestial Hierarchy* 201A (1987, p.161).

14. Pseudo-Dionysius, *The Celestial Hierarchy* 205B & C (1987, pp.161-62).

15. *Kena Upanishad* 2.3. Compare this from the *Tao Te Ching* 56: 'Those who say do not know; those who do not know say.'

16. *Brhadāranyaka Upanishad* 4.3.30. On the idea of a "second" or "other" the Qur'an says: 'Were there other gods in heaven or earth besides God, both heaven and earth would be ruined' (21:22).

17. Erigena cited in Snodgrass, *ATE1*, 1990, p.17, n.48.

18. Palamas, *Triads* 1.3.4, 1983, p.32.

19. Swami Ramdas, *Guide to Aspirants*, Anandashram Series no.13, Kanhangad, 1949, p.32, cited in Perry, *TTW*, 2000, p.221.

20. *Yoga Darshana*, 3.3.

21. Shiva Samhitā, cited in Daniélou, *Yoga, The Method of Re-Integration*, 1949, p.95.

22. Coomaraswamy, 'On the One and Only Transmigrant': *SP2*, 1977, p.78. On the question of self-sacrifice see ibid passim, '*Ākimcañña*: Self-Naughting' and '*Ātmayajña*: Self-Sacrifice', all in the same volume.

23. Boehme, *Signatura Rerum*, XI.72, cited in Perry, *TTW*, 2000, p.233.

24. *Hadīth qudsī*, cited in Perry, *TTW*, 2000, p.861.

25. St. Augustine, *Soliloquies* II, cited in Perry, *TTW*, 2000, p.860.

26. Meister Eckhart, from Blackney (ed.), *Meister Eckhart: A Modern Translation*, 1949, p.259, cited in Perry, *TTW*, 2000, p.861.

27. McGinn, Intro. to *Meister Eckhart: The Essential Sermons, Commentaries, Treatises and Defenses*, 1981, p.31. As McGinn remarks the *durchbrechen* in a sense mirrors the "inner emanation" of the *bullitio* (p.47). See McGinn, 'The God beyond God: Theology and Mysticism in the Thought of Meister Eckhart': *Journal of Religion* 61, 1981, pp.1-19.

28. Meister Eckhart, Sermon 52, (Colledge & McGinn, 1981, p.203).

29. Shabistarī, *The Secret Rose Garden*, cited Perry, *TTW*, 2000, p.753.

30. Cited in Burckhardt, *ISD*, 1976, p.30, n.2.

31. Cited in Nicholson, *Studies in Islamic Mysticism*, 1921, p.152.

32. In the Islamic tradition this is *al-Ahadiyah* (the Divine or Transcendent Unity). This is to be distinguished from *al-wāhidiyah* (the Divine Unicity). The Divine Unity is beyond all distinctive knowledge whereas the Unicity appears in the differentiated just as principial distinctions appear in it.

33. The *Zohar* remarks, 'the knowledge of the Creator is not like that of His creatures, for whom knowledge is distinct from the subject. This differentiation is designated by the following three terms: thought, that which thinks, and the thing thought of. The Creator, on the other hand, is in Himself knowledge, He who knows, and that which is known. In fact, His manner of knowing does not consist in applying His thought of things outside of Him; rather, it is by understanding and knowing himself that He knows and perceives all that is' (Franck, *The Kabbalah*, 1979, p.100).

34. Hermes, *Libellus* XI (ii), 20b, cited in Perry, *TTW*, 2000, p.752.

35. *Theologia Germanica*, XLII.

36. *Yoga-Vasishtha* cited in Perry, *TTW*, 2000, p.753.

37. *Mundaka Upanishad* 3.2.9.

38. *Brhad-āranyaka Upanishad* 4.4.6.

39. *Paradisio*, XXXIII, 124.

40. Uncited reference in Schuon, *SPHF*, 1987, p.170.

41. Boehme, *Signatura Rerum*, XVI, 8.

42. Hermes (*Lib*. XVI. 3) following Coomaraswamy, 'On the One and Only Transmigrant': *SP2*, 1977, p.71, n.21.

43. *Tao Te Ching* 42.

44. On the diremption of the complementary principles see Snodgrass, *ATE1*, 1990, p.60; see also Guénon, 1975, Chs.6 & 7.

45. Aristotle's "unmoved mover." Meister Eckhart is here quoting Aristotle, *On Heaven and Earth* 1.22 (270a33-35).

46. Meister Eckhart, *Par. Gen.* 21 (Colledge & McGinn, 1981, p.101). The opening word of *Genesis*, *Berashith* ("In the beginning"), contains the word, *rē'shīyth*, "the first," as in principial. This word derives from the root, *rō'sh*, indicating "the *head*."

47. Meister Eckhart, *Par. Gen.* 20 (Colledge & McGinn, 1981, p.101).

48. Guénon, *MB*, 1981, p.164. In this context Perry notes the Vedàntic doctrine of *bhedābheda* or 'Distinction without Difference' (*The Widening Breach*, 1995, p.15).

49. *Yang* is the active principle and *yin* the passive principle. In traditional texts *yin* is generally mentioned before *yang*. This accords with the cosmological point of view.

50. See Guénon, *RQ*, 1995, Ch.1 & *passim*.

51. See *The Widening Breach*, 1995, *passim*.

52. Fohr, *Adam and Eve*, 1986, p.43.

53. On the symbolisms of the whale-fish see Guénon, *FS*, 1995, Chs.20, 21, 24, 25, 39 & 40.

54. Skinner, *The Source of Measures*, 1982, p.219.

55. See also Guénon, 'Concerning the Two Saint Johns', *FS*, 1995, Ch.40.

56. See Scott, 'Remarks on the universal symbolism of the number 72', *Eye of the Heart: A Journal of Traditional Wisdom* 1, 2008, pp.119-140. The relationship-identification between 70, 71 and 72 is developed in Drummond, *Oedipus Judaicus* (1811), 1996, pp.344-46.

57. This symbolic web is further enriched by the suggestion, offered by *Strong's*, that the word *yōwnāh* derives from *yayin* (יין; "to *effervesce*," as *wine* fermented), where, as noted, wine is a symbol of the Divine Essence, just as bread is Substance.

58. Unterman, *Dictionary of Jewish Lore & Legend*, 1991, p.181. The "wings of the *Shekhinah*," which are seen as the "wings of a dove" spread out and embrace the Jewish People. Thus, as Unterman remarks elsewhere, the dove is also a symbol of the people of Israel (see p.65).

59. On the *gunas* see Daniélou, *MGI*, p.1985, pp.23-24.

60. Fohr, *Adam and Eve*, 1986, p.43.

61. Guénon, *GT*, 1994, pp.24-25.

62. Perry, *The Widening Breach*, 1995, pp.18-19.

63. Guénon, *SC*, 1975, p.28.

64. *Zohar* I, 21b-22a, cited in Scholem, *MTJM*, 1995, p.226, n.72. See also *Zohar* I, 49b-50a.

65. On the Alchemical Wedding see Burckhardt, *Alchemy*, 1974, Ch.11.

66. Perry offers a lists of complementaries that, as he remarks, could be expanded endlessly; see *The Widening Breach*, 1995, p.3.

67. Meister Eckhart, *Comm. Gen.* 26 (Colledge & McGinn, 1981, p.91).

68. Schuon, *IFA*, 1989, p.73.

69. Schuon, *IFA*, 1989, p.73.

70. See for example, in the Hindu tradition: *Chāndogya Upanishad* 6.2.1, *Brhad-āranyaka Upanishad* 2.5.19. In the Semitic traditions we find this affirmation repeated often, for example, *Isaiah* 45:5 & 46:9, and in the Qur'an: 'There is non divinity but Divinity' (*La ilaha illa 'Llah*); 'Say He is the one God' (*Qul hua 'Llahu ahad*).

71. This is Copenhaver's 1992 translation (*Hermetica*, 2000, p.58) of the quotation cited above by Coomaraswamy. Meister Eckhart remarks, 'Unity acting as a principle of the number six does not make six more than itself, but makes it exactly and absolutely six' (*Par. Gen.* 20, Colledge & McGinn, 1981, p.100).

72. God made man "in the image."

73. Mathers, *KU*, 1991, pp.22-23.

74. Macrobius, *Commentary on the Dream of Scipio*, 1.6.7-9.

75. Hermes Trismegistus, *Asclepius* III.21.

76. Schuon, *SME*, 2000, p.16.

77. For one argument for the appropriateness of applying gender symbolism at this level see James Cutsinger's reply to the criticisms of Martin Lings and Alvin Moore, Jr. in the Reader's Forum, *Sophia*, Vol.7, No.2, 2001, pp.235-240.

78. Guénon, *GT*, 1994, p.19, n.7.

79. *1 Enoch* 54.8. E. Isaac remarks that this section is believed to be part of the lost "Book Noah" (Charlesworth (ed.), *OTP1*, 1983, p.38).

80. For various mythological examples of the Androgyne see Eliade, *Patterns in Comparative Religion*, 1958, p.420; also Campbell, *The Hero with a Thousand Faces*, 1975, pp.128-29; *Primitive Mythology*, 1982, p.103-8.

81. Campbell, *The Hero with a Thousand Faces*, 1975, p.128.

82. *Symposium* 180e.

83. *Genesis Rabba*, 8.1.

84. *Zohar* 1:35b following Matt (tr.), *Zohar*, 1983, p.56.

85. See al-Jīlī, *al-insān*, 1983; see also Guénon, *SC*, 1975, Ch.2. In his introduction to *al-insān* Burckhardt says, 'the cosmos is, then, like a single being; – "We have recounted all things in an evident prototype" (Qur'an 36). If one calls this "Universal Man," it is not by reason of an anthropomorphic conception of the universe, but because man represents, on earth, its most perfect image' (p.iv).

86. Govinda observes that the *Ādibuddha* is 'the symbol of universality, timelessness and completeness of the enlightened mind' (*Foundations of Tibetan Mysticism*, 1969, p.99). He cites H. V. Guenther (*Yuganaddha, the Tantric View of Life*, Banaras, 1952, p.187): '*Ādibuddha* is best translated as the unfolding of man's true nature.'

87. Schaya, *UMK*, 1971, p.126.

88. Scholem, *MTJM*, 1995, p.215.

89. Scholem, *MTJM*, 1995, p.265.

90. Mathers, *KU*, 1991, pp.26-27.

91. Halevi, *Adam and the Kabbalistic Tree*, 1974, p.21. Halevi notes the four laws as follows: (1) All is One; (2) the action of the supernal trinity; (3) the law of sequence as defined by the Great Octave; and (4) the four worlds, each containing a secondary Tree in its own right.

92. *Anthologia Graeca ad Fiden Codices*, Vol.II; Ovid, *Metamorphoses*, IV, 288 ff.; *et al*, cited in Campbell, *The Hero with a Thousand Faces*, 1975, p.128, n.88.

93. Campbell, *Primitive Mythology*, 1982, p.417. Of course, Hermes' counterpart in the Norse tradition is Loki whose androgynous nature is demonstrated by the story of his transformation into a mare so as to seduce the stallion, Svadilfaeri, the end result of which is the eight-hoofed horse, Sleipnir.

94. Schaya, *UMK*, 1971, p.68.

95. 'So shall the last be first, and the first last' (Mt.20:16).

96. Unterman, *Dictionary of Jewish Lore & Legend*, 1991, p.181.

97. Guénon, *GT*, 1994, p.14. Guénon remarks that 'certain more or less heterodox Christian sects have made the Holy Spirit out to be feminine–often with the specific intention of providing it with characteristics comparable to those of the Mother [of the ternary Father, Mother and Son]' (pp.13 & 14); see Ch.1.

98. Guénon, *LW*, 1983, p.15; see 'Shekinah and Metatron', Ch.3.

99. On *līlā* as "cosmic play" see Coomaraswamy, SP2, 1977, '*Līlā*' (pp.148-158).

100. Karapātrī, "Śrī Śiva tattva," *Siddhānta*, II, 1941-42, 114, cited in Daniélou, *MGI*, 1985, p.203.

101. *Symposium* 190b.

102. Parmenides, *Frag*.VIII.

103. Guénon, *SC*, 1975, p.29.

104. Guénon, *FS*, 1995, p.186.

105. *Gylfaginning*, 42 in Sturluson, *Edda*, 1998, p.35.

106. *Symposium* 180e.

107. *Republic* 521c. Clement says that this expresses 'a conversion and turning about of the soul from a day whose light is darkness to the true day—that ascension to reality of our parable which we will affirm to be true philosophy' (*Stromata*, 5.105.2; 133.5).

108. Snodgrass, *ATE1*, 1990, p.157; see Chs.11-14.

109. Sūrah 25, *al-furquan*.

110. Schuon, *IFA*, 1988, p.187.

111. Schuon, *IFA*, 1988, p.187, n.1.

112. Burckhardt, *MI*, 1987, pp.193-94.

113. Nasr, *ICD*, 1978, p.269. Nasr observes that the use of the Aristotelian language of form and matter is here transposed into the spiritual domain to symbolise the inner experiences of the traveler.

114. Ibn Sina, cited in Nasr, *ICD*, 1978, p.269. Nasr is quoting from Henry Corbin's, *Avicenna and the Visionary Recital*, Pantheon Books, New York, 1960. The 1980 Spring Publications (Texas) edition follows the original French edition omitting pages 279-380 of the 1960 edition, which include this translation of the "Recital of Hayy Ibn Yaqzan."

115. For a full exposition of this symbolism see Guénon, *SC*, 1975.

116. See the *Bardo thos grol*, 'The Great Book of Natural Liberation Through Understanding in the Between', or as it is commonly known in the West, 'The Tibetan Book of the Dead'.

117. *Matsya Purana* 3 tells of the birth of Sandhyā from Prajapati, the lord of progeny; cited in Daniélou, *MGI*, 1985, p.236.

118. Guénon, *MB*, 1981, p.88, n.1.

119. Al-Jīlī, *al-insān*, 1983, p.xviii.

120. On the *yin-yang* symbol see Guénon, *SC*, 1975, Ch.22; *GT*, 1994, Ch.4.

121. Guénon, *FS*, 1995, p.208. On *T'ai-chi* see Chan, *A Source Book in Chinese Philosophy*, 1969, p.263, passim.

122. Guénon, *GT*, 1994, p.34, n.12.

123. Perry, *TTW*, 2000, p.650.

124. Cited in Burckhardt, *MI*, 1987, p.194.

125. Rappoport, *AII*, 1995, p.210.

126. *Inferno*, XXXIV, 90.

127. Burckhardt, *MI*, 1987, p.194.

128. Burckhardt, *ISD*, 1976, p.123.

129. Burckhardt, *MI*, 1987, p.196.

130. Burckhardt, *MI*, 1987, p.197.

131. Cited here from Shaikh Al-'Alawī in Lings, *A Sufi Saint of the Twentieth Century*, 1971, p.160.

132. *Summa Theol.*, 1.63.3, cited in Perry, *TTW*, 2000, p.208.

133. The reader is directed to Coomaraswamy's essay, 'Symplegades': *SP1*, 1977. This essay offers an extensive bibliography on this subject. See also the related essay in the same volume, '*Svayamātrnnā*: Janua Coeli'.

134. For various accounts of the motif of the Symplegades in the Hero's journey see Campbell, *The Hero with a Thousand Faces*, 1975, pp.79-80.

135. Guénon, *FS*, 1995, p.110.

136. Coomaraswamy, 'Symplegades': *SP1*, 1977, p.526, n.12.

137. *Argonautica* II.549-609.

138. Compare Sleipnir, the winged "horse-ship"; in this connection one thinks of Pegasus in Greek tradition and Buraq in Islamic tradition.

139. See here Stoddart, 'Mysticism' originally published in Fernando (ed.), *The Unanimous Tradition*, 1991; republished in *Sacred Web* 2, 1998.

140. Coomaraswamy, '"Satan" and "Hell"': *SP2*, 1977, p.30, n.26.

141. *Chāndogya Upanishad* 8.4.1, cited in Perry, *TTW*, 2000, p.979. Swāmī Gambhīrānada's translation has "dam" instead of "bridge." This simply reflects a shift in perspective, for the *barzakh*, is both barrier and bridge.

142. Coomaraswamy, 'Symplegades': *SP1*, 1977, p.531.

143. Coomaraswamy, 'Symplegades': *SP1*, 1977, p.522, n.5.

144. Coomaraswamy, 'Symplegades': *SP1*, 1977, p.522, n.5.

145. Shakespeare, *Anthony and Cleopatra*, 5.2.297.

146. Coomaraswamy, 'Symplegades': *SP1*, 1977, p.528.

147. Parmenides Frag.1.

148. Drummond, *Oedipus Judaicus*, 1996, p.98.

149. Unger, "Hebrews" in *Unger's Bible Dictionary*, 1965, p.465.

150. See Drummond's dissertation on the Paschal Lamb (VI), *Oedipus Judaicus*, 1996.

151. Meister Eckhart cited in Perry, *TTW*, 2000, p.876.

152. Guénon, *SC*, 1975, p.32; see Ch.7.

153. Perry, *The Widening Breach*, 1995.

154. Coomaraswamy, 'Symplegades': *SP1*, 1977, p.542.

155. Guerber, *Greece and Rome*, 1985, p.356. Guerber tends towards interpretation of these myths as simply "nature allegories"; however, Guerber's view does not necessarily mean his reading is incompatible with mine–merely that it is limited.

156. This use of the term "space" is purely symbolic. As Schuon remarks, 'There is no common measure between manifestation and the Principle, and consequently there cannot be an intermediate point which is situated as it were "mathematically" in the centre. This centre exists only in relation to the world and in a purely symbolic manner. It appears either as "the Principle made manifest" or as the "manifestation of the Principle"' (*SPHF*, 1987, p.174).

157. The resting place of Deucalion's Ark is commonly accepted as Parnassus although Robert Graves remarks that some tell it was Mt. Etna or Mt. Athos or Mt. Othrys in Thessaly (*The Greek Myths Vol.1*, 1960, p.139).

158. Dalley (ed.), *MM*, 1991, p.96.

159. *Antiquities* 1.3.92.

160. Whiston's notes to his translation of Josephus, *The Complete Works of Josephus*, 1981, p.33-34.

161. This potentiality must be sacrificed in the act of Creation, as witnessed in the Mithraic mysteries; see Cumont, *The Mysteries of Mithra*, 1956.

162. "Darkness" is the other exemplary symbol of Substance, although, as noted, this more accurately refers to the transcendent nature of Substance.

163. See, as a more obscure example, *Zohar* II, 64b-65a.

164. See Tishby, *WZ2*, 1989, p.507, n.302.

165. Coomaraswamy, 'The Inverted Tree': *SP1*, 1977.

166. Coomaraswamy, 'The Inverted Tree': *SP1*, 1977, p.396. Most interestingly Coomaraswamy cites Holmberg on the tradition of the Inverted Tree: 'The Lapps sacrificed every year an ox to the god of vegetation, represented by an uprooted tree so placed on the altar that its crown was downward and roots upward.' (p.396) The "sacrifice" of the *aleph* (ox) to the *resh* cannot go unnoticed here.

167. See Chevalier & Gheerbrant, *DS*, 1996, 'forty' (pp.401-402).

168. *Rosh Hashanah* 21b, cited in Gikatilla, *SO*, 1994, p.323

169. Schaya, *UMK*, 1971, p.69, n.1.

170. Skinner, *The Source of Measures* (1894), 1982, p.250.

171. Note that both *Binah* and *Tiferet* are known by the Holy Name YHVH, although in the case of *Binah* this name is vocalized as ELoHIM (see Rabbi Gikatilla, *SO*, 1994, passim.).

172. According to Christian tradition St. Peter was presented the "keys of the kingdom of heaven" (Mt.16:19).

173. See Coomaraswamy, '*Svayamātrnnā:* Janua Coeli': *SP1*, 1977; Guénon, *FS*, 1995, Chs.20, 39, 40 & 60.

174. Guénon, *FS*, 1995, p.90.

175. Guénon, *FS*, 1995, p.92.

176. Cited in Rappoport, *AI1*, 1995, p.260.

177. *Midrash Tanchuma, Genesis*, 8, 16 per Rappoport, *AII*, p.275.

178. Guénon, *FS*, 1995, p.92.

179. Perry, *The Widening Breach*, 1995, p.18, n.1.

180. "Virtual" inasmuch as it is distinct from the Union achieved by the solar hero in the passage through the Sundoor.

181. The same is true of the "two" accounts of the creation of man in *Genesis* Chapters One and Two, which rather than being separate accounts are in fact the two complementary expressions of the anthropomorphic cosmogenesis viewed respectively *ad extra* (*Genesis* Ch.1) and *ad intra* (*Genesis* Ch.2). These correspond to the two "contradictory" theories in contemporary embryology: "recapitulation" and "neoteny." On this notion see Lawlor, *Sacred Geometry*, 1989, pp.90-91.

182. The Ark is popularly known as "the Ark of the Covenant (*beriyth*)," and so have I referred to it. However, it is referred to in the Hebrew Scriptures as "the Ark of the Testimony (*ēdūwth*)" (Ex.25:22, 26:33, 40:21). The words *beriyth* (ברית; "in the sense of *cutting*"; a *compact* made by passing between two pieces of flesh—cf. the Symplegades) and *ēdūwth* (from *'ūwd*; "to duplicate") bare comparison. The Ark also contains the pot of manna and Aaron's rod.

183. These tablets symbolism, among other things, the Written Law and the Oral Law.

184. Cited in Lawlor, *Sacred Geometry*, 1989, p.56.

185. In Renaissance depictions of Eden this enclosure was often depicted as a fence. See for instance Fra Angelico's famous and very beautiful *Annunciation* at San Marco.

186. The word in question is קרן, *qāran*, a primitive root meaning "to *push* or gore"; as *qeren*, it means to "*shoot out horns*," and figuratively a "ray of light."

187. On the symbolism of horns see Guénon, *FS*, 1995, Ch.30.

188. Campbell, *Primitive Mythology*, 1982, p.436. With respect to the "triple jewel" or *Triratna* see Guénon, *GT*, 1994, Ch.24.

189. Chevalier & Gheerbrant, *DS*, 1996, p.514.

190. Chevalier & Gheerbrant, *DS*, 1996, p.515.

191. Chevalier & Gheerbrant, *DS*, 1996, p.515.

192. The Hebrew omits from verse one, 'come up to me on the mountain', but this instruction is found again at verse two, 'at dawn come up Mount Sinai and wait for me there at the top of the mountain.'

193. According to the Latin MSS, *Vita* 50.1-2, in Charlesworth (ed.), *OTP2*, 1983, p.292.

194. *2 Enoch* 33.8-12, in Charlesworth (ed.), *OTP1*, 1983, p.156.

195. *Antiquities*, 1.2.3.

196. Rabbi Gikatilla, *SO*, 1994, p.125.

The Ternary: *Unity in Plurality*

Introduction

Immanence articulates itself through the "triple immanent principle": Principle-Essence-Substance. This is reflected or realised in the ternary, Essence-Substance-Manifestation. Manifestation, in turn, is comprised of the "three worlds" of the microcosm: earth-midspace-heaven. The symbolisms of both the Ark of Noah and the Ark of the Covenant suggest the triple immanent principle through that which they contain. In the former case the triple immanent principle is expressed by the three sons of Noah. In the latter case this is expressed by 'the gold jar containing the manna, Aaron's branch that grew the buds, and the tablets of the covenant' (Heb.9:4). Similarly each of these Arks expresses the microcosmic "three worlds." The Ark of Noah expresses the "three worlds" by the three "decks" of the Ark (Gen.6:16) and the division of "all living things" into "birds," "animals" and "every kind of creature that creeps along the ground" (Gen.6:20). In the Ark of the Covenant, the "three worlds" are expressed horizontally by the three main divisions of the Temple (the Portico, the Great Chamber and the Sanctuary), and vertically by the three "storeys" of the Temple (1Kgs.6:8). The Temple, like the mountain, is an *imago mundi*. This chapter begins with a consideration of the relationship between the Trinity, as an expression of the Absolute, and the ontological ternary. We then turn to a more detailed symbolic exegesis of the two biblical Arks in light of the ideas above.

The Trinity

> Of the first principle the Egyptians said nothing, but celebrated it as a darkness beyond all intellectual conception, a thrice unknown darkness.
>
> Damascius[1]

> No sooner do I conceive of the One than I am illumined by the splendour of the Three; no sooner do I distinguish them than I am carried back to the One.
>
> St. Gregory Nazianzen[2]

> These three are one.
>
> *1 John* 5:7

The supreme prefiguration of all positive ternaries is the Trinity: Absolute, Infinite, Good. This can be likened to the Christian Trinity: Father, Son and Holy Spirit. However, one must be careful when considering the Christian Trinity, for the dogmatism of Trinitarian theology can often bring more dissension than not; thus the doctrinal disputes between the Latin and the Greek Churches concerning the *filioque*, and the arguments concerning "modalism" in the Trinity.³ Again, there is debate over the identification of the Trinity with the Divine Essence and the idea of a Godhead above and beyond the Trinity.⁴ For our purposes it is enough to distinguish, as does Meister Eckhart, between the trinitarian Godhead (*Gottheit*) and the personal God (*Gott*); where the former does, in fact, equate with the Divine Essence—without this in anyway limiting the Trinity to a single "Essence"—with the latter equating with Being as such, or from a more limited point of view, the Demiurge; again, the distinction here is that between The One and the monad.

Schuon offers an understanding of the Trinity that has proved controversial but which is nevertheless insightful where metaphysics are at issue.⁵ He writes:

> The Trinity can be envisaged according to a "vertical" perspective or according to either of two "horizontal" perspectives, the former of them being supreme and the other not. The "vertical" perspective—Beyond-Being, Being and Existence—envisages the hypostases as "descending" from Unity or from the Absolute—or from the Essence it could be said—which means that it envisages the degrees of Reality; the supreme "horizontal" perspective corresponds to the Vedantic triad *Sat* (supra-ontological Reality), *Cit* (Absolute Consciousness) and *Ananda* (Infinite Bliss), which means that it envisages the Trinity inasmuch as it is hidden in Unity; the non-supreme "horizontal" perspective on the contrary places Unity as an essence hidden within the Trinity, which is then an ontological Trinity representing the three fundamental aspects or modes of Pure Being, whence we have the triad: Being, Wisdom, Will (Father, Son, Spirit).⁶

Schuon's "vertical" Trinity echoes Plotinus' three consubstantial hypostases: the One, the Intellect and the World Soul, of which Vladimir Lossky says: 'Their consubstantiality does not rise to the trinitarian antinomy of Christian dogma.'⁷ Lossky's view reflects a dogmatism—valid in itself—which, in the final analysis, is concerned with what is properly an ineffable and apophatic Reality, such that descriptions of it necessarily involve the antinomy and paradox that see the Trinity being a single Unity with Three Persons that are absolutely distinct and yet absolutely equal. Moreover, the apophatic nature of the Trinity alerts one to the fact that this, as Schuon says, is what the Buddhists call an *upāya*, a "provisional means," or a way.⁸ Apophatic and cataphatic theology are, regardless of the absoluteness of their goal, still "ways" to this goal. Thus, to call the Trinity an *upāya* is no disservice, for any human conception, be it negative or positive, of the Divine as "other," is contingent or provisional. The Trinity of Itself—one might say, in Its Essence—is not contingent; nevertheless, insofar as we may conceive of it, this conception is precisely an *upāya*; moreover, for the Christian it constitutes, along with the Person of Christ, the *upāya par excellence*, which is to say, the Revelation. In the end this is summed up by a quote from St. Gregory Nazianzen which, it might be noted, Lossky uses to argue the case against the type of conception that some feel Schuon expounds. St. Gregory Nazianzen: 'To us there is one God, for the Godhead is One, and all that proceedeth from Him is referred to One, though we believe in Three Persons ... When, then, we look at the Godhead, or the First Cause, or the Monarchy, that which is conceived is One; but when we look at the Persons in whom the Godhead dwells, and at those who timelessly and with equal glory have their being from the First Cause—there are Three whom we worship.'[9] The very nature of "believing in" and "worshipping" express the idea of "otherness" and show the contingent nature of the Trinity *thus envisaged*; the shift from "looking" at the Godhead to "looking" at the Persons, shows that what is at issue here is a matter of perspective. These are not criticisms of St. Gregory Nazianzen but recognition of the distinction between worshipper and the Worshipped, creature and God, the servant (*al-'abd*) and Lord (*al-rabb*).[10]

It might be contested that the Essence in itself, or the *hyperousia*, as St. Gregory Palamas terms it, is beyond relationship, "incomprehensible and ineffable," and thus the absolutisation of the Trinity, while theologically acceptable, is metaphysically inadmissible. However, as envisaged by St. Gregory Palamas the Godhead has two coessential modalities: Essence and Energies (δυναμεις). The Essence in Itself might be termed the interiority of God, and to be correct this is "unknowable,"[11] but God in His Essence also possess certain modalities of expression, Energies, which, while remaining uncreated, nevertheless are figured by the Trinity. In this sense the Trinity is the uncreated "expression" of the Godhead. Let it be stressed that this "expression" is still "uncreated" and thus must be distinguished from the created world insomuch as it is the created "expression" of the Absolute—"made in the image," with the emphasis on being "made." Now, one might suppose to see the Essence as the Divine considered *ad intra* and the Trinity as the Divine *ad extra*, but this would be incorrect, for the Divine viewed *ad extra* is the Personal God, the Demiurge and by extension, Creation itself, where the Trinity also embraces Creation. In fact the Divine considered *ad intra* is both Trinitarian Essence and uncreated Trinitarian Energies.

One might say that the Essence is apophatic, exclusive and interioris-ing, while the Trinity is cataphatic, inclusive and exteriorising, and it is precisely this that the Energies express. Again, one might talk of the unity of the Essence-Trinity and the Trinitarian Energies. As Meister Eckhart remarks, 'the one essence is their root, and these three are the one essence.'[12] Better still we should say that there is only the Trinity, apophatic and cataphatic. The Essence and the Trinity may be likened to the Absolute and the Infinite, which are, so to speak, the intrinsic dimensions of each other. In the final analysis there is, as Schuon says, 'no need to consider a trinity formed by the aspects "Good," "Absolute," "Infinite"; but rather, what ought to be said is that the Sovereign Good is absolute and, therefore, that it is infinite.'[13]

According to Kabbalah the ineffable and unknowable "Trinity" is described as three veils of the "Negative Existence." These are not three separate veils each being comprised of "negative existence" but three veils or aspects of the one "negative" Reality: *Ain* ("Negativity"; Abso-lute), *En Sof* ("the Limitless"; Infinite), and *En Sof Aur* ("the Limitless Light"; Good). *Ain* is "Negativity" insomuch as the Absolute is beyond all affirmation. It is "nothingness," the absence of any definite or condi-tioned reality,[14] *neti neti*, "neither this nor that." As Alain Daniélou re-marks, with respect to *Brahman*, 'We can only define it negatively, say-ing that it is nothing of what man can know or conceive, neither god, nor man, nor thing. It is thus spoken of as nondual, unknowable, formless, changeless, limitless, etc.'[15] Pseudo-Dionysius goes further yet, saying that the "transcendent Cause" (the Absolute) is 'beyond privations, be-yond every denial, beyond every assertion.'[16]

The Trinity, *Ain*, *En Sof*, *En Sof Aur*, prefigures the onto-cosmolog-ical "articulation" of the *Sefirot*. Mathers says that 'in themselves they [the Negative Trinity] formulate the hidden ideas of the *Sefirot* not yet called into being'.[17] Mathers:

> The first veil of the negative existence is the AIN, *Ain* = Nega-tivity. This word consists of three letters, which thus shadows forth the first three *Sefirot* or numbers. The second veil is the AIN SVP, *Ain Soph* = the Limitless. This title consists of six letters, and shadows forth the idea of the first six *Sefirot* or num-bers. The third veil is the AIN SVP AVR, *Ain Soph Aur* = the Limitless Light. This again consists of nine letters, and symbol-ises the first nine *Sefirot*, but of course in their hidden idea only. But when we reach the number nine we cannot progress farther without returning to the unity, or the number one, for the num-ber ten is but a repetition of unity freshly derived from the nega-

tive, as is evident from a glance at its ordinary representation in Arabic numerals, where the circle 0 represents the Negative, and the 1 the Unity. Thus, then, the limitless ocean of negative light *does not proceed from a centre, for it is centreless, but it concentrates a centre* [the *tsimtsum*], which is the number one of the manifested *Sefirot, Keter*, the Crown, the First *Sefirah*; which therefore may be said to be the *Malkhut* or number ten of the hidden *Sefirot*.

The Trinity expresses the "articulation of the Essence"[18] through the coessential hypostases: Father, Son and Holy Spirit. The three divine hypostases, as St. Gregory Palamas says, possess one another 'naturally, totally, eternally and indivisibly, but also without mixture or confusion, and they co-penetrate each other in such a way that they possess one energy.'[19] The Absolute is by definition Infinite, comprising the Infinite Substance (*ousia* or *hyperousia*) or All-Possibility, which, by virtue of its absolute inclusiveness, is the Divine Perfection or the Good. The Father can be equated with the Absolute and the Son with the Infinite, insomuch as Christ is the Word, the Divine Substance, through whom 'all things came in to being' and without which 'not one thing came in to being' (Jn.1:3). The Holy Spirit is then the Good insomuch as it is the projection of the Absolute into Relativity, which achieves the perfection of the Infinite. We could equally say that the Son is the Good insomuch as it is in Him that Relativity is actualised, or "made flesh." Likewise, the Holy Spirit can be recognised as the Infinite insomuch as it is the infinite projection of the Absolute. Again, the Absolute is the Supreme Good, being the Ultimate Perfection. 'These three are one' (1Jn.5:7),[20] which is to say with St. Augustine that 'the works of the trinity are indivisible.'[21]

The Divine Essence is the principle of Being, which is to say, Being *per se*. Being is the same with the Essence but the Essence is not limited to Being. At the level of Being the Trinity is the intrinsic nature of the extrinsic Personal God. Here the Christian Trinity may be likened by symbolic transposition to the Hindu *Saccidānanda, Sat* (Being), *Cit* (Consciousness), *Ānanda* (Beatitude). This is the Trinity envisaged with respect to Schuon's supreme "horizontal" perspective. Guénon observes that this Trinity has its equivalent in the Arabic terms, *al-'aql* (Intelligence), *al-'āqil* (the Intelligent) and *al-ma'qūl* (the Intelligible): 'the first is universal Consciousness (*Cit*), the second is its subject (*Sat*) and the third is its object (*Ānanda*), the three being but one in being "which knows Itself by Itelf."'[22] As Guénon says, *Sat, Cit, Ānanda* are 'but one single and identical entity [*Saccidānanda*], and this "one" is *Ātman*'.[23]

174

Furthermore, as the Trinity is identical to the Essence so, says Guénon, is *Ātman* identical with *Brahman* Itself.[24] Likewise, Schaya observes that in the final analysis the principial *Sefirah Keter* is "in itself" *Ain*.[25]

The Ternary

In the beginning God created heaven and earth.
Genesis 1:1

The Tao produced one; one produced two; two produced three.
Tao Te Ching, Ch.42

Bringing or coming into being is based on a triplicity, or rather a bipolar triplicity, one being of the Reality, the other of the creature.
Ibn al-'Arabī[26]

Being is "one that is three," the Trinity envisaged as *Saccidānanda*. At the principial level this is a "distinction without difference" (*bhedābheda*); Being, Consciousness, and Beatitude are not three separate entities but one reality. This ternary is prefigured at the highest level by the principle of the Trinity (Absolute, Infinite, Good), which is Supreme Unity. *Saccidānanda*, the supreme "horizontal" Trinity gives rise to the ontological ternary. Now, as Schuon remarks, 'the centre-present [that is, the ontological principle] is expressed by the ternary, and not by unity, because unity is here envisaged in respect to its potentialities and thus in relation to its possibility of unfolding; the actualisation of that unfolding is expressed precisely by the number two. The number three evokes in fact not absoluteness as does the number one, but the potentiality or virtuality which the Absolute necessarily comprises.'[27]

To talk of the Trinity envisaged ontologically is to talk of Immanence as the articulation of Transcendence. In the Judaic tradition Immanence articulates Itself through what Leo Schaya has termed "the triple immanent principle," *Shekhinah-Metatron-Avir*. Schaya:

Shekhinah is the immanence of *Keter*, the presence of divine reality in the midst of the cosmos. *Metatron*, the manifestation of *Hokhmah* and the active aspect of the *Shekhinah*, is the principle form from which all created forms emanate; *avir*, the ether, is a manifestation of *Binah*: it is the passive aspect of *Shekhinah*, its cosmic receptivity, which gives birth to every created substance, whether subtle or corporeal. The triple immanent principle, *Shekhinah-Metatron-Avir*, in its undifferentiated unity, constitutes the spiritual and prototypical "world of creation": *olam haberiyah*.[28]

According to Schaya, '*Keter* wraps itself in its first casual emanation, *Hokhmah*, and surrounds *Hokhmah* with its receptivity, *Binah*; and the radiation of the active principle completely fills the receptivity of the passive cause.'[29] He is quick to emphasise that, '*Hokhmah* and *Binah* emanate simultaneously from *Keter*, the dark receptivity of the "mother" being entirely filled with the luminous fullness of the "father"; these two complementary principles are never in any way separate. They are not, therefore, really two; the created being, man, sees them as differentiated, being himself subject to distinction. In reality, *Hokhmah* and *Binah* are indivisible and inseparable aspects of *Keter*, the One.'[30]

Strictly speaking the Trinity refers to Transcendence—allowing for the fact that the Trinity embraces Immanence *in divinis*—whereas the "triple immanent principle" pertains to Immanence. It is in this sense that I offer a distinction between the terms Trinity as such and the notion of ternary. Thus, the term "Trinity" connotes the notion of the Unity of the Godhead; to say Trinity is to say one with three coessential Persons or "aspects." The term "ternary" describes the fundamental elements of creative Being; to say ternary is to talk of three "entities"—for want of a more satisfactory term—, two of which are the polarisation of the third. Two things emerge from this distinction between Trinity and ternary. Firstly, one might pedantically object that the Trinity is in fact a ternary, given the etymological derivation of the word "ternary" from the Latin, *terni* ("three at once"). I will not argue, but instead reiterate that the present distinction between Trinity and ternary is contrived with a view to expedient clarification. Secondly, all ontological polarisations are, in the final analysis, resolvable in the *coincidentia oppositorum*, through which the ternary dissolves in the Unity of the Trinity.

There are two fundamental forms of the ternary, of which the polarisation of the Principle into Essence and Substance is the exemplar and archetype of the first. This first ternary is comprised of three terms in a relationship such that two terms derive from or contrive to a third term. The principal image of this type is the triangle with its apex situated at the top. 'In India' observes Robert Lawlor, 'the triangle was called the Mother, for it is the membrane or birth channel through which all the transcendent powers of unity and its initial division into polarity must pass in order to enter into the manifest realm of surface. The triangle acts as the mother of form.'[31]

This type of ternary consists of two complementary and, strictly speaking, analogous ternaries. The first is comprised of a first principle that gives rise to two complementary principles; this is figured by a triangle with its apex above (fig.2). The ternaries Androgyne, Father, Mother or Principle, Essence, Substance are of this sort. In the

Chinese tradition this is the ternary *T'ai Chi* ("Great Extreme"), *T'ien* ("Heaven), *Ti* ("Earth"). 'And this' says Guénon, 'is not the end of the matter: *T'ai Chi*, transcendental Being or Unity, itself presupposes another principle—*Wu Chi*, Non-Being or the metaphysical Naught. But it is impossible for this principle to enter into relationship with anything beside itself in such a way as to become the first term of a ternary, for no relationship of this sort could possibly exist prior to the affirmation of being or Unity.'[32]

The second and complementary ternary of this type is comprised of two complementaries and a third term which rises as a result of their union; this is figured by a triangle with its apex below (fig.3).[33] The ternaries Father, Mother, and Son and the Chinese "Great Triad," *T'ien*, *Ti* and *Jen* (Heaven, Earth and Man) are of this sort.[34]

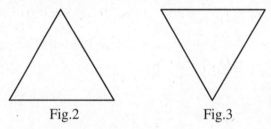

Fig.2   Fig.3

The polarisation of the Divine Androgyne into the sexual principles (Father, Mother) is answered, so to speak, by the union of the sexes in the "Son," the 'royal child more perfect than its parents,' the *Rebis* of the alchemists. The *Rebis*—from *res bina*, "twofold matter"—is so called because 'it is made of two substances, namely of male and of female … although at bottom it is the same substance and the same matter … and these two separate substances derived from the same source are really one homogenous whole.'[35]

Guénon remarks that the two complementary or opposed terms—according to the perspective adopted—express, as the case may be, either a horizontal opposition (between right and left) or vertical opposition (between higher and lower). Guénon:

> Horizontal opposition occurs between two terms which share the same degree of reality and are, so to speak, symmetrical in every respect. Vertical opposition indicates, on the contrary, a hierarchical relationship between the two terms. Although still symmetrical in the sense of being complementary, they are related in such a way that one of them must be considered to be higher, or superior, and the other lower or inferior.[36]

'It is important' says Guénon, 'to notice that in a vertical opposition the first term of a ternary of the first type [Principle, Essence, Substance] cannot be placed between the two complementaries or in the middle of the line that joins them: this can only be done with the third term of a ternary of the second type [Essence, Substance, Manifestation]. The reason is that the principle can never be situated at a lower level than the one of the two terms that derive from it; it is necessarily higher than, or superior to, them both.'[37] Thus it is only in the case of the second type of ternary that we can re-arrange it in the form of a vertical line (fig.4) where Essence and Substance are respectively the upper and lower poles of Manifestation.

The Great Triad

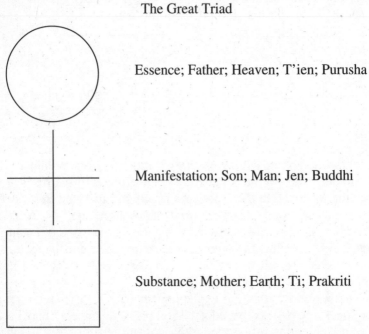

Essence; Father; Heaven; T'ien; Purusha

Manifestation; Son; Man; Jen; Buddhi

Substance; Mother; Earth; Ti; Prakriti

Fig.4

Essence is represented by a circle, both Centre (the first point) and circumference. Substance is represented by a square expressing a plane of Existence delineated by the extent of its four direction, which correspond to the Four Elements (Ether not being included corresponding as it does to the Centre). Manifestation is represented by the cross expressing the meeting of the "vertical" Essence and the "horizontal" Substance.[38]

The second fundamental ternary is comprised of a hierarchy of constituent elements of the microcosm, *corpus*, *anima*, *spiritus*; *soma*, *psyché*, *pneuma*; or *tamas*, *rajas*, *sattva*. This ternary, says Schuon, is based on the 'qualitative aspects of space measured from the starting point of consciousness which is situated within it: ascending dimension or lightness, descending dimension or heaviness, horizontal dimensions open to both influences.'[39] These are again what Guénon refers to as the "three worlds," the Hindu *Tribhuvana*, *Bhu* (Earth), *Bhuvas* (Air) and *Svar* (Heaven).[40] The fundamental difference here is that whereas Essence and Substance (*T'ien* and *Ti*, or *Purusha* and *Prakriti*) are 'outside of manifestation, and indeed are the immediate principles behind manifestation, the "three worlds" signify the totality of manifestation itself, divided in to its three basic categories–the realm of supra-formal manifestation, the realm of subtle manifestation and the realm of gross or corporeal manifestation.'[41] Snodgrass refers to Earth, Midspace and Heaven;[42] from a slightly different perspective, these are Netherworld, Earth and Heaven; again, these are Dante's Inferno, Purgatory and Paradiso.

A certain awkwardness arises here, as Guénon observes, inasmuch as we are somewhat obliged to use the terms "heaven" and "earth" to refer both to Essence and Substance and to the supra-formal and gross realms of manifestation. However, as Guénon remarks,

> to justify this dual application or connotation of the same terms we need only point out that the supra-formal realm of manifestation is clearly the realm in which celestial influences are predominant, while terrestrial influences will obviously predominate in the gross realm. ... We can also say—and this amounts to saying the same thing in a different way—that the supra-formal realm is closer to essence while the gross realm is closer to substance, although of course this in no way entitles us to identify them with universal Essence and universal Substance themselves.[43]

Between the first type of ternary we have considered and the ternary figured by the "three worlds" there is a fundamental difference, being specifically evident in their order of production. Thus in the ternary Principle-Essence-Substance, the terms Essence and Substance result from the diremption of the biune Principle. In the Great Triad, *Jen* (Man) or Manifestation is the product of the fundamental masculine and feminine principles. In contrast, each term of the *Tribhuvana*, considered in descending order, has its immediate principle in the term that precedes it.[44]

Allowing for these fundamental differences, one can nevertheless say that there is commonality between the Great Triad and the "three worlds." In the first instance, and as we have just noted, "heaven" and "earth" of the "three worlds" are, so to speak, "influenced" by Heaven and Earth of the Great Triad. As for what the Vedantists call *antariksha* or the "intermediary world" (*Bhuvas*, Air, Midspace), this, as Guénon remarks, is 'a combination of the two different classes of mutually complementary influences, balanced and intermingled to such an extent that it is impossible–at least when one is speaking of this intermediary world as a whole—to say which set of influences is stronger than the other.' Nevertheless, as Guénon stresses, 'On no account must this middle term of the *Tribhuvana* be confused with the middle term of the Great Triad, Man.'[45] This is not to say that these terms have nothing in common, for in fact they share a correlation of "function"—precisely that of "intermediary."[46]

One might describe the difference under consideration as that between verticality and horizontality. This is to say that the Great Triad must be seen as vertical inasmuch as Essence, first and foremost, must be considered as "upper" by virtue of its "excellence" and Substance as "lower" by virtue of its "density." In contrast the "three worlds" are the elements of a horizontal plain of Existence. Nevertheless from the point of view of man, that is, viewed from within Manifestation itself, the "three worlds" appear vertical, and here it is a matter of effective and adequate symbolism. From another point of view, when considered metaphysically the "three worlds" contract, so to speak, from the exoteric to the esoteric, from Earth to Midspace to Heaven. This contraction returns us to the symbolism of the circle: the circumference is the realm of gross manifestation; the radii are the subtle realm; the centre is the supra-formal realm. The combination of horizontal contraction and the symbolic verticality of the "three worlds" is epitomised by the symbolism of the mountain: as one moves upwards from the base to the apex, one simultaneously moves inwards from the circumference to the centre. At the centre-apex one stands at the heart (*barzakh*) of the Man of the Great Triad, none other than Universal Man. From here one is brought into the presence of the Divine (cf. Moses on Mt. Sinai, Ex.24:12-18), through which and in which one may "taste" without "touching" the Unmanifest Trinity.

The Three Worlds of the Ark

Put the entrance in the side of the ark, which is to be made with lower, second and third decks.

Genesis 6:16

The Ark is the receptacle of Divine Immanence, which is to say, it is the receptacle of Manifestation or the "three worlds." This tripartite structure is symbolically figured in the accounts of both the Ark of Noah and the Ark of the Covenant, and again with the accounts of the tabernacle and the Temple. The Ark of Noah is constructed, in conformity with God's commands, with 'lower, second and third decks' (Gen.6:16). Here the "three worlds" are contained *within* the Ark, expressing the virtuality of onto-cosmological existence during the Flood. Moreover, these three "decks" or "storeys," from *ma'alah* (מעלה; "*elevation*"), imply a verticality that is proper inasmuch as in this state—the state of virtuality during the intermission of the Flood—the "three worlds" are more closely influenced by the Great Triad. The idea of three ascending "worlds" is further implied by the division of "all living things" into "birds," "animals" and "every kind of creature that creeps along the ground" (Gen.6:20), which demonstrates three successive vertical distinctions being from what is most upper to what is lower. These divisions can be compared respectively to the *Tribhuvana* (Heaven, Air, Earth), where we keep in mind that "birds" commonly refer to the angelic realm,[47] and that "animals," by virtue of being "elevated" upon their legs, are thus placed in the "air" or in Midspace.

The word translated variously as "decks" or "storeys" (*ma'alah*) derives from *'ālāh* (עלה; "to *ascend*"), which as *'ălāh* (עלה) means "a *holocaust*," that is, a "burnt offering." In the context of the story of Noah one thinks immediately of the "burnt offerings on the altar," which Noah offered to Yahweh after disembarking from the Ark (Gen.8:20). This altar prefigures the altar of the tabernacle. The three "decks" of the altar of the Ark are explicit in the Vedantic symbolism of the Fire Altar, where they are the three "Self-perforates" (*svayamātrnnā*). Coomaraswamy remarks that these represent Earth, Air and Sky. These "Self-perforates" are referred to as "stones" or "dry stones,"[48] which, as Coomaraswamy notes, appear to have a baetylic origin, as predicated in *Taittirīya Samhitā* V.2.6.2.[49] The *svayamātrnnā* are, moreover, related to the symbolism of the Sundoor, as is evident by the title of Coomaraswamy's essay, '*Svayamātrnnā*: Janua Coeli.'

With respect to the tabernacle, and beginning from what is most "outer" and moving to what is most "inner," that is from Earth to Heaven, the "three worlds" are expressed by, the court,[50] the Holy Place, and the Most Holy or the Holy of Holies (see Ex.26-27). Schaya:

> These three hierarchic aspects of the universal dwelling place of God have their image here below in the tripartite division of the sanctuary: the "divine" Holy of Holies, the "heavenly" Holy, and the "earthly" outer court. Here the vestibule of the temple symbolises the "earthly paradise." Here below God dwells in

the darkness of the Holy of the Holies, for "above" also His absolute essence rests in eternal invisibility, from out of which His shining being and its indwelling [*Shekhinah*] reveal themselves. The light of His indwelling radiates from His Holy of Holies to the Holy and shines upon the sevenbranched candlestick, just as God descends from His infinity in order to sit in state above the seven heavens as Lord of the worlds, in the radiant crown of the seven all determining, all illuminating aspects of His countenance. Finally, the outer court, like the whole earth, serves as a "footstool for His feet."[51]

By extension to the Temple the "three worlds" are the Portico (*ulam*); the Great Chamber (*hekal*); and the Sanctuary (*debir*) (see 1Kgs.6; cf.Ezk.40 & 41). With the Ark of Noah the "three worlds" are static or simultaneous *within* the Ark. They are, so to speak, vertically superimposed upon each other. In comparison the accounts of the tabernacle and Temple show the "three worlds" as successive horizontal stages surrounding or veiling the Ark, expressing the fact that cosmic existence is here being considered *in actu*, or in respect to its extension along a horizontal plane of Existence. With the Ark of Noah the "three worlds" exist "internally," the Ark therefore being the "container." With the tabernacle and the Temple the "three worlds" must be seen as either contracting into the Ark or emanating from it, depending on the perspective adopted. The emphasis here is on the Ark as Centre or Heart. 'Neither My earth nor My heavens contain Me, but I fitted into the believing heart.'[52] Furthermore, Manifestation *in actu* proceeds not only along the horizontal plane but also demonstrates, at its level, a symbolic verticality. Thus we read, 'The entrance to the lowest storey was at the right-hand corner of the Temple; access to the middle storey was by a spiral staircase, and so from the middle storey to the third' (1Kgs.6:8). The verticality of the Temple is in proportion to its vicinity to the Centre, as explained above with respect to the symbol of the mountain. This symbolism, displayed by the Temple, is epitomised by the symbolism of the ziggurat.[53] Again, this same symbolism is displayed by the pyramid, which, as we have noted, was seen by some to have been the form of the Ark of Noah. From a purely terrestrial perspective one can also see that the horizontal and vertical expansion of the Temple expresses the three dimensions of spatial existence.

The symbolism of the heart is informative here. According to the Hindu tradition *Brahman* is said to dwell in the smaller ventricle (*guhā*) of the heart (*hridaya*); to be more precise, it is the cavity (*dahara*) that is here in question as the symbolic "location" of *Brahman*.[54] Here again there is a three-fold symbolism: *hridaya, guha, dahara*. The "cavity" or "emptiness" of the *dahara* speaks of the Unmanifested at the heart of manifestation. Similarly, it is precisely in the "empty space" between the wings of the *cherubim* that man meets God (Ex.25:22). In his commentary on the *Chāndogya Upanishad*, Śankarācārya teaches that this space that fills the nothingness is *ākāśa* (ether) and furthermore that this is called *Brahman*: '*Brahman* is like space because of unembodiedness, and because of the similarity of subtleness and all-pervasiveness.'[55] *Ākāśa* is the same with the "Ether in the Heart"[56] of which Guénon says that it is, 'the primordial element from which all the others proceed being naturally taken to represent the Principle.' He adds, 'This ether (*Akaśā*) is the same as the Hebrew *Avir*, from the mystery of which gushes forth the light (*Aor*), which realises all extent by its outward radiation'.[57] This recognises the connection between *ākāśa* and the *Shekhinah* with respect to the relationship *Shekhinah-Metatron-Avir* and the symbolic association of the *Shekhinah* with Light. The *Fiat Lux* determines the measure of the cosmogenesis by the radiation of light (*Aor*), which is the "visual" expression of *avir* or *akaśā*. As Guénon remarks, *ākāśa* not only fills space but also, via its measure, determines it, and thus is space.[58] Both the Judaic and Hindu symbolisms present a hierarchical ternary that reflects the triadic nature of the universal dwelling place of God, the *mishkan* (dwelling) of the *Shekhinah*: onto-cosmological Existence.

The triple structure of cosmic existence is reflected in the triple nature of man, *corpus, anima, spiritus* or, *soma, psyché, pneuma*. Here we are still concerned with the "three worlds." However, man comprises another ternary, which by virtue of the potential equality of its constituents transcends the "three worlds" and endows man with the quality of objectivity that allows him to be a witness to the Absolute.[59] This is the ternary: Will, Sentiment, Intelligence, or, activity, love, knowledge.[60] Here we have the three "ways" of the Hindu tradition, respectively, *karma, bhakti, jñāna*. These are recognised by the Christian tradition in Christ's commandment to 'Love the Lord your God with all your heart (*bhakti*), with all your soul (*karma*), and with all your mind (*jñāna*)' (Mt.22:34).[61] Schuon:

> This doctrine of the three human dimensions can be expressed in a quite simple and immediately plausible way as follows: the good that man is capable of knowing he must also will in so far as this good can be the object of the will; in addition he must love this good and at the same time the knowledge of it as well as the will towards it; just as he must will and love the earthly and contingent reflections of this good according to

what is required or permitted by their nature. One cannot devote oneself to knowledge without loving it and willing it, any more than one can will something without knowing it and loving its realisation; and one cannot love without knowing an object or without wishing to love it. This interdependence shows that the immortal soul is one and that its modes have one and the same significance, that of manifesting God by realising Him.[62]

Microcosmically man is formed of the ternary *corpus*, *anima*, *spiritus*; macrocosmically, Cosmic Man is formed of the ternary Earth, Air, Heaven. At the centre of man is the Heart-Intellect, which is a tri-unity: Will, Intelligence and Love; at the Centre of the Universe is the triune Principle: Being, Consciousness, Beatitude. Man, and by extension the Universe, is tripartite by virtue of being made "in the image" of the Principle; but the "three worlds" are not directly equivalent to the three aspects of the Principle, for, in the first place, they pertain to a lower level of existence, and in the second place, it is true that an "image" is always less than its source.

The Nine-Fold Division

I provided her with six decks,
Dividing her (thus) into seven parts.
Her floor plan I divided into nine parts.

Gilgamesh, XI.ii

To talk of the Ark of Noah in terms of the "three worlds" is symbolically adequate and justified if we are considering its description as presented in *Genesis*. However, one might question the appropriateness of this reading applied to Ark symbolism in general. Here it would seem to be enough to show that not all mythological "arks" have tripartite form. While this is in fact the case it nevertheless takes nothing away from the general thesis of the Ark as the receptacle of Divine Immanence and as a prefiguration of onto-cosmological existence. Here it is a matter of symbolic emphasis, so that while one tradition might emphasise the triple structure of both the Principle-Centre and of Manifestation another might foreground the four directions of a plane of Existence, or the five Elements, or the six directions of cosmological space, etc. Each mythology presents an appropriate emphasis for the purpose for which it was intended. Often several, if not all, of the symbolic elements we have mention are combined in various ways. By way of example we might consider the description of the Ark of Ut-napishtim from the *Epic of Gilgamesh*, which is constructed "with six decks" thus "dividing her into seven parts" and with a "floor plan" that divides it in to "nine parts."[63]

The relation of the numbers six and seven to the Centre has already been discussed. It is, however, worth remarking that the six "decks" are what is "solid" or explicit while the number seven is associated with the space "between" the "decks," or what is implicit. All this is again to recall the words of Coomaraswamy: 'this use of symbols which are contrary in their literal but unanimous in their spiritual sense very well illustrates the nature of metaphysics itself, which is not like a "philosophy," systematic, but is always consistent.'[64]

There is of course a further link between the three decks or storeys of the Ark of Noah and the six decks of the Ark of Ut-napishtim. This is the symbolic relationship between the numbers three and six. In the first place, the Ark is principally metaphysical Unity or the monad; this is a triunity, having three fundamental aspects (Being, Consciousness, Beatitude); this gives rise to the ontological ternary, Principle, Essence, Substance; the union of the masculine Essence and the feminine Substance produces the hermaphroditic Manifestation, which in turn is comprised of the ternary Heaven, Midspace, Earth, where each of these elements must be thought of as androgynous to varying degrees, so that each of the "three worlds" must be seen as having its respective "expression" or *śakti* (energy), to use the Hindu term.[65] At the level of Manifestation the "three worlds" are expressed by and within the six directions of space, these being prefigured by the principle of the "three worlds" and their respective *śakti*. This symbolism is found in the account of Noah through his three sons and their respective wives.

There is another way of looking at this that takes account of the nature of the fundamental numbers and the symbolic progression or unfolding of number by means of either addition or multiplication. As Guénon remarks, in both the Chinese tradition of the Far-East and the Pythagorean tradition of the West, odd numbers are said to be masculine or active (*yang*), while even numbers are feminine or passive (*yin*).[66] Because they are *yang*, odd numbers can be termed "celestial"; even numbers, because they are *yin*, can be described as "terrestrial." 'But apart from this broad generalisation' says Guénon, 'there are certain individual numbers that have a specific affinity either with Heaven or with Earth, and this calls for explanations of a different kind.' He continues,

> To begin with, it is worth emphasising that it is chiefly the *first* odd number that is traditionally viewed as the number of Heaven and as an expression of the nature of Heaven–just as it is chiefly the first even number that is viewed as the number of Earth and as an expression of the nature of Earth. The reason for this is not hard to find: it is simply that each of these numbers holds

pride of place at the head of its own particular "order," so that all the other numbers are in a sense merely derivatives of them, holding second place in relation to them in the particular series to which they belong. ... Now what we must also bear in mind is the fact that unity, or the number one, is strictly speaking the principle of number and so cannot be counted as a number itself. ... So while the first even number is 2, the first odd number is considered to be, not 1, but 3. ... 2, then is the number of Earth, and 3 the number of Heaven.[67]

This means that Earth comes before Heaven, just as *yin* comes before *yang*, which is another example of the cosmological view mentioned earlier.[68]

There is an obvious relationship between the numbers three and two that produces the number six. By this relationship we can see that the three decks of the Ark of Noah and the six decks of the Ark of Ut-nap-ishtim are related by the manner in which three symbolises Heaven or Essence in and of itself, while six represents this same principle from the standpoint of Manifestation. This might seem to suggest a problem with the idea that even numbers are "terrestrial," but here it is a matter of a "kind of inversion," as Guénon says and which we have noted as proper to symbolism in general.[69] Guénon:

Whereas 2 and 3 represent Earth and Heaven in themselves, 5 and 6 represent Earth and heaven in their reciprocal action on and reaction to each other. In other words, 5 and 6 represent Earth and Heaven from the standpoint of manifestation, which is in fact the product of this action and reaction. We find this very clearly expressed, for example, in the text that says: 'In 5 and 6 we have the central union (*chung ho*, that is, the union oc-curring in the centre) of Heaven and Earth.'[70]

Both five and six are formed by the numbers two and three, but in the case of five these two numbers are combined by addition (2 + 3 = 5) whereas in the case of six they are combined by multiplication (2 x 3 = 6). Guénon expands on the symbolism of the distinction between addi-tion and multiplication:

The action of Heaven on Earth gives rise to a straightforward addition of the celestial number 3 and the terrestrial number 2, for the simple reason that the action of Heaven is strictly "ac-tionless," and can be described as an "action of presence." As to the reaction of Earth with regard to Heaven, this gives rise to multiplication of the celestial number 3 by the terrestrial number 2, because the potentiality inherent in substance is the very root of multiplicity.[71]

Whereas three and two are respectively expressions of the intrinsic natures of Heaven and Earth, six and five are expressions of the "measure" or extension of Heaven and Earth.[72] This is to say that space, which is defined by its six directions, is the "measure" (Guénon notes that the very notion of "measure" is directly associated with manifestation[73]) or extension of Heaven; which is to say that Heaven manifests as Earth; which is again to say that Essence and Substance are almost synonymous in practice.

Heaven has two aspects: Uncreated and created. Here one might say that the Uncreated Heaven is Pure Essence, while the created heaven corresponds, in a limited sense, to the heaven of the "three worlds." The Uncreated Essence is the triune Principle; the created Essence is the sextuple expression. The actionless action of Heaven, as Principle, upon heaven, as expression, can therefore be described by addition, as Guénon says above, in which case Heaven is described in its totality by the number nine, as indeed it is by Dante and others.[74] The Principle with respect to both its Uncreated and created aspects is expressed by the number nine $(3 + 6 = 9)$. From another perspective, the infinite possibilities of the number three, the number of Heaven, are expressed by the complete permutations—the full internal unfolding—of this number, and this is found by the square of a number; thus $3^2 = 9$ or, $3 \times 3 = 9$.[75]

The number nine is universally regarded as the number of perfection or fulfilment. This is the perfection of Essence or Heaven and there are many examples where nine is the number of Heaven.[76] Again, each of the "three worlds" is a microcosmic reflection of the triune Principle and thus, as the *Dictionary of Symbols* remarks, is symbolised by the ternary figure of a triangle, with nine therefore being the totality of the "three worlds." This same image is found with the *Sefirotic* Tree of Kabbalah, which has three ternaries—a ternary of ternaries—that are finally reflected in the tenth *Sefirah*, *Malkhut*, the Kingdom or Creation. According to Pseudo-Dionysius the heavenly beings are divided in to three triads: thrones, cherubim and seraphim; authorities, dominions and powers; and, angels, archangels and principalities.[77] To talk of the totality of the "three worlds" is to talk of their perfection, and this can never be achieved in their unfolding expression but only in their principle, that is, only *in divinis*, "in Heaven," or in Essence.

The symbolism of the number nine is found in various forms throughout many of the world's Ark mythologies. According to Robert Graves, the ark of Deucalion 'floated about for nine days until, at last, the waters subsided, and it came to rest on Mount Parnassus'.[78] Noah died at the age of nine hundred and fifty, combining the number nine with the number fifty, the number of "all" (*kol*), of totality, of the Jubilee. With the account of the Ark of Ut-napishtim the symbolism is explicit: 'Her floor plan I divided into nine parts.' This nine-fold division is found again, with greater emphasis still, in the Chinese story of Yū the Great, where it is the key to saving mankind from the "flood."

The story of Yū the Great comes mainly from the *Shu Ching* (The Book of History). The eighth emperor, Ti Yao (the Divine Yao), was celebrated for having 'united and harmonized the many states'.[79] 'However,' as Campbell remarks, 'in spite of his great virtue and the cosmic influence of his sagely character, all was not quite perfect in the period of Yao; for there was a terrible spate of inundations'.[80] The number eight, as we have noted, is the number of "balance," particularly cosmic balance, but the perfection of the created cosmos still presupposes the Great Uncreated. Ti Yao, set Kun ("the Great Fish"), one of the eight sons of the earlier monarch, Chuan Hsū, to work for nine years to stop the flooding, but Kun failed by making the mistake of violating nature: 'He damned up the inundating waters and thereby threw into disorder the arrangement of the five elements.'[81] His son Yū assumed his task under the reign of the emperor Yao and his successor the emperor vice regent, Shun. According to the tradition, Heaven gave Yū the "Great Plan with its nine divisions" by which he was able to order the empire into nine divisions and thereby stop the flooding.[82]

According to legend the inspiration for this division into nine came from a diagram called *Lo Chu*, the "Writing of the Lake." 'This diagram' say Guénon, 'was brought to him [Yū the Great] by a tortoise, and it shows the nine primary numbers arranged in the form of the so-called "magic square."[83] By applying this division to the empire, Yū the Great turned it into an image of the universe.'[84]

4	9	2
3	5	7
8	1	6

Fig. 5

The basic property of this "magic square" is that the numbers on every line—vertical, horizontal and diagonal—always add up to fifteen.[85] Not surprisingly the different sets of primary numbers that produce fifteen are all highly suggestive: 3X5: the relationship of Heaven and Earth, where Earth is seen from the viewpoint of Manifestation; 7 + 8: the relationship of the Centre with the Harmony of the Circle; 6 + 9: the relationship of Heaven from the viewpoint of Manifestation considered with respect to its complete unfolding. Guénon further remarks that if we replace the number at the centre by the *yin-yang* symbol[86] and the other numbers by the eight *kua* or trigrams, we end up with a square or "terrestrial" equivalent of the usual circular or "celestial" diagram.[87] This is to say that this "magic square" represents, at least in one sense, a "terrestrialisation" of the celestial archetype; or, from another point of view, a "celestialisation" of the terrestrial plane. Heaven expressed through Earth, and Earth made in the image of Heaven.[88]

The nine-fold division of China is again reflected in the design of the *Ming T'ang*, the residence of the Chinese Emperor.[89] The *Ming T'ang*, as with any true Palace or Temple, is an *imago mundi*. At the heart of the *Ming T'ang* resides the semi-divine Emperor, who, like the Tabernacle, is the "meeting place" of God and man. This image of the world is directly comparable to that presented in the Kabbalah: 'The Tabernacle of the Holiness of *Jehovah* in which the *Shekhinah* resides is the Holy of Holies, which is the heart of the Temple, which in turn is the centre of

Zion (Jerusalem), just as Zion is the centre of the Land of Israel and the Land of Israel is the centre of the world.'[90] Moreover, the central number of the "magic square" of *Lo Chu* is five, the number of "true man" (*chen jen*), who, as Guénon remarks, 'contains within himself everything that is manifested in the state of existence with whose centre he is identical.'[91] Which is to say that "true man" is identical with the Ark.

Yū the Great did not "build an ark" in the sense of Noah. Nonetheless, there are several striking similarities. Noah is the tenth generation beginning with Adam. He is also the last of the antediluvian patriarchs. Yū the Great became the tenth and last emperor of the Chinese "Golden Age."[92] They are both in this sense, and in accordance with the symbolism of the number ten, the end of their respective series and the potential beginning of the "new" Age. Again, Noah became lame after being bitten by the lion on the Ark; Yū likewise became lame in saving the world. In the account of Noah it was the raven and the dove that effectively signalled the remission of the flood; Yū is said to have had a long neck with a "mouth like a raven's beak."

Of further interest here is the Native American Huichol story of the flood, mentioned previously. Tako'tsi took with her "a parrot and a macaw"[93] on top of the box containing the body of the man. When they finally landed on Mount Toapu'li it is these birds that excavated river valleys with their beaks allowing the water to run off. Similarly, according to Mencius, it was Yū himself, with his "raven's beak mouth" that 'dug the soil and led the water to the sea'.[94] Moreover, the parrot and the macaw are said to have created "five oceans" through their work.[95] Five: the number of Heaven seen through Earth; this is to say that they brought cosmic order by the celestialisation of the chaotic (flooded) earth.

Yū the Great is attributed with the casting of the "Nine Cauldrons of Hsia";[96] the cauldron, like the Grail, is a potent homologue of the Ark. According to tradition these "nine cauldrons" were cast using metal brought from the nine regions of China, created following the "nine-fold plan." Five of these cauldrons were *yang* and four *yin*, and they are said to symbolise the uniting of the nine regions at their centre, and hence the whole world, a description that fits with the general theory of the Ark being developed. Moreover, these cauldrons 'moved about of their own accord and boiled without any fire and were filled through influence of Celestial Powers.'[97] That is to say, they are the domain of uncreated power or "non-acting activity" (*wei wu wei*), which is precisely the power of Heaven. During the decadent Chou Dynasty, the 'three-legged cauldrons took refuge under water, and their virtues and knowledge were lost.'[98] The theme is universal: at the end of the age, when mankind has declined to a point of requiring divine purification, then the seeds of all virtue and knowledge retreat into a receptacle or Ark of some form. Of further interest is the account of the first emperor, Ch'in Shih Huang Ti, who tried to recover one of the cauldrons from the River Sseu, but was prevented by a dragon. His virtue, it is said, was insufficient to obtain a cauldron. Here again is the association of the water and the dragon and the "treasure" that it guards.

The description of these cauldrons as "three-legged" immediately evokes the relationship of the Ark and the ternary. One is tempted to say that the "legs" express the foundations upon which the bowl of the cauldron rests in a manner that corresponds to the way that the Centre rests "upon" the foundation of the tripartite world. This description of the nine cauldrons as "three-legged" and as moving "of their own accord" is almost identical with the description offered by Homer of the cauldrons of Hephaestus: 'He was making a set of twenty tripods to stand along the wall of his strong-built house, and had fitted with golden wheels under each leg, so he could have them moving of their own accord, running by themselves to where the gods gathered and then returning again to his house—a miraculous sight.'[99] Roger Sworder argues that the cauldrons of Hephaestus represent the fifth Platonic element, *ether*, represented by the dodecahedron.[100] According to Plato, the dodecahedron is 'used for embroidering the constellations on the whole heaven'.[101] Elsewhere he associates it with the Earth.[102] Similarly, in the Chinese tradition the cauldron corresponds to the trigram *k'uen*, Earth, the passive principle, the receptacle.[103] For Sworder the dodecahedron is reserved for one purpose alone, 'to serve as the outermost shape of the whole universe';[104] that is to say, as the receptacle of the universe.

According to Chinese Inner Alchemy (*Nei Tan*) the human body is a three-legged cauldron in which the elixir of immortality is brewed. The human body is a homology of the Ark. In this regard we note that, according to a *hatha-yoga* text, the human body is seen as 'a house with a pillar and nine doors'.[105] The Tibetan Wheel of Life depicts the body as a house with six windows corresponding to the six senses.[106] One sees here a difference similar to the various descriptions of the Ark. The cauldron as the source of the "elixir of immortality" recalls the Ark in its guise as the Grail. Among the Celts the cauldron corresponds to the *Cornucopia* or Horn of Plenty, not only supplying inexhaustible food but also limitless knowledge.[107] Again, the Celtic goddess, Kerriwen, goddess of poets, smiths, and physicians, also owed a magical cauldron.[108] Returning to the Chinese tradition, the *Dictionary of Symbols* observes that 'the first three-legged cauldron was cast by Shang Ti and from it he gained the powers of divination, of controlling the cycle of the seasons and finally immortality.'[109]

The Ternary Projection

The sons of Noah who came out of the ark were Shem, Ham and Japheth–Ham being the father of Canaan.

Genesis 9:18

Divine Immanence: Principle, Essence, Substance; Essence, Substance, Manifestation. These are the two complementary ternaries by which, through which and in which creation comes about. However, in describing these there can be a confusion arising from the fact that both of these ternaries can be expressed by the same three symbolic forms: a point, a vertical line "descending" from this point, and a horizontal line, being a limit to the vertical line.

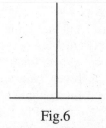

Fig.6

In the first case the point is the Principle; Essence is then represented by the vertical line, expressing what we might call the Divine Activity or Divine Power, Essence *in actu* (the Divine Ray; the *Fiat Lux*); the horizontal line represents the "reflective" surface or passive Substance (the Waters) upon which Essence "acts." In this symbolism Manifestation is implied by the meeting point of Essence and Substance.

The second case is that of the Great Triad: the point is Essence, inasmuch as this is extrinsically identifiable with the Principle which it intrinsically implies; the horizontal line remains Substance; however, in this symbolism the vertical line represents the union of Essence and Substance, that is to say, Manifestation. There is a certain crossover between these symbolisms for in the first case what represents Essence *in actu*, which is to say Principial Being, in the second case represents Manifestation, which is to say, Being *qua* cosmological existence.

Unity, Polarisation and Limitation. Unity is represented by the point, intrinsically implying Transcendence (*ad intra*) and extrinsically expressing Immanence (*ad extra*). As Keith Critchlow remarks, 'The point of emergence does not necessarily reveal its causation either in the field of its emergence ... the point represents a unitary focus of conscious awareness; in the physical world it represents a focal event in a field which was previously uninterrupted.'[110] The point (*bindu*) implies

192

the bi-unity, Essence-Substance. The externalisation of the point signifies the diremption and thus polarisation of these principles, and this is expressed by the "line-path." Critchlow: 'The line-path can be taken as representing the point "externalising" itself. A line, i.e. when a point has moved outside and away from its original position, symbolises the polarity of existence'[111]. This "line-path" is symbolically vertical, where this implies the dual movements "downwards," away from the Source, and "upwards," returning to the Source. On the one hand this line is infinite in virtue of participating in the Unity. On the other hand this line is limited by virtue of departing from the Origin. This limitation is figured by the horizontal line, which delimits the descending extension of the vertical line. The horizontal line extends indefinitely.

The symbolisms being considered here concern what might be called the "projection" of Immanence. This idea of a ternary projection is born out by the symbolisms of both the Ark of Noah and the Ark of the Covenant. With the account of Noah this is expressed by his three sons, Shem, Ham and Japheth (Gen.6:11), who are precisely the "projection" or "extension" of Noah. Here the three sons can be considered either inasmuch as they exist in the Ark (*in potentia*) or, and this is more to the point being considered, inasmuch as they emerge from the Ark after the Flood (*in actu*). Regarding the symbolism of the Ark of the Covenant the projection outwards is expressed, as noted, by the Holy of Holies, the Holy Place and the court, or, by extension, the Sanctuary, the Great Chamber and the Portico. However, the ternary under consideration may also be found, *in potentia* expressed by the contents of the Ark: the Tablets of the Law, the pot of manna and Aaron's rod (Heb.9:4; cf. Ex.25;16; Ex.16:34; Nm.17:25).

The sons of Noah: *Shēm* (שם; "*name*"), *Chām* (חם; "*hot*"), *Yepheth* (יפת; "*expansion*"). Immanence is the expression or "name" of the Divine Reality and this symbolism is explicit with the Hebrew *Shēm* ("*name*"). It is informative here to recognise the correspondence between Shem and *Metatron*, the angel of the Name of God.[112] This correspondence is reinforced by the identification of Melchizedek—who we have already noted as conflated with Metatron—and Shem, the Midrash referring to "Shem-Melchizedek."[113]

On the one hand we might say that the Name is the Principle—"In the beginning was the Word."[114] Meister Eckhart: 'This is in the Greek: "In the principle was the Word"'.[115] On the other hand the Name is the Divine Influence—'through whom all things came into being'—who, as Meister Eckhart remarks, is identical with the *Fiat Lux*: 'First note that "In the beginning was the Word, and the Word was with God," [is] contained in the words: 'And God said, "Let there be light…"'.[116] 'The word was the real light that gives light to everyone; he was coming into the world' (Jn.1:9).

The Principle or Essence is, from a certain perspective, identical with Heaven; note, then, the close relationship between the words *Shēm* (שם) and *shāmayin* (שמין), meaning "heaven." *Shāmayin* derives from the unused root *shāmayim* (שמים), which is the dual form of the singular *shāmeh* (שמה; "sky"). The shift in the finals is informative: *Shāmeh* (the "sky") has as its final a *he*, which is symbolically a "window"; the sky is a window through which one "sees"—in the sense that intimated realities are "seen"—the Unmanifested Heaven. *Shāmayim* has as its final a *mem*, symbolically "water," which evokes the passive potentiality of the Unmanifested Principle. *Shāmayin*, "heaven," has as its final a *nūn*, symbolically a "fish," which evokes the active potentiality or the creative principle of Heaven; this inasmuch as the symbolism of the fish expresses the notion of "life" associated with water; moreover, concerning the symbol of the fish, this is the Christian *Ichthus*, the essential symbolism here being that of the *vesica piscis*: the geometric expression of the germinating seed and formative power which gives rise to the "polygonal world."[117]

Shāmayin, "heaven," is almost identical—differing basically by the inclusion of a *yod*—to the word *shāman* (שמן), a primitive root which means "to *shine*," recalling of course that Heaven is the source of the Divine Light. *Shāman* ("to *shine*") gives rise to the word *shemen* (שמן), meaning "oil," especially that of the olive, the allusion being that oil or grease is used to polish and thus to make shine. This connection is not unrelated to the meaning of *Shēm* as "name." As we read in *The Song of Songs*, 'your name is an oil poured out' (1:3). According to Rabbi Gikatilla, the symbolism of "oil" is that of 'the essence of all the Spheres [the *Sefirot*]'.[118] He cites the vision of Zechariah of the two olive trees from which flow "golden oil" through the two golden "openings" or "tubes" (Zc.4:12). These two olive trees and subsequent two openings express the symbolism of duality,[119] through which the Essence flows forth to enlighten the world, which, moreover, is expressed in Zechariah's vision by the "seven lamps" (the seven onto-cosmological "directions") that are fed by this oil. Furthermore, these seven "lamps" are identical with the "seven eyes of Yahweh" that are on the "stone," as mentioned above.

'Your name is an oil poured out': this "oil" is none other than the Word, the Divine Light of the *Fiat Lux*, poured out on creation. In this context note that the word for the "window" of Noah's Ark, *tsōhar* (צהר; "a *light*"), derives from the primitive root, *tsāhar* (צהר; "to *glisten*")— used only as a denominative of *yitshār* (יצהרי; "*oil*," as producing *light*;

194

figuratively, *anointing* oil). Recall, also, the meaning of the term Messiah as being "the *anointed* one." This web of meanings is further complemented by the word *shāma‘* (שמע; "to *hear*"), demonstrating the relationship between light and sound.[120] Moreover, this word differs principally by its final, *ayin*, which is symbolically an "eye" or "fountain," from which the "Waters of Life" pour out.

Rabbi Dr. I. Rapaport observes the equivalence between the Hebrew word *shēm* and the Akkadian word *suma*, which had the meaning of "offspring" or "child."[121] Here again there is a connection to Metatron, who is known as *na'ar* ("boy" or "lad") because of his cyclic regeneration.[122] This alludes to the complementary currents (*catabasis* and *anabasis*) of the vertical axis; that is to say, the potentiality of the "child" manifests itself in the form of the "adult," who must then return to the child state to regain its perfection. 'In truth I tell you, anyone who does not welcome the kingdom of God like a little child will never enter it' (Mk.10:15, Lk.18:17).

Finally, with respect to the name *Shēm*, let us recall the symbolism of the name Noah, as "rest," and thus the connection to the Centre envisaged as the seventh point; *Shem*, then, as the expression of Noah, should, from a certain perspective, be associated with the number eight, and in fact this is the case with the Hebrew word for "eight" being *sh^emīynīy* (שמיני). Note, then, that the essential "oil" flows forth through the fifty gates of *Binah*, which, as Rabbi Gikatilla reveals, 'can be eight or fifty.'[123]

Chām ("hot"): from this, *chammāh* (חמה; "the *sun*"), where the sun is a well-recognised symbol of the Centre. We might well remark that the difference between *Chām* and *chammāh* is the final *he*, which as noted in the case of *shameh*, is symbolically a "window"; as the sky is a "window" to Heaven, likewise the sun is a "window" to the central Principle. *Chām*, as the sun, suggests the point or Essence identified with the Principle, but the sun is known by its infinite rays, which each act as the Divine Ray and *axis mundi* for the "world" that they illumine, and in this sense we have *chammān* (חמן), which word means "a *sun*-pillar" (the Hindu *skambha*). This word has as its final a *nūn*, which, as in the case of the word *Shāmayin*, implies an active expression of the Principle; moreover, the ideogram for the final *nūn* (ן) expresses the idea of a pillar or axis. Both *Shem* and *Chām* contain the dual sense of the point and the vertical line, interchangeable to the extent that they either express the Principle or Essence *in actu*.

Yepheth ("expansion"), from the primitive root *pāthāh* (פתה; "to *open*"), corresponds to the horizontal line of the above schema, for it is this that expresses the expansion of the vertical axis upon the horizontal axis. The horizontal expansion of the Divine Ray is equally the limitation and reflection that allows the *Fiat Lux* to be known as such; in this sense note the connection between *Yepheth* (יפח) and *yāpha'* (יפע), which is a primitive root meaning "to *shine.*"

On the one hand we have *Shem, Chām, Yepheth*: Principle, Essence, Substance, and on the other hand, *Shem, Chām, Yepheth*: Essence, Manifestation, Substance. Now, insomuch as these principles may be envisaged as interchangeable they express a metaphysical reading and must be thought of primarily in respect of their unified principle within the Ark. However, the Noah narrative is chiefly cosmological and in this regard the three sons have a precise order: Shem, Ham, Japheth, which is attested to by tradition (Gen.5:32; 6:10; 10:1). Here we have our second ternary, the Great Triad: Essence, Manifestation, Substance. However, this ternary is still anterior to creation *per se*. When considering the relationship of the three sons and cosmic existence a further symbolism is needed and this is found precisely in the account of Noah's drunkenness and the actions of his sons. Thus, *Genesis* 9:18: 'The sons of Noah who came out of the ark were Shem, Ham and Japheth–Ham being the father of Canaan.' Ham is not mentioned again in this narrative with Canaan effectively replacing him; furthermore, Canaan is here given as the youngest son (Gen.9:24), the order becoming Shem, Japheth, Canaan. I have suggested that Ham expresses the principle of Manifestation; Canaan, the "son" of Ham, expresses the realisation of Manifestation, and this is none other than Creation. The change in the order further suggests the idea of Canaan as a resultant of the principles embodied by Shem and Japheth. Shem, Japheth, Canaan: Essence, Substance, Manifestation (Creation).

Canaan or *K^ena'an* (כנען) means "*humiliated*"; this meaning evokes the sense in which Creation is a "Fall"—thus the Christian *contemptus mundi* and the negative connotation of the Hindu *Māyā*. *K^ena'an* derives from the primitive root *kāna'* (כנע; "to *bend*"), thus "to bend the knee" and hence "to humiliate." Furthermore, this implies the sense of "humbling" oneself; in this respect recall Christ's *kenosis* (Ph.2:6-11), his "emptying himself," which corresponds, as I have shown elsewhere, to the "withdrawal" of the *tsimtsum*.[124] *Philippians* 2:8: 'he was humbler yet, even to accepting death, death on the cross.' Christ's being "humbler yet" implies a first "humbling," so to speak, and this is none other than His (the Unmanifest Word's) taking "the form of a slave" (Ph.2:8), accepting limitation, which is to say, becoming the manifested; for to say manifestation is to say limitation. To this verse 10 adds: 'so that all beings in the heavens, on earth and in the underworld, should bend the knee in the name of Jesus'. This echoes Is.45:23: 'All shall bend the knee to me'. In both it is the case that Manifestation, which is on the one hand "All" (the "lesser Absolute"), and on the other hand the "three worlds" (Heaven, Earth, Underworld; alternatively, Heaven, Midspace, Earth), must "bend the knee,"[125] must be "humiliated" or "humbled," precisely so that it may be.

The Hindu term *Māyā* connotes both a negative and a positive sense. Note, then, the Hebrew word *chānan* (חנן), which, like *kāna'*, is a primitive root meaning "to *bend*," the difference being that *chānan* connotes the idea of bending down to an inferior, and thus the positive sense of "to *favour* or *bestow*." The act of creation implies God's "bending" down, which is both an act of humbling and of bestowing favour; one thinks of Michelangelo's famous image of the creation of Adam. A connection presents itself here that is pertinent in its suggestiveness: St. Luke records of the annunciation that the angel Gabriel greeted Mary with the words: 'Rejoice, you who enjoy God's favour! The Lord is with you' (Lk.1:28). The Greek word here for "favour" is *charis* (χάρις), but the Evangelist could not have been ignorant of the Hebrew *chānan*, which for that matter, is related to the Hebrew *chānāh* ("to *incline*"; "to *decline*," especially of the slanting rays of the evening sun); and this is the root of the name Hannah or *Channāh* ("*favoured*"), which in turn is the Hebrew origin of the name Anna, who, according to the *Protevangelium of James*, was the mother of Mary. In a sense the symbolisms of the names Anna and Mary are interchangeable.[126]

Regarding the meaning of the word *chānan* as "to *bend*," this is also the meaning of the root of the Hebrew word *qesheth* (קשת), that is "bow" or "rainbow": 'I now set my bow in the clouds and it will be a sign of the covenant between me and the earth' (Gen.9:13). The rainbow, as remarked, is generally considered as expressing the union of heaven and earth, and this "union" is none other than Manifestation. Moreover, the root in question is *qāshāh* (קשה; "to be *dense*"), where Manifestation implies the sense of solidification or becoming "dense"; and this in turn derives from the original sense of the primitive root *qōwsh* (קרש; "to *bend*"), which in turn connotes the idea of "bending a trap or snare," and thus *yāqōsh* (יקש; "to *ensnare*"); this being precisely the negative role of Manifestation as implied by the Hindu term *Māyā*, the "web of seeming."[127]

The word *chānāh* further connotes the sense of "to *pitch* a tent" and thus "to rest in a tent." We have already discussed the idea of "rest" and acknowledged the tent as a symbol of the *Shekhinah*. This returns us to the account of Noah's drunkenness and the "sin of Canaan," for it is written: 'Noah, a tiller of the soil, was the first to plant the vine. He drank some of the wine, and while he was drunk, he lay uncovered in his tent' (Gen.9:20, 21). Noah is the "seed" (*quinta essentia*) planted in the "soil" (*prima materia*) from which springs forth the "vine" (*axis mundi*); the "wine" made from this vine is itself none other than the conduit of the *quinta essentia*, so that Noah's "drunkenness" (*gnosis*) signifies the state of his union with the Divine Essence—in a sense, his union with himself; and this occurs in the heart of his tent (*Shekhinah*), "uncovered" and "naked." Thus, cosmologically speaking, this passage refers to the transcendent Essence at the heart of Immanence—Meister Eckhart's "something in the soul." It is Ham, father of Canaan, who sees his father "naked" and tells his two brothers outside. According to the symbolism under consideration, Ham represents the principle of Manifestation, which is to say Immanence, and this is to say *Shekhinah*. As the principle of Manifestation Ham is none other than Essence, in the sense in which *Chām* may be identified with the Divine Sun, and this explains his "seeing" his father in this state, which is to say that this is a matter of identity; but Ham is also Immanence as such, symbolised by the "tent," which is to say he represents the recognition of this state within Manifestation. His brothers, Shem and Japheth remain "outside" Manifestation in the sense we have observed above, being here, as they are, identical to ontological Essence and Substance.

Ham tells his brothers of their father's nakedness whereupon they took a cloak and, "without looking upon him," covered their father's nakedness. This is to say, that the coming together of Essence (Shem) and Substance (Japheth) brings forth the *paragod* (the cloak), which veils cosmic existence. The word translated variously as cloak or garment is *simlāh* (שמלה; "a *dress*," especially "a *mantel*"); *Strong's* conjectures that this comes "through the idea of a *cover* assuming the shape of the object beneath," with this deriving from the word *cēmel* (סמל) meaning "to *resemble*" or "a *likeness*"—'God created man in the image of Himself.' To say man is to say creation; the veil of creation is the "image" or "likeness" of its Source. We might further remark on the fact that the word *simlāh* contains the name Shem (שמ-לה), which it might be said to veil.

According to St. Paul the Ark of the Covenant holds 'the gold jar containing the manna, Aaron's branch that grew the buds, and the tablets of the covenant' (Heb.9:4). The Ark of the Covenant principally expresses the receptacle of Divine Immanence in efficient mode, which is to say that the emphasis here is necessarily on the ternary Essence, Substance, Manifestation, or the Great Triad.

The Tablets of the Law: on the one hand these are the Divine Word, identical to the Divine Name (Shem); on the other hand the Tablets of the Covenant are the "Word made flesh" or stone, as it is, and this suggests the idea of Substance; of course the symbolism of "stone" and "*the*

198

stone" involves the identification of Substance and Essence. Recall, then, that the Hebrew word translated as "tablet" derives from the root *lūach* (לח; "to *glisten*")—*lūach* ("to *glisten*"): *shāman* ("to *shine*"). Again, recall the word *Lūwz* (לוז): 'Jacob took the stone he had used for a pillow, and set it up as a pillar, pouring oil over the top of it. He named the place Bethel, but before that the town had been called Luz'. 'Your name is an oil poured out'. As observed, between *lūwach* and *Lūwz* there is a shift in finals from *heth*, "a fence or enclosure" and the eighth Hebrew letter, to *zayin*, "a sword" and the seventh Hebrew letter. This symbolism is that of the "wall of Paradise" and the "fiery sword"; this pertains to the *coincidentia oppositorum*, and thus it is specified that there were two tablets (Ex.31:18). Moreover, this is the mystery of the *hashmal*, which is the mystery of the *Fiat Lux* and of the Divine Essence.

A further connection arises if we instead move from *heth*, the eighth letter, to *teth*, the ninth Hebrew letter, which is associated with the symbolism of the "serpent." This gives us *lūwt* ("to *wrap*") and from this, *lōwt* ("a *veil*"), suggesting the substantial veil of the *paragod*; moreover, the inclusion of the serpent in this symbolism suggests the serpent in the Garden, which is, in a sense, the seed of the Fall and thus of cosmological existence as such. *Lōwt*: this is also the name Lot, and this is not unconnected, for it is Lot who survived the destruction of Sodom and Gomorrah to be the seed of his generations, just as Noah does with the Flood.

The jar of manna: 'Moses then said to Aaron, "Take a jar and put in it a full homer of manna and store it in Yahweh's presence, to be kept for your descendants." Accordingly, Aaron stored it in front of the Testimony' (Ex.16:33-34). On the one hand manna is "bread" (Substance); on the other hand manna is *soma* and *nogah* (Essence). Furthermore, the Hebrew word *mān* (מן) is formed by the union of a *mem* (the passive water) and a *nūn* (the active fish). This word means literally "a *whatness*," a name which is thought to have been derived from the question the Israelites asked when presented by Moses with this food: 'What is that?' (*mān hu'*) (see Ex.16:15). Now, without in any way trying to suggest an etymological connection that does not exist, let us simply remark that the term "Quiddity," used in reference to the Essence, comes from the scholastic *quidditas*, "what-it-is."[128]

The "jar," like the Kabbalists Urn, is a homologue of the Ark. The word "jar" is in Greek, *stamnos* (σταμνος; "a *jar* or earthen *tank*"), from the base *stao* (σταω; "to *stand*"); this is likewise the base of *stasis* (στασις; "a *standing position*"), which means, by implication, "existence." Again, *stao* is also the base of *stauros* (σταυρος; "a *stake* or *post*, as set upright"), by implication, the Cross of Christ. As Guénon has observed, the cross is the expression of the realisation of Universal Man, where the cross 'very clearly represents the manner of achievement of this realisation by the perfect communion of all the states of the being, harmoniously and conformably ranked, in integral expansion, in the double sense of "amplitude" and "exaltation."'[129]

The Hebrew word translated as "jar" is *tsintseneth* (צנצנח; "a *vase*"),[130] from *tsēn* (צן; "a *thorn*"). The Christian symbolism of "thorns" is primarily that of the negative aspect of Manifestation, so that 'the seed sown in thorns' represents the 'worry of the world and the lure of riches' (Mt.13:22). In this connection, and recalling the destruction of the world by fire, St. Paul says of the 'field that grows thorns' that it 'will end by being burnt' (Heb.6:8). Now, the jar (Manifestation) contains or "surrounds" the manna (the Principle; Essence-Substance) in the same way that the circumference surrounds the centre, and this evokes the image of the crown of thorns placed upon Christ's head (Mt.27:29; Mk.15:17; Jn.19:2). Here the head of the Divine Man is none other than the Centre, being identical also to the Heart; the crown of thorns forms a circumference to this Centre. Moreover, the royal symbolism of the crown is not affected by the ignorant mockery of the Roman soldiers so that here we also have the positive aspect of Manifestation in its guise as the majestic Glory of God, and this reading finds correspondence to the image of Moses with the "rays of light" or "horns" shooting from his head. Furthermore, the sense of the idea that the divine Seed-Point (*bindu*) is both the Centre and "everywhere" is expressed by the derivation, suggested by *Strong's*, of the Greek word for "thorn" (*akantha*; ακανθα), from the word *akmēn* (ακμην), which in turn is akin to *akē* (ακη; "a *point*"); this is to say, that the "circumference" of thorns is made up of individual thorns, which are each "a point," reflective of *the* Point, the Centre.

Thus: 'Yahweh spoke to Moses and said, "Tell the Israelites to give you a branch for each of their families, one for each family: twelve rods. Write the name of each on his branch; and on the branch of Levi write Aaron's name, since the head of the Levite families must have a branch too. You will then put them inside the Tent of meeting in front of the Testimony, where I will make myself known to you."' (Num.17:16-20 [1-5]). By the sprouting of his branch was Moses confirmed as leader of the Israelites, while Aaron and his line where chosen as the guardians of the sanctuary. 'Moses went to the Tent of the Testimony and there, already sprouting, was Aaron's branch, representing the House of Levi; buds had formed, flowers had blossomed and almonds had already ripened' (Num.17:23-24 [8-9]).

The Hebrew word translated as "branch" or "rod" is *matteh* or the feminine *mattāh* (מטה; "a *branch*," as *extending*). This derives from the primitive root *nātāh* (נטה; "to *bend*"), recalling our earlier comments on this meaning. Again, note that the difference here is a shift from a *nūn* to a *mem*. Moreover, this is especially to bend "downwards" with the word *mattāh* also meaning "*downward, below* or *beneath*." To this we can add that the word *muttāh*, also from the root *nātāh*, means "expansion," recalling the meaning of the name *Yepheth*. The symbolism here is of the horizontal expansion commensurate to the vertical descent; that is, the symbol of the triangle apex upward or the pyramid, which is a symbol of Manifestation and the Ark.

Mattāh, in the sense that it means "downwards," derives from the primitive root *'āvar* (עור; "to *blind*," through the idea of a *film* over the eyes), which is to say "a veil"; moreover this is also *'owr* ("*skin*" or "*hide*"), as in the "tunic of skins" with which Yahweh clothed Adam and Eve on expelling them from the Garden (Gen.3:21). At the same time this derives from the root *'uwr* ("to be *naked*"), which shows again that the naked Transcendence rests "beneath" (*mattāh*) the veil of Immanence.

Aaron's blossoming rod expresses Manifestation in all its fructuous glory. This symbolism is again found with the miracle of Joseph's rod signalling his betrothal to Mary (*The Protevangelium of James* 9.1). According to this account, a dove came forth from Joseph's rod and flew on to his head. This alludes to *Matthew* 3:16 and the baptism of Christ.[131] Of course, as St. Peter says, baptism corresponds precisely to "traversing the waters" of the Flood (1Pt.3:21), and this recalls the dove that signalled the end of the Flood. The image of a rod that bursts into flowers, usually lilies, is also an attribute of St. Mary the Virgin.[132] This symbolism is again found with the blooming of Christ's Cross at the Crucifixion.[133] And, according to popular legend, the staff of St. Christopher—who carried Christ across the Waters and is thus a homologue of the Ark—blossomed into a palm-tree when Christ planted it on the shore after their crossing the Waters.[134]

The account of Aaron's rod comes just after the rebellion and punishment of Korah. We are told here that Aaron 'stood between the living and the dead' (Num.17:13 [48]), an image that portrays him with one foot in either realm, a bridge between worlds. In the story of the betrothal of Joseph and Mary, Joseph is especially reminded of the punishment of Korah if he should not obey God's command to accept Mary. In a sense, just as Aaron, and with him the priestly caste, act to bring man to God and God to man, so too does Joseph act to bring the Virgin Mother and Child to mankind. Guénon has remarked on the curious fact that it was a "Joseph" who possessed the "oracular cup" (Gen.44:5) and a Joseph, of Arimathaea, who possessed the Grail.[135] Note that it is another

Joseph, husband of Mary, who possessed, so to speak, Mary, herself a well known symbol of the Grail and the vessel of the blood of Christ.

The symbolism under consideration is that of Aaron's rod, and this requires us to consider the name Aaron or *'Ahărōwn* (אהרון). According to *Strong's*, this word is of uncertain derivation, but let us note the striking comparison here to the Hebrew word, *'ārōwn* (ארון) or *'ārōn* (ארן), which is the word translated as "ark," as in the Ark of the Covenant. This word means "a *box*" and is derived from the primitive root *'ārāh* (ארה; "to *pluck* or gather"). In this connection one thinks of Guénon's treatment of the symbolism of the "gathering of what is scattered": the "scattering" or dis-membering of the primordial Being, which is the passage from unity to multiplicity, and the consequent "gathering," that is, the return to unity.[136] To gather that which is scattered, says Guénon, 'is the same thing as "to find the lost Word"'.[137] Recall, then, that both the Ark of Noah and the Ark of the Covenant contain "the Word." This "gathering" is the *coagula* of the alchemists, the condensation of Taoism, and the "re-memberment" of Christ—"do this is remembrance of me." All of this is to observe once again that the Ark constitutes the point of retraction of multiplicity to unity.

The name *'Ahărōwn* differs from the word *'ārōwn* only by the inclusion of a *he*. This suggests the idea whereby Aaron might be seen as a "window" through which the principle of the Ark is to be seen. In fact this is in perfect accord with the symbolism at hand. Firstly, Moses— who was "plucked" from the waters[138]—is analogous, at the appropriate level, to Noah, and thus, like Noah, is an expression of the Ark; secondly, Moses and Aaron, as "brothers," must be seen as two aspects of the one principle. Moreover it is perfectly in accord with Scripture to say that it was "through" Aaron that Moses acted. Manifestation is none other than the "act-uality" of the Ark, and this "activity" is symbolised by the vertical axis; thus the symbolism of the "rod of Aaron."[139]

It will not be out of place to conclude these observations with a few words about the symbolism of the "anointing oil." Oil is synonymous with the Divine Name and with Essence. At the same time Essence is "almost synonymous in practice" with Substance; thus it is not surprising to find that Shinto tradition regards oil as the symbol of the primeval undifferentiated state, the primordial Waters being here "oil."[140]

The ingredients of the "holy anointing oil," which consecrate the Ark of the Covenant, the Tabernacle and all its accessories, and finally Aaron and his sons (Ex.30:26-31), is given in the scroll of *Exodus*: "Yahweh spoke further to Moses and said, "Take the finest spices: five hundred shekel of fresh myrrh, half as much of fragrant cinnamon, two hundred and fifty shekels of calamus, five hundred shekels (reckoning by the sanctuary shekel) of cassia, and one hin of olive oil' (Ex.30:22-24).

Myrrh or *mōwr* (מור) means, in the first case, "*distillation*," evoking the idea of the alchemist's *coagula* and the Taoist condensations, and again the sense of the Hebrew *qāshāh* ("to be *dense*"); in the second case, this means "*bitter*," evoking the negative sense of creation, a notion that is evident in the Hindu term *Māyā*—"that which" (*yā*) "is not" (*mā*)—which evokes the notion of illusion or unreality. Recall that myrrh was presented to the baby Jesus by the Magi (Mt.2:12) symbolising the coming into created existence of the Divine Principle.[141] Moreover, the gift of myrrh to the baby Jesus was seen by the Church Fathers to symbolically prefigure the bitterness of the Passion. *Mōwr* derives from the root *mārar* (מרר), which is also the root of the name Miriam, the sister of Moses and Aaron, and, in turn, the root of the name Mary. Furthermore, *mōwr* also has the form, *mōr* (מר), which is the same as *mar* (מר; "a *drop*"), recalling the *bindu* ("a drop").

Cinnamon, *qinnāmōwn*, (קנמון) from the unused root, "to *erect*." One thinks of Jacob erecting—"setting up as a pillar"—the stone upon which he slept. The related word calamus, *qāneh* (קנה) means "a *reed*" and by resemblance, "a *rod*" recalling this symbolism. Moreover, this derives from the primitive root *qānāh* (קנה; "to *erect*," in the sense of "to *create*"). Cassia, *qiddāh*, (קדה) from the root *qādad* (קדד; "to *shrivel*," in the sense of "to *contract* or *bend*," as in deference). Finally, the olive oil, which, as discussed, means "*illuminating*" from an unused root indicating *brightness*.

The Receptacle of Sound

The essence of all beings is earth,
the essence of earth is water,
the essence of water is the plants,
the essence of the plants is man,
the essence of man is speech,
the essence of speech is the *Rg Veda*
the essence of the *Rg Veda* is the *Sāmaveda*,
the essence of the *Sāmaveda* is the *Udgīta* (which is *OM*).
That *Udgīta* is the best of all essences, the highest,
Deserving the highest place, the eighth.
Chāndogya Upanishad 1.1.1-3

The symbolisms considered above are found with many homologues of the Ark. By way of examples: the Arabic letter *nūn*, the conch shell, the trumpet and the sacred word, *Om*, which, moreover, are further linked by their respective associations with the notion of "sound."

According to Guénon, the form of the Arabic letter *nūn* is fundamentally associated with the symbolism of the Ark.[142]

Fig.7

The lower half-circumference of the letter *nūn* figures 'an ark floating on the waters' and the point within it 'represents the seed enveloped or contained therein.'[143] Guénon:

> The central position of this point shows, moreover, that in reality it is a question of the "seed of immortality," or indestructible "kernel" which escapes all the outward dissolution. It may be noted, too, that the half-circumference, with its convexity turned downwards is a schematic equivalent of the cup, like which it thus has, so to speak, the significance of a "matrix" in which the not-yet-developed seed is enclosed and which ... is to be identified with the lower or "terrestrial" half of the World Egg.'[144]

The upper half-circumference of the World Egg is to be seen in the rainbow, the analogue, in the strictest sense of the word, of the Ark.[145]

The form of the Arabic *nūn* alerts us to an important qualification on the schema of point, vertical line and horizontal limit. In fact this qualification is already alluded to by the fact that the horizontal line is analogous to the Waters of *Genesis*. Thus, to be precise the horizontal line should be represented as a wave or, that which is the principle of a wave, a curve, as it is with the *nūn*. In the first case, a wave expresses the primordial vibration field (*nāda*);[146] in the second case, a single curve implies the indefinite limit of Substance, which has at its extremes a tendency to "bend" back towards Essence, much as a flower tends to bend towards the Sun. Critchlow describes this curve or arc in terms of its essential relationship with the point of origin.

> Having a limited departure from the point of origin, polarity expresses itself in the relationship of the central (essentially passive) "original" point and the outer projected (active) point. This expression forms an arc with the line representing out original departure as radius. ... The arc implies the control exercised by the centre point and expresses the demarcation of the active

outer limits; the movement expresses an expansion. As the arc closes, another primordial "threeness" becomes evident: a centre point of origin (the controlling element); departure from this centre as direction or field; and boundary to the domain.[147]

By a shift in perspective the horizontal line becomes a horizontal plane. The most adequate form to express this plane, in terms of the relationship between the original point and the boundary, is the circle. The circle expresses a unity that reflects the unity of the original point. 'The circle' says Critchlow, 'expresses "threeness" in itself, i.e. centre, domain, periphery; and "fourness" in a manifest context, i.e. centre, domain included, boundary, domain excluded.'[148] The circle "in itself": centre, radii, circumference; Principle, Essence, Substance. The circle "in a manifest context": Essence, Manifestation, Substance; in this respect the "domain excluded" is none other than the Unmanifested.

According to Kabbalah, the Hebrew letter *nūn* is associated with the idea of birth; it is understood, says Guénon, as a "new birth" or "regeneration" of the being, individual or cosmic.[149] It is interesting to remark, then, that the Arabic *nūn* is immediately preceded by the letter *mīm*, which, as Guénon writes, 'has amongst its principle significations that of death (*al-mawt*), and whose form represents the being completely folded up in himself, reduced in a way to a pure virtuality, to which the position of prostration corresponds ritually.'[150] In the Hebrew alphabet *nūn* is preceded by the letter *mem*, symbolically signifying water. The correspondence of water and death is particularly obvious in the symbolism of the flood. By inverse analogy the "waters of birth" are the "death waters" of the previous state of being, an instance of the malefic and benefic aspects of the symbolism of the Flood. The numerical value of *mem* is forty recalling the associated symbolism of this number.

Al-Jīlī associates the final letter *nūn* of the Divine Name *ar-Rahmān* (The Compassionate") to the Divine Quality, the Speech, which is the manifestion of the Divine Word, *Om*.[151] In Hindu mythology Speech (*Vāc*) is the daughter of *Prajāpati* (the manifesting form of *Brahmā*).[152] *Vāc* is also called *Sandhyā* (Twilight)—corresponding thus to Venus (Aphrodite)—which shows that form is manifest through her, as through the *coincidentia oppositorum*. *Vāc* is again called *Gāyatri* (the triple-hymn), a name that reveals the triadic nature of Speech as the creative power. According to the *Matsya* and *Śiva Purānas*, it was from the the incest of *Brahmā* and *Sata-rūpā* (*Vāc*) that Svāyambhuva Manu, the progenitor of man and flood hero of the Hindu tradition, was born.

The letter *nūn* is the fourteenth letter of both the Arabic and Hebrew alphabets; in both alphabets it has the numerical value of fifty. Both fourteen and fifty develop from the symbolism of the number seven, the number of the Centre. The Centre is both created and Uncreated; thus, from the celestial perspective, the fullness of the Centre is expressed by the symbolic addition of seven and seven ($7 + 7 = 14$); from the terrestrial perspective, the actuality of the Centre is expressed by the symbolic multiplication of seven by seven ($7 \times 7 = 49$), with the potentiality of the Centre being expressed by the "fullness" (*kol* = "all"), of the number fifty, the number of *Binah* and the Jubilee.

The term "Jubilee" derives from the word *yōbēl* (יבל; "the blast of a *horn*"). There is one notable exception to this derivation, Lev.25:9, where the word translated variously as "jubilee" or "trumpet" derives from *t*ᵉ*rūw'āh* ("a *clamor*," especially "a *clangor* of trumpets"). This word derives from the primitive root *rūwa'* (רוע; "to *mar*"; figuratively, "to *split* the ears"). In this connection, recall that the Jubilee is analogous with *Yobel* and, again, *Binah*, and thus is the *coincidentia oppositorum*. Not only does duality resolve into unity in the *coincidentia oppositorum* but this is also the point from which unity "splits" into duality. Observe the close connection between *rūwa'* and *rūwach* (רוח), the "Divine Spirit" (*Rūh*), which is also identifiable with the *coincidentia oppositorum*.

The Jubilee signals *Rosh ha-shanah*, the Hebraic civil New Year (Num.29:1); this coincides with the celebration of the "The Feast of the Trumpets" (*yom terauh*, "*day of blowing*"), also the festival of "The Seventh New Moon." On the Day of Atonement (*kol shofar*, the "voice of the trumpet") Elijah will blow the "great shofar" to inaugurate the ingathering of the exiles and the Resurrection of the Dead.[153] This "ingathering" echoes the symbolism of "gathering what is scattered." In Hebraic tradition, trumpets are made from the "horn" of the ram or goat. The blowing of the ram's horn echoes the sacrificial replacement of Isaac by the ram 'which was caught by its horns in a bush' (Ex.22:13); thus the blowing of the *shofar* "frees" man from his debts. A connection presents itself when we recall that the ram is a solar symbol,[154] for the word *shōphār* (שפר) derives from *shāphār* (שפר) meaning "to *glisten*," which gives rise to *shiphrāh* (שפרה; "*brightness*").

There are three basic sounds for the blowing of the *shofar*: *tekiah*, a long plain note; *shevarim*, three broken undulating or wavering notes; and *teruah*, a series of nine short staccato notes.[155] These can be viewed with respect to the above schema: point, vertical line and horizontal line. Thus, the *tekiah* suggests the infinite Principle (the point)—its length suggests the infinite, while its single note suggests the idea of unity; the *shevarim* suggests the three vertical elements (the Great Triad); and *teruah*, with its nine staccato notes, suggests the horizontal "nine-fold division," the symbolism of the completion of a particular cycle of existence, and thus the perfection of the "nine-fold plan." Again, the *teruah* might be seen as like the nine *sefirot* vertically descending from *Keter*; the three wavering notes of the *shevarim* equally suggests the three horizontal aspects—here the "wavering" of the notes expresses the primordial vibration of Substance (*nāda*).

The association of the trumpet and the "end of time" is clearly shown in Norse mythology. Heimdall, who guards Bilfrost, the rainbow-bridge, blows upon his trumpet, *Giallarhorn*, to awaken the gods to the battle of *Ragnarok*.[156] *Giallarhorn* is the same horn that Mimir used to drink from his well, 'which has wisdom and intelligence contained in it'.[157] Odin hung upside down from the branches of the World tree, *Yggdrasil*, so as to drink from the well of Mimir.[158] However to gain his drink he had to sacrifice one of his eyes, depositing it 'in that renowned well of Mimir.'[159] This symbolism of being "one-eyed" echoes the symbolism of lameness. Interestingly, then, Heimdall refers to himself as both Hod—"He is blind"—and also Vidar—"He has a thick shoe"—that is, "He is lame."[160] The "blindness" of Hod should be seen as being "one eyed," recalling not only Odin but also the Cyclopes, the servants of Hephaestus.[161] Furthermore, Heimdall says of himself in *Heimdalar-galdr*: 'Offspring of nine mothers am I, of nine sisters am I the son.'[162] So too Hephaestus spent nine years under the sea in Thetis' cave, which is both a womb and a "mother."

According to the Hindu myth of the deluge, Viśnu, in the guise of *Matsya-avatāra* (the Fish-Incarnation) conducted the Ark of Manu to safety after Manu fastened the vessel to *Matsya's* "horn," using the great serpent Remainder (*Sesa-nāga*) as a rope.[163] Yet again it is said that *Matsya* told Manu to secure the Ark to a tree trunk, advising him to allow the craft to float down with the receding waters.[164] The image of *Matsya* with a horn suggests the one-horned narwhal, the horn of which was traditionally taken as being the horn of the unicorn. Commenting on fifteenth-century Christian "unicorn tapestries," E. C. Marquand remarks that these always contained a central tree, the Tree of Life, whose "axial" significance is in accord with that of the single horn.[165]

Hebraic tradition of Noah's Ark offers an interesting comparison to the Hindu tradition. It is said that among the animals Noah brought to the Ark was the rhinoceros, which, although only being one day old, was too large—forty-four and a half miles long—to fit in the Ark. Thus, Noah tied the horn of the rhinoceros to the side of the Ark, along which the beast swam.[166] Another tradition tells of how the young David was wandering in the desert when he came upon a reem (rhinoceros) asleep. Unaware that it was a rhinoceros he took it for a mountain (symbol of Manifestation) and began to climb it; the rhinoceros awoke and rose, lifting David up to the sky (Heaven). Seized with fear he vowed to the Lord that if God would save him he would build a temple as high as the horn of the rhinoceros, namely, one hundred cubits. His vow was heard and he was saved.[167] In the first tradition the rhinoceros (mountain, Temple, Manifestation) is saved by virtue of being connected to the Ark (the Centre-Principle) by the axial horn. In the second tradition the Temple is modelled upon the axial horn, which links earth and heaven.

The use of the horn to create a trumpet is paralleled by the similar use of the shell. The conch shell, still used as a ceremonial horn by Brahmins, Tibetan lamas and Maoris, is particularly relevant here. According to Hindu tradition, during the cataclysm that separates this *Maha-Yuga* from the previous one, the Veda was enclosed in a state of envelopment in the conch (*shankha*), one of the chief attributes of Viśnu.[168] The *Dictionary of Symbols* notes an analogy between the conch shell and the three *matras* of the monosyllable *Om* (A-U-M): 'Some traditions group together the three elements of the monosyllable as a spiral (the conch), a point (the seed which it holds) and a straight line (the development of the potential contained within the shell).'[169] These might be compared to the three ways of blowing the *shofar*. In terms of the symbolism of the shell, the point or seed is the hidden "pearl"; then, on the one hand, the vertical line is figured by the spiral of the conch and the straight line is the horizontal development of the potentiality of a state of Being; or, on the other hand, the straight line is the vertical Divine Ray with the spiral expressing the primordial vibration (*nāda*).

In Greek mythology the conch is the shell from which Aphrodite was born.[170] In Cambodia the conch explains the *salagrama*, 'the counterpart of the lingam in the worship of Śiva.'[171] This female sexual symbolism is best seen in the cowie shell of Malaysia.[172] In Hinduism the conch is one of the twenty-four icons of Viśnu. Daniélou remarks that it is the symbol of the origin of existence: 'It has the form of a multiple spiral evolving from one point into ever-increasing spheres. It is associated with the element water ... When blown, it produces a sound associated with the primeval sound from which creation developed.'[173] The spiral of the conch echoes the spiral staircase of the Temple (1 Kg. 6:8). The conch of Viśnu is the compliment to the *vajra* (thunderbolt).[174] The conch is the 'relatively passive and receptive aspect of a principle of which the *vajra* is the active aspect.'[175] As Guénon remarks, the *vajra* corresponds to the *baetyl* and to the World Axis.[176]

The conch is also connected to the moon through its whiteness. According to the *Dictionary of Symbols*, in China, 'a huge shell was used "to draw the waters of the Moon," or "celestial dew," and also the *yin* element; *yang*, fire was drawn from the Sun by means of a metal mirror.'[177] In another example of inverse analogy the moon that reflects the sun's light also corresponds to the mirror. The "waters" of *Genesis* 1:2 act as a mirror to the divine Ray of the *Fiat Lux*.

In Tibet the bell (*dilbu*) plays the role of the conch, as the complement to the *vajra*.[178] The shape of a bell resembles an inverted cup. This is a most eloquent cosmological symbol. At the "centre" or "heart" of the bell *rests* the clapper (the *bindu*), suspended via a chain (*axis mundi*) to the "top" of the bell. The same image is found in Operative Freemasonry in the plumb line suspended from the cupola of the Lodge by the Great Architect of the Universe.[179] The hemispherical shape of the bell is analogous to the upper hemisphere of the World Egg. In Islamic tradition the "Ringing of the Bell" (*salsalat al-jaras*) expresses the creative Sound, as heard by the Prophet at the time of the revelation of the Qur'an.

Notes

1. Per Thomas Taylor, *The Mystical Hymns of Orpheus*, 1896, p.xxiv, n.16, cited in Perry, *TTW*, 2000, p.997.

2. *Oratio* XL, 41, cited in Lossky, *The Mystical Theology of the Eastern Church*, 1968, p.46.

3. On these points see Lossky, *The Mystical Theology of the Eastern Church*, 1968, Ch.3.

4. Such accusations are levelled at Meister Eckhart. On Meister Eckhart's understanding of the Trinity see McGinn, *The Mystical Thought of Meister Eckhart*, 2001.

5. For an example of those who disagree with Schuon here see Timothy A. Mahoney, 'Christian Metaphysics: Trinity, Incarnation and Creation', *Sophia* 8.1, 2002, p.87 particularly n.30. A characteristic Schuonian passage which has attracted criticism from some orthodox Christians can be found in *LT*, 1975, pp.106-109.

6. Schuon, *UI*, 1976, p.54.

7. Lossky, *The Mystical Theology of the Eastern Church*, 1968, p.49.

8. Schuon, *LT*, 1975, p.107.

9. *Oratio* XXXI (Theologia V), 14, cited in Lossky, *The Mystical Theology of the Eastern Church*, 1968, p.59.

10. In the final analysis these are one and the same. According to al-Jīlī, 'if the servant (*al-'abd*) is elevated by cosmic degrees towards the degrees of the Eternal Reality and he discovers himself, he recognises that the Divine essence is his own essence, so that he really attains the Essence and knows It, as the Prophet expresses it thus: 'He who knows himself (*nafsah*), knows his Lord,' (*man 'arafa nafsahu faqad 'arafa rabbahu*)' (*al-insān*, 1983, p.13).

11. Schuon: 'Man cannot love God in His Essence, which is humanly unknowable, but only in that which God makes known to him' (*SPHF*, 1987, p.157).

12. Meister Eckhart, *Comm. Jn.* 67 (Colledge & McGinn, 1981, p.146).

13. Schuon, *SME*, 2000, pp.22-23.

14. Schaya, *UMK*, 1971, p.36.

15. Daniélou, *MGI*, 1985, pp.20-21.

16. Pseudo-Dionysius, *The Mystical Theology*, 100B (1987, p.136).

17. Mathers, *KU*, 1991, p.20.

18. Samsel, 'A Unity with Distinction: Parallels in the Thought of Gregory Palamas and Ibn al-'Arabī', *Sophia* 7.2, 2001, p.100.

19. St. Gregory Palamas, cited in Meyendorff, *A Study of Gregory Palamas*, 1998, p.239.

20. According to the Vulgate: 'So there are three witnesses *in heaven: the Father, the Word and the Spirit, and these three are one; there are three witness on earth*: the Spirit, the water and the blood; and the three of them coincide' (vv.7-8) The words in italics are not found in the early Greek MSS. Cf. Jn.14:11, 10:30: 'The Father and I are one.'

21. Augustine, *Comm. Jn.* 95.1.

22. Guénon, *MB*, 1981, p.107, n.1.

23. Guénon, *MB*, 1981, p.107.

24. Guénon, *MB*, 1981, p.38.

25. Schaya, *UMK*, 1971, p.36.

26. Ibn al-'Arabī, *Fusūs* (1980, p.142).

27. Schuon, *IFA*, 1989, p.143.

28. Schaya, *UMK*, 1971, p.68.

29. Schaya, *UMK*, 1971, p.75. *Keter-Hokhmah-Binah* are the 'first and transcendental causes' of which *Shekhinah-Metatron-Avir* are the immanent causes.

30. Schaya, *UMK*, 1971, p.75, n.1.

31. Lawlor, *Sacred Geometry*, 1989, p.12.

32. Guénon, *GT*, 1994, p.19.

33. These two ternaries have been discussed in detail by Guénon, *GT*, 1994, Ch.2, from which much of the following is drawn with due reference.

34. The Egyptian triad Osiris, Isis and Horus is perhaps the most famous mythological example of this type.

35. Pertnety, *Dictionnaire mytho-hermétique*, Paris, 1972, pp.426-7, cited in Chevalier & Gheerbrant, *DS*, 1996, p.791.

36. Guénon, *GT*, 1994, p.22.

37. Guénon, *GT*, 1994, p.22.

38. This diagrammatical representation follows Guénon, *GT*, 1994, p.22.

39. Schuon, *EPW*, 1981, p.67.

40. See Guénon, *GT*, 1994, Ch.10.

41. Guénon, *GT*, 1994, p.70.

42. See Snodgrass, 'The Symbolism of the Levels' in *SS*, 1985, (pp.233-250). Snodgrass: 'Midspace extends from the surface of the Earth to the first of

the heavens ... Midspace is vertically coextensive with the Cosmic Mountain' (p.234).

43. Guénon, *GT*, 1994, pp.70-71.

44. Guénon, *GT*, 1994, p.72.

45. Guénon, *GT*, 1994, p.71.

46. See Guénon, *GT*, 1994, p.73.

47. Ezk.31:6; Ps.104:12; see Guénon, *FS*, 1995, Ch.9.

48. *Śatapatha Brāhmana* VIII.7.3.20; VIII.7.4.1, cited in Coomaraswamy, *SP1*, 1977, p.465.

49. Coomaraswamy, *SP1*, 1977, p.485.

50. The Hebrew here is *chatser* (חצר; "to *surround*"). This primitive root is directly related to the word *chatsorer* (חצרר; "to *trumpet*"), which suggests two relevant connections. The first is the capture of Jericho achieved by circumscribing or "surrounding" the city with the Ark of the Covenant seven times accompanied by the blowing of seven trumpets (Jos.6:6-16). The second is again the connection to *yobel*.

51. See Schaya, 'The Meaning of the Temple' in Needleman (ed), *The Sword of Gnosis*, 1974, p.363. The "footstool" is a symbolic cognomen of the cosmic manifestation of Immanence: 'Thus speaks Yahweh: The Heaven is my throne and the earth is my footstool' (Is.66:1); King David declared: 'I have set my heart on building a settled home for the ark of the covenant of Yahweh, for the footstool of our God...' (1Ch.28:2). 'I have set my heart' says King David, which is as if to say, this is where my Heart will be "set." Schaya remarks that the "footstool" is none other than the "foundation stone" of the *Zohar* (*Vayehi* 23.1a), which 'is made up of fire (spiritual light), water (subtle substance) and air (ether, the quintessence of the corporeal elements)'. Schaya: 'The divine "footstool" or "foundation stone" is none other than the revelation of the supreme tri-unity here below' (*UMK*, 1971, pp.101; see also p.104).

52. Cited by Ibn al-'Arabī, *Lubb* (1981, p.42). Ibn al-'Arabī explains this *hadīth qudsī* citing "a lover" with the following: 'The heart is a pearl which looks at God. / The heart is the place of manifestation of the Name and the Named. / The heart is a falcon, or a bird of marvel. / The heart is the being of the Ipseity of God.'

53. See Snodgrass, *SS*, 1985, II. 19; Chevalier & Gheerbrant, *DS*, 1996, p.1145. Eliade: 'When the pilgrim climbs [the temple or ziggurat], he is coming close to the centre of the world, and on its highest terrace he breaks through into another sphere, transcending profane, heterogeneous space, and entering a "pure earth"' (*Patterns in Comparative Religion*, 1958, p.376). "Pure earth": that is, the primordial state or the Garden of Eden, which is of course, the Heart. When the desire for union with the Divine becomes perverted to a lust for the power of the gods the ziggurat becomes the Tower of Babel.

54. See *Chāndogya Upanishad* 8.1.1.

55. Śankarācārya commentary on *Chāndogya Upanishad* 8.1.1.

56. See Guénon, 'The Ether in the Heart', *FS*, 1995, Ch.75.

57. Guénon, *FS*, 1995, p.297. Guénon notes 'This is the *Fiat Lux* (*Yehi Aor*) of *Genesis*, the first affirmation of the Divine Word in the work of creation– the initial vibration which opens the way to the developments of possibilities contained potentially in the state 'without form and void' (*thohu va bohu*), in the original chaos' (n.13).

58. See Guénon, *RQ*, 1995, Ch.3; *SC*, 1975, Ch.4.

59. We say "potential equality" for these three dimensions of man are respectively predominant according to the disposition of the individual and are only "equal" inasmuch as the realisation of their ends, that is the union with God, corresponds to their unity in the Principle.

60. See Schuon, 'The Triple Nature of Man' in *EPW*, 1981.

61. See Schuon, 'The Supreme Commandment' in *EPW*, 1981.

62. Schuon, *EPW*, 1981, p.95.

63. See *Gilgamesh* XI, ii, in Dalley (ed.), *MM*, 1991, p.111.

64. Coomaraswamy, 'Some Pali Words': *SP2*, 1977, p.324.

65. On *Śakti* see Daniélou, *MGI*, 1985, Ch.20 passim.

66. Guénon, *GT*, 1994, p.58. What follows is essentially a paraphrase of Ch.8 of this work.

67. Guénon, *GT*, 1994, pp.58-59. The 1994 edition has an *erratum* here reading '5 the number of Heaven' corrected to '3 the number of heaven'.

68. The "second" biblical account of the creation of man expresses this cosmological viewpoint. Thus we read, 'At the time when God made earth and heaven' (Gen.2:4b). Compare Gen.1:1, 'In the Beginning God created heaven and earth.' Again, these are not two separate accounts but the complementary perspectives: cosmological and metaphysical respectively.

69. Following the "law of inverse analogy."

70. Guénon, *GT*, 1994, p.61. Guénon is citing *Ch'ien Han-chu*.

71. Guénon, *GT*, 1994, p.62.

72. Thus terrestrial man is symbolised by the pentagon, with its five points that measure out the body of man, while celestial man is symbolised by the six-point star or the Star of David.

73. See Guénon, *RQ*, 1995, Ch.3.

74. See Guénon, *ED*, 1996, pp.47-8.

75. Two further symbolic numbers deserve mention here: 72 (7 + 2 = 9), which we have had numerous occasion to mention, and the square of 9, 81 (8 + 1 = 9); moreover, (9 + 9 =18; 1 + 8 = 9).

76. See "nine" in Chevalier & Gheerbrant, *DS*, 1996, p.702.

77. Pseudo-Dionysius, *The Celestial Hierarchy*, 6, 200D, 201A (1987, p.160-61).

78. Graves, *The Greek Myths*, *Vol.1*, 1960, p.139. One of the more esoteric associations between the number nine and the "flood" is that developed by Plato in the *Critias* where "nine thousand years of flooding" (a complete cycle) have elapsed (*Crit.* 111) since 'the declaration of war between those who lived outside and all those that lived inside the Pillars of Heracles' (*Crit.* 108); which

is to say, between potentiality ("inside") the "Pillars of Heracles" (the Symplegades) and actuality ("outside").

79. Campbell, *Oriental Mythology*, 1973, p.385.

80. Campbell, *Oriental Mythology*, 1973, p.385. This is the same Yao whom Guénon recalls from the *Tchoang-tseu* (Chuang-Tzu): 'The emperor Yao took a great deal of trouble, and sincerely believed he had reigned in an ideal way. However, after his visit to the four masters on the distant island of *Ku-shih* he realised he had spoilt everything.' Guénon offers this explanation: 'The ideal, [Yao] discovered, consists in the indifference (or rather the detachment in action that is non-action) of the superior man who allows the cosmic wheel to turn' (Guénon, *LW*, 1983, p.55). On the four cardinal points see Ch.9.

81. *Shu Ching* 5.4.1, following Campbell, *Oriental Mythology*, 1973, p.388.

82. *Shu Ching* 5.4.1, following Campbell, *Oriental Mythology*, 1973, p.389.

83. See "magic square" in Chevalier & Gheerbrant, *DS*, 1996, p.623. For a discussion of the cosmological significance of magic squares see Critchlow, *Islamic Patterns*, 1976, Ch.3.

84. Guénon, *GT*, 1994, pp.110-11; see Ch.16.

85. Guénon remarks it should further be observed that every number added to its (symmetrically) opposite number produces 10; moreover, the odd or *yang* numbers occupy the central position on each side of the square (the cardinal points) and form a cross (dynamic aspect); while, on the other hand the even or *yin* numbers occupy the corners of the square (the intermediary points) and delimit the square itself (static aspect) (see Guénon, *GT*, 1994, p.111, n.8).

86. This is fully justified inasmuch as 5 is the sum of 3 or Heaven (*yang*) and 2 or Earth (*yin*).

87. Guénon, *GT*, 1994, p.111, n.6.

88. This is at least one of the meanings, positive in this case, of the Hermetic "squaring of the circle."

89. Guénon, *GT*, 1994, Ch.16.

90. Cited in Guénon, *GT*, 1994, p.112, n.12.

91. Guénon, *GT*, 1994, p.100-101; see ibid Ch.14.

92. See Campbell, *Oriental Mythology*, 1973, p.382-89 for an account of these ten emperors; cf. also the ten Sumerian kings.

93. The long red feathers of the macaw have meant that it is regarded as a solar symbol (Chevalier & Gheerbrant, *DS*, 1996, p.623). It is worth conjecturing that, because of its habit of imitation, the parrot may well have been seen as a lunar symbol. The moon reflects (imitates) the sun. Here then are the two elements of the *Ming T'ang*.

94. *Mencius* 3.1.4.7. cited in Campbell, *Oriental Mythology*, 1973, p.389.

95. Jordan, *Myths of the World*, 1993, p.114-15.

96. *Tso chuan*, cited in Eliade (ed.), *The Encyclopedia of Religion Vol.11*, 1996, p.540; see also "cauldron" in Chevalier & Gheerbrant, *DS*, 1996, p.166.

97. Chevalier & Gheerbrant, *DS*, 1996, p.166.

98. "Cauldron" in Chevalier & Gheerbrant, *DS*, 1996, p.166.

99. *Iliad* 18.373-79.

100. See Sworder, 'Homer's Smith God' in *Mathematical Cosmologies of Newton, Homer and Plato*, 1997.

101. *Timaeus* 22.

102. *Phaedo* 110b.

103. Chevalier & Gheerbrant, *DS*, 1996, p.166.

104. Sworder, 'Homer's Smith God' in *Mathematical Cosmologies of Newton, Homer and Plato*, 1997, p.13.

105. *Goraksha Shataka* cited in Eliade, *Sacred and Profane*, 1987, p.173. The perfectly valid physiological explanation for this description only goes to confirm the analogy of man and the universe.

106. "House" in Chevalier & Gheerbrant, *DS*, 1996, p.530.

107. Chevalier & Gheerbrant, *DS*, 1996, p.165.

108. Chevalier & Gheerbrant, *DS*, 1996, p.165.

109. Chevalier & Gheerbrant, *DS*, 1996, p.165.

110. Critchlow, *Islamic Patterns*, 1976, p.9.

111. Critchlow, *Islamic Patterns*, 1976, p.9.

112. B.T. *Hagigah*, 15a; B.T. *Sanhedrin*, 38 a; B.T. *Avodah Zarah*, 3b.

113. *Midrash Tanchuma, Genesis*, 8, 16. *Genesis Rabba*, 44 recounts Gen.14:18 yet says that it was Shem 'who was now priest of the most high God and ruled at Salem under the name of Melchizedek' (cited in Rappoport, *AI1*, 1995, p.260). See also *Jerusalem Targum* Gen.14:18 cited in Cohen, *ET*, 1995, p.236.

114. For numerous examples of this idea in the various traditions of the world see Perry, *TTW*, 2000, pp.1031-1036.

115. Meister Eckhart, *Comm. Jn.* 4 (Colledge & McGinn, 1981, p.123). 'In its principle,' i.e. *in principio*. As Bernard McGinn notes, the Latin *principium* means both "beginning" and "principle," a semantic ambiguity that Eckhart plays with throughout his treatment of John (see n.8).

116. Meister Eckhart, *Comm. Jn.* 4 (Colledge & McGinn, 1981, p.123).

117. Lawlor, *Sacred Geometry*, 1989, p.34. For a detailed discussion of the *Vesica* see Critchlow, *Time Stands Still*, 1979.

118. Rabbi Gikatilla, *SO*, 1994, p.314.

119. Again, these two trees are 'the two anointed ones in attendance on the Lord of the whole world', which the *NJB* says are Joshua and Zerubbabel, the spiritual and temporal powers respectively, prefigured by Melchizedek, who holds both powers in his single being, and who is thus the *coincidentia oppositorum*.

120. *Tsōhar* can also be compared to *tsāhal* (צהל), which means "to *gleam*" and by transference, "to *sound*."

121. Rabbi Rapaport, *The Hebrew Word Shem and Its Original Meaning*, 1976, passim.

122. See Tishby, *WZ2*, 1991, p.626-29.

123. Rabbi Gikatilla, *SO*, 1994, p.314.

124. See Scott, 'Withdrawal, Extinction and Creation: Christ's *kenosis* in light of the Judaic doctrine of *tsimtsum* and the Islamic doctrine of *fana'*, *Sophia* 7.2, 2001, pp.45-64, pp.45-64; revised and republished in *The Essential Sophia*, (ed.) S.H. Nasr & K. O'Brien, 2006, pp.58-77.

125. The Hebrew word for "knee" is *bārek* derived from *bārak*, primitive root meaning "to *kneel*" and by implication "to *bless*"; in this connection note the Islamic term *al-barakah*, the blessing or spiritual influence, and the similarity here to the word *barzakh*, insomuch as it is precisely in the mystery of the isthmus that existence is "blessed" with its very being.

126. According to Epiphanius, Jesus had two sisters, the name of the first being either Mary or Anna and the second being Salome (*Ancor.* 60; *Pan.* 78.8; cited Schneemelcher (ed), *New Testament Apocrypha, Vol.1*, 1991, p.472). In the first case there is identification between that from which Jesus "comes forth"; in the second case we have Salome who the *Protevangelium of James* says was one of the midwives at Jesus' birth, that is, that which "brings forth."

127. Oldmeadow, 'Śankara's Doctrine of *Māyā*': *Asian Philosophy*, Vol.2, No.2, 1992, p.133.

128. The technical term translated as "what" (*quod quid est*) depends on Aristotle, eg. *Metaphysics* 1.8 (988b29).

129. Guénon, *SC*, 1975, p.10.

130. The ancient Egyptian hieroglyph for the heart is a vase; see Guénon, *FS*, 1995, Ch.5 in which he discusses in some detail Charbonneau-Lassay's article 'The Ancient Iconography of the Heart of Jesus'.

131. See Schneemelcher (ed.), *New Testament Apocrypha*, 1991, p.430.

132. "Flowering rod" in Metford, *DCLL*, 1983, p.101.

133. "Cross, legends of the" in Metford, *DCLL*, 1983, p.76.

134. As per Mershman, *The Catholic Encyclopedia, Vol. III* Online Edition. See also "St. Christopher" in Metford, *DCLL*, 1983, p.67-8.

135. Guénon, *FS*, 1995, pp.198-99.

136. See Guénon, 'Gathering What Is Scattered', *FS*, 1995, Ch.48.

137. Guénon, *FS*, 1995, p.207.

138. Popular etymology gives the Hebrew name *Mōshel* from the root *māshāh*, "to draw out." The *NJB* rejects this on the grounds that the Pharaoh's daughter did not speak Hebrew, but this is simply another case of being ignorant of the symbolic import of the Scriptures for the sake of appearing historically accurate. This qualification is not to ignore the analogous stories of infants drawn from water, such as Agade of Mesopotamia, but simply to stress that Truth is Truth wherever it is found and that it cannot but appear in almost identical forms.

139. Note the account of Aaron's death "on the frontier of Edom" (recalling the symbolism of Edom) where Aaron was "gathered to his people" (Nu.20:22-29). It is hard to deny the connection between *'Aharōwn* and *'ārōwn* considering the insistence placed on it in this passage.

140. Chevalier & Gheerbrant, *DS*, 1996, p.715.

141. The gifts of gold, frankincense and myrrh again express the three aspects of Immanence. Myrrh we have discussed; gold is a common symbol of the divine Essence; and frankincense, which derives from the Hebrew *lᵉbōwnāh* (from "*whiteness*"), implies firstly purity and light (the *Fiat Lux*) and secondly the idea of "smoke," which, by way of the smoke of the sacrifice, is an axial symbol. Similarly, the Church Fathers see these as symbols of the royalty (gold), divinity (frankincense) and Passion (myrrh) of Jesus.

142. As noted, the Hebrew *nūn* is associated with the fish, which is itself a potent homologue of the Ark.

143. Guénon, *FS*, 1995, p.110.

144. Guénon, *FS*, 1995, p.110.

145. Guénon, *FS*, 1995, p.112.

146. Coincidentally, Lawlor understands the Egyptian god Nun as expressive of 'the primordial vibrational field (called *nāda* in India)'. He explains that this "primal ocean" is 'the One imaged as undifferentiated cosmic substance, the source of all creation' (*Sacred Geometry*, 1989, p.22). *Nāda* is the sound of the sacred monosyllable, *Om* (see Daniélou, *MGI*, 1985, p.203). It might also be remarked that the god Nun advises Ra in the myth of "The Slaying of Men," a purification myth similar to the Flood (Spence, *Egypt*, 1994, p.166). For the text see Budge, *Legends of the Gods*, 1994, Ch.2 where he uses the name Nu instead of Nun.

147. Critchlow, *Islamic Patterns*, 1976, p.9.

148. Critchlow, *Islamic Patterns*, 1976, p.9.

149. Guénon, *FS*, 1995, p.110.

150. Guénon, *FS*, 1995, p.111.

151. Al-Jīlī, *al-insān*, 1983, p.5. On the connection in the Hindu tradition between Speech and *Om* see Daniélou, *MGI*, 1985, p.37-40.

152. 'In the beginning this [world] was just water. That water emitted the Real (*satya*) and the Real is the Immense-Being (*Brahmā*). From the Immense-Being came forth the lord-of-progeny (*Prajā-pati*), and from the lord-of-progeny the gods' (*Brhad-āranyaka Upaniśad* 5.5.1. [451], cited in Daniélou, *MGI*, 1985, p.239).

153. Compare the "seven trumpets" of Rev.8 that herald the Apocalypse.

154. On the symbolism of the ram see "The Sheep" in Charbonneau-Lassay, *The Bestiary of Christ*, 1992, pp.67-82.

155. See "shofar" in Unterman, *Dictionary of Jewish Lore & Legend*, 1991, p.184.

156. *Gylfaginning* from Sturluson, *Edda*, 1998, p.54.

157. *Gylfaginning* from Sturluson, *Edda*, 1998, p.17.

158. This reveals something of the meaning of the inverted nature of the twelfth card of the Tarot, the Hanging Man.

159. *Voluspa* quoted in Sturluson, *Edda*, 1998, p.17.

160. *Gylfaginning* from Sturluson, *Edda*, 1998, p.26.

161. For further examples and comments on these various symbols see "blindness," "cyclops," "lameness," "one-eyed" & "one-legged" in Chevalier & Gheerbrant, *DS*, pp.99, 270, 586, 721 & 721.

162. *Heimdalargaldr* quoted in Sturluson, *Edda*, 1998, p.26.

163. See Daniélou, *MGI*, 1985, p.166-7.

164. See Jordan, *Myths of the World*, 1993, p.115.

165. *Parnassus*, October, College Art Association of America 1938, cited in Charbonneau-Lassay, *The Bestiary of Christ*, 1992, p.370.

166. *Zebachim*, 113b, cited in Rappoport, *AI1*, 1995, p.221.

167. Midrash Tehillim, 22, 28, cited in cited in Rappoport, *AI3*, 1995, pp.13-14.

168. Guénon, *FS*, 1995, p.107.

169. Chevalier & Gheerbrant, *DS*, 1996, p.229. On *Om* see Guénon, *MB*, 1981, Ch.16; Daniélou, *MGI*, 1985, pp.39, 174, 338 & 340; "aum" & "*Om*" in Chevalier & Gheerbrant, *DS*, 1996, pp.57 & 717.

170. Chevalier & Gheerbrant, *DS*, 1996, p.228. Graves notes this as a "scallop" shell. Botticelli's 'Birth Of Venus' (c.1480) shows Venus (Aphrodite) upon what is obviously a scallop shell, yet it is nevertheless referred to as a conch (see Gardner, *Art Through the Ages*, 1970, p.442). Aphrodite is analogous to the pearl, meaning that the shell should in fact be that of an oyster. However, any discrepancy here can be reconciled when it is realised that the conch, the scallop and the oyster share a common symbolism, of which Botticelli was more than likely aware. Moreover, concerning the symbolism of the horn, Aphrodite is also said to be blowing a triton-shell (see Graves, *The Greek Myths Vol.1*, 1960, p.50).

171. Chevalier & Gheerbrant, *DS*, 1996, p.228.

172. "Cowie" in Chevalier & Gheerbrant, *DS*, 1996, p.236.

173. Daniélou, *MGI*, 1985, p.155.

174. Chevalier & Gheerbrant, *DS*, 1996, p.228. On the associated symbolism of the *vajra* see Guénon, *FS*, 1995, Chs.27 & 28.

175. Chevalier & Gheerbrant, *DS*, 1996, p.228.

176. See Guénon, *FS*, 1995, Ch.27.

177. Chevalier & Gheerbrant, *DS*, 1996, p.228.

178. Guénon notes that the *dilbu* 'often has depicted on it a feminine figure who represents *Prajna-paramita* or "transcendental Wisdom." The bell is her symbol, just as the *vajra* is the symbol of the "Method" or the "Way"' (*GT*, 1994, p.50, n.26).

179. This symbolism is found in the iconography of Piero della Francesca's *Brera Alterpiece* (c.1475). Here an egg/pearl—the symbolism is complementary—is suspended from the centre point of an ornamental scallop shell that forms the cupola above the seated Virgin and Child. This "upper scallop" shell finds its lower half in the scallop of Botticelli's Venus. Whether or not it is intentional on behalf of Botticelli it is worth noting that his shell is reversed to that of della Francesca's in accordance with the law of inverse analogy.

The Quaternary: *The House of God*

Introduction

Immanence is realised by cosmic existence. This is symbolised by the stability of the square or rectangle, or, in terms of three-dimensional symbolism, the cube. The dimensions of the Ark of Noah and the Ark of the Covenant express this symbolic rectangularity. This symbolism is again found with the Temple and the "Heavenly Jerusalem" of *Revelations*, and is most immediately evident in the Islamic "House of God" *par excellence*, the *Ka'bah*. The symbolism of the quaternary, which underpins the geometric symbolism of the rectangle/cube, influences the very nature of temporal and spatial existence, for example: the four seasons and the four principle directions of the compass. Numerically, the unfolding of the quaternary, through the Pythagorean *Tetraktys*, shows the "fullness" of the quaternary, which contains and realises the symbolic decad. In turn, the number ten expresses the return of onto-cosmological existence back to the unmanifested potentiality; that is to say, the return of the monad to the metaphysical zero. The Ark of the deluge comes to rest upon the "twin peaked" mountain; the triple immanent principle effects creation; creation is perfected in the image of the House of God.

The Quaternary as Ontological Unfolding

A river flowed out of Eden to water the garden, and there it divided and became four rivers.

Genesis 2:10

Existence stands upon quaternity.

Ibn al-Arabī[1]

The ternary is completed by and finds its realisation in the quaternary.[2] The three negative veils (*Ain*, *En Sof*, *En Sof Aur*) give birth, so to speak, to a "fourth": the positive universe. This quaternary is echoed in the Kabbalistic doctrine of the "Four Worlds,"[3] which distinguishes four "Worlds" placed between the *En Sof* (the Limitless) and the earthly cosmos.[4] The Four Worlds are: *Azilut* (Emanations), *Beriah* (Creation), *Yezirah* (Formation) and *Asiyyah* (Making).[5] One must not commit the error of seeing these Four Worlds as analogous with the total of the three veils of negativity and the positive universe. The Four Worlds correspond, in a general way, to the schema Principle-Essence-Substance-Manifestation. According to Guénon, this fundamental quaternary is enumerated in the *Rasā'il Ikhwān as-Safā'* as follows: '1 – the Principle, which is designated as *al-Bāri'*, the Creator (which indicates that it is not the supreme principle, but only Being, inasmuch as it is the first principle of manifestation which is, in fact, metaphysical Unity); 2 – the universal Spirit; 3 – the universal Soul; and 4 – the primordial *Hyle*.'[6] Similarly, Scholem notes that *Asiyyah* ("Making", *Hyle*) is comparable to Plotinus' hypostasis of Nature, being 'conceived as the spiritual archetype of the material world of the senses.'[7]

Ibn al-'Arabī talks of five "presences" (*al-hadarāt al-khamsa*) the first of which expresses the Uncreated, embracing the three negative veils of Kabbalah, with the second, third, fourth and fifth presences corresponding to the Four Worlds. The First Presence is *al-Ghayb al-Mutlaq* (Absolute Unknowableness). The Second Presence is *'Ālam al-Jabarūt* (the Universe of Omnipotence), also known as the Presence of the First Unveiling, the First Jewel (*al-jawhar al-fard*, "The Singular Jewel"; the Unmanifested Intellect), the Qualified Spirit and the Universe of Quiddities. This is the ontological Principle, Being. It is also called the Great Isthmus, being the meeting place of the manifested and the Unmanifested. The Third Presence is *'Ālam al-Malakūt* (Angelic Universe), Firstness, the Second Unveiling, the Universe of Orders. It is also called the small Isthmus, being the meeting place of the created and the Uncreated. This is Essence. The Fourth Presence is *al-Shuhūd al-Mutlaq* (Absolute Observation, Vision, Witnessing), the Universe of Witnessing, Universe of Possession, Universe of Creation. 'This station' says Ibn al-'Arabī, 'circumscribes the totality of the universe of forms.'[8] He also says that the Great Throne (*al-Arsh al-Azīm*) is of this station. This is Substance. The Fifth Presence is *al-Insān al-Kāmil* (Perfect Man), who is Manifestation.

The ternary Principle-Essence-Substance is reflected in the ternary Essence-Substance-Manifestation. This may be expressed by the image of two inverted triangles sharing the same base, where the base is formed of the polarity of Essence and Substance. This image reveals how the ontological ternary as "completed" by the unfolding of the quaternary.

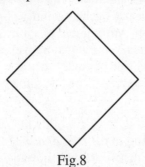

Fig.8

When considering the ternary Essence-Substance-Manifestation, or Father-Mother-Son, we must keep in mind that the "Son" (the *Rebis*) is androgynous, so that this ternary also implies the quaternary, or if you will, quaternity Father-Mother-Son/Daughter. However, a similar transition from ternary to quaternary cannot be made with the ternary Principle-Essence-Substance, for here the Principle (*Keter Elyon*, *Wu Chi*, *Para-Brahman*) is neuter. Still, beyond distinctions of sexual symbolism one can say, as does Schuon, that "the Essence" (Schuon is referring to the Divine Essence, which can be likened by analogy to the Principle in the above schema) comprises four qualities or functions: 'firstly Purity or Vacuity, Exclusivity; secondly, as the complementary opposite … Goodness, Beauty, Life or Intensity, Attraction; thirdly Strength or Activity, Manifestation; and fourthly … Peace, Equilibrium or Passivity, Inclusivity, Receptivity.'[9] The relationship between this quaternity and the quaternary as an expression of ontological unfolding might be likened—but not equated—to that between the Trinity and the ternary.

When describing Immanence in terms of numerical hypostases the quaternary, in a general sense, represents universal manifestation. 'In this respect,' remarks Guénon, 'it therefore marks the very starting point of cosmology, while the numbers that precede it, one, two and three, are strictly related to ontology.'[10] Guénon:

> the quaternary … is held to be presupposed by manifestation, in the sense that the presence of all its terms is necessary for the complete development of the possibilities which manifestation comprises; and this moreover is said to be why, in the order of manifested things, the mark of the quaternary, we might say its "signature," is always especially noticeable—whence, for example, the four elements (Ether not being counted here, for it is a question only of the "differentiated" elements), the four cardinal points (or the four regions of space which corresponds to them, with the four "pillars" of the world), the four phases into which each cycle is naturally divided (the ages of human life, the seasons in the yearly cycle, the lunar phases in the monthly cycle, etc), and so on. Any number of applications of the quaternary are there, all interconnected moreover by rigorous analogical correspondences, for basically they are just so many more or less specialised aspects of the one same general "schema" of manifestation.[11]

The number four is said to have a worldwide symbolic quality of passive substance. According to the *Dictionary of Symbols*, 'Four does not create, but contains all that is created subsequently. Its property is potentiality.'[12] Potentiality: Substance, *materia prima*, the "face of the Waters"; this, as the last cognomen indicates, is a horizontal plane (face) of Existence, where a plane is delineated precisely by expansion in the four cardinal directions.

The quaternary represents the totality of manifestation: 'the earthly, the totality of the created and the revealed'.[13] Its symbolism is, firstly, that of the totality of created things and, secondly, that of the perfection of creation. In the former case the totality of created things is also the totality of all that perishes; this explains why in Japanese the same word, *shi*, means both "four" and "death," and this in accord with the ambiguous nature of *Māyā*. In the latter case, the symbolism of the quaternary is the source of the perfection of the number eight; moreover, the number four, by its development through the *Tetraktys* and its subsequent relation to the number ten, implies the return of the manifested one to the Unmanifested zero.

The Cross and the Square

God, in his suffering, opened his arms and embraced the circle of the world.

Lactantius[14]

The Divine Ray "descends" to the "point" at which it strikes a horizontal plane of Existence; the point of intersection is the fixed Centre for this plane of existence. The Centre, envisaged as the monad, is the first representation of onto-cosmological existence in its purely virtual state (the "seed"). From the Centre the Divine Ray expands to generate the four arms of the horizontal cross (the four "rivers" of *Genesis*, the "beams" of light of the *hashmal*, the "four winds", etc.). The horizontal cross, and by association the number four, represent the indefinite potentiality of universal manifestation. On earth this cross is represented by the directions North, South, East, and West. Certain versions of the Flood myth recall how the Ark sailed or drifted to the extent of the four directions before returning to land at the centre of the world.[15] The Ark thus measures the extent of cosmological space, by which it creates space.[16] This is to say that space exists within the scope of the Ark, which, in a manner of speaking, is to say that the Ark "contains" space, and even that the Ark is space.[17] Similarly, the Divine House creates space through being the central orientation by which all spatial position is referred. This idea is best expressed by the Islamic *qiblah* (the direction of prayer), which centres on the *Ka'bah*. The word *qiblah* is derived from the root QBL, which also gives *al-qābil* ("receptacle") and, by metathesis, *al-qalb* ("heart").

To take all this further: the number five—the centre of the nine principal numbers—expresses the Centre envisaged as a synthesis of a horizontal plane. In several myths the Ark contains five "stones" or "seeds" demonstrating the relationship between the number five and the monad (stone, seed) envisaged as the Centre.[18] The manifested world, comprised of the complementary dimensions of space and time, is measured by the six directions of space, with the number seven expressing the Centre envisaged as the point of return to the Unmanifested. The number eight expresses the perfection of the manifested world; this is developed from the number four and the horizontal cross, for each of the four arms of this cross have both a centrifugal and centripetal movement, the former indicating the totality of manifestation and the latter, by virtue of returning to the Centre, the perfection of manifestation.

The arms of the horizontal cross become the radii of the circle, where the circumference is made up of an indefinitude of points representing multiplicity or the manifest world.[19] Guénon: 'The cross, when it turns around its own centre, engenders the circumference which, with the centre, represents the denary, which itself … is the complete numerical cycle.'[20]

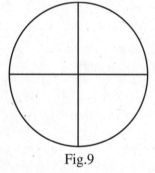

Fig.9

'God, in his suffering, opened his arms and embraced the circle of the world'.

Guénon remarks that the figure of the cross inscribed in a circle is the hermetic symbol of the vegetable kingdom.[21] This alludes to a further symbolism: the relationship between the "Earthly Paradise" and the "Heavenly Jerusalem".[22] In the first case, the Earthly Paradise, corresponding to the beginning of a cycle, is described as a garden, has vegetable symbolism and is traditionally depicted as circular.[23] In the second case, the Heavenly Jerusalem, corresponding to the end of a cycle, is described as a city, has mineral symbolism and is square: 'The plan of the city is perfectly square, its length the same as its breadth' (Rev.21:16). Concerning these symbolisms, Guénon says that 'vegetation represents the development of seeds in the sphere of vital assimilation, while minerals represent results that are fixed definitely—"crystallized" so to speak—at the end of a cyclic development.'[24] Guénon also remarks that 'the presence of the same "Tree of Life" in the centre in each case shows clearly that it is only actually a question of two states of one and the same thing'.[25] According to Christian tradition the Tree of Life corresponds to the Cross of Christ.[26] The *Dictionary of Symbols* notes that the symbol of the cross becomes one of the basic themes of the Old Testament: 'It is the Tree of Life (*Genesis* 2: 9), Wisdom (*Proverbs* 3: 18), the wood of Noah's Ark,[27] the rod with which Moses struck water from the rock, the pole on which the brazen serpent hung or the tree planted beside running water.'[28] In another link between the cross and the Ark, St. Justin recognises the "hidden" symbol of the cross (*cruces dissimulatae*) in, among other things, the ship's mast.[29] This brief survey connects the idea of the fixed Centre with the primordial Garden, the traversing Ark, the redeeming Cross and the eschatological City.

The symbolism of the cross inscribed in a circle is connected to that of the *swastika*. Guénon:

> If it [the *swatstika*] is compared with the figure of the cross inscribed in the circumference of a circle, it will be seen that these are really equivalent symbols in certain respects; but in the *swastika* the rotation round the fixed centre, instead of being represented by the circumference, is merely indicated by short lines joined to the ends of the arms of the cross and forming right angles with them; these lines are tangents to the circumference which marks the direction of movement at the corresponding points. As the circumference represents the manifest world; the fact that it is as it were "suggested" (or "understood") indicates quite clearly that the *swastika* is not a symbol of the world, but rather of the Principle's action upon the world.[30]

Fig.10

The tangent lines in the swastika indicate movement in a particular direction; if each tangent line be taken with the tangent line representing its diametrically opposed movement then we have an image of perfect stasis and balance. This figure is the square.

Fig.11

The quaternary is expressed by both the cross and the square; the latter is static and the former, like the *swastika*, dynamic. Schuon:

> Quaternity signifies stability or stabilization; represented by the square; it is a solidly established world, and a space which encloses; represented by the cross, it is the stabilizing Law that proclaims itself to the four directions, indicating thereby its character of totality. The static square is the Sanctuary, which offers security; the dynamic quaternity is the radiation of ordaining Grace, which is both Law and Benediction. All of this is prefigured in God, in the Essence, in an undifferentiated manner, and in Being, in a differentiated manner.[31]

On the three dimensional plane the point-circle is expressed by the sphere and the square by the cube. The sphere, remarks Guénon, 'can be said to be the most universal form of all, containing in a certain sense all other forms, which will emerge from it by means of differentiation taking place in certain particular directions'.[32] In contrast to the sphere, the cube is the most "arrested" form of all. Guénon: 'The cube is also the form which is related to the earth as one of the elements, inasmuch as the earth is the "terminating and final element" of manifestation in the corporeal state, and consequently it corresponds also to the end of the cycle of manifestation, or what has been called the "stopping point" of the cyclical movement.'[33] The point-circle represents the virtuality of Essence, whereas the square represents the potentiality of Substance. As Guénon remarks, 'Immobility or stability thus understood, and represented by the cube, is therefore related to the substantial pole of manifestation, just as immutability, in which all possibilities are comprehended in the "global" state represented by the sphere, is related to the essential pole'.[34]

The cross is dynamic, implying change and thus, not only space, but also time. Thus Schuon remarks that the quaternary refers not only to equilibrium, but 'also determines unfolding, and so time, or the cycles: hence the four seasons, the four parts of the day, the four ages of creatures and worlds. This unfolding cannot apply to the Principle, which is immutable; what it entails is a successive projection, in the cosmos, of the principial and consequently extra-temporal [quaternary].'[35] The Ark is the static Now (*nunc stans*) coincident with Eternity. As Eternity gives rise to aeviternity (from the Latin *aevum*), or the indefinite extension of time, so the journey of the Ark on the Waters of Potentiality gives rise to the cosmic cycles that measure time. This is born out by the Hebrew Flood, which, as *The New Bible Commentary* demonstrates, measures an exact solar year:[36]

There were 40 days during which the rain fell (Gen.7:12) ...   40 days
Throughout another 110 days the waters continued to rise,
   making 150 days in all for their "prevailing" (7:24) ...   110 days
The waters occupied 74 days in their "going and decreasing"
   (AV mg.). This was from the 17th of the seventh month
   to the 1st of the tenth month (8:5). There being 30 days
   to a month, the figures in days are 13 plus 30 plus 30 plus 1 ... 74 days
Forty days elapsed before Noah sent out the raven (8:6, 7) ... 40 days
Seven days elapsed before Noah sent out the dove for the first
   time (8:8). This period is necessary for reaching the total and
   is given by implication from the phrase "other seven days"
   in verse 10 ...   7 days
Seven days passed before sending out the dove
   for the second time (8:10) ...   7 days
Seven more days passed before the third sending
   of the dove (8:12) ...   7 days
Up to this point 285 days are accounted for, but the next episode
   is dated the 1st of the month in the 601st year. From the date
   in 7:11 to this point in 8:13 is a period of 314 days; therefore
   an interval of 29 days elapses ...   29 days
From the removal of the covering of the ark to the very end
   of the experience was a further 57 days (8:14) ...   57 days
                                      Total ...   371 days

According to *The New Bible Commentary*,

The calendar month was one of 30 days; thus from the 17th of the month in the 600th year to the 27th of the second month in the 601st year was one calendar year and 11days, that is, 371 days. The whole of this is purely calendar reckoning. If the trouble be taken to investigate the real days as measured by the sun a remarkable fact emerges. There were only 29   real days to a lunar month; but for calendar purposes the first 24-hour day of the month was counted twice, half belonging to the preceding month and half to the following. Twelve lunar months were actually only 354 days. If then the 11 days (from the 17th to the 27th of the second month) be added the figure 365 is reached. The fact then comes to light that the flood occupied exactly one solar year.[37]

The Temple likewise suggests a spatio-temporal symbolism. According to Josephus, if one looks upon the description of the tabernacle and the Temple, "without prejudice and with judgment," one will find these 'made by way of imitation and representation of the universe.'[38] He interprets the seventy parts of the candlestick as the *Decani*; the seven lamps as the course of the planets; the sardonyxes as the sun and the moon; and the twelve stones as the Zodiac. Drummond presents an interesting and detailed examination of the tabernacle and Temple in this light.[39] The very word "temple" is linked to the movement of the stars: '*Templum* originally meant that quarter of the sky which the Roman augur marked out with his staff and in which he watched either natural phenomena or the flight of birds.'[40] Eliade notes the etymological kinship between *templum* and *tempus*: '*templum* designates the spatial, *tempus* the temporal aspect of the motion of the horizon in space and time.'[41]

The Tetraktys

Ten is the royal number: it is born from one and nothing;
When God and creature meet, this birth takes place.
Angelus Silesius[42]

The "totality" of the number four is developed by the "quaternary number," the Pythagorean *Tetraktys*, being the symbolic formula by which the sum of the first four numbers equal ten, $1 + 2 + 3 + 4 = 10$. The number ten is the perfect number representing the complete and total process of manifestation expressed by the return of the one to the uncreated zero (1 0).

The *Tetraktys*, observes Guénon, is a "triangular number": 'those numbers obtained by adding the consecutive whole numbers from unity to each of the successive terms of the series. Unity is the first triangular number ... The second triangular number is $1 + 2 = 3$, which shows, moreover, that once unity has produced the binary by its own polarisation, the immediate result is the ternary ... the fourth triangular number is: $1 + 2 + 3 + 4 = 10$, namely, the *Tetraktys*'.[43] Envisaged in this sense, the *Tetraktys* 'was naturally represented by a symbol, which taken as a whole, was of ternary form, each of its outer sides comprising four elements; and this symbol was comprised of ten elements in all, represented by as many points, of which nine were on the perimeter of the triangle and one at its centr.'[44]

Fig.12

This representation is equivalent, despite the difference in geometric form, to the representation of the denary by the circle, as in each case one corresponds to the centre and nine to the circumference. Guénon notes that 'it is because 9 and not 10 is the number of the circumference that its [the circumference's] division is normally calculated in multiples of 9 (90 degrees for the quadrant and subsequently 360 degrees for the entire circumference)'.[45] The correspondence of the circumference (Manifestation) to the number nine recalls the "nine-fold plan" of Yū the Great, the nine-fold plan of the *Ming T'ang*, the nine parts of the floor plan of the Ark of Ut-napishtim, the nine *Sefirot* (*Binah* to *Malkhut*) envisaged in terms of Divine Radiation or *ad extra*, the nine circles of heavens, the nine days (cycles) during which the Ark of Deucalion floated on the waters of the Flood, the nine years (cycles) Hephaestus spent in Thetis' cave,[46] the nine notes of the *teruah*, etc.[47] In the mythology of the Ancient Mexicans there are nine rivers which bar access to the "eternal house of the dead,"[48] an image that recalls the river as the circumference of the World (Oceanus) and, in turn, the serpent as the circumference (the Ouroboros), for various traditions associate the serpent with the number nine.[49] The nineth letter of the Hebrew alphabet, *teth*, is a serpent.

According to Guénon, the formula of the *Tetraktys* is related to that of the "square of four", which is simply to recognise this as expressing another form of the general schema of manifestation.[50]

Fig.13

'The square of four' says Guénon, 'is, geometrically, a square of which the sides contain four elements like those of the already mentioned triangle. ... These two figures can then be united by making the base of the triangle and the upper side of the square coincide'[51]. This schematic

representation can be figured in two ways, which give rise to complementary symbolisms. In the first case the points of the "triangle" and
the "square" are envisaged according to the integrity of the respective
forms, thus:

```
            •

         •     •

      •     •     •

   •     •     •     •

   •     •     •     •

   •     •     •     •

   •     •     •     •
```

Fig.14

This form, comprised of the numbers 10 (the triangle) and 16 (the square)
has, as its sum, 26; this, says Guénon, 'is the total numerical value of the
letters forming the Hebrew Tetragrammaton *yodh*, *he*, *vau*, *he*. ...What
is more 10 is the value of the first letter (*yodh*) and 16 is that of all the
three other letters *he*, *vau* and *he*.'[52]

In the second case, the base of the triangle and the upper side of
the square are recognised in terms of their identity so that the figure
obtained is thus:

```
            •

         •     •

      •     •     •

   •     •     •     •

   •     •     •     •

   •     •     •     •
```

Fig.15

This form has as its total sum 22, which is, of course the number of letters in the Hebrew alphabet, from which the world was created. Moreover, the twenty-two letters of the Hebrew alphabet "contain" the *Torah*
which, according to Rabbi Menahem Recanati, is the exoteric form of

the Decalogue, which in turn is written on the four sides of the two stone Tablets.[53]

A further connection develops when we consider that the triangle is properly "vertical," expressing the "descent" from one to four, while the square is "horizontal," being a plane of Existence. Considered thus the resultant form is a pyramid—recall the Ark of Noah as a pyramid—with a base measured by the number four and three levels of ascent. This pyramid may be thought of as developed from the second form with the triangle and the square sharing a base and an upper side. One may also develop the first form—where the triangle and the square are considered in terms of their integrity—into a three dimensional form; here the triangle gives rise to the same pyramid of base four and three levels, while the square gives rise to a cube of side four. The resultant form is a cube surmounted by a pyramid, which is the general form of a "house" and its "roof." This is the form given to the Ark of Noah, the body of which is "cubic-rectangular," with a roof rising to "a cubit higher," which is generally taken as indicating that it rises to an apex.

The House of God

I can descend and restrict My *Shekhinah* within a square cubit.
Exodus Rabba XXXIV. I[54]

The house ascends and takes up its position, and joins itself to both realms … and the house shines with six lights that cast radiance on every side.
Zohar I, 172a-172b[55]

'What is God?' asks Bernard of Clairvaux, 'He is length, width, height and depth'.[56] Onto-cosmological existence emanates from the Centre, bringing forth the six principle directions: 'the house shines with six lights that cast radiance on every side'. These directions measure three-dimensional space, which, in a sense, is thus the container of cosmological existence.[57]

The measurements of space symbolically describe the nature of Divine Immanence. The Ark of Noah, for example, is length three hundred cubits, breadth fifty cubits and height thirty cubits; Origen interprets this by saying that its length expresses simultaneously the number one hundred and the number three: the first signifies the fullness of unity, the second the Trinity; its breadth is interpreted as the symbol of the Redemption (cf. the Jubilee). As to the height of its roof, which was built one cubit higher, Origen says that this symbolises the number one, by reason of the unity of God.[58] This reading puts the emphasis on the Principle. Isidore of Seville points out that three hundred cubits equals

229

six times fifty, thus the length is six times the breadth and symbolises the six ages of the world.[59] This puts the emphasis on the spatio-temporal expression. Similar interpretations can, and have, been offered concerning other homologues of the Ark. That two valid interpretations differ simply shows that the Divine Nature is simultaneously multivalent and consistent.

The potentiality of three-dimensional space is best expressed by the sphere; its fullness and perfection is best expressed by the cube. The symbolism of the receptacle envisaged as a cube is most famously found with the Islamic *Ka'bah*, which means "cube" in Arabic. The *Ka'bah* is 'the first house built for mankind ... to bless and guide all worlds.'[60] It defines space by virtue of the *qiblah*; moreover, as Schuon says, the *Ka'bah* 'becomes space as soon as one is in the interior of the building: the ritual direction of prayer is then projected towards the four cardinal points.'[61] The *Ka'bah* is orientated so that one axis points to the summer solstice sunrise and the winter solstice sunset, while the other axis aligns to the rising position of the star Canopus. Canopus was originally the Alpha star of the ancient constellation Argo, the astrological expression of the ship on which Jason sailed.[62] In Hindu tradition Canopus (*Agastya*) is the helmsman of Argha, the "Water Vessel"; in Arab tradition this star is the "Ship of the Desert." The "house" is none other that the terrestrial reflection of the celestial "ship." The name *Canopus* comes from the ancient Egyptian meaning the "jar" or "vase" used for holding the entrails of the embalmed body during the soul's journey across the waters of death.

The *Ka'bah* has eight corners, expressing both balance and perfection. The corners of the lower or base square of the *Ka'bah* (Formal Manifestation or the sensible level) are connected to the corners of the upper square (Formless Manifestation or the supra-sensible level) by means of four "pillars" (*arkān*) which, according to Snodgrass, 'connect the sensible and intelligible levels, and are the means of communication between Heaven and Earth.'[63] This recalls the role of the octagon as the "intermediary world" between the circle of Heaven and the square of Earth. 'The house ascends and takes up its position, and joins itself to both realms'.[64]

'The *Ka'bah*' remarks Snodgrass, 'is the visible representation of Allah's Throne (*al-'arsh*) which stands on the Waters and is the first metaphysical entity to emanate from the Supreme Principle.'[65] Allah's Throne–the "throne of glory," epithet of the *Shekhinah*—corresponds to the *Merkabah*, the Throne-Chariot of Ezekiel's vision, which is surrounded and supported by and identifies with the *Tetramorphs*. In Hindu mythology, the throne of Śiva, the *simhāsana*, is likewise borne by four animals, corresponding to the four ages of the world and the four colours.[66] The *Tetramorphs* are in turn the *hashmal*, which 'radiates its beams of light to the four corners'.[67]

Sūrah 11 (*Hūd*)—which contains the account of the building of the Noah's Ark—says this: 'And it is He Who created the Heavens and the earth in six days, and His Throne was upon the water' (11:6). Snodgrass:

> A *hadīth* of the Prophet expands the image: 'Verily, the Throne was on the Water, and when Allah created the Heavens, He placed it above the seven Heavens, and placed the clouds as a sieve for the rain, if it were not so, the earth would be submerged.' The "clouds" (*ghamām*) are the division or partition (*barzakh*) that separates two cosmic levels, without this partition the lower level would be "submerged," that is, reabsorbed into the higher level. The "rain" is the down pouring of spiritual, psychic and even physical graces from the Throne, symbolically represented by the dome of the sky. … The Throne on the waters is the homologue of the Lotus in the Hindu and the Buddhist traditions. The Lotus, which grows from the Waters of cosmic potentiality, is simultaneously the centre and the container of the universe; its opening is the actualization of the potentialities contained in the Waters.[68]

Another *hadīth* compares the *Ka'bah* to the heart.[69] The Ark is the heart of the Temple and the Ark is the Temple. The House of God is the formal realisation of the formless potentiality of the Throne on the Waters. The House of God contains the unfolding of onto-cosmological existence and is this unfolding. This unfolding is expressed through the cosmic cycles. At the end of a cycle the House becomes the Ark of the Flood. This is most explicit in the case of the Ark of Ut-napishtim: 'Tear down (this) house, build a ship!'.[70] This divine command was delivered to Ut-napishtim by the "house" itself, which is here a "house that speaks" (cf. the "talking stones").[71] This is moreover a "reed hut," recalling the symbolism of the reed and showing that this is the Divine Spirit, the Spirit that moves on the Waters, which is identical to the Divine Throne.[72]

Notes

1. Ibn al-Arabī, *Futūhāt* (2002, p.52).

2. See Mathers (tr.), *KU*, 1991, p.35.

3. It is not my intention to debate the historical drama of the doctrine of the Four Worlds, although this is not without importance. On this the reader should see Scholem, *MTJM*, 1995, p.272. The schemata of the Four Worlds overlays

the ten-fold sefirothic tree; the analogical and metaphorical interplay involved in such Kabbalistic schema means that these Four Worlds may be adequately envisaged at various levels.

4. Scholem, *MTJM*, 1995, p.272. Scholem notes that there is no trace of such a doctrine in the major part of the *Zohar*, which is not to dismiss it but to acknowledge the organic nature of what is, after all, a living tradition.

5. See Scholem, *MTJM*, 1995, p.272; Mathers (tr.), *KU*, 1991, Plate VI for 'The analogy between The Soul, The Letters of The Teragrammaton & The Four Worlds'.

6. Guénon, *FS*, 1995, p.75. Guénon says that these terms 'correspond to the four "worlds" of the Hebrew Kabbalah, which also have their exact equivalents in Islamic esoterism'.

7. Scholem, *MTJM*, 1995, p.272.

8. Ibn al-'Arabī, *Lubb* (1981, p.11). These comments on the Five Presences are drawn from this work (pp.9-14).

9. Schuon, *EPW*, 1981, p.70. These, says Schuon, are the Qur'anic Names *Dhu 'l-Jalal, Dhu 'l –Ikram, Al-Hayy, Al-Qayyum*.

10. Guénon, *FS*, 1995, p.75.

11. Guénon, *FS*, 1995, p.75.

12. Chevalier & Gheerbrant, *DS*, 1996, p.405.

13. Chevalier & Gheerbrant, *DS*, 1996, p.402.

14. Lactantius, *Divine institutiones* 4: 26, 36, cited in Chevalier & Gheerbrant, *DS*, 1996, p.254.

15. In the native American Huichol myth the Ark drifted for a year in each of the four directions before coming to rest on the top of the sacred mountain mountain, Toapu'li (Jordan, *Myths of the World*, 1993, pp.114-15).

16. God 'ordered all things by measure, number and weight' (Ws.11:20). This is the idea of the "geometrician God." On the relation of "measure" to manifestation see Guénon, *RQ*, 1995, Ch.3.

17. Thus, in the *Timaeus*, Plato calls his receptacle of becoming (49A) space, 'eternal and indestructible' providing 'a position for everything that comes to be' (52).

18. The symbolism of the four directions of a plane of Existence is again evident in the Hebrew creation of Man in which dirt (earth; Substance) was taken from the four corners of the world, with a fifth handful coming from the site of the Temple (see *Pirke de Rabbi Eliezer* Ch.11 & 20, cited in Rappoport, *AI1*, 1995, p.140). The four handfuls of earth were coloured red, black, white and yellow recalling the symbolism of these colours as discussed earlier.

19. See Snodgrass, *SS*, 1985, p.22.

20. Guénon, *FS*, 1995, p.76. The manifest centre or first point is, as we have noted, represented by either a vertical line (the West) or a horizontal line (the East); the line and the circumference combine to represent the denary (1 0).

21. Guénon, *ED*, 1996, p.63.

22. On these two symbolisms and their relations to the extremes of a cosmic cycle see Guénon, *ED*, 1996, pp.63-66.

23. See for example the depiction of the Creation of the Garden of Eden in the Luther Bible, 1534.

24. Guénon, *ED*, 1996, p.65, n.88.

25. Guénon, *RQ*, 1995, p.173.

26. 'The death came by the tree, the life by the cross' (de Voragine, *The Golden Legend*, *Vol.1*, 'The Passion of our Lord', 31, 1900).

27. 'Make to thee an ark of tree' (de Voragine, *The Golden Legend*, *Vol.1*, 'The History of Noah', 83, 1900). The connection between the Ark and the tree is again found in the account of Osiris, where the coffin (Ark) containing his body was enclosed in a tamarisk tree. According to Ibn al-'Arabī, the name Moses (*Mūsā*) means both water and tree, *mū* meaning water and *sā* meaning a tree, in Coptic; this because his basket (Ark) was found stopped by a tree at the water's edge (*Fusūs*, 1980, p.254).

28. Chevalier & Gheerbrant, *DS*, 1996, p.254.

29. St. Justin, *Apologia* 1: 55, cited in Chevalier & Gheerbrant, *DS*, 1996, p.254.

30. Guénon, *SC*, 1975, p.55.

31. Schuon, *EPW*, 1981, p.71.

32. Guénon, *RQ*, 1995, p.170.

33. Guénon, *RQ*, 1995, p.171.

34. Guénon, *RQ*, 1995, p.171.

35. Schuon, *EPW*, 1981, pp.71-72.

36. See Davidson, et al, *The New BIBLE Commentary*, 1968, pp.84-85.

37. Davidson, et al, *The New BIBLE Commentary*, 1968, p.85.

38. *Antiquities,* 3.7.7 (180).

39. See Drummond's dissertation 'Concerning the Tabernacle and the Temple' (III), *Oedipus Judaicus*, 1996.

40. Chevalier & Gheerbrant, *DS*, 1996, p.979, quoting G. de Champeaux and S. Dom Sterckx (O.S.B.), *Introduction au monde des symboles*, Paris, 1966, p.455.

41. Eliade, *Sacred and Profane*, 1987, citing Werner Müller, *Kries und Kreuz*, Berlin, 1938, p.39.

42. Angelus Silesius, *Cherubinischer Wandersmann*, V.8, cited in Perry, *TTW*, 2000, p.888.

43. Guénon, *FS*, 1995, p.76

44. Guénon, *FS*, 1995, pp.76-77.

45. Guénon, *FS*, 1995, p.77.

46. This "cave" beneath the "sea" is a potent homologue of the Ark (on the related symbolism of the cave see Guénon, *FS*, 1995, Chs.31-36). This is, of course, the womb, where the nine is the nine months of gestation.

47. There are numerous other relevant examples of the symbolism of the number nine (see "nine" in Chevalier & Gheerbrant, *DS*, 1996, p.702).

48. Chevalier & Gheerbrant, *DS*, 1996, p.297.

49. See Chevalier & Gheerbrant, *DS*, 1996, p.703.

50. Guénon, *FS*, 1995, p.75.

51. Guénon, *FS*, 1995, p.77.

52. Guénon, *FS*, 1995, p.78.

53. Rabbi Menahem Recanati, *Sefer Ta'amei ha-Mizvot*, 3a, cited in Tishby, *WZ1*, 1989, p.284.

54. Cited in Cohen, *ET*, 1995, p.43.

55. Tishby, *WZ1*, 1991, p.390.

56. Bernard of Clairvaux, *On Consideration*, cited in Lawlor, *Sacred Geometry*, 1989, p.6.

57. Recall the qualification, mentioned earlier, that 'there is no space outside the Cosmos and the Universe cannot be said to be in space.'

58. Cited in Chevalier & Gheerbrant, *DS*, 1996, p.43.

59. Cited in Chevalier & Gheerbrant, *DS*, 1996, p.43. Many of the early Church Fathers considered there to be six ages of the world, corresponding to the six days of Creation. The first age is from Adam to Noah; the second from Noah to Abraham; the third from Abraham to David; the fourth from David to the Babylonian captivity; the fifth from the Babylonian captivity to the advent of Jesus Christ; with Christ's coming the sixth age is said to have entered on its process. The difference between there being "six ages" or "four ages", as we might more commonly think of, is a difference in symbolic emphasis.

60. Sūrah 3: 90 (*āl-'imrān*).

61. Schuon, *G:DW*, 1990, p.16.

62. In more modern times the constellation of Argo was broken into three parts, *Carina* (the Keel), *Puppis* (the Stern), and *Vela* (the Sails). Canopus fell into *Carina*, and is therefore now *Alpha Carinae*.

63. Snodgrass, *ATE2*, 1990, p.419. On the identification of the lower and upper squares with the sensible and supra-sensible levels of existence see pp.416-17, & fig.94.

64. *Zohar* I, 172a-172b.

65. Snodgrass, *ATE2*, 1990, p.410. For a detailed exposition of the stellar and Shi'ite symbolism of the *Ka'bah* see pp.409-424.

66. "Throne" in Chevalier & Gheerbrant, *DS*, 1996, p.998.

67. *Zohar Hadash*, *Yitro*, 38a & d.

68. Snodgrass, *ATE2*, 1990, p.410, n.1. See Snodgrass, *SS*, 1985, 97 ff.

69. 'The heart is a Divine *Ka'bah*'; cited in Ibn al-'Arabī, *Lubb* (1981, p.42).

70. *Gilgamesh*, XI, in Dalley (ed.), *MM*, 1991, p.110.

71. The god Ea was unable to communicate directly with Ut-napishtim because of an oath of secrecy he had sworn to the other Gods.

72. Snodgrass: 'The Throne is the place of the Divine Presence: the Spirit (*al-rūh*) is at its centre, but is also the Throne as a whole. ... The Throne symbolises the "relationship" of the supreme Principle to Its manifestation' (*ATE2*, 1990, p.412-13).

Conclusion

The Container and the Contained

The colour of the water is the colour of the vessel containing it.
Abu'l-Qāsim al-Junayd[1]

Did not the sea make friends with Noah and Moses?
Jalāl al-Din Rūmī[2]

To talk of the Ark as a "receptacle" implies two related notions: that of "container" and that of "receiving." In the first case, Immanence is a possibility of the Infinite and is thus "contained" by the Infinite.[3] The Infinite is identical with Transcendence. Thus one can say that Transcendence is the container of Immanence. Transcendence cannot "receive" Immanence, which it already possesses *in divinis*; rather Immanence flows forth from Transcendence according to the Scholastic maxim *bonum diffusivum sui*, "the Good diffuses itself." It does not flow "out" of Transcendence, for this flowing forth remains a possibility of the Infinite, even if it is now, so to speak, an actualised or realised possibility. God (Infinite and Transcendent) sends forth His Ipseity (Immanence) by Himself (as a possibility of His Infinitude) from Himself (from the Infinite) to Himself (to the Infinite). This flowing forth of Immanence— which is simultaneously a "withdrawal" (*tsimtsum*) of Transcendence— is received *a priori* by Being. Between Immanence and Transcendence there is both discontinuity and continuity. Discontinuity for the container surpasses the contained in extent; continuity for Being is essentially identical with Transcendence.

In the case of Being the container and the contained are identical.[4] The container of Being is Substance, inasmuch as Being is manifested through or "in" Substance; from another perspective, Being contains Substance, inasmuch as Substance is prefigured in Being. In turn, Substance, as Schuon remarks, 'has two containers, space and time, of which the first is positive and the second negative'.[5] Space and time are contained in Being *in divinis*, prefigured by the Infinite and the Eternal. They are "received" and made manifest by cosmological existence, of which they are the defining conditions. Space and time do not "contain" cosmological existence in the sense of being "beyond"; instead they are the receptacle of cosmological existence.[6]

The *Mundaka Upaniṣad* describes these ideas through the symbolism of the spider and its web: 'a spider spreads and withdraws (its thread) … so out of the Immutable does the phenomenal universe arise.'[7] The spider contains the thread and is identical with the thread; the web receives the thread and is identical with the thread; but between the spider and the web there is distinction. Ibn al-'Arabī offers a similar metaphor in his *Diwan of Shashtarī*: '"We are like the silkworm, our obstacles are the result of our own work," an allusion to the worm which creates its own prison by surrounding itself with its own thread'.[8] If this has the virtue of recalling the symbolism of the worm as Essence and as Centre, then the eight-legged spider has the virtue of signalling the relationship between the Centre and the number eight.

The Absolute is like a sea (Infinite; Beyond-Being) within which there is a glass of water, which here stands for Being. The glass is itself an illusion (*Māyā*), its substance being also water; here one might consider the glass as formed of ice, which in substance, if not in state, is still water, and this is to recognise that illusion is a state and not a substance.[9] The water in the glass and the water of the sea are identical in essential substance (*ousia*) but not in extent. One might say that there is a difference or discontinuity in extent of substance but an identity or continuity of essence. The sea is "beyond" the water of the cup in its extent; at the same time it contains and intimately identifies with the water of the cup so that they are not other than each other or, better to say, there is only the Sea.[10]

The Ark, which is synonymous with the Throne, rests upon the Waters and is the Waters. 'Have you not considered the Throne,' asks Ibn al-'Arabī, 'how it rests on the water and derives from it?'[11] 'The Throne' remarks Snodgrass, 'is "the place of the Divine Presence," the most secret and hidden (*bātin*), it is also the most outward (*zāhir*). It is simultaneously the centre and the circumference of the cosmos; it is surrounding and surrounded, containing and contained; it stands at the centre of the Waters and is also the Waters themselves, as designating the totality of creatures, spiritual, subtle and gross; it stands at the fulcrum of the Waters but includes the Waters within itself.'[12]

The Ark of Noah and the Ark of the Covenant receive the Word *a posteriori*, that is to say, they are made manifest through their experience of the Word; they contain the Word and they are the Word. 'In the beginning was the Word, the Word was with God and the Word was God. He was with God in the beginning. Through him all things came into being, not one thing came into being except through him' (Jn.1:1-3). The *Brahma-Sūtra* says, 'The repository of Heaven and earth, etc. (is the supreme Self) on account of the word denoting Itself.'[13] 'Moses', remarks Schaya, 'erected the tabernacle for God's "indwelling" (*shekhinah*), and Solomon erected the temple for God's "name" (*shem*). Thus their two works were essentially one, just as God is truly present in His name, this being precisely His "indwelling" or "habitation".'[14] Al-Jīlī

236

says: 'The perfection of the Named One is eminently manifested by the fact that He reveals Himself through His Name to the person who does not know Him, so that the Name is to the Named as the outward is to the inward; and in this respect the Name is the Named One Himself.'[15] '*Om* is *Brahmā*.'[16] 'God is the Word which pronounces itself.'[17] In the Judaic tradition the Word is synonymous with the Torah, which leads the Kabbalist Abraham Abulafia to say that the Torah 'is wholly in thee and thou art wholly in it.'[18] As the Word is the source of creation It is also the place of return. In the words of the *Zohar*: 'Blessed is the person who utterly surrenders his soul for the name of YHWH to dwell therein and to establish therein its throne of glory.'[19]

The relationship of Transcendence and Immanence is one of identity and distinction. Schuon: 'That we are conformed to God,—"made in His image,"—this is certain; otherwise we should not exist. That we are contrary to God, this is also certain; otherwise we should not be different from God. Without analogy with God we should be nothing. Without opposition to God we should be God.'[20] Ibn al-'Arabī: 'God says, *There is naught like unto Him*, asserting His transcendence, and He says, *He is the Hearing, the Seeing*,[21] implying comparison [Relativity and Immanence].'[22] 'The Father is greater than I' (Jn.14:28), but, at the same time, 'The Father and I are one' (Jn.10:30).[23]

Identity means that the Cosmos is not other than God. Thus, in his chapter on Noah, Ibn al-'Arabī says, 'the Reality never withdraws from the forms of the Cosmos in any fundamental sense, since the Cosmos, in its reality, is implicit in the definition of the Divinity'.[24] This recalls Meister Eckhart: 'if there were anything empty under heaven, whatever it might be, great or small, the heavens would either draw it up to themselves or else, bending down, would fill it themselves'.[25] The essential identity of the Cosmos with God, however, must not be mistaken for the limitation of God to the Cosmos. To say, as Schuon does, that 'if the relative did not exist, the Absolute would not be the Absolute'[26] does not mean that the Absolute is limited to the Relative. This leads to the error of pantheism. Schuon: 'If God is conceived as primordial Unity, that is, as pure Essence, nothing could be substantially identical with Him; to qualify essential identity as pantheistic is both to deny the relativity of things and to attribute an autonomous reality to them in relation to Being or Existence, as if there could be two realities essentially distinct, or two Unities or Unicities.'[27] In the words of the Rabbis: 'God is the dwelling place of the universe; the universe is not the dwelling place of God.'[28]

Mercy and Charity

Let us, then, come boldly unto the throne of grace to receive mercy
and to find grace when we are in need of help.

Hebrews 4:16

My mercy encompasses all things.

Qur'an, 7.156

The quality of mercy is not strain'd, it droppeth as the gentle rain
from heaven upon the place beneath: it is twice bless'd; it blessed
him that gives and him that takes.

Shakespeare[29]

When the seas of Mercy begin to surge, even stones drink the
Water of Life.

Jalāl al-Din Rūmī[30]

Charity is to recognise the eternal Word in creatures.

Titus Burckhardt[31]

According to Islamic tradition, the first word written by the Pen (*al-Qalam*) upon the Guarded Tablet (*al-Lawh al-Mahfūz*) was "Mercy"
(*Rahmān*).[32] Mercy, as Ibn al-'Arabī says, is 'the Throne that encompasses all things, while the Merciful is its occupant, by whose reality
Mercy permeates the Cosmos'.[33] This distinction between the Mercy
and the Merciful may be likened to that between Immanence and Transcendence. In a difficult passage, Ibn al-'Arabī expands on this distinction while at the same time confirming the identity of Mercy and the
Merciful:

> Mercy is, in reality, an attribution of the Merciful that necessitates control, being indeed that which is merciful.[34] He Who
> causes it to exist in the recipient of Mercy does not bring it into
> existence to have mercy on the recipient by it, but only to have
> mercy by it on that which resides within it. God is not a locus
> for phenomena, nor yet a locus for the bringing of mercy into
> existence. He is the Merciful, and the merciful is only such by
> the residing of mercy within it. Thus is it confirmed that He is
> the very Mercy Itself.[35]

He also says, 'He whom the Mercy remembers, it has mercy upon.'[36]
That is, He whom the Mercy remembers is brought forth into creation in
Mercy. 'And God remembered Noah, and every living thing, and all the
cattle that were with him in the ark: and God made a wind to pass over
the earth and the waters assuaged' (Gen.8:1).

Mercy is most commonly symbolised by "water" or "breath." These are the "receptacles" of the divine Essence (the Merciful). As Ibn al-'Arabī says, 'From the water of Mary or from the breath of Gabriel, / In the form of a mortal fashioned of clay, / The Spirit came into existence in an essence / Purged of Nature's taint'.[37] The container and the contained identify. Thus, Snodgrass recognises the Throne as 'the Spirit (*al-Rūh*), the same spirit of God (*Ruahh Elohim*) that in *Genesis* "moved on the face of the Waters", the Waters being the totality of cosmic potentialities, the Ocean of primordial Substance.'[38]

In Kabbalah, the most common meaning of water is "mercy" or "blessing."[39] According to *sefirotic* symbolism, the *sefirot* are portrayed as "vessels" (*kelim*) or pools" (*braichah*)[40] into which the "river" of Mercy flows from the fountain of the Godhead, through the fifty gates of *Binah*.[41] As each vessel fills it overflows causing a continuous stream to water the "garden" of the created world, *Malkhut*. Isaac Luria developed his doctrine of "The Breaking of the Vessels" (*Shevirath Ha-Kelim*) based on this symbolism.[42] For Luria the "vessels" or "shells" (*kelipot*) express the sense of limitation associated with the judgment of the *sefirot Din*. 'If I create the world only with the attribute of mercy, sins will multiply beyond all bounds; if I create it only with the attribute of justice, how can the world last? Behold, I will create it with both attributes; would that it might endure!'[43] These "shells" of judgment untempered by compassion correspond to the Kings of Edom.[44] The *Shevirah*, as Scholem says, 'is compared to the "break-through" [Meister Eckhart's *durchbrechen*] of birth ... In this manner, the mystical "death of the primordial kings" is transformed into the far more plausible symbol of a mystical "birth"'.[45] Indeed, for Ibn al-'Arabī and al-Jīlī the term "mercy" (*rahmah*), which derives from the Arabic root RHM, evokes the word *rahima*, which means, the womb.[46] The womb is a potent homologue of the Ark. Burckhardt notes that the simplest word from this root is *rahīm*, which means "matrix."[47]

Although the *sefirah Din* first imposes judgment and limitation, the first vessel, as such, is the *sefirah Hesed*, which symbolises pure Mercy and here identifies with *Binah*. In Hebrew, the word *Hesed* (*checed*; חסד) also means "favour," which recalls our earlier observations on *chānan*, meaning "to *favour* or *bestow*" by "bowing down," as in God's bending down in the act of creation, and His bending down in humbling Himself to become man (Christ's *kenosis*). In this connection, *checed* derives from *chācad* (חסד), a primitive root meaning "to bow."

'Rejoice, you who enjoy God's *favour*! The Lord is with you' (Lk.1:28). The Virgin is the receptacle of God's out flowing Mercy. She is the Mother of Mercy (*Madonna della Misericordia*). She sits enthroned beside God the Son.[48] The enthroned Virgin is prefigured in the Hebrew Scriptures by Bathsheba, who was placed upon a throne by her son.[49] The throne of the Virgin is the Sun, which is also her "robe" (Rev.12.1). The rays of the Sun are the flowing forth of God's Mercy. The *Ka'bah*, the terrestrial Throne, is likewise "robed" by the black curtain of the *kiswa*, which here expresses the "rays" of the "Black Sun," shining with the "Light Inaccessible." This is the Black Virgin, 'I am black, but beautiful.'

The Virgin sits upon the Throne and is the Throne. The Ark is synonymous with the Throne, which is Mercy. Again, the Ark is synonymous with the Heart. Yet according to a distinction developed by Ibn al-'Arabī, the Heart is greater than the Throne. This returns us to the distinction between that which "contains" and that which "receives," for Mercy, like the womb (*rahima*), receives, even though this is, in the final analysis, the receiving of the ever-flowing Infinite from Itself to Itself by Itself. The Heart, however, contains in the manner of Its absoluteness. The distinction might be likened to the exclusive Absolute (the Centre) and the inclusive Infinite (the Circumference). Ibn al-'Arabī: 'Know that the heart, by which I mean the Heart of the gnostic, derives from the Divine Mercy, while being more embracing than it, since the Heart encompasses the Reality, exalted be He, and the Mercy does not. ... The Reality is the subject and not the object of the mercy, so that the latter has no determining power with respect to the Reality.'[50] According to Austin, 'The reason for the greater capacity of the Heart is that, whereas the Mercy symbolises the whole manifestation and its resolution into unity, the Heart symbolises the whole experience of Oneness of being, as including not only the creative process and its resolution, but also that inalienable and unalterable aspect of the Reality which knows nothing of cosmic becoming.'[51]

Divine Mercy is the eternally flowing forth of the Infinitude of God from God to God. It is this that gives birth to Existence and returns creation back to God. This birth and return (*durchbrechen* and *reditus*) is expressed by the Divine Names: *ar-Rahmān* (The Compassionate, He whose Mercy envelops all things) and *ar-Rahīm* (The Merciful, He who saves by His grace).[52] Ibn al-'Arabī also describes these as "the mercy of unobligating giving" and "the mercy of binding obligation."[53]

The divine Mercy is God's gift of Himself to creation. Man—"made in the image"—responds to this gift by firstly, giving himself to God (inverse analogy) and secondly, giving himself to mankind (direct analogy). These then are summed up in the first two commandments, as expressed in the Gospels: 'You must love the Lord your God with all your heart, with all your soul and with all your mind. This is the greatest

240

commandment. The second resembles: You must love your neighbour as yourself. On these two commandments hang the whole of the law, and the Prophets too' (Mt.22:37-40; Lk10:25-28; Jn.13:34-34a).[54] The mercy of loving one's neighbour is expressed in the virtue of charity. The *sefirah Hesed* (Mercy) corresponds to the patriarch Abraham, who is the personification of charity, as shown by his entertainment of the three strangers at the Oak of Mamre:

> Yahweh appeared to him at the Oak of Mamre while he was sitting by the entrance of the tent during the hottest part of the day. He looked up, and there he saw three men standing near him. As soon as he saw them he ran from the entrance of the tent to greet them, and bowed to the ground. "My lord," he said, "if I find favour with you, please do not pass your servant by. Let me have a little water brought, and you can wash you feet and have a rest under the tree. Let me fetch a little bread and you can refresh yourselves before going further, now that you have come in your servant's direction." They replied, "Do as you say."'(Gen.8:1-8)[55]

'Remember always to welcome strangers, for by doing this, some people have entertained angels without knowing it' (Heb.13:2).[56]

According to Judaic tradition, Abraham once questioned his teacher, Shem-Melchizedek,[57] on the virtue that merited the saving of his father, Noah, and his brothers on the Ark. Shem-Melchizedek replied that their merit consisted in having practiced "charity" in feeding the needy.[58] 'Charity' says a Jewish tradition, 'doth deliver from death—not merely from unnatural death but from death itself'.[59] The Talmud distinguishes two categories of charity, which correspond, at the appropriate level of analogy, to the two types of Mercy. The lesser charity is almsgiving (*Tzedakah*). Cohen notes that the proper meaning of this word is "righteousness":

> ...assisting the poor is not an act of grace on the part of the donor, but a duty. By giving alms he is merely practicing righteousness, i.e. performing a deed of justice. All man's possessions are but a loan from the Creator of the Universe, to Whom belong the earth and the fullness thereof, and by his charity he merely secures a more equitable distribution of God's gifts to mankind.[60]

'For all things come of Thee, and of thine own have we given Thee' (1Ch.29:14). One recalls here that Noah was precisely saved for being the "righteous" man in his generation (Gen.7:1).

The second, and superior, category is called *Gemiluth Chasadim* ("the bestowal of loving acts"; benevolence). 'The Pentateuch begins with an act of benevolence and concludes with an act of benevolence. At the beginning it is said, "And the Lord God made for Adam and his wife coats of skin, and clothed them" (Gen.3:21); and at the end it is said, "And he buried him (Moses) in the valley" (Deut.34:6)'.[61] This meta-cosmic Charity corresponds to *ar-Rahmān* (The Compassionate).

Of the acts that constitute benevolence one is given special attention: the "entertainment of wayfarers," of which virtue Abraham is the embodiment and epitome. There is a tradition concerning Abraham in this light that is particularly interesting in the context of the tamarisk tree as a homologue of the Ark. In the Scriptures we are told that Abraham planted a tamarisk (*'ēshel*; אשל) in Beersheba (Gen.21:33).[62] According to *Genesis Rabba*, 'Eshel means a lodging-place where Abraham used to receive passers-by, and when they had eaten and drunk, he would say, "Stay the night and bless God"'.[63] The term *eshel* is accordingly explained as made up of the initial of the three words: *achilah* "eating," *shethiyah* "drinking," and *linah* "lodging overnight."[64] The tamarisk is the Ark which sustains through the "dark night of the Flood"; it sustains by the act of charity with which it is, in a sense, identical.

The deepest truth of charity is the truth of unity. Love of God is realisation of the unity of God. 'Hear, O Israel: the Lord our God is one Lord. You must love the Lord our God with all your heart, with all your soul, with all your strength' (Dt.6:4-5). Love of one's neighbour is realisation of God in them. As Burckhardt says, 'Charity is to recognise the eternal Word in creatures.' Love of God is realisation of the exclusivity of the Absolute; love of one's neighbour is recognition of the inclusiveness of the Infinite. To love God is to know that the Absolute alone is real; to love one's neighbour is to know that the Relative is granted contingent reality by the fact that nothing can be other than God. 'Love of one's neighbour' says Schuon, 'receives all its meaning through the love of God'.[65] Schuon again: 'To love God … is to realise in ourselves that which, by virtue of the analogical correspondences, is conformable to the divine Presence.'[66] To love God is to realise ourselves as receptacles of the Divine Immanence, which is to say, to realise ourselves as the Ark and, in the final analysis, to realise ourselves as God. As Meister Eckhart says, 'We love God with his own love; awareness of it deifies us.'[67]

The unity of God is the heart of the revelation of Abraham, who turned from the idol worship of his father, Terah, to the worship of the one true God. Several Judaic traditions tell of how Abraham deduced the unity of God by a sort of apophatic reasoning. According to one story, when he revolted against idolatry, his father took him before King Nimrod that he might punish him for his iconoclasm.

> "If," said Nimrod, "thou will not worship the God of thy father, then at least worship fire." Abraham replied: "We should rather worship water which extinguishes fire." Nimrod then said: "Then worship water." Abraham retorted: "If so, we should worship the cloud which carries the water!" Nimrod said: " Then worship the cloud." Abraham retorted: "If so, we should worship the wind which disperses the cloud!" Nimrod said: "Then worship the wind." Abraham retorted: "Rather should we worship the human being who carries the wind!"[68]

According to another account, after his birth Abraham had been hidden in a cave for three years.[69]

> When he left the cave, his heart kept reflecting upon the creation of the Universe, and he determined to worship all the luminaries until he discovered which one of them was God. He saw the moon whose light illumined the darkness of night from one end of the world to the other and noticed the vast retinue of stars. "This is God," he exclaimed, and worshipped it throughout the night. In the morning when he beheld the dawn of the sun before which the moon darkened and its power waned, he exclaimed: "The light of the moon must be derived from the light of the sun, and the Universe only exists through the sun's rays." So he worshiped the sun throughout the day. In the evening, the sun sank below the stars and the planets. He thereupon exclaimed: "Surely these all have a master and God!"[70]

Abraham's iconoclasm is directly related to his virtue of charity. As the Mishnah says, 'Whoever shuts his eye against charity is as though he worshipped idols'.[71] For Meister Eckhart, the account of Abraham's charity to the three strangers hints at Abraham's appreciation of unity. Meister Eckhart cites *Genesis* 18:2 as: 'He saw three and adored one'.[72]

'Charity' says Schuon, 'starts from the truth that my neighbour is not other than myself, since he is endowed with an ego; that in the sight of God he is neither more nor less "I" than myself; that which is given to "another" is given to "myself"; that my neighbour is also made in the image of God; that he carries within him the potentiality of the Divine presence and that this potentiality must be revered in him'.[73] This truth is central to the Noachic covenant: 'He who sheds the blood of man, by man shall his blood be shed, for in the image of God was man created' (Gen.9:6). To shed the blood of another is to shed one's own blood, for humankind is a single being in the image of the one God.[74] 'Inasmuch as ye have done it unto one of the least of these my brethren, ye have done it unto Me' (Mt.25:40).

The virtue of charity, which merited the salvation of Noah and his sons, is the knowledge of the unity of Being. Charity, understood thus, is Supreme Identity. It presupposes union with God: the union of the *gnosis* of Noah's "drunkenness"; the union of contraries by which one knows God; the union of *Yobel*, "the state of supreme illumination and identity"; the union of the Ark.

The Ark is the place of the *Shekhinah*, described as divine Light. Julian of Norwich saw charity as a divine light, which she understood after three manners. 'The first,' she says, 'is Charity unmade; the second is Charity made; the third is Charity given. Charity unmade is God; Charity made is our soul in God; Charity given is virtue. And that is a precious gift of working in which we love God, for Himself; and others, in God; and that which God loveth, for God.'[75] These three modes of divine Charity correspond to the divine Mercy, which is unmade in the Heart, but which flows forth upon the Throne and is made as a gift of grace. For Richard of St. Victor the Ark of the Covenant signifies nothing less than Grace.[76]

According to Schuon, 'the extrinsic charity of God consists *a priori* in His "putting Himself in the place" of nothing, that is of unreality or of impossibility, and He does so in creating the world, which is none other than nothingness to which God has lent a particle of His being.'[77] This recalls Meister Eckhart's saying, cited earlier, that all creatures are "nothing."[78] This particle of being (the *reshimu*) is His divine gift of Love. Thus the Persian Sufi, Abū Yazīd Tayfūr al-Bastāmī, says, 'A single atom of the love of God in a heart is worth more than a hundred thousand paradises.'[79] To realise the nothingness of creation is to rend the illusion of the Relative and see only the Absolute. To see the Absolute is to see the Relative in the Absolute, to see God in creation. Ibn al-'Arabī: 'He who is universal is particular, and He Who is particular is universal. There is but one Essence, the light of the Essence being also darkness.'[80] In the words of the Buddhist saint, Milarepa: 'If you realise the Voidness, Compassion will arise within your hearts; if ye lose all differentiation between yourselves and others, fit to serve others ye will be; and when in serving others ye shall win success, then shall ye meet with me; and finding me, ye shall attain to Buddhahood.'[81]

If God's extrinsic Charity, which is the same as His Mercy, is His "putting Himself in the place of nothing," then His intrinsic Charity is the realisation, made in the "Heart of the gnostic," that "nothing" is not and that there is only God.

Summary and Synthesis

The principle which is symbolised by the Ark is prefigured in the first case by the Absolute or Transcendence, by virtue of the All-Possibility of the Infinite. That is, Immanence is prefigured or "contained" *in divinis* by the Infinitude of the Absolute. Thus one can say that Transcendence is the Supreme Ark. On the one hand, All-Possibility is symbolised by Darkness, expressing its unknowablity; on the other hand, it is symbolised by the supreme Waters (*hyperousia*), expressing the plenitude of the Infinite. The possibility of Immanence "contains" Immanence by identity; this is what we might call the second valence of the Ark principle and it is not different from Transcendence.

The possibility of Immanence is the "seed" or "egg" (*Hiranyagarbha*) of Immanence afloat on the waters of Possibility. This seed gives rise to, and is identical with, Being. Being is the third valence of the Ark. Being contains universal existence by virtue of being its principle. Being is both Transcendent and Immanent. It is the Ark envisaged as "bridge" and as "dam": the Christian *Logos* and the Islamic *barzakh*. Being is the Throne that rests upon the Waters and is identical with the Waters. Here the Waters are firstly Possibility (the Infinite) and secondly Virtuality and Potentiality, or ontological Substance (*Prakriti*). Again, Being is the Divine Sea and the river, *fons et origio*. The Divine Sea is identical with the Waters of Possibility. The river is *Yobel*, the *Fiat Lux*, ontological Essence (*Purusha*). Essence acts upon Substance; the Spirit "moves on the Waters." This act is an actionless action (*wei wu wei*). The Throne "rests" on the Waters. Being is at "rest" by virtue of its primordial Unity.

The Sea is the receptacle from which the river gushes forth and the final end to which it returns. The Sea "contains" the river and "receives" the river: it is the Ark of the river. Being is expressed by onto-cosmological existence or becoming, which is spatio-temporal existence. This is prefigured *in divinis* by the Centre and the Origin. The Centre is the principle and container of space. The Origin is the principle and container of time. Time implies a change of position from one qualified space to a second; each space is contained in the principle of the Centre: hence, space contains time. The unfolding of time produces a qualified direction by which two points in space may be referenced; this unfolding is contained in the Origin: hence, time contains space. The matrix of space and time is becoming or *Samsāra*. Being is the Centre and the circumference; it is the Beginning and the End. Being is the Ark of becoming. Becoming is the Ark of cosmic existence.

To say Virtuality is to say immutability or "rest." Virtuality is "actualised" or "realised" through cosmic potentiality, which is the potentiality of the cosmic seed or the World Egg. Schuon: 'Being cannot not include efficient Possibility, because it cannot prevent the Absolute from including the Infinite.'[82] Ontological possibility, or potentiality, gives rise to the play of creatural existence. The creature is "made in the image" of its Principle, which it contains in its heart. 'Relativity is only real through its contents which, for their part, pertain to the Absolute.'[83] By identity with the Principle human beings realise that they are, in fact, themselves the receptacles of Divine Immanence.

Immanence *qua* Immanence is firstly Unity and secondly the possibility for multiplicity or distinction. This possibility is realised via the polarisation of the creative principles: Essence and Substance. Prior—logically rather than temporally—to this diremption, Essence and Substance reside in the biunity of Being, fused but not confused. This biunity is the *coincidentia oppositorum*, by which Creation is born and through which the soul must return in its quest for Unity (the passage through the Symplegades). The outflowing of ontological possibilities via the *coincidentia oppositorum* ("two by two") projects simultaneously "downwards" and "outwards" giving rise to the triangle, apex up, which is the "mother of form" and which is symbolised principally by the Cosmic Mountain (the "twin-peaked mountain"). This is the ternary, Principle-Essence-Substance. This ternary is in turn reflected—in the mirror of the Lower Waters—by the ternary Essence-Substance-Manifestation. These two ternaries produce the quaternary Principle-Essence-Substance-Manifestation. Manifestation imitates the triunity Principle-Essence-Substance, being "made in the image"; it does so in its tripartite structure, being formed of three levels or "storeys," Heaven-Midspace-Earth or Heaven-Earth-Underworld. These are in turn envisaged as a ternary of ternaries giving rise to the perfection of Manifestation being expressed by the number nine. This ternary of ternaries is not Manifestation *per se* but the "container" of it; for Manifestation is realised fully *a posteriori* in Man. The symbolism of the ternary, or of Manifestation thus conceived, finds its completion in the quaternary, and thus the *Tetraktys* and the number ten, which indicates the return of the one to the metaphysical zero. The quaternary is thus the end and achievement of Manifestation; it "receives" and "contains" all that precedes it in the sense of being the totality of the process of Manifestation. To paraphrase Schuon: duality "engenders" and trinity "projects" or "sets into motion," while quaternary suffices unto itself, being a result or an achievement.[84]

To generalise: metaphysically speaking, the Ark is God, and more specifically Transcendence; ontologically speaking, the Ark is Being or Immanence; cosmologically speaking, the Ark is firstly, space and time, secondly, the Sun—the divine Centre—and thirdly, Mother Earth; spiritually speaking, the Ark is firstly, Mercy and secondly, Charity. At the deepest level of understanding, the Ark is the "heart of the gnostic," which embraces the Divine Reality. In the words of the *hadīth qudsī*: 'Neither My earth nor my heavens contain Me, but I fitted into the believing heart.'

> If the creature submits to you,
>   It is the Reality Who submits.
> And if the Reality submits to you,
>   The created may not follow Him in that.
> Therefore realise what we say,
>   For all I say is true.
> There is no created being
>   But is endowed with speech.
> Nor is there aught created, seen by the eye,
>   But is essentially the Reality.
> Indeed, He is hidden therein,
>   Its forms being merely containers.

Ibn al-'Arabī[85]

Notes

1. Al-Junayd, cited in Nicholson, *Studies in Islamic Mysticism*, 1921, p.159.

2. Rūmī, *Mathnawī*, I, 2137 (Gupta (tr.), *Vol.1*, 1997, p.194).

3. In discussing the possibilities of the human individuality, Guénon remarks that, 'Taken literally, the relationship of container to contained is a spatial relationship; but here it should be only taken figuratively, for what is in question is neither extended nor situated in space' (*MSB*, 2001, p.41, n.1). In discussing the Infinite we are discussing Possibility as such, and thus the same proviso applies.

4. Ibn al-'Arabī: 'So the world is both carrier (*hāmil*) and carried (*mahmūl*). As carried it is form (*sūra*), body (*jism*), and active (*fā'il*); as carried it is meaning (*ma'nā*), spirit (*rūh*), and passive (*munfa'il*)' (*Futūhāt*, 2002, p.52).

5. Schuon, *G:DW*, 1990, p.97.

6. Plato's "receptacle" or "nurse" of becoming (*Timaeus*, 49A; 52).

7. *Mundaka Upaniśad*, 1.1.7.

8. This tentative English translation comes from a paper delivered in French by Jaafar Kansoussi, Director of al-Quobba Zarqua publishing house in Marrakech, at the Ibn 'Arabi Society's Ninteenth Annual Symposium (2002). He kindly directed me to his French translation of Ibn al-'Arabī's, *Diwan of Shashtari*, p.74.

9. Al-Jīlī: 'In parable, the creation is like ice, and it is Thou who art gushing water. The ice is not, if we realised it, other than its water, and is not in this condition other than by the contingent laws. But the ice will melt and its condition will dissolve, the liquid condition will establish itself, certainly' (*al-insān*, 1983, pp.28-29).

10. This extended analogy comes from my essay 'The Logic of Mystery & the Necessity of Faith' in *The Betrayal of Tradition: Essays on the Spiritual Crisis of Modernity*, 2004.

11. Ibn al-'Arabi, *Fusūs* (1980, p.213).

12. Snodgrass, *ATE2*, 1990, p.411.

13. *Brahma-Sūtra*, 1.3.1.

14. Schaya, 'The Meaning of the Temple', 1974, p.360.

15. Al-Jīlī, *al-insān*, 1983, p.8.

16. *Taittirīyà Upaniśad*, 1.8.

17. Meister Eckhart, from Pfeiffer, 1924, *Vol.1*, pp.69-70, cited in Perry, *TTW*, 2000, p.1005.

18. Abraham Abulafia, cited in Scholem, *MTJM*, 1995, p.141.

19. *Tikkune Zohar* 3b., cited in Scholem, *MTJM*, 1995, p.369, n.137.

20. Schuon, *SPHF*, 1987, p.167.

21. Qur'an, 42:11.

22. Ibn al-'Arabi, *Fusūs* (1980, p.75).

23. On the interplay of the hypostases see Schuon, *FDH*, 1982, pp.41-42.

24. Ibn al-'Arabi, *Fusūs* (1980, p.74). St. Augustine, in his *Confessions*, says 'He [God] did not create and depart, but the things that are from Him are in Him' (4.12.18).

25. Meister Eckhart, Sermon 4 (Walshe, *Vol.1*, 1987, p.44).

26. Schuon, *SPHF*, 1987, p.108.

27. Schuon, *TUR*, 1993, p.41

28. Cited in Radhakrishnan, *Selected Writings on Philosophy, Religion and Culture*, 1970, p.146.

29. *Merchant of Venice*, 4.1.184.

30. Rūmī, *Mathnawī*, V, 2282 (Nicholson (tr.), cited in Perry, *TTW*, 2000, p.611).

31. Burckhardt, *Études Traditionnelles*, 1953, p.174, cited in Perry, *TTW*, 2000, p.596.

32. Snodgrass, *ATE2*, 1990, pp.410-11. Snodgrass notes that the Pen and the Guarded Tablet are the Islamic equivalents of Essence and Substance or *Purusa* and *Prakrti*, the polar complementaries by whose union phenomena come to be manifested (p.411, n.2).

33. Ibn al-'Arabī, *Fusūs* (1980, p.278).

34. The Merciful is the Active Participant or agent of mercy, distinct here from the mercy itself. Its activity is a "non-acting activity" (*wei wu wei*). The Merciful is uncreated whereas the Mercy is the very power of creation, which it embraces.

35. Ibn al-'Arabī, *Fusūs* (1980, p.225).

36. Ibn al-'Arabī, *Fusūs* (1980, p.225).
37. Ibn al-'Arabī, *Fusūs* (1980, p.174).
38. Snodgrass, *ATE2*, 1990, p.411.
39. This is particularly evident with the symbolism of "rain". Rain is the symbol of the celestial influences which the earth receives. See "rain" in Chevalier & Gheerbrant, *DS*, 1996, p.782; see also Guénon, 'Light and Rain', *FS*, 1995, Ch.62.
40. According to Rabbi Gikatilla the word "blessing" (*brachah*) comes from the word "pool" (*braichah*), see *SO*, 1994, p.16.
41. Rabbi Gikatilla, *SO*, 1994, p.245.
42. See Scholem, *MTJM*, 1995, pp.266-68; see n.68 where he refers to Tishby's analysis of this doctrine.
43. *Genesis Rabba*, 12.15.
44. Scholem, *MTJM*, 1995, p.266.
45. Scholem, *MTJM*, 1995, p.267.
46. See Al-Jīlī, *al-insān*, 1983, 'Of the Compassionate Beatitude (*ar-rahmāniyah*)'. In his introduction to the *Fusūs*, Austin remarks, that for Ibn al-'Arabī, the term "mercy" 'did not simply denote an attitude or feeling of compassion, as usually understood, but rather the very principle of creation by which all created things exist and by which all the latent possibilities within the "divine mind" are released into actuality, as objects of the divine perception and witness' (1980, p.29).
47. Burckhardt, *ISD*, 1976, p.123.
48. The Virgin is typically shown enthroned in Renaissance art. See "Coronation of St. Mary the Virgin"in Metford, *DCLL*, 1983, p.67-8.
49. "Mary the Virgin, St." in Metford, *DCLL*, 1983, pp.170-171. *Bath-Sheba'* (בת-שבע; *"daughter of an oath"*). This name derives from two words. The first is *bath* ("a *daughter*") as the feminine form of *bēn* ("a *son*"), which derives from the primitive root, *bānāh* ("to *build*"). The second is *sheba'*, which is taken as "*oath*." This is the feminine form of *shib'āh* ("*seven*," as the sacred *full* one). It derives from the primitive root, *shāba'* ("to *be complete*"). It is taken as "*oath*" in the sense of "to seven oneself," i.e. to swear by repeating the declaration seven times. The name Bathsheba expresses the feminine nature of the complete building of cosmic existence through the "seven", which correspond to the seven cosmological *sefirah*. From one perspective, these are the "throne" upon which the triunity *Keter-Hokhmah-Binah* rests; from another perspective these are the "throne" on which the Virgin *Malkhut* is enthroned.
50. Ibn al-'Arabī, *Fusūs* (1980, p.147).
51. Austin, Introductory Note to Ch.12 of Ibn al-'Arabī, *Fusūs* (1980, p.145).
52. See Ibn al-'Arabī, *Fusūs* (1980, p.190).
53. Ibn al-'Arabī, *Fusūs* (1980, p.189).
54. On the "Supreme Commandment" see Schuon, *EPW*, 1981, pp.151-157.

55. Abraham is the head of the Semitic patriarchy and corresponds in the Greek tradition to Zeus, who is not only the head of the Greek pantheon but also the "protector of wayfarers."

56. Again, Lot when he meets the angles who come to Sodom (Gen.19:1-4).

57. Halevi refers to Melchizedek as Abraham's "teacher" (*The Way of Kabbalah*, 1967, p.16; *Kabbalah*, 1996, p.14. Presumably this follows the tradition whereby Metatron (Yahoel) is seen as Abraham's spiritual teacher, see Scholem, *MTJM*, 1995, p.69. For the original tradition see *The Apocalypse of Abraham* where Iaoel (Yahoel) reveals the secrets of heaven to Abraham (15.4).

58. *Midrash Tanchuma*, *Genesis*, 8, 16, cited in Rappoport, *AI1*, 1995, p.275. The textual context is Melchizedek's "feeding/blessing" of Abram with bread and wine (Gen.14:18).

59. *Sabbath* 156b, cited in Cohen, *ET*, 1995, p.221.

60. Cohen, *ET*, 1995, p.219.

61. *Sotah* 14a, cited in Cohen, *ET*, 1995, p.225.

62. *Be'ēShaba'* (באר שבע; *"well of an oath"*) is also *"well of seven"*; that is, the seven "wells" or vessels of the cosmological *sefirot*.

63. *Genesis Rabba*, 54.6, cited in Cohen, *ET*, 1995, p.225.

64. Cohen, *ET*, 1995, p.225, n.1.

65. Schuon, *EPW*, 1981, p.153.

66. Schuon, *SW*, 1995, p.93.

67. Meister Eckhart, from Pfeiffer (ed.), *Meister Eckhart Vol.1*, 1924, p.147, cited in Perry, *TTW*, 2000, p.614.

68. *Genesis Rabba*, 38.13, cited in Cohen, *ET*, 1995, p.1-2 & Rappoport, *AI1*, 1995, p.xxix. See Rappoport, *AI1*, 1995, pp.238-245 for various other accounts of Abraham's iconoclasms.

69. Compare Moses hidden for three months (Ex.2:1-2).

70. *Midrash Hagadol*, cited in Cohen, *ET*, 1995, p.2. This tradition can also be found in the *Apocalypse of Abraham*, 7.1-12 (Charlesworth (ed.), *OTP1*, 1983, p.692) and Qur'an 6:75-79.

71. *Baba Bathra* 10a, cited in Cohen, *ET*, 1995, p.223.

72. Meister Eckhart, *Comm. Jn.* 37 (Colledge & McGinn, 1981, p.135).

73. Schuon, *SPHF*, 1987, p.24. See also 'The Supreme Commandment', *EPW*, 1981; 'Complexity of the Concept of Charity', *SW*, 1995.

74. Discussing Meister Eckhart's idea of the "image," Richard Woods remarks, 'we are created both *Imago Dei* and *ad imaginem Dei*, the second as creatures distinct from but wholly dependent upon God for our existence, and the first as identical with the Word of God and thus with but indistinct from God in the depths of the divine nature itself' ('Eckhart's Imageless Image: Art, Spirituality, and the Apophatic Way', 2003, p.11).

75. Julian of Norwich, *Revelations of Divine Love*, cited in Perry, *TTW*, 2000, p.598.

76. Richard of St. Victor, *Benjamin Major* (*The Mystical Ark*), 1979, p.152.

77. Schuon, *SW*, 1995, p.97.

78. See Meister Eckhart, Sermon 4 (Walshe, *Vol.1*, 1987).

79. Bāyazīd al-Bistāmī, cited in Perry, *TTW*, 2000, p.617.

80. Ibn al-'Arabī, *Fusūs* (1980, p.150). Again: 'All becoming is an imagination / And in truth also a reality / Who truly comprehends this / Has attained the mysteries of the Way' (p.197).

81. Milarepa, cited in Perry, *TTW*, 2000, p.601.

82. Schuon, *IFA*, 1989, p.38.

83. Schuon, *EPW*, 1981, p.48.

84. Schuon, *SME*, 2000, p.64.

85. Ibn al-'Arabi, *Fusūs* (1980, p.130).

Sources

Albertus, Frater, *Alchemist's Handbook*, New York: Weiser, 1974
———, *Praxis Spagyrica Philosophica & From "One" to "Ten"*, Maine: Weiser, 1998
Al-Ghazali, *The Nintey-Nine Beautiful Names of God*, (tr.) D. B. Burrell and N. Daher, Cambridge: The Islamic Texts Society, 1995.
Anonymous, *The Prilgrim's Tale*, (tr.) T. A. Smith, Mahwah: Paulist Press, 1999.
Apollodorus, *The Library of Greek Mythology*, (tr.) R. Hard, Oxford: Oxford University Press, 1997.
Barks, C., *The Essential Rumi*, New York: HarperCollins, 1995.
Bailey, L. R., *Noah The Person and the Story in History and Tradition*, South Carolina: University of South Carolina, 1989.
Bernhard, W. A., *The Living World of the Old Testament*, Fourth Edition, Essex: Longman, 1975.
Becker, U. (ed.), *The Element Encyclopedia of Symbols*, Dorset: Element Books, 1994.
Bentley, J., *Hindu Astronomy Pt.1* 'The Ancient Astronomy', Osnabruck: Biblio Verlag, 1970.
Boethius, *The Consolation of Philosophy*, (tr.) V. E. Watts, Middlesex: Penguin Books, 1969.
Brahma-Sūtra-Bhāsya of Śankarācārya, (tr.) Swami Gambhiranada, Calcutta: Advaita Ashrama, 1792
Brown, J. E. (ed.), *The Sacred Pipe: Black Elk's Account of the Seven Rites of the Oglala Sioux*, Norman: University of Oklahoma Press, 1989.
Bruno, G., *Cause, Principle and Unity And Essays on Magic*, Cambridge: Cambridge University Press, 1998.
Budge, W. E. A., *Legends of the Gods*, New York: Dover, 1994.
———, *The Book of the Dead: 'The Hieroglyphic Transcript and English Translation of the Papyrus of Ani'*, New Jersey: Gramercy Books, 1995.
Bulfinch, T., *Bulfinch's Mythology*, New York: Avenel Books, 1979.
Burckhardt, T., *Alchemy*, Baltimore: Penguin, 1974.
———, *An Introduction to Sufi Doctrine*, Wellingborough: The Aquarian Press, 1976.
———, 'Abd al-Karīm al-Jīlī, *al-insān al-kamīl* (Universal Man), (tr.) T. Burckhardt, Gloucester: Beshara Publications, 1983.
———, *Mirror of the Intellect*, Cambridge: Quinta Essentia, 1987.
Campbell, J., *The Masks of God: Oriental Mythology*, London: Souvenir Press, 1973.

————, *The Hero with a Thousand Faces*, London: Abacus, 1975.

————, *The Masks of God: Occidental Mythology*, Middlesex: Penguin, 1978.

————, *The Masks of God: Primitive Mythology*, Middlesex: Penguin, 1982.

Chāndogya Upanishad (With the Commentary of Śankarācārya), (tr.) Swāmī Gambhīrānada, Calcutta: Advaita Ashrama, 1992.

Chadwick, H., *Boethius: The Consolations of Music, Logic, Theology, and Philosophy*, Oxford: Clarendon Press, 1990.

Chan, W-t (tr.), *A Source Book in Chinese Philosophy*, New Jersey: Princeton University Press, 1969.

Charbonneau-Lassay, L., *The Bestiary of Christ*, (tr.) D. M. Dooling, Middlesex: Arkana Books, 1992.

Charlesworth, J. H. (ed.), *The Old Testament Pseudepigrapha* (2 Vols.), New York: Doubleday, 1983.

Chevalier, J. & Gheerbrant, A., *Dictionary of Symbols*, (tr.) J. Buchanan-Brown, Middlesex: Penguin, 1996.

Cicero, *De Re Publica; De Legibus*, (tr.) C. W. Keys, Loeb Classical Library, London: Harvard University Press, 1994.

Cohen, A., *Everyman's Talmud*, New York: Schocken Books, 1995.

Coomaraswamy, A., *Selected Papers Vol.1: Traditional Art and Symbolism & Selected Papers Vol.2: Metaphysics*, (ed.) R. Lipsey, New Jersey: Princeton University Press, 1977.

————, *Time and Eternity*, New Delhi: Munshiram Manoharlal, 1993.

Coomaraswamy, A. & Sister Nivedita, *Hindus and Buddhists*, London: Senate, 1994.

Copenhaver, B. P., *Hermetica*, Cambridge: Cambridge University Press, 1992.

Corbin, H., *Avicenna and the Visionary Recital*, Texas: Spring Publications, 1980.

Craig, A., Evans, C. A., Webb, R. L. & Wiebe, R. A., *Nag Hammadi Texts and the Bible: A Synopsis and Index*, Leiden: E. J. Brill, 1993.

Critchlow, K., *Islamic Patterns An Analytical and Cosmological Approach*, London: Thames and Hudson, 1976.

Cumont, F., *The Mysteries of Mithra*, New York: Dover, 1956.

Dalley, S. (ed.), *Myths from Mesopotamia: Creation, The Flood, Gilgamesh, and Others*, Oxford: Oxford University Press, 1991.

Daniélou, A., *The Myths and Gods of India: Hindu Polytheism*, New York: Inner Traditions, 1985.

————, *Yoga, The Method of Re-Intergration*, London: Christopher Johnson, 1949.

Dante, *The Divine Comedy*, (tr.) C. H. Sisson, Oxford: Oxford University Press, 1993.

Davies S., *Uncreated Light: The Traditional Doctrine of the Intellect in Dante and Blake*, Bendigo: La Trobe University, 1997.

Davidson, F., Stibbs, A. M., & Kevan, E. F., *The New BIBLE Commentary*, London: Low & Brydone Ltd., 1968.

Dionysius, (the Areopagite), *Pseudo-Dionysius The Complete Works*, New Jersey: Paulist Press, 1987.

Drummond, Sir W., *Oedipus Judaicus: Allegory in the Old Testament* (1811), London: Bracken Books, 1996.

Eckhart, *A modern translation*, (tr.) R. B. Blakney, New York: Harper & Row, 1941.

————, *Meister Eckhart: The Essential Sermons, Commentaries, Treatises, and Defence*, (tr.) E. Colledge, O.S.A. and B. McGinn, New Jersey: Paulist Press, 1981.

————, *Meister Eckhart Sermons & Treatises* (3 Vols.), (tr.) Walshe, Dorset: Element Books, 1987.

Eisenman, R. & Wise, M., *Dead Sea Scrolls Uncovered*, New York: Penguin Books, 1993.

Eliade, M., *Patterns in Comparative Religion*, London: Sheed and Ward, 1958.

————, 'Methodological Remarks on the Study of Religious Symbolism', from M. Eliade & J. M. Kitagawa (eds.), *The History of Religion: Essays in Methodology*, Chicago: University of Chicago Press, 1959, pp.86-107.

————, *Images and Symbols: Studies in Religious Symbolism*, New York: Sheed and Ward, 1969.

————, *Australian Religions: An Introduction*, London: Cornell Uni. Press, 1973.

————, *The Myth of the Eternal Return* or, *Cosmos and History*, New York: Princeton Uni. Press, 1974.

————, *The Forge and the Crucible*, Chicago: The University of Chicago Press, 1976.

————, *Essential Sacred Writings From Around the World* (Previously, *From Primitive to Zen*), New York: HarperCollins, 1977.

————, *A History of Religious Ideas Vol.1: From the Stone age to the Eleusinian Mysteries*, Chicago: The University of Chicago Press, 1978.

————, *A History of Religious Ideas Vol.2: From Gautama Buddha to the Triumph of Christianity*, Chicago: The University of Chicago Press, 1984.

————, *A History of Religious Ideas Vol.3: From Muhammad to the Age of Reforms*, Chicago: The University of Chicago Press, 1985.

————, *Shamanism: Archaic techniques of ecstasy*, Middlesex: Arkana, 1989.

————, *Sacred and Profane: The Nature of Religion*, San Diego: Harcout Brace & Company, 1987.

————, *Symbolism, the Sacred, and the Arts*, New York: Continuum, 1992.

————, (ed.), *The Encyclopedia of Religion* (16 Vols.), New York: Simon & Schuster Macmillan, 1995.

Fernando, R. (ed.), *The Unanimous Tradition: Essays on the essential unity of all religions*, Colombo: The Sri Lanka Institute of Traditional Studies, 1991.

Frazer, Sir J. G., O.M., *The Golden Bough: A Study in Magic and Religion*, London: Macmillan, 1976.

Fohr, S., *Adam and Eve: The Spiritual Symbolism of Genesis and Exodus*, London: University Press of America, 1986.

Gardner, H., *Art Through the Ages*, Fifth Edition, New York: Harcourt, Brace & World, 1970.

Gaskell, G. A., *Dictionary of All Scriptures & Myths*, New Jersey: Gramercy Books, 1960.

Gaster, T. H., *Myth, Legend, and Custom in the Old Testament*, New York: Harper & Row, 1969.

Gikatilla, Rabbi J., *Gates of Light (Sha'are Orah)*, (tr.) A. Weinstein, Walnut Creek: AltaMira, 1994.

Govinda, Lama A., *Foundations of Tibetan Mysticism*, Maine: Samuel Weiser, 1969.

Graves, R., *The Greek Myths* (2 Vols.), London: Penguin, 1960.

Guénon, R., *Crisis of the Modern World*, London: Luzac and Co. Ltd., 1975.

————, *Symbolism of the Cross*, London: Luzac & Co. Ltd., 1975.

————, *Man and his Becoming According To The Vedānta*, New Delhi: Oriental Books Reprint, 1981.

————, *The Lord of the World*, Yorkshire: Coombe Springs Press, 1983.

————, *The Great Triad*, New Delhi: Munshiram Manoharlal, 1994.

————, *The Reign of Quantity & The Signs of the Times*, New York: Sophia Perennis et Universalis, 1995.

————, *Fundamental Symbols: The Universal Language of Sacred Science*, Cambridge: Quinta Essentia, 1995.

————, *The Esoterism of Dante*, New York: Sophia Perennis, 1996.

————, *The Multiple States of the Being*, New York: Sophia Perennis, 2001.

Gunkel, H., *The Legends of Genesis*, New York: Schocken Books, 1970.

Halevi, Z. b. S., *The Way of Kabbalah*, London: Rider & Co., 1976.

————, *Adam and the Kabbalistic Tree*, Maine: Samuel Weiser, 1991.

————, *Kabbalah The Divine Plan*, New York: HarperCollins, 1996.

————, *Tree of Life*, Bath: Gateway Books, 1997.

Hall, M. P. (tr.), *Codex Rosae Crucis*, n.s.: The Philosophical Research Society, 1974.

Harmon, N. B.(ed.), *The Interpreter's Bible Vol.1*, Tennessee: Abingdon Press, 1952.

Hesiod, *Works and Days* from *Hesiod and Theognis*, (tr.) D. Wender, London: Penguin, 1973.

Ibn al-'Arabī, Muhyī al-Dīn, *The Bezels of Wisdom* (*Fusūs al-hikam*), (tr.) R. Austin, Mahwah: Paulist Press, 1980.

———, *Kernel of the Kernel* (*Lubbu-l-Lubb*), (tr.) I. H. Bursevi, Roxburgh: Beshara Publications, 1981.

———, *The Meccan Revelations* (*al-Futūhāt al-Makkiya*), (ed.) M. Chodkiewicz, (tr.) W. C. Chittick & J. W. Morris, New York: Pir Press, 2002.

Al-Jīlī, *al-insān al-kamīl* (Universal Man), (tr.) T. Burckhardt, Gloucester: Beshara Publications, 1983.

Jones, B. E., *Freemasons' Guide and Compendium*, London: Harrap, 1956.

Jordan, M., *Myths of the World: A Thematic Encyclopedia*, London: Kyle Kathie, 1993.

Josephus, *The Complete Works of Josephus*, (tr.) W. Whiston, Grand Rapids: Kregel Publications, 1981.

Kaplan, A., *Sefer Yetzirah: The Book of Creation In Theory and Practice*, York Beach: Weiser, 1997.

Kelley, C. F., *Meister Eckhart on Divine Knowledge*, New Haven: Yale University Press, 1977.

Kirk, G. S. & Raven, J. E., *The Presocratic Philosophers*, Cambridge: Cambridge University Press, 1957.

Klossowski de Rola, S., *The Secret Art of Alchemy*, London: Thames and Hudson, 1992.

———, *The Golden Game: Alchemical Engravings of the Seventeenth Century*, London: Thames and Hudson, 1997.

Lawlor, R., *Sacred Geometry: Philosophy and Practice*, London: Thames and Hudson, 1989.

Lempriere, J., *A Classical Dictionary*, New York: George Routledge and Sons, 1906.

Lings, M., *A Sufi Saint of the Twentieth Century*, London: Allen & Unwin, 1971.

Lossky, V., *The Mystical Theology of the Eastern Church*, Cambridge: James Clarke & Co., 1968.

Mathers, S. L. (tr.), *The Kabbalah Unveiled*, Middlesex: Arkana Penguin Books, 1991.

McGinn, B., 'The God beyond God: Theology and Mysticism in the Thought of Meister Eckhart', *Journal of Religion* 61, 1981, pp.1-19.

————, *The Mystical Thought of Meister Eckhart*, New York: Crossroad, 2001.

Matt, D. C. (tr.), *Zohar: The Book of Enlightenment*, New York: Paulist Press, 1983.

Metford, J. C. J., *Dictionary of Christian Lore and Legend*, London: Thames and Hudson, 1983.

Meyendorff, J., *A Study of Gregory Palamas*, New York: St. Vladimir's Seminary Press, 1998.

Nasr, S. H., *Ideals and Realities of Islam*, London: Allen & Unwin, 1966.

————, *Sufi Essays*, London: Allen & Unwin, 1972.

————, *Knowledge and the Sacred*, Edinburgh: Edinburgh University Press, 1981.

————, *An Introduction to Islamic Cosmological Doctrines*, London: Thames & Hudson, 1978.

Needleman, J. (ed), *The Sword of Gnosis*, Baltimore: Penguin, 1974.

Nicholas of Cusa, *Nicolas of Cusa Selected Writings*, (tr.) H. L. Bond, Mahwah: Paulist Press, 1997.

Nicholson, R. A., *Studies in Islamic Mysticism*, London: Cambridge University Press, 1921.

Northbourne, Lord, *Religion in the Modern World*, London: J. M. Dent, 1963.

————, *Looking Back on Progress*, London: Perennial Books, 1970.

Oldmeadow, K., ' ankara's Doctrine of *Māyā*', *Asian Philosophy*, Vol.2, No.2, 1992, pp.131-146.

————, *Traditionalism: Religion in the light of the Perennial Philosophy*, Colombo: Sri Lanka Institute of Traditional Studies, 2000.

Ovid, *The Metamorphoses of Ovid*, (tr.) M. M. Innes, Middlesex: Penguin, 1961.

Palamas, G., *Gregory Palamas: The Triads*, Mahwah: Paulist Press, 1983.

Pallis, M., *A Buddhist Spectrum*, London: George Allen & Unwin, 1980.

Perry, W. N., *The Widening Breach: Evolutionism in the Mirror of Cosmology*, Cambridge: Quinta Essentia, 1995.

————, *A Treasury of Traditional Wisdom*, Louisville: Fons Vitae, 2000.

Perry, M., 'The Forbidden Door', *Sophia*, Vol.7, No.2, 2001, pp.139-185.

Plato, *The Collected Dialogues*, New Jersey: Princeton University Press, 1980.

Plotinus, *The Enneads*, (tr.) S. MacKenna, Middlesex, Penguin, 1991.

von Rad, G., *Genesis*, (tr.) J. H. Marks, London: SCM Press Ltd, 1963.

Radhakishnan, S., *Selected Writings on Philosophy, Religion and Culture*, (ed.) R. A. McDermott, New York: E. P. Dutton, 1970.

Rapaport, Rabbi I., *The Hebrew Word Shem and Its Original Meaning*, Melbourne: The Hawthorn Press, 1976.

Rappoport, A. S., *Ancient Israel* (3 Vols.), London: Senate, 1995.

Richard of St. Victor, *The Twelve Ō Patriarchs Ō The Mystical Ark Book Ō Three of the Trinity*, (tr.) G. A. Zinn, Mahwah: Paulist Press, 1979.

Robinson, J. M. (ed.), *The Nag Hammadi Library*, New York: HarperCollins, 1990.

Rūmī, Jalāl al-Din, *Maulan Rum's Masnawi* (6 Vols.), (tr.) M. G. Gupta, Agra: M. G. Publishers, 1997.

————, *Kulliyat-e Shams* (8 Vols.), (ed.) Badi-uz-Zaman Furuzanfar, Teheran: Amir Kabir Press, 1957-66.

Samsel, P., 'A Unity with Distinction', *Sophia*, Vol.7, No.2, 2001, pp.95- 137.

Schaya, L., *The Universal Meaning of the Kabbalah*, (tr.) N. Pearson, New Jersey: Allen & Unwin, 1971.

————, 'The Meaning of the Temple', J. Needleman (ed), *The Sword of Gnosis*, 1974.

————, 'The Eliatic Function': *Studies in Comparative Religion* Winter-Spring, 1979, pp.31- 40.

Scholem, G., *Kabbalah*, New York: Meridian, 1978.

————, *Origins of Kabbalah*, New York: Princeton, 1990.

————, *Major Trends in Jewish Mysticism*, New York: Schocken Books, 1995.

————, *On the Kabbalah and Its Symbolism*, New York: Schocken Books, 1996.

Schwaller de Lubicz, R. A., *The Temple in Man: Sacred Architecture and the Perfect Man*, New York: Inner Traditions International, 1981.

Schneemelcher, W. (ed), *New Testament Apocrypha* (2 Vols.), Louisville: Westminster/John Knox Press, 1991.

Schuon, F., *Light on the Ancient Worlds*, London: Perennial Books, 1965.

————, *Dimensions of Islam*, London: Allen & Unwin, 1969.

————, *Logic and Transcendence*, New York: Harper & Row, 1975.

————, *Understanding Islam*, London: Mandala Books, 1976.

————, *Islam and the Perennial Philosophy*, London: World of Islam Festival Trust, 1976.

————, *Esoterism as Principle and as Way*, Middlesex: Perennial Books, 1981.

————, *Sufism: Veil and Quintessence*, Bloomington: World Wisdom Books, 1981.

————, *From the Divine to the Human*, Bloomington: World Wisdom Books, 1982.

————, *Logic and Transendence*, London: Perennial Books, 1984.

————, *Spiritual Perspectives and Human Facts*, London: Perennial Books, 1987.

————, *In The Face Of The Absolute*, Bloomington: World Wisdom Books, 1989.

————, *Castes and Races*, Middlesex: Perennial Books, 1989.

————, *Gnosis: Divine Wisdom*, Middlesex: Perennial Books, 1990.

————, *To Have a Centre*, Bloomington: World Wisdom Books, 1990.

————, *The Transcendent Unity of Religions*, Wheaton: The Theosophical Publishing House, 1993.

————, *Treasures of Buddhism*, Bloomington: World Wisdom Books, 1993.

————, *Stations of Wisdom*, Bloomington: World Wisdom Books, 1995.

————, *Language of the Self*, Bloomington: World Wisdom Books, 1999.

————, *Survey of Metaphysics and Esoterism*, Bloomington: World Wisdom Books, 2000.

Scott, T., 'Understanding "Symbol"', *Sacred Web* 6, 2000, pp.91-106.

————, 'Preliminary Remarks on Reclaiming the Meaning of "Religion"', *Sacred Web* 7, 2001, pp.59-66.

————, 'Withdrawal, Extinction and Creation: Christ's *kenosis* in light of the Judaic doctrine of *tsimtsum* and the Islamic doctrine of *fana*', *Sophia* Vol.7, No.2, 2001, pp.45-64; revised and republished in *The Essential Sophia*, (ed.) S.H. Nasr & K. O'Brien, Bloomington: World Wisdom Books, 2006, pp.58-77.

————, 'Notes on the mystery of the *coincidentia oppositorum*', *Sacred Web* 9, 2002, 11-35.

————, 'The Logic of Mystery & the Necessity of Faith' in *The Betrayal of Tradition: Essays on the Spiritual Crisis of Modernity*, (ed.) K. Oldmeadow, Bloomington: World Wisdom Books, 2004, 123-145.

Sharpe, E., *Understanding Religion*, London: Duckworth, 1975.

Shabistarī, *The Secret Rose Garden of Sa'd Ud Din Mahmud Shabistari*, (tr.) F. Lederer, Lahore: Ashraf, n.d.

Skinner J., *A Critical and Exegetical Commentary on Genesis*, New York: Charles Scribner's Sons, 1925.

Skinner, J. R., *The Source of Measures: Key to the Hebrew-Egyptian Mystery* (1894), San Diego: Wizard's Bookshelf, 1982.

Smart, N., *The World's Religions*, London: Cambridge University Press, 1992.

Smith, H., *The Religions of Man*, New York: Harper & Row, 1965.

Smith, W., *Smith's Bible Dictionary*, Michigan: Zondervan Publishing House, 1948.

Smith, W. C., 'Objectivity and the Humane Sciences' in (ed.) W. G. Oxtoby, *Religious Diversity: Essays by Wilfred Cantwell Smith*, New York: Harper & Row, 1976.

Snodgrass, A., *The Symbolism of the Stupa*, New York: South East Asia Program, 1985.

———, *Architecture, Time and Eternity: Studies in the Stellar and Temporal Symbolism of Traditional Buildings* (2 Vols.), New Delhi: Sata-Pitaka Series, 1990.

———, *Patterns of Symbolism in Traditional Architecture*, Sri Lanka: Sri Lanka Institute of Traditional Studies, 1998.

Spence, L., *The Encyclopedia of the Occult*, London: Bracken Books, 1988.

———, *Egypt Myths and Legends*, London: The Guernsey Press, 1994.

Strong, J., *The Comprehensive Concordance of the Bible together with Dictionaries of the Hebrew and Greek Words of the original, with references to the English words*, World Publishing, Michigan, n.d.

Stoddart, W., 'Mysticism' originally published in R. Fernando (ed.), *The Unanimous Tradition*, 1991; revised version published in *Sacred Web* 2, 1998, pp.65-77.

Sturluson, S., *Edda*, London: Everyman, 1998.

Sworder, R., *Mining, Metallurgy and the Meaning of Life*, Sydney: Quaker Hill, 1995.

———, *Mathematical Cosmologies of Newton, Homer and Plato*, Bendigo: La Trobe University, 1997.

Taylor, T., *The Theoretic Arithmetic of the Pythagoreans*, Maine: Samuel Weiser, 1991.

Theon of Smyrna, *The Mathematics Useful for Understanding Plato*, (tr.) R. & D. Lawlor, San Diego: Wizard's Bookshelf, 1979.

Tillich, P., 'Religious Symbols and Our Knowledge of God' (1955) in Rowe & Wainwright (eds.), *Philosophy of Religion: Selected Readings*, New York, 1973.

Tishby, I., *The Wisdom of the Zohar* (3 Vols.), Oxford: Oxford University Press, 1991.

Thurman, R. A. F. (tr.), *The Tibetan Book of the Dead*, New York: Bantam Books, 1994.

de Troyes, C., *Arthurian Romances*, Middlesex: Penguin, 1991.

Unger, M. F., *Unger's Bible Dictionary*, Chicago: Moody Press, 1965.

Urban, H., '*Oblatio Rationabilis*: Sacrifice in East and West', *Sophia* Vol.8 No.1, 2002, pp.153-196.

Unterman, A., *Dictionary of Jewish Lore & Legend*, London: Thames and Hudson, 1991.

Vermes, G., *Scipture and Tradition in Judaism*, Leiden: E. J. Brill, 1983.

————, *The Dead Sea Scrolls In English*, London: Penguin Books, 1988.

de Voragine J., *The Golden Legend or Lives of the Saints* (1275), (tr.) William Caxton, (ed.) F. S. Ellis, n.s.:Temple Classics, 1900 (Reprinted 1922, 1931).

Waite, A. E., *The Holy Kabbalah*, Hertfordshire: Oracle Publishing, 1996.

————, *A New Encyclopaedia of Freemasonry*, New Jersey: Wings Books, 1996.

————, *The Hermetic Museum*, Maine: Weiser, 1999.

Westcott, W. W., *Collectanea Hermetica*, Maine: Weiser, 1998.

Westermann, C., *Genesis 1-11*, Minneapolis: Augsburg Pub. House, 1984.

Wise, M., Abergg, M. Jr. & Cook, E., *The Dead Sea Scrolls A New Translation*, Rydalmere: Hodder & Stoughton, 1996.

Woods, R., 'Eckhart's Imageless Image: Art, Spirituality, and the Apophatic Way': *Eckhart Review* No.12, 2003, pp.5-20.

Yu, A. C., *The Journey West* (4 Vols.), Chicago: University of Chicago Press, 1980.

Zeitlin, I. M., *Ancient Judaism: biblical Criticism from Max Weber to the Present*, Cambridge: Polity Press, 1984.